Pitt Series in Composition, Literacy, and C

DAVID BARTHOLOMAE AND JEAN FERGUSON CARR, E

Gertrude Buck

Toward a Feminist Rhetoric: The Writing of Gertrude Buck

Edited by JoAnn Campbell

University of Pittsburgh Press

Published by the University of Pittsburgh Press, Pittsburgh, Pa. 15260
Copyright © 1996, University of Pittsburgh Press
Manufactured in the United States of America
Printed on acid-free paper

Library of Congress Cataloging-in-Publication Data

Buck, Gertrude, 1871–1922.
    Toward a feminist rhetoric : the writing of Gertrude Buck / edited
by JoAnn Campbell.
        p.   cm.
    Includes bibliographical references.
    ISBN 0-8229-3900-2 (cloth : acid-free paper).
    —ISBN 0-8229-5573-3 (pbk.)
    1. Rhetoric—History.   2. Rhetoric—Study and Teaching (Higher)
3. Criticism.   4. Feminism and literature.   I. Campbell, JoAnn L.
II. Title.
PN183.B83   1996
808'.0092—dc20   95-23511
                                                      CIP

A CIP catalogue record for this book is available from the British Library.

Eurospan, London

Frontispiece: Courtesy of Special Collections, Vassar College Libraries.

Contents

Acknowledgments   vii

Introduction   ix

I. THEORY OF ORGANIC EDUCATION

The Organic Curriculum   3

The Religious Experience of a Skeptic   19

II. A SOCIAL RHETORIC AND POETICS

Genesis: Poetic Metaphor   31

The Present Status of Rhetorical Theory   45

What Does "Rhetoric" Mean?   52

The Social Criticism of Literature   56

III. COMPOSITION INSTRUCTION WITH PURPOSE

Recent Tendencies in the Teaching of English Composition   91

The Basis of Exposition   101

Argumentation   112

Marks in Freshman English   123

IV. HOLISTIC GRAMMAR INSTRUCTION

The Sentence-Diagram   131

The Psychology of the Diagram   141

Make-Believe Grammar   145

V. POETRY, PLAYS, AND FEMINIST FICTION

Preface to *Poems and Plays*   159

Poems   163

    The Road to Nowhere

    A Maine Road

    Fishing

    Berlin

    An Epitaph

    The Return

Mother-Love   167

The Girl from the Marsh Croft   187

The Funeral   240

    V. WORKING DOCUMENTS

Correspondence and Department Reports   253

    Works Cited   283

Acknowledgments

I was introduced to Gertrude Buck in an eighteenth- and nineteenth-century rhetoric class with Jerry Bump at the University of Texas at Austin, encouraged by Jim Berlin to pursue my interest, and guided through a dissertation on her writing by Lester Faigley, James Kinneavy, and John Ruszkiewicz. Nancy MacKechnie, curator of Rare Books and Manuscripts, Special Collections of Vassar College Libraries, and Nancy Bartlett at the Bentley Historical Library, University of Michigan, provided assistance and permissions for the materials to be published. At the University of Pittsburgh Press, Jean Ferguson Carr, David Bartholomae, and Catherine Marshall have been extraordinarily knowledgeable and supportive editors. Thanks to Mary Trachsel, Sue Carter Simmons, Vickie Ricks, Sharon Crowley, Pat Brantlinger, Kathryn Flannery, and Barry Kroll for commenting on earlier versions of this project. For the daily love and support essential to any academic endeavor, I thank Lori Campbell and Laura Galloway.

This book is dedicated to my mother, Ann Louise Campbell, and to the memory of my grandmother, Anna Sophia Carlson, who graduated from St. Cloud Teachers College in 1920.

Introduction

In calling this book *Toward a Feminist Rhetoric*, I intend to highlight Gertrude Buck's efforts to rethink a patriarchal rhetorical tradition, reshape teacher-centered classrooms, and revise intellectual and social issues of concern to women. Susan C. Jarratt has argued that "if the Western intellectual tradition is not only a product of men, but constituted by masculinity, then transformation comes not only from women finding women authors but also from a gendered rereading of that masculine rhetoric" (2). Not only is Gertrude Buck an important woman author, but she revised a masculine rhetoric in her dissertation, by rereading the treatment of metaphor by male rhetoricians, and continued to reread masculine cultural practices throughout her career. Buck's writing illustrates the range of materials that can comprise a rhetoric, including fiction, academic articles, and classroom textbooks, and her thinking and presentation in these works exemplify what I call a feminist rhetoric. That is, although Buck wrote against the grain of nineteenth-century conventional wisdom about teaching writing, literature, and grammar, she did so with more humor than indignation, using whatever of value might be saved from the masculine tradition in which she worked. Buck was a productive scholar, publishing six textbooks, a book of literary criticism, and over a dozen pedagogical articles that focused on language, grammar, rhetoric, and teaching. She also wrote fiction, poetry, plays, and edited a volume of John Ruskin's writing. The range of genres included in this collection allows us to see how Buck integrated her rhetorical theory with her teaching and literary interests. Buck represents more than an interesting footnote in the history of composition, and her writing reflects more than a development of the feminist rhetorics and pedagogies that challenged dominant rhetorics. The problems Buck addressed persist in the academy today: models of learning are too mechanical, students are frequently alienated from their studies and particularly their writing, insufficient financial and emotional rewards are given to instructors at the bottom of the academic hierarchy, theories of language are insufficient to account for the social realm that language is a creature of and creates.

Drawing from all Buck's published writing—composition textbooks, pedagogical articles, rhetorical treatises, literary criticism, professional correspondence, poetry and fiction—this collection provides material with which to explore a number of questions: How do issues of instruction change over time? How does one's theory play out locally in the daily work of teaching and administrating? How do various genres support or limit the development of an idea? How can a woman negotiate power within an institution? What roles do communities of women play in supporting the work of female academics? How might one work within an institution to transform the kinds of knowledge that are perceived, privileged, and produced? In working with Buck's plays, articles, and textbooks for the past seven years, I have come to appreciate the way she integrated aspects of her work and her life; it seems that her academic work was guided by the same principles with which she lived her life, and her life was shaped by the theories she produced in her work. Today, when fragmentation seems to be magnified and celebrated, I welcome Buck as a model who feminizes rhetoric, a study that has historically sought connections among speaker and listener and context. Buck's feminism helped her to balance concerns about the individual and society, to analyze the social and institutional forces that prevent people from writing, and to monitor the effects of hierarchy and imbalances of power on those with the least academic authority. She argued that the university had a responsibility to interact with and contribute to the welfare of its surrounding communities, and she analyzed education and rhetorical theories for the effect they had on those with least power, namely students.

This edition answers a call to recover women theorists and to develop a history of women in rhetoric. Patricia Bizzell has outlined three ways scholars can find or create a feminist tradition in what has been an exclusively male tradition of rhetoric. She advocates reading the canon of male writers as a resisting reader, thus bringing a feminist perspective to twenty-five hundred years of texts and practices. She suggests we find women who were writing at the same time and in parallel traditions, and, finally, that scholars look outside the sites of school and public office, which have served as the location of rhetorical tradition, to find evidence of women's rhetorical and literate activities (51). Within Bizzell's rubric, this project falls into the second group: Buck produced texts that rivaled the male-authored rhetorics that dominated composition classrooms in U.S. academies during the late nineteenth century.

Because rhetoric has historically been defined and practiced as a public performance, it may be appropriate that the Gertrude Buck I construct on these pages is based primarily on her published writings. Although I researched the archives of both institutions with which she was associated, the University of Michigan and Vassar College, I found little autobiographical material. We know she was born on 14 July 1871, the daughter of Anne Bradford and George M. Buck, an attorney and judge in Kalamazoo, Michigan, who presumably encouraged her education. She entered the University of Michigan in 1890, first studying Greek and then medicine. Only in her junior year did she switch to English (Wylie, "Some Early Writings" 21). Buck earned all three of her degrees at the University of Michigan: A.B. in 1894, M.S. in 1895, and Ph.D. in 1898. In graduate school she worked with Fred Newton Scott, who at that time was defining rhetoric as a tool for democracy in the Midwest in distinction to the definitions and classroom practices issuing from Harvard and Amherst, the "cutting edge" of rhetoric in the East. There she studied the history of rhetoric, graded student themes, and developed her own reading of the rhetorical tradition.

Buck's dissertation project consisted of a revision of rhetoric's canon that centered on a critique of the treatment of metaphor, and she used the new subject of psychology to address what might be called feminist concerns: what happens to the *person* in a theory of metaphor and the praxis that grows out of that theory? As a rhetorician, Buck observed more than the words of a text; she analyzed strategies, anticipated effects, and observed the conditions that could best facilitate the production of text. Virginia Allen writes that "the subject matter of her life was not merely rhetoric, grammar, and literature, but the society in which those vital disciplines was practiced" (156). Buck's concerns as a teacher were rhetorical and feminist; she wanted her women students to learn to speak and write effectively about public matters.

> At a time when women were accused of abandoning their traditional roles to assume "male" social roles, Buck's theory of discourse offers a clear social dimension to female experiences, giving women room to locate themselves in new social roles, not by abandoning their past but by rewriting it. Always appropriating the past to usher in change, Buck's theory suggests that women and men, like characters in a complex narrative, are creations of a complex interaction of habit, environment, social circumstances, and, of course, gender. (Ricks 14)

Whether Buck called herself a feminist or not, the treatment of women and women's rights figure centrally in her pedagogical and imaginative work.

In her one-act play *Mother-Love*, Buck dismantled essentialist notions of womanhood, particularly the equation of "good woman" with "mother," by portraying an unmarried woman tenderly caring for her mentally disabled older sister. Their "real" mother's selfish devotion to a runaway son deprives the family of material and emotional support. Buck advocated women's rights in limericks published in *The Masses*, her textbooks offered feminist claims for students to support, and her rhetorical theory challenged a two-thousand-year tradition that defined persuasion as an act of war.

I have labeled Buck's writing as moving *toward* a feminist rhetoric rather than embodying one entirely because I think a feminist rhetoric should be created collectively. No single writer or theorist can offer an exhaustive definition, no single orator can be the ideal rhetor, and no one teacher should be the model of an ultimate practitioner. Feminist gains have always come from collective, collaborative work to create social and institutional change. This is not *toward* a feminist rhetoric because of some lack on Buck's part. I offer this edition of her work as a site for feminist rhetoricians to articulate a tradition of women in the academy and to practice feminist criticism so that by connecting with the women who have historically produced feminist rhetorical theory and radical pedagogy we can encourage the efforts of writers, teachers, and rhetoricians today.

Gertrude Buck taught composition, rhetoric, and literary theory at Vassar College from 1897 until her death in 1922.[1] As a rhetorical theorist, Buck seems prescient; sixty years before composition professionals began teaching students a writing process in addition to grading written products, she suggested that teachers "postpone [criticism] until the writing-process has thereby gained a freedom and vigor which can defy its paralyzing effect" ("Recent Tendencies" 379). As a feminist, she developed an organic vision of writing in community that challenged the tenets of the more popular "mechanical" rhetorical theories and practices of her day. Traditional rhetoric relied on

1. Laura Wylie wrote to Fred Scott on 23 November 1921: "You will be sorry to hear that Miss Buck is seriously ill, having had a stroke last August, from the results of which she is still almost completely incapacitated. We have every reason to hope for her ultimate recovery, however, as she is gaining both in speech and the power of motion, but there is no immediate prospect of her being able to take up any work" (Bentley Historical Library, University of Michigan, Ann Arbor). At Buck's memorial service, her colleague Katherine Warren described her "physical frailty against which she made constant and most gallant war [so that] bodily ailments incapacitating to ordinary mortals seemed to affect her productivity little or not at all" ("In Remembrance" 19). Buck's obituary in the *New York Times* records that she died "after a long illness" (10 January 1922).

"warlike" qualities, where the speaker's goal was to annihilate the opposition; Buck advocated a more communal model of communication, where listeners and speakers worked together to reach truth. She argued that student writers should choose topics that interested *them*, that an audience should be determined for each writing assignment, that literature was an activity, and that writing and reading were inherently connected.

To some extent, Buck represents a generation of white women, among the first to graduate from colleges in the United States, whose positive intellectual and social experiences at women's colleges or coeducational universities suggested they might devote themselves to a "life of the mind." Michigan had been a leader in the education of women, becoming a coeducational institution in 1870, and its president, James Angell, had publicly supported the intellectual abilities of women students.[2] I qualify the extent to which Buck might be said to represent a generation of women with Ph.D.s because she published more than most other turn-of-the-century women professors of rhetoric and composition; thus, it is easier to trace her thinking and her career. Little documentation exists for those teachers who did not publish widely in academic or popular journals, although we have records in student memoirs, departmental reports, and records of memorial services.[3] Like other "re-

2. "There is no department of study in which some of our female students do not excel; and in none have they, as a class, failed to do fine work. It is possible that those now here are under a special stimulus. As pioneers, they doubtless feel that the reputation of their sex is, to a certain extent, staked upon their efforts. And they labor with great fidelity; we have been constrained to caution some of them against over-work. But I think that substantially the same zeal may be expected of their successor" (qtd. in Tyler 268).

3. The following profiles may offer a sense of Buck's written production in relation to other women teaching under similar conditions. Clara Stevens, a Mount Holyoke Female Seminary graduate of 1881, taught at her alma mater until she went to graduate school. Like Buck, Stevens was a student of Fred Newton Scott and John Dewey at the University of Michigan, earning a Masters of Philosophy in 1894. She published only two articles on pedagogy, yet was an active chair of the Rhetoric Department at Mount Holyoke, formed in 1897, until her retirement in 1921. Margaret Ball, another Mount Holyoke graduate, was professor of rhetoric at Mount Holyoke College from 1906 until 1943. Ball published a textbook, *The Principles of Outlining*, a literary study, *Sir Walter Scott as a Critic of Literature*, and at least sixteen articles, many in popular magazines such as *Scribner's* and *Atlantic Monthly*. Mary Augusta Jordan, a Vassar College graduate, taught writing at Smith College from 1884 until 1921. She edited a collection of Ralph Waldo Emerson's essays, wrote a book, *Correct Speaking and Writing*, and contributed five articles to Smith and Vassar alumnae publications. She also published four articles on teaching in journals such as *School Review* and *Atlantic Monthly*. At her death, Smith College President Nielson remarked that, "Sacrificing contributions to scholarship that she might give herself to her teaching and other academic duties, Miss Jordan published comparatively little." Sophie Hart, a Radcliffe College graduate of 1892, also earned an M.A. at the University of Michigan and taught at Wellesley College from 1892 until 1937. Hart lectured widely to alumnae clubs around the country and published most of her half dozen articles in Wellesley magazines.

covered" early feminists, Buck comes to us not without contradictions; as an unmarried woman financially dependent on an institution, she wrote suffrage limericks and was active in the suffrage league of Poughkeepsie, yet she seems not to have been an activist on the college campus. She did not, for instance, sign a 1913 petition that the Vassar faculty circulated protesting what was perceived as undemocratic actions by the administration.

Rather than working to change her institution, Buck focused on creating alternative communities outside the academy. Her special project, the Vassar Dramatic Workshop (and, later, the Poughkeepsie Community Theatre), provided a perfect vehicle for the democratic connection between college and community that Buck advocated. She once called it "an example of what all colleges should do for their communities" (letter to MacCracken, 3 June 1920). The Community Theatre brought together her many theoretical and educational concerns; it combined art with a democratic social structure, blending and balancing the two so that they were inextricably connected, just as Buck believed they were all along. In her chair's words, "all classes of townspeople" were involved and "the possibilities of a really democratic participation in this movement and of genuine artistic achievement seem almost limitless" (letter to MacCracken, 19 April 1920). Buck saw her role in the theatre much as she did her role as a teacher, "supervising the work of the untrained committees on the two productions, [and] using to best advantage the work of all members of the community who are interested and developing their latent powers" (letter to MacCracken, 3 June 1920). As the theatre took more of her time and proved more immediately rewarding, Buck's publications in composition and rhetoric ceased.

Major Themes

Over the course of twenty-five years of teaching at Vassar College, Buck never lost her passionate beliefs in the possibility of harmony among people and in the natural abilities of the individual. From her textbooks to fiction, from her literary theory to committee reports, several themes emerge and endure despite teaching pressures and institutional roadblocks. Buck insisted on the *organic unity* in all things and all people, a concept that grew from romanticism and informed the progressive age. As she explained in an article on grammar, "thought is not a heap of shreds and patches, a whole made up of previously separate parts, but a single, differentiating organic process" ("Foundations" 485). In an essay she wrote as a student for Michigan's magazine, *The Inlander*, Buck described Shakespeare's character Menenius to illustrate her organic theory of society:

Each man's life is so subtly intertwined with the life of the whole that his deed, whether good or evil must inevitably return upon himself; and consequently, not only positive crimes but "envy, hatred, malice and all uncharitableness" become simply irrational, as if one hand should maim the other. ("Ethical Significance" 221)

Early in her career Buck articulated this organic perspective in a book she wrote with Harriet Scott, *Organic Education.* Her interest in the psychology, process, and consequences of thought led her to develop a curriculum for elementary students and a theory of reading literature that reconciled the conflicting theories of the day: "One must listen closely to hear, amid the jangle of conflicting theories as to what literary criticism really is, the still small voice of their harmonious relation to one another. Once heard, however, it cannot be disregarded" (*Social Criticism of Literature* 16).

Because she believed people could achieve harmony if they only listened to themselves and nature, she concluded that education could foster *cooperation* as a logical or natural mode of action. Describing the Detroit Normal School which Harriet Scott ran, Buck recorded that the curriculum adhered to a "principle of cooperation, which has been more or less explicitly recognized throughout the grades as the underlying principle, not only of political but also of industrial and social development" ("Another Phase" 383). Buck's later working environment, the English Department at Vassar College, was governed democratically and cooperatively, shaping and shaped by Buck's theories and practices. This emphasis on the good of the community, evident also in the new socialism at the turn of the century, was a central tenet of the English Department, as the chair, Laura Johnson Wylie, reported in 1921: "From 1896 at least, we have worked co-operatively whenever co-operation was possible. Matters affecting the interest of the whole group have in every case been made subjects for joint discussion, and whenever it was practical have been jointly determined. Smaller units acting together in any capacity have invariably made the organization of their common task a definite part of their work" (1921 "Report").

Cooperation plays a key role in Buck's 1916 monograph, *The Social Criticism of Literature,* and is evident on several levels—as the motivation for her writing the book, as the foundation of the act of reading and consequent definition of good literature, and as the function and duty of the critic who makes literature more accessible to society. She hoped that "the long war of critical theories [will] end in the active peace of cooperation" (15), yet she recognized that there was a tendency for literary concerns to be elite, aristocratic, or snobbish, and she therefore argued that the critic had "one priceless possession—a vitalized, *democratized* conception of literature" (31). Here, then, is a combination of romantic and social views: the critic's role was to level up conditions between the poet and reader so that all could share in the concentrated experience of the writer and gain her or his educational and experiential advantages. By this means the "poet's individual gain in perception or emotion has been socialized" (39). Buck also viewed reading as an act of cooperation between reader and writer. Her fiction reflected her belief that cooperation and goodness could prevail, and that women were too frequently hindered from achieving their potential. In her dramatization of Selma Lagerlöf's story "The Girl from the Marshcroft," a country woman who had a child outside marriage overcomes social censure to prove her worth to the audience and ultimately to the man she loves.

In addition to her belief in unity and the importance of cooperation, Buck emphasized *accepting the individual* as the starting place for any teaching, and she urged teachers to allow their students to read materials that interested them and write about their own concerns to their "spiritual peers." A teacher's job was to help students awaken to their individuality and reach their potential to serve society. Her mentor at the University of Michigan, Fred Newton Scott, remembered that her comments on student themes "were never mere perfunctory annotations. They were attempts to bring out the individuality of the student in his writing, and to suggest ways and means by which he might improve himself through his writing. They were counsels of encouragement as well as a means of correcting errors ("Address" 3). Practices that cut students off from their interests slowed that progress, and Buck advocated "the gradual education of readers through the very reading which now interests and satisfies them" (*SCL* 57).

The goal and result of individuals working together cooperatively was greater *service to the community*, which could be achieved if education elevated people beyond their individual interests and current tastes to a "higher" more communal level. Buck called her rhetoric "social" and grounded it in her reading of Plato, where discourse itself furthered the common good. She believed language, of "unrivaled importance to the social order," had the power to establish communities ("Make-Believe Grammar" 33). Like many nineteenth-century women faculty, her life reflected the important place of connections with women; she and Laura Wylie, English Department chair, lived together for years, traveling to Europe, having students for supper each Sunday evening, and entertaining other teachers regularly.[4] Buck helped to found organizations that would support creative and political interests and confirm connections. To nurture the creative side of their writing, members of the department formed a Journal Club, which met to read their own short stories, novels, poems, and plays. To create stronger ties with the community outside the college, Buck formed a club with the town teachers of English to discuss conditions and methods of teaching. More politically active was the Women's City and County Club of Pough- keepsie, which Buck helped form and over which Wylie presided for ten years. Buck also started the Vassar Dramatic Workshop and founded the Community Theatre of Poughkeepsie. It is ironic that she has been singled out for her advanced views, when she herself credits her accomplishments and ideas to her community.[5]

What sets Buck apart from many composition teachers today is the ex- plicitly spiritual orientation of her writing. As one colleague recalled, Buck "acknowledged in her own life the existence in the universe of a divine idea ascertainable to human reason, and taught us by example that the day's work could never be futile, but was to its last detail and in its apparently most irrelevant moment, eternally worthwhile" (Reed 2). Early in her career she connected the theological and rhetorical: "The organic unity of all creation, and the evolution of the universe according to discernible laws, were ideas which ultimately revolutionized my theological conceptions" ("Religious Ex- perience" 26). Those beliefs influenced her theory of rhetoric, her classroom practices, and her work in a community of teachers as well. For instance, Buck's optimism about society's progress, which was, of course, a trait of the

4. The relatively low salaries of teachers at women's colleges made communal living a necessity. When Vassar College opened in 1865, male teachers and their families lived in apart- ments in the pavilion and lower-ranked female instructors lived in single rooms on corridors with students. "By the turn of the century, [President] Taylor relented and allowed women faculty the right to live outside college residences, but the college granted women $100 less than men for a rent allowance because women had the option of living in college" (Horowitz 187). The salary for full professors at Vassar College was $3,200 in 1918 and $3,600 in 1920. Associate professors made between $2,400 and $2,600, assistant professors earned $2,000, and instructors made $1,400–$1,600 per year.

5. In a careful examination of Buck's ideas, Gerald Mulderig, for instance, comments that "our profession has changed much as Buck's work suggested that it would. . . . Buck thought she stood at a turning point in composition teaching, but it was a turning point still more than half a century away" (101). Virginia Allen writes that Buck traced the "mental processes during the act of composing at the turn of the century and that she did so from an epistemological self- consciousness that was unparalleled before the late 1960s in composition research" (157). These comments, while accurate, point to a way of doing history that values most the unique, the first, or the anomalous.

progressive era, was based on the following belief: "[When] society shall come to recognize that which in the New Testament phrase is called love, in our practical modern vernacular co-operation, as essentially the law of its life, then it may fairly be said in the psychological phrase, to have come to self-consciousness, to a sense of its own individual character, as a complex, highly-differentiated, organic unity" ("Ethical Significance" 222).

By emphasizing love or cooperation as a law, Buck removed it from a romantic realm of emotion and placed it on a par with the psychological principles just being codified. Society, she thought, was evolving, and if individuals could recognize the laws upon which that growth depended, progress would be assured. Believing that love, or cooperation, was the primary law, Buck looked for it everywhere and objected to any teaching or theory that did not have a cooperative basis; to view rhetoric as persuasion for its own sake, without regard to the truth or the listener, was a form of violence. She wanted all language to build society, or rather she knew that language, like literature, "is not alone a creature but also a creator of the society it serves" (*SCL* 60). Language users, especially the socially elite, should be aware of the power of language so that "a reader who understands the place of literature in the social economy cannot relegate it to the category either of private yachts or of ward politics, but must definitely take account of its relations to himself" (*SCL* 55).

Buck believed that the pursuit of truth—whether writing a description or diagramming a sentence—helped a person maintain integrity, and such consistency was crucial because every activity affected the whole, the organism, of which the individual was a part. The integration of theory and practice, what might more accurately be called Buck's praxis, was recalled by her colleague, Amy Reed:

> It was her habit to think much quite by herself, and to think far ahead, to remain as much as possible in that reflective solitude until she had hold of some large thought—a thought which was not merely a vague generality but quite clear in many details of its application, and which was of a size to warrant perhaps years of work. Emerging then, she would talk the matter over with fellow workers, until through their reaction or criticism the best means of carrying out the idea also became clear to her. Then, always asking help of friends and colleagues—for her thoughts were increasingly social and always involved cooperation—she would proceed with unfailing patience and thoroughness to carry out her theory, teaching others to carry on at first with her help and then if possible without it, in order that she might be free to pursue the next plan, then already forming. (2)

Unlike the usual practice, where a teacher became so associated with a course that taking the course meant taking that teacher, she developed courses, taught them with others, and then left to teach something new. That her colleagues recognized the ideas guiding her activities and accepted the integration of theory and practice is testimony to the eloquence of her life.

Early Development

As an undergraduate at Michigan, which admitted women in 1870, Buck wrote for the campus newspaper, the magazine *The Inlander*, and was active in debate. As a graduate student, she worked as a reader of themes and was the first Ph.D. student in rhetoric to graduate from Fred Newton Scott's program. (It is most likely through her association with Scott, the first president of the National Council of Teachers of English and a past president of the Modern Language Association, that she came to the attention of scholars.) She taught high school in Indianapolis for a year, worked with Scott's sister, Harriet, at the normal school for teachers in Detroit, and most likely attended John Dewey's course at the University of Chicago before going to Vassar College.

Buck's student writing was characterized by the same confident, unapologetic, direct, and often humorous tone as her later professional writing. These characteristics seem all the more remarkable when compared to the writing of some of her female contemporaries, as the following example illustrates. In an article for *The Inlander*, Buck edited a collection of responses from American writers to the question, "What do you think of athletic education for women?" The authors were told that their answers would be published in *The Inlander*, that proceeds of sales of the magazine would go to the women's gymnasium, and that their autographs would be sold to raise money. Twenty-six writers replied. Ten of them were women, whose presentation of self differed markedly from that of the men. Mary Hallock Foote, a well-known illustrator, had been elected to the National Academy of Women Painters and Sculptors, and had published seven books. She wrote, "I wish I could put something less stupid above my autograph. On the whole I think I will give it to you on a separate piece of paper," and she did so ("Athletic" 292). Harriet Prescott Spofford, who published widely in *Harper's Bazaar, Atlantic Monthly*, the *Knickerbocker, Cosmopolitan*, and juvenile magazines, had published fourteen books when she wrote, "I am ashamed to send you such an unworthy contribution to the Inlander, but such as it is, it goes with my warmest wishes for the success of your undertaking" (294).

Another writer, Mrs. Schuyler Van Rensalaer, authored a popular series on recent American architecture for the *Century Magazine* in the 1880s and 1890s and by 1894 had published six books on architecture and art. To Buck's inquiry she replied: "I am gratified by the request you make of me, and gladly comply with it, although it seems odd to be told that my autograph can have any pecuniary value. The chance that it may, as attached to an entirely worthless answer to the question you put, seems so very remote that I venture to enclose another sheet with a borrowed sentiment on another subject which has far more intrinsic value, hoping in this vicarious way to contribute a mite toward the good work you have in hand" (296). Two passages from Sir Thomas More followed Mrs. Van Rensalaer's entry. Louise Imogen Guiney had published six volumes of poetry and essays in 1895 and was part of the literary circle of Boston, which included Annie Adams Fields and Sarah Orne Jewett. She responded, "You will, I hope, get your gymnasium; but I can hardly believe that the autograph of this inadequate poet and pretty fair sprinter will do much towards that admirable end! Believe me" (299).

Contrast these with the response from Robert Grant, an author whose response cast him in the role of suitor: "The admiration which, according to your letter, the girls of Michigan University have for me, would be ardently reciprocated, I feel sure, were I to meet them in person" (297).

Buck's master's thesis, *Figures of Rhetoric, a Psychological Study*, was the first publication in Scott's series, Contributions to Rhetorical Theory. Her Ph.D. thesis extended that work, and *The Metaphor: A Study in the Psychology of Rhetoric* was fifth of the nine publications in the series. In this book, Buck examined theories of metaphor from Aristotle to the present, and found them lacking in psychological validity. In his important study of rhetoric and composition in the nineteenth century, Albert Kitzhaber admired Buck's "courage in brushing away the accumulated dust of well over two thousand years" (290). At one point she faulted Cicero for assuming metaphors give pleasure simply because they are brief. Buck defined metaphor as vital. "It is not compounded like a prescription with intent to produce a certain effect upon the person who swallows it, but it springs spontaneously out of a genuine thought-process and represents with exactness a certain stage of a growing perception. . . . It is not an artificial, manufactured product, but a real organism, living, growing, and dying" (Metaphor 35).

The spontaneous element of metaphor interested Buck, and she found it the most "natural" form of speech. Historically, she wrote, there have been two explanations for metaphor: (1) to make up for the poverty of language, allowing a speaker to use a similar word when a new item had no name; and

(2) to ornament speech and give pleasure to the hearer. Chiefly relying on the psychological theories of William James and John Dewey, she argued that both were false. The first implied that spiritual and material conceptions were so sharply distinct that a speaker saw two separate ideas, a resemblance between them, and lacking a word for the latter concept, used an available word from the former object. Buck believed that psychological studies of children's development refuted the poverty of language argument and proposed instead that the child uses the same word because she or he can not differentiate between the objects; only later do the objects become distinct. She discounted the second theory, that metaphors were created to give pleasure to a reader, as being too mechanical. Such a view of composition might account for metaphors in lesser poetry, but the "mechanical," "crude," and "essentially cheap" image of Shakespeare groping for an appropriate object with which to compare the sun dissuaded Buck of this theory (27).

Years at Vassar College

Laura Wylie, chair of Vassar's English Department, read Buck's dissertation, was impressed, and hired her to run the composition and rhetoric program there. When she arrived on campus in 1897, Vassar College had been educating women for thirty-two years and took pride in being the first endowed college for women. Vassar's first president had the job of defining the role education would play in women's lives. John Howard Raymond adopted a middle position, whereby women would be encouraged to develop their mental powers but discouraged from using those increased powers to change their traditional role in society. In an 1870 address to the Baptist Educational Convention, Raymond assured his audience that by being granted education and ennobling her mind, the Vassar woman "will not need to handle the ballot . . . or to take orders in the church or prefix a 'rev.' to her name" (51). He advocated a liberal education for women of the educated class so she could become "more of a woman . . . a fit companion for a wiser and nobler man . . . she will fill a larger space and be felt as a greater power. She will have a wider information, will think more correctly, decide more wisely, converse more understandingly, and in every way make larger contributions to the intelligence and the improvement of the community to which she belongs" (43). Into this environment Buck stepped as a young instructor, with a Ph.D. in rhetoric and a vision of a harmonious, working community.

THE VASSAR ENVIRONMENT

The Vassar College English faculty was in some ways typical of educated women's communities at the turn of the century; they were the first and second generations of women to attend college. Laura Wylie, department chair from 1896 until 1922, was Vassar's valedictorian in 1877 and in 1894 was the first woman granted a Ph.D. from Yale. Others held degrees from Cornell, Columbia, Barnard, Wellesley, Bryn Mawr, Mount Holyoke, and Michigan. They were all unmarried, as were 75 percent of the women who earned Ph.D.'s between 1877 and 1924 (Harris 101). A life of service and sacrifice was expected of single women, whose devoted service to an institution at times literally took up all their personal space. While Buck and Wylie lived in a house in town, not all the teachers could afford to, and because there was not enough office space for all the instructors, many conducted conferences and kept papers in their rooms. In yearly reports Wylie asked for more space for her instructors because it was "inadequate" to have "but a single room in which to sleep, study, and carry on one's business and one's social life" (1915 "Report").

Numerous department reports and personal accounts indicate that the English Department was democratically run. An elected executive committee made personnel decisions; all other matters were discussed by the entire department and voted upon by the members. At the center of the democratic harmony within the department was the relationship between Buck and Wylie. Shortly after Buck's arrival, Wylie argued for her promotion, for she felt from the beginning that Buck was an equal and was grateful for the administrative duties she performed. In an annual report two years after her promotion to professor, Wylie urged "that Professor Buck's salary be made equal to that of the head of the department" because "Miss Buck does her full share" of administrative work, "relieving me entirely of a great deal of it" (1909 "Report"). The request was denied. Records indicate that Buck and Wylie shared a household from 1908 on and had a very stable relationship—at one time they considered adopting a child.[6] Their partnership served as a reference point for the close connection between rhetoric and literature within the curriculum. A colleague recalled that "the completeness of their cooperation made the growth of an integral relation between their courses in

6. Their relationship might have been what Carroll Smith-Rosenberg has called an "intense female friendship," and today we might call them lesbians, given their woman-centered lives and commitment to each other. Problems with using contemporary labels for the past should not erase the lives of woman-identified women. After Wylie's death *The Poughkeepsie Courier* (17 April 1932) reported that her will directed "that her body be cremated and the ashes buried in the grave of her friend, Gertrude Buck, in Woodlands Cemetery, Philadelphia. She then directs that sufficient money be given the cemetery to care for the permanent upkeep of the grave." Wylie also established a Gertrude Buck Fund with $10,000 "to perpetuate the friendly relations between city and college."

literature and in writing a natural process, and formed a nucleus for similar relations in the department as a whole" (Warren, "Retirement" 2). Elsewhere English departments were battling out the supremacy of rhetoric or literature, but the Vassar department combined three branches of language study: history of the language, rhetoric, and literature. In the same request for equivalent salary, Wylie commented on the healthy consequences of their relationship.

> Indeed, if we did not work together in entire harmony, it would probably be necessary either for me to do considerably less teaching, or to divide the department, as has been unfortunately done in many places, into the departments of English or Rhetoric, and of Literature. The present union of the two subjects in a single department has many advantages of economy and efficiency, and it seems unfortunate that in order to preserve these, one of the people concerned should suffer serious and permanent financial loss. (1909 "Report")

According to Wylie, what set her department apart from others was that rather than conducting their work "perfunctorily, or with a view of the interests of the individuals conducting it," the Vassar English faculty "work disinterestedly and intelligently for the common good, and through this intelligent co-operation make the ideas on which we act effective in the various spheres to which they are applied" (1921 "Report"). This cooperative strategy might also have served as a means of survival within a hostile environment. Wylie protested in the 1921 annual report that while the English department put in more hours for less pay, "the budget for labor and for material equipment [had] been exceeded again and again," and she began to see the limitations of their cooperative attitude.

A debate over women's suffrage highlighted differences in administrative style between the college and the department, differences that directly affected the faculty's relationship with students. In January 1908, President James Taylor received a letter from M. Carey Thomas, president of Bryn Mawr, asking him to allow Jane Addams to speak on "The Working Woman's Need of the Ballot." In addition to speaking at Bryn Mawr, Addams was scheduled to speak at Mount Holyoke, Radcliffe, Smith, and Wellesley, and President Thomas inquired when could she schedule the well-known reformer for Vassar. Taylor rejected the invitation, replying that Addams "comes as a representative of a 'movement,' and I cannot myself think that it is a wise project, for . . . it seems to me an effort on the part of a most admirable body of women to exploit the colleges in connection with what they and many others regard as a most needed reform" (letter to Thomas, 9 January 1908).[7] Taylor had also refused to allow a chapter of a suffrage club to be formed on Vassar's campus, and this new controversy forced him to explain his views to the alumnae at their 1909 meeting.

The transcript of Taylor's address was printed and distributed to faculty and other alumnae under the title "The 'Conservatism' of Vassar." Taylor argued that he did not oppose suffrage per se, but rather opposed exploiting young, unformed minds for whatever cause came along. The purpose of the college, he said, was to lay a "broad and liberal foundation" upon which the graduate could discuss social or political issues: "The chief mission of the college is to train the young, not for special fields of work or any special theories of reform, but to enlighten and broaden and inspire, to train to the careful weighing of evidence, to the scholarly knowledge of facts and the experiences of history, to the testing of theories of what has been already tried, and all as the basis for individual independence in thought and life. It is not the chief mission of an undergraduate to deal with the untried." Until they had the training and information to make decisions and act upon them, the college should protect these unformed minds: "Vassar recognizes the right of everyone to do her own thinking, and her *right* to *withhold the results* till she knows what she thinks. It *encourages* this reticence in the young." He wrote to a parent in June 1912 that "one of the fundamental mistakes of our whole American system is this crowding of young people to the front before they have had time to think or to gather fair material upon which to base their conclusion." President Taylor concluded his address by quoting the first acting president, John Raymond: 'The mission of Vassar College was not to reform society but to educate women.' In his own words, Vassar believed in "the home and in the old-fashioned view of marriage and children and the splendid service of society wrought through these quiet and unradical means."

Taylor received praise for his outspokenness from many colleagues, including the president of Princeton, Woodrow Wilson, President Seelye of Smith, the presidents of Michigan, Brown, and Baltimore Women's College. Several antisuffrage groups requested multiple copies of the pamphlet, but in keeping with his stance of "neutral" education, Taylor refused them, main-

7. In contrast, at Wellesley College, Addams's visit was reported as "so distinctly social and economic rather than political in its character, that it may perhaps be regarded as the most important of the contributions to the department made by allied organizations" (*Wellesley College President's Report*, 1907–08).

taining that "the question of suffrage is in no way involved, save as an accident" (letter to faculty, 24 March 1909).

Many faculty members, however, saw suffrage at the center of the controversy and spoke about the issue at a student meeting. Inez Milholland, a student activist who later become prominent in the women's suffrage movement, had earlier called a meeting in a graveyard adjacent to the campus in compliance with Taylor's decree that suffrage not be discussed on college grounds; faculty and students gathered to hear Harriet Stanton Blatch, Charlotte Perkins Gilman, Helen Hay, and Rose Schneiderman of the Capmakers Union.[8] In 1909 Taylor allowed use of a campus room but warned that the students "must not admit any outsiders and it must be a private meeting; that is, without public report" (Memorandum). While he assumed that "both sides and students only would have a talk over the issue," faculty members spoke at the meeting, and only those in favor of suffrage had been invited. There followed a heated faculty meeting during which Taylor reiterated that "in no sense was the question of suffrage at issue save that it chanced to be the burning point attracting popular attention and newspaper reporters, and so involved us with the critical public." He was concerned about faculty speaking out on public issues and reminded them "we were all bound, if need be for the interest of the college, to withhold any organized expression of opinion as if official and authoritative, as it was sure to be considered" (Memorandum). He recorded that in response to this view, "a section of the faculty very strongly opposed this as an attack on individual freedom."

Taylor sent a memorandum to those faculty members most vocal during the meeting, including Laura Wylie. Invoking a rhetoric of service, he justified "the proper restraining imposed on that liberty by considerations of the larger welfare of the college, in relation not only to its students but to its constituency." He strongly advised his faculty to put aside their personal beliefs for the good of the college: "In any heated state of the popular mind it is wise for the college faculty to avoid the encouragement of one side, and for it to give its endeavors, if given at all, to the fair putting of both sides in an academic attitude. That is indeed putting the college above ourselves, but

8. A 1920 account of this incident: "Now, nothing is so sure to make young people want to do a thing as an order that it must not be done, and Vassar girls were no exception to this rule. Not being permitted to meet in the college a number of students organized a suffrage society, which held its meetings by night in a graveyard. Result—the passion for suffrage flew like a white flame through the student body. The most stunning and attractive of the leaders joined the movement. A new outlet for the spirit of adventure had been found" (Bennett 13).

that, I trust, we are all of us doing in very many of our relationships, and in connection with very many of our personal opinions" (Memorandum). With this move, Taylor encouraged silence from the faculty, just as he had from Vassar students. Caroline Furness, who had spoken at the meeting in favor of suffrage, immediately sent Taylor a note, writing, "hereafter I shall be more guarded than in the past in any public expression of my opinion." While Laura Wylie was heading the Poughkeepsie suffrage movement, Furness anticipated Taylor's reaction, and she acknowledged that "I have even refrained from taking an active part in the work in Po'Keepsie which my interest might lead me to do, on account of my connection with the college" (letter to Taylor, 9 March 1909).[9]

Throughout the discussion of the suffrage issue, Taylor treated the students and faculty like children who needed to be protected from anything foreign, upsetting, or "social." Of course, he had to answer to parents, like George Swain, a professor at Harvard, who considered sending his daughter to Vassar so "she would not be brought under the influence of what I consider the modern fads of socialism, women's suffrage, etc. but where she would learn to be pre-eminently a home-maker and to look upon the home and the family as the main safeguard of our national life" (letter to Taylor, 8 March 1913). But he made clear his own belief that the college should keep women from the seductiveness of the outer world where they might "be led aside . . . by any of the alluring or insistent demands of the service or reforms which are better suited to the mature than to those in the process of education" ("Conservatism"). In a letter to faculty, he asked, "Suppose now that every explorer of new views and every adherent of new isms have a chance at will to attack these young and comparatively inexperienced minds?" (24 March 1909). As male protector, he felt a moral responsibility to keep the women isolated in a pristine environment: "Every one that has a cause wishes naturally to get at our young people, and in turn if one resists and holds to a belief in a steady development and training to fit one to examine every cause, to 'prove all things, and to hold fast that which is good,' then one must expect to meet in turn the accusations of a lack of interest and breadth, now in political reform, now in social reform, and now, alas, also in religion" ("Conservatism"). His language indicates how these "young minds" were attached

9. Martha Vicinus has observed that "university women followed 'the conventionalities of the age' even more firmly than other career women lest they attract further negative criticism" and that ultimately attacks on women's education had a "dampening effect on the individual participants" (607).

to equally young female bodies. Reformers wishing to agitate the Vassar students resemble men seeking sexual favors, men for whom the desire "to get at" the women comes "naturally." The good woman student "resists," finding strength in her "belief in a steady development" of intellect in the college world, or of strong moral character in the social realm. Taylor's description of Vassar's "old-fashioned preparatory education" parallels the kind of sexual standards traditionally referred to when women are encouraged to "be patient," as Taylor advised his students to be.

How effective was Taylor's "neutral" stand on suffrage, which included banning a suffrage club and discouraging prosuffrage faculty from addressing students? A poll taken by the student newspaper, the *Vassar Miscellany News*, found that 27 percent of the first-year students favored suffrage and 27 percent declared themselves ignorant of the issue; among seniors 57 percent were in favor and only 1 percent ignorant (Ellis 43). Clearly the issue was being discussed, although it is interesting to note that the percentages against suffrage (46 percent in the first year, 42 percent in the senior year) remained fairly constant. Records indicate that Taylor granted permission to members of the class of 1912 to form a chapter of the College Equal Suffrage League, a decision that drew telegrams from happy alumnae around the country who had been working for the vote for women. But other records maintain that it was not until 1914 that the faculty, "administering the college in the absence of a president, finally allowed the students to form a Woman's Suffrage Club" (Ellis 47).

Although as far as I can tell Buck did not speak at the suffrage meeting of 1909 and did not sign a petition for a more democratic college structure that circulated in 1913, she did address the issue. In 1912, under the title "Anti-Suffrage Sentiments," she published the following limericks in *The Masses*, a socialist magazine (she did not include this publication on the list she submitted to the president at the end of the year):

A delicate Angora cat
Had whiskers: but, pray, what of that?
"I don't want to vote,"
To a friend she once wrote:
"My place is at home on the mat."

"Let me hold the umbrella, my dear,"
Mrs. Hen said to kind Chanticleer.
" 'Tis man's privilege, love."

And he held it above

His own head, so it dripped in her ear.[10]

She also encouraged students to think about suffrage in her writing classes. Her 1899 textbook on argument included the following possible conclusions for an a priori argument: "Women will be allowed to vote on all questions in all States," "Every woman should be able to earn her own living," and "Women who desire to do so should enter the profession of medicine."

TEACHING CONDITIONS

The teaching environment at Vassar College was unlike that at all-male institutions, where students were antagonistic to their instructors, the structure of departments was more hierarchical, and the textbooks were less concerned with student interests and designed far less interactively than the three written by Gertrude Buck. One colleague remembered Buck as having "a quality of respect for her students' capacities which gave them confidence and evoked from them latent powers and swift flashes of new understandings, in which they often surprised themselves by doing better than they had ever done before!" Like Fred Newton Scott, she was able to develop "to a remarkable degree her students' aptitudes" (Paton). Scott had defined the teacher's role as not "simply to teach a language," but "to develop human personality—to draw it out, to give it freedom of expression, and when it has thus been developed, to know it through and through and to estimate it for itself" ("What the West Wants"). Buck's method of drawing students out was described by her colleague and co-author Elisabeth Woodbridge (Morris): "There was something Socratic in the way she led a class through tangled fields of thought, appreciating delicately and warmly any least bit of honest work, no matter how beset by what was false or confused. Something Socratic, yet possessing none of the Socratic over-astuteness which leaves one, at the end of some of those matchless dialogues, feeling tricked rather than led. Her classes were really and truly led—led and not pushed, led and not dragged—led by the gradual release in each participant of her own best powers, to her own best achievement" (9).

To help students produce something they cared about, Buck assigned topics from their own interests: "However trivial they may be in the teacher's eyes, [these topics] are for him and to his spiritual peers worth communicating" ("Recent Tendencies" 374). And George Pierce Baker, a Harvard instructor whose playwriting workshop she attended in 1916, remembered that "Miss Buck knew that it is the teacher's business not to set a model that is to be

---

10. I want to thank Julie Allen for bringing these limericks to my attention.

copied. It is to coax, it is to suggest, it is to draw out from the individual something that is that individual's; then that individual, with certain standards gained, may go out safely" (13).

The actual work of college teaching took up a great deal of the instructors' time, more than they would have chosen, as evident in the annual department reports and tallies of hours spent in various academic tasks. The specific conditions under which they worked included heavy teaching loads and large class sizes. As Wylie recorded, "each of the freshman teachers gives, during each semester, about three hundred interviews, varying in length from ten minutes to an hour. She receives nearer two thousand than fifteen hundred papers during the semester; and these papers have to be kept in a place convenient for reference" (letter to MacCracken, 30 September 1916). In light of these numbers, it is remarkable that the curriculum did not turn toward what has been called "current-traditional rhetoric," in which papers were marked solely for mechanical correctness.[11] Wylie recalled the situation during her first year (1894) when she "taught four sections of freshman averaging forty-five students each, and two classes in argumentation . . . averaging sixty each." Vassar still operated with assistants who didn't lead classes but criticized the written work, and Wylie concluded that "under such conditions good teaching was . . . manifestly impossible" (1915 "Report"). Adding up the time spent for each class, she concluded that each section required at least nine and one-half hours each week for conferences, classwork, and theme reading.

During Buck's first semester at Vassar, 1897–1898, she taught four sections of the required argumentation class, one section of advanced composition/description, a section of freshman English, and an independent study graduate course. Second semester found her with the same schedule plus a section of advanced argumentation and oral debate. She continued with seven courses each semester until 1902, when she was promoted to associate professor and her teaching load was dropped to four courses each semester. In addition to teaching, Buck's duties included directing the first-year English program, maintaining relations with secondary schools, organizing department lectures, and serving on various university committees and national committees, such as NCTE's committee to revise grammatical terminology.

COMPOSITION INSTRUCTION

The first-year course at Vassar was designed to give students broad exposure to language, and Buck lectured to the incoming class on "The Social Function

11. For a discussion of these practices see Robert Connors, "Mechanical Correctness."

of Language" and "The Functional Study of English." According to Wylie's 1910 report, the aim of first-year English at Vassar was

> to emphasize equally the development of the constructive, creative faculties and of the power of proportion and appreciation. Required of all students, based on a varied and often very inadequate preparation and preliminary to later elective English work of all sorts, it must provide training for both intelligent reading and clear writing, and in each of these cases for girls of average ability and practical bent as well as for those of marked artistic power. Practice in expository writing, with study of modern essays, is, by common consent of college teachers of English, best fitted to meet the psychological needs of the students at this stage of their progress and to train them in the accuracy and honesty of reading and writing which are the conditions of their later development.

The "psychological needs" of students were ascertained by the psychology department, which tested freshwomen their first semester, beginning with "students about whose grading we are doubtful" (Wylie, 1919 "Report"). The English Department hoped to use the results of the tests to place students more accurately in sections according to ability and need.

A good indication of the nature and emphasis of the required writing course is Buck's textbook, *A Course in Expository Writing* (1899), which she co-authored with Elisabeth Woodbridge. (Woodbridge and Buck also wrote *A Course in Argumentative Writing* [1899], and Buck wrote *A Course in Narrative Writing* [1906]; all three were used in Vassar courses.) In addition to using Buck and Woodbridge's book, all classes read some texts in common. For the 1910–1911 school year, for example, the texts were Huxley's "Piece of Chalk," Carlyle's *Heroes and Hero Worship*, Emerson's "American Scholar," Newman's "Literature," Arnold's "Sweetness and Light," *Beowulf*, Pater's "Essay on Style," and Stevenson's or Lamb's *Essays* (Wylie, 1911 "Report").[12] But this philosophy apparently changed, for in 1913 Wylie reported that "there is no single essay read by every section" with the result that "the classes . . . are much more interested in the reading when it is more varied and better

12. These texts were reconstructed for classroom consumption; Arnold's *Culture and Anarchy* was limited to "Sweetness and Light," Emerson's essay became a "book" of comparable weight with his British peers, and Huxley's evolutionary text is represented by a section. Arnold's essay and possibly the others were in teaching editions. Mary Augusta Jordan of Smith College edited a teaching edition of Emerson's writing, Buck edited a collection of Ruskin's work, and she notes in her textbook that Arnold's essay could "be found in a number of cheap editions; it has been reprinted with Pater's *Essay on Style*, by the MacMillan Company" (*Expository* 284).

adapted to their individual needs" (1913 "Report"). Evidently, the readings were selected after the class had met.

Pedagogically, in addition to discussions of the literature, students had individual and group interviews for criticism of themes and further discussion of the readings, three each semester on the average of twenty-five minutes each.[13] Consequently, teachers of English 1 spent "an average of three hours a week in reading the themes of each section, three and one-half hours in interviews with each, and three hours in class-work" (Wylie, 1911 "Report"). Buck noted that the amount of time in interviews was almost doubled because "preparation for their interviews takes about the same length of time as do the interviews themselves" (Wylie, 1904 "Report"). Groups were formed in class also because subsections permitted "more effective discussion and criticism of themes" (Wylie, 1915 "Report"). In other courses, lectures were "only given when absolutely necessary to supplement the results attained by the students alone," and in the first-year course they were never given at all. Quizzes were not given because they were considered "incompatible with free discussion" (Wylie, 1907–08 "Report"). Students from the composition course contributed to a publication, *The Sampler*, established in 1917, which offered them a venue for their writing and a real audience.

The original title of the course, Exposition Through Description, indicates Buck's approach. In line with her interest in psychology, she believed that sense impressions formed the basis of knowledge and that description was the transference of that knowledge to others: "For all our own convictions have been gained through sense-experience, and we unconsciously recognize this when we revert to experience in communicating with others" (*Expository* 4). Difficulty in writing came when students relied on others' accounts of an experience or memories rather than their own immediate experience. Many of the exercises in the text attempted to remedy the problem by having students see something as if for the first time, so they could trace the process of coming to know something and share that in writing. Buck believed that description was "successful just so far as it follows the actual order of the sensuous experience it describes" (25). So, for example, she suggested ways to discover just what that order was by retarding the initial experience or interrupting it at stages:

> Suppose we take first a bunch of leaves of various kinds, and expose them to view for an instant. If the exposure has been sufficiently short, it will be found

13. Often called the "Princeton Plan" of tutorials, these interviews were in place at Vassar before that institution made the technique famous.

that the spectators have received little more than an impression of something green. On a second exposure, this will have defined itself into a perception of form sufficiently clear to involve the recognition of the object as leaves. On a third exposure the impressions will have gained further definiteness both in perceptions of color, form, and even texture, and the spectators will now perceive that the leaves are of different kinds. . . . It will be seen here as in the case of gradual approach, there is a clear progression from the vague to the definite, from the general to the detailed. It will, moreover, be apparent that each stage of perception contains all that went before, but what is at the first implicit is at the last explicit. (13)

After discovering their own process of sensory perception, students were asked to help others who had never seen the object see it through their writing. Buck suggested that students send descriptions of buildings to architects to learn how specific and detailed they had been. In a discussion of the epistemology underlying such exercises, Buck wrote that she did not assume "any antithesis . . . between appearance and reality. Appearance rightly understood is reality. But because this right understanding does not always inhere in the immediate sense-impressions, because the reality is implicit rather than explicit in their sensuous appeal, the record of this appeal, where its full significance has been perceived, ought to be so made as to carry this significance with it" (63).

The typical exercise in *Expository Writing* is short, and students produced about twenty-five themes each semester, including two long papers which required that they gather new material. Otherwise, the topics were "connected with the students' individual experience—whether gained through 'nature, books, or action': and the aim is for clear, precise expression of well organized, individual thought" (Wylie, 1911 "Report"). Drawing upon the student's experience was a technique common to textbook writers, but few texts aggressively took on controversial topics of the day such as suffrage, unions, or coeducation as did Buck's.[14]

Writing topics in *A Handbook for Argument and Oral Debate* (1906) by Buck and Kristine Mann fell into three main categories: issues of education, current affairs, and gender. Buck encouraged young writers to examine the institution with which they were most familiar, the school, and suggested topics such as the nature of examinations, the elective system, and arguments for and against kindergarten or industrial education. For political issues, she

---

14. Robert Connors notes that "by 1900 personal writing assignments . . . had gained all but complete acceptance" ("Personal Writing" 177).

included prose passages by William Lloyd Garrison for abolition, a proslavery speech by John Calhoun in the Senate, descriptions of the lives of graduates of Tuskegee Institute, and excerpts from W.E.B. Dubois's *The Training of Black Men* for students to discuss, debate, and consider. She suggested students write to "a factory owner to improve the conditions of his employees" (13), or that students try their persuasive abilities by writing to people of wealth to leave money to some cause or institution. Pedagogically, defining an audience made for sound rhetoric, and by encouraging her women students to address political issues, articulate their own positions, and develop a sense of their right to have reasoned opinions, Buck trained women to take part in debates as citizens.

Not surprisingly, these controversial topics appeared in Buck's *Course in Argumentative Writing* (1899) more frequently than in her expository text. Yet the prose samples that she analyzed, imitated, and discussed in the latter might be read as controversial when placed within contemporary textbook culture. Although most are by well-known male writers, in the selection and use of samples by women writers Buck's texts stand apart from the more widely used textbooks of John Genung of Amherst and A. S. Hill of Harvard. A count of the works by women in these texts may be deceiving: in *Working Principles of Rhetoric* (1900), Genung used samples from six women writers; Hill's *Principles of Rhetoric* (1895) offers twenty; and Buck's *Expository Writing* only seven, although many passages by male authors discuss women. Frequency alone, however, doesn't tell us much about the way women were portrayed in these textbooks. How the author framed the selection influenced how the students interpreted the material. Genung, for instance, used a passage from Jane Austen in a negative manner, to demonstrate a rambling style. Buck used the same excerpt from *Emma*, but selected ten pages rather than just one, and asked students to formulate "suggestions of character" from the passage. Hill used women writers almost exclusively to illustrate styles to avoid. While it is true that he used male writers for the same purpose, holding up published women writers as examples to avoid would have had a particularly inhibiting effect on women students.

Buck's texts included long passages about women—Queen Elizabeth I, Joan of Arc—excerpts from American women writers, and a passage from C. F. Woolson's *Anne* that described single women in a sympathetic light: "But who goes into the woods, explores the rocky glens, braves the swamps? Always the ardent-hearted old maid, who, in her plain garb and thick shoes, is searching for the delicate little wild blossoms the world over" (173). A different stereotype of women was addressed in a nine-page passage by Walter

Besant that described the "typical" girl of 1840, one who possibly "through the shutting up of all the channels for intellectual activity [was] snappish, impatient, and shrewish" (203). The Besant passage presented a cultural view of women's mental abilities that had recently been used to argue against higher education for women.

> In her presence, and indeed in the presence of ladies generally, men talk trivialities. There was indeed a general belief that women were creatures incapable of argument, or of reason, or of connected thought. It was no use arguing about the matter. The Lord had made them so. Women, said the philosophers, cannot understand logic; they see things, if they do see them at all, by instinctive perception. This theory accounted for everything, for those cases when women undoubtedly did "see things." Also it fully justified people in withholding from women any kind of education worthy the name. A quite needless expense, you understand. (*Expository* 196)

Of this passage Buck said, "The following description will be found excellent in material, but unevenly good in presentation" (195). Assuming instructors might hesitate to use such controversial material, Buck encouraged them with a footnote, unique to this passage also: "This can be made very interesting in a class discussion, after the students have done some independent study on it" (195).

While Genung included six women writers in his prose examples in *Working Principles*, only one less than Buck, many of his selections perpetuated negative stereotypes about women. For instance, to illustrate "failure to keep an end in view" Genung cited William James's comment about "those insufferably garrulous old women, those dry and fanciless beings who spare you no detail, however petty, of the facts they are recounting" (570). One of the passages by George Eliot (indexed under "G") concerned Rosamond's egoism (568); in the selection by Elizabeth Ward, filed under "creating emphasis by repetition," the speaker confesses that "before an audience I am an abject coward, and I have at least concluded to admit the humiliating fact" (252); a sentence from Mrs. Humphrey Ward's *David Grieve*, selected to demonstrate "an extreme of what is admissible in writing, and far beyond what is natural to a spoken utterance" concludes a description of Leicester with the clause "Dora shrank into herself more and more" (165). In addition to self-deprecating comments about or by women, Genung supplied his own examples: to demonstrate how the use of the indicative sounds "raw and crude" when used contrary to fact, he offered, "It is time some contempt was shown to ladies; they have shown it to servants long enough" (233). Genung's texts were among the most frequently used books in composition courses between 1890 and 1910. In a sampling of thirty-three schools, as many as eighteen used his *Principles* for an average of three to five years (Wozniak 279).

Yet not all the examples in Buck's textbooks challenged traditional women's roles. Consider the following, from *Expository Writing*: "Describe your first impression of a shop window full of spring hats" (34); "Expound some of the following subjects by generalized narration—Going shopping with a bargain-hunter" (205); "Write an exposition of character from dress—Mrs. M—— when not dressed for company" (97). These gendered prompts make it clear that her audience consisted of the upper classes: "Write an exposition of character from dress—a cook, the description being sent to a married friend who has asked you to get her a servant" (97); "contrast, so as to bring out their characters . . . the way in which two servants sweep a room, or wash dishes, or wait on the table" (114). Students using this book would soon be in positions of authority, and Buck suggested that they write "a confidential report on a servant or a clerk" (115). Throughout the assignments she asked them to pay careful attention to life around them: "Make a stenographic report of an actual conversation, such as takes place at table or between classes. . . . the report may be brief, but should be exact, including abbreviations, slang, etc." (114). Unlike the textbooks of Genung and Hill, Buck's indicate respect for students' interests, their lives, and their abilities.

For greater efficiency in teaching, the first-year course in composition at Vassar was eventually divided into sections according to ability. By tracking students and providing for a deficient section with a limited enrollment, the department was able to offer the kind of individual instruction it believed important. Buck commented that a course finally limited to twenty students provided the "opportunity for the class discussion of every student's work at frequent intervals and enabled me to know intimately the capacities and peculiar difficulties of each member of the class" (Wylie, 1914 "Report"). Such attention to the individual was difficult with large classes, and the debate on class size between Wylie and President Taylor and later President MacCracken will sound familiar to teachers in the 1990s. Describing the early situation of the department, Wylie noted that "neither literature nor composition can be taught, in any real sense of the word, to college students by lecturing to them about it in regiments of fifty to one hundred and fifty" (1914 "Report"). The 1914 departmental report cites national studies on class size which indicated that a maximum of fifteen students per composition section was ideal, and Wylie recorded that Vassar's courses numbered twenty-one to twenty-five. The emphasis on educational efficiency at the turn of the century, based on Frederick Taylor's work, no doubt influenced Wylie's arguments for smaller class sizes and lower teacher course loads. At Bryn Mawr, she notes, composition students per teacher were reduced to forty apiece, "not at all for the sake of indulging or sparing the teachers, but in order to increase the efficiency of their teaching" (1914 "Report").[15]

Buck's Rhetorical Theory

In a professional conversation concerned mostly with grammar, and a dominant pedagogy largely divorced from practical application, Buck insisted that all learning be purposeful, that writing assignments be rhetorical, and that grammar instruction by holistic, that is, that it take account of the students' motivations. Typical nineteenth-century grammar exercises asked students to identify and correct erroneous sentences, thus teaching them that "the main activity one performed with a sentence was knocking it to pieces to prove it bad" (Connors, "Mechanical Correctness" 63). By incorporating a romantic belief in the organic nature of language, Buck hoped to make composition useful and vital to a changing student population.

Her emphasis on the organic nature of language prompted Buck to examine classroom practice. When asked how had they perceived grammar and sentences as school children, her students replied that sentences were artificial constructs written solely for the purpose of parsing. Buck thought current instructional practices were not conveying a communicative function of

---

15. Regarding class size and teacher workloads, Wylie referred to NCTE guidelines in her 1915 annual report: "it is essential that the maximum number of students in Freshman English Composition assigned to a single instructor should in no case exceed 60." One gets a sense of the pace of academic progress when next considering the CCCC 1989 draft report on professional standards which recommended that "no English faculty members should teach more than 60 writing students a term. In developmental writing classes, the maximum should be 45" (64). The unacceptable working conditions that Wylie named year after year were persistent nationally, so that participants of the 1986 Wyoming Conference on English presented a resolution to the Conference on College Composition and Communication charging the organization to formulate professional standards for writing instruction, a procedure for hearing grievances, and a censure procedure for those schools not complying with the minimum conditions of employment. For a story of the Wyoming Resolution see *College English* 49 [March 1987, 274–80]; for an analysis of the changing language and priorities of the original resolution, see Gunner's essay in *Writing Ourselves into the Story*; for a history of exploitive conditions for writing teachers, see Connors in *The Politics of Writing Instruction*.

language when she got answers such as: "I always saw a sentence in the form of a train of cars . . . I never thought a sentence was for anything but to study"; and "A sentence looked to me like squares ruled off on paper and fitted together somehow—always in a different pattern, it seemed. I saw no use for it as I saw no use for grammar at all" ("Foundations" 482). One focus of Buck's concern was the practice of diagramming sentences. She argued that the typical diagram for sentences was not an accurate reflection of the thought the sentence expressed. For her, the linear sentence diagram indicated that the sentence "has not grown, but has been manufactured. . . . [we then regard it] as a thing dead and static, a manufacture instead of a growth" ("Sentence-Diagram" 251). She argued that teachers should not use what was untrue: "we dare not willfully mislead [students] by the use of any 'device,' however temptingly 'convenient' that does not truthfully represent so far as we can judge, the reality which it symbolizes" ("Sentence-Diagram" 260). Her emphasis on truthfulness is quite like the romantic insistence on integrity, and her belief in the organic nature of language contrasted with an approach she termed "a science of crystallized or fossilized thought-structure, the anatomy, not the physiology, of sentential expression" ("Psychology of the Diagram" 470). In order to capture the growing nature of thought through language, and especially through grammar diagrams, she devised a branching amoebalike scheme that began with a single thought or sense perception, such as "ouch," and then indicated how the thought was delineated into a subject "I" and a predicate "cut myself." Teachers, however, continued to use linear diagrams rather than Buck's amoebas, perhaps for reasons such as those expressed by F. A. Barbour: "In high schools, and in normal schools with large classes, the diagram is an indispensable aid in the rapid conduct of recitation; and to the teacher overburdened with much manuscript it is a sort of god-send as a system of stenography" (242).

The editor of Buck and Scott's *Brief English Grammar* (1905) acknowledged the nonmainstream beliefs held by Buck and worried that they would hurt the book's sales. After reading the contracted manuscript, the editor wrote to Buck:

> You seem to me to try so hard to consider grammar as a logical process that you forget that it is often merely a formal process; and I think at times this leads to confusion of ideas. . . . I query the prominence that you have given to what you call the "branching idea." I suppose this is essential to your view of the way in which the subject should be presented. But I question whether the process is not one, in point of fact, of growth by loose aggregation, develop-

ment rather than branching. After all, this branching matter is in the main, I
think, a figure of speech, and I believe you somewhat overwork it. (Damon)

Despite this criticism, Buck maintained her organic view of language. Chapter 2, for instance, "How the Subject Grows," continues the branching metaphor: "As the main limbs of the tree keep dividing into smaller branches,
then into twigs and leaves, so does the sentence. The subject and the predicate
divide and subdivide into clauses, phrases, and finally into words" (27).

Virginia Allen has commented that *A Brief English Grammar* "is disap-
pointingly traditional. Such concessions to the marketplace in the textbooks
of the reformers were, however, all too common" (150). She nevertheless sees
two characteristics that set the book apart from most grammar texts: its
descriptive rather than prescriptive approach to grammar, and its social
responsibility. "It neither advocated nor promoted elitist language forms but
spoke of choosing certain usages to avoid the appearance of eccentricity or
ignorance" (150).

In "The Present Status of Rhetorical Theory" (1900), Buck explored the
organic (i.e., good) nature of language and its role in the social organism by
contrasting Platonic and Sophistic rhetorical theory. She was clearly influenced in her rhetorical theory by her mentor and dissertation director, Fred
Newton Scott, who challenged the ideal rhetoric teacher as someone who
"put into the hands of the pleader the keen knife of persuasion" ("Two
Ideals" 161). Scott argued that composition teachers should instead work
toward the ideal of social service, for "as long as we hold to the idea of mere
success or achievement of the individual writer, composition has no solid
foundation" (166). Buck shared his distrust of persuasion and interpreted
rhetoric as a truer form of communication, taking an epistemic approach
whereby both speaker and hearer learn something. Throughout Buck's career, Scott was her mentor, from whom she sought counsel, guidance, and
suggestions for teaching associates. In composition history, Scott and Buck
are frequently linked, with little distinction made between their theories.
Buck did credit Scott in print for the beginnings of many of her ideas, and
undoubtedly Scott's confidence in her contributed to her productivity and
the authoritative voice evidenced in many articles. Still, when comparing
herself with her well-known mentor, Buck occupied the subject position of
many women writers, identified primarily by what she lacked. In one letter to
Scott, for instance, she characterized Lane Cooper's article "On the Teaching
of Written Composition" as "a tissue of fallacies but with such superficial

plausibility that I wondered whether some answer ought not to be made by someone." She suggested that he write a response because "if you would do this yourself of course it would have greatest weight. . . . I long to do so, but simply cannot undertake anything of the sort even if my answer would be effective, as it would not at all in comparison with yours" (23 April 1910).

The democratic strain in her work seems to end with the question of taste, for although Buck did not attribute differences in taste to a biological or innate distinction, she believed that education, upbringing, and experience all contribute to finer sensibilities. She wrote that "progress is the law of mental life. The human mind is a developing organism; under normal conditions it neither stands still nor retrogrades. . . . if the literature adapted to further its progress is at hand, it tends to seize upon this literature in preference to that which either fails to quicken or actually stultifies it" (*SCL* 57). While such a notion holds all individuals to be equal, it still privileges the cultural capital of the elite, an asymmetry that Buck was unable to observe in her elite institution.

In a 1918 letter to Vassar President MacCracken, Buck described an instance of the development of taste. School boys in the music settlement in New York chose to perform a concert of ragtime music, and the conductor, rather than imposing his taste, agreed, but he trained them "just as he would have trained them to play really good music." The boys became dissatisfied with the numbers they had chosen, "asked for something not so 'jingly,'" and ended up with a program much like the conductor would have selected. Her point was that the students' own abilities and tastes could evolve to the desired level of refinement if they were nourished and not stifled. She avoided value judgments about taste by viewing differing tastes as different stages of growth, again employing an organic model, and held that all stages were equally valuable to the process. Describing her varying stages of metaphor, she wrote that "each is as essential, as dignified and as honorable as any other" (*Metaphor* 44).

In defining good literature, Buck suggested that standards could not be mechanically applied from tradition, nor found in the works themselves, nor in the readers' responses alone. Discussing standards of criticism, she modified Matthew Arnold's influential definition of literature as the best that is known and thought in the world: "the best, that is, not absolutely, but at this moment for himself and for the readers he addresses, the best calculated to satisfy their perhaps unrecognized needs, and to carry them a step beyond their present experience or powers" (*SCL* 41). The critic was a teacher.

Buck's Theory in Relation to "Current-Traditional Rhetoric"

Historians of writing instruction have labeled the most widely used pedagogy and rhetorical theory of the nineteenth century "current-traditional" and have primarily drawn upon rhetoric and grammar textbooks and rhetorical treatises to understand how writing was taught at the University of Michigan, Harvard, Amherst, and other eastern colleges for men. Current-traditional rhetoric's emphasis on the form of writing rather than the content meant that students received little instruction in invention, wrote in the modes of discourse (description, narration, exposition, argumentation), and received comments on the mechanical features of their prose rather than on their ideas. In rhetoric classes during the first half of the century, elite students memorized texts and recited the principles of rhetoric. While these students frequently graduated to become ministers or lawyers, their education was unrelated to their future rhetorical performances. A changing student population and the institution of an elective system in universities altered rhetoric instruction, and by the 1870s the classical curriculum with its belletristic focus "was forced to move away from the abstract educational ideal of 'mental discipline' and toward more immediate instructional goals" (Connors, "Mechanical Correctness" 64). By the 1890s Harvard's Committee on Composition and Rhetoric had issued three reports to the Harvard Board of Overseers, emphasizing problems in spelling, punctuation, handwriting, and grammar in the writing of incoming students. The consequence of the reports' focus on superficial (often called mechanical) correctness was that educators turned their focus to little more than the forms of discourse and the concepts of unity, coherence, and emphasis.

The type of literacy instruction employed in English departments corresponded to the economic changes of corporate capitalism and the emerging "meritocracy" of universities, according to James Berlin.

> The best that can be said of this model is that students were indeed writing. The worst that can be said is that this model severely restricts the student's response to experience. Current-traditional rhetoric dictates that certain matters cannot be discussed because they are either illusory—not empirically verifiable—or they cannot be contained within acceptable structures—rational categories, for example. This very exclusion, meanwhile, encourages a mode of behavior that helps students in their move up the corporate ladder—correctness in usage, grammar, clothing, thought, and a certain sterile objectivity and disinterestedness. (*Writing Instruction* 75)

The focus on mechanical features of writing also helped to maintain instructors' authority in a shifting pedagogical scene, creating a useful barrier for male professors unaccustomed to the presence of women in their classrooms, for example. In a detailed treatment of the role of invention in current-traditional rhetoric, Sharon Crowley argues that lack of instruction in choosing and developing topics undermined the student writer's authority because the writer was not selecting the rhetorical situation she would address. A focus on appearances, the etiquette of writing, usurped from students any power they might have derived from addressing issues they found important to real readers. "Students were systematically taught that they were not to say anything to anybody but were to write about preselected topics as correctly and (if they got past 'correctly') in as elegant a manner as they could muster. Their discourse was forever and always in bondage to someone else's, if not that of a model text, then that of textbook prescriptions or the instructor's enforcement of them" (Crowley, *Methodical Memory* 152).

While keeping her conversation within the parameters of the field, focused on grammar instruction, Buck nevertheless challenged the mechanical assumptions of current-traditional rhetoric. Her psychological, feminist rhetoric at Vassar College was a product of the cooperative, democratic system of governance practiced by the English Department faculty, and it served her student population better than a managerial rhetoric, for women graduates had few employment opportunities and graduated to teach or serve their families and communities through volunteer service. Buck's rhetoric was more closely aligned with the Greek ideals of civic service than the mercantile and mechanical goals of current-traditional rhetoric.

Buck's Place in Composition Studies: The Feminist Dimension

Historians of composition have judged that Buck's alternative views for instruction and theory were simply squeezed into obscurity by the dominant rhetoric. Rebecca Burke, for example, concluded that because of the emphasis on mechanical correctness "there was no room for thinkers like Scott and Buck, who brought fresh ideas to rhetoric—ideas that linked rhetoric to new, poorly understood and little accepted disciplines, such as psychology and linguistics" (4). Like Burke's comment that "there was no room" for Buck's ideas, Kitzhaber believes that she was "undoubtedly ahead of her time. So radically different an approach to one of the rhetorical staples could not be assimilated by rhetoricians contemporary with her" (289), and Mulderig writes that she "questioned the conventions according to which writing was being taught at a time when many of those conventions . . . were ascending in importance. Perhaps that is why her work did not receive the attention it deserved" (101). These perceptions may be valid, but they ignore the marginalization of women in the profession, just as the histories of writing instruction have ignored women's colleges. For much of the history of western culture, to be a woman has meant to be quiet, docile, and remain in the domestic sphere. To be a rhetorician, on the other hand, meant being public, vocal, and occupying a privileged position (Glenn 180). A masculine rhetorical tradition was instituted in schools as well, with good writing being equated with manliness and bad writing with femininity (Brody 3). Buck, former president of the Oratorical Association at the University of Michigan, brought the power of public discourse to her students, teaching them specific skills, inviting their knowledge of other spheres, and encouraging them to add their voices to public debate.

Perhaps what allowed Buck to write more than other women scholars of her time, to challenge pedagogical traditions equated with excellence in education, and to link individual psychology with larger laws of language was her sense of herself not as an individual leader but as a member of an entire community interested in progressive education. Although she once characterized herself as a "hopeless radical" ("Review of Carpenter" 406), more often, regarding grammar and writing instruction, she saw herself less as a maverick or innovator and more as a spokesperson for the most progressive ideas of the day, part of the mainstream or "dawn [which] is just breaking in this subject" ("Psychological Significance" 277). In language as optimistic as any pragmatist writer, she concluded an argument for a more psychologically accurate diagram of the sentence by telling those who objected to her approach that they "seem not to realize that they are fighting the flood of irresistible progress in education" ("Psychology of the Diagram" 470). In "The Sentence-Diagram" she wrote that "it is surely high time that this idea of growth, now dominant in other fields of investigation, dawn upon the darkness of grammar. We have been too long bound by the mechanical notions of an earlier and a cruder philosophy" (259).

In what we may call a feminist strategy of scholarship, Buck devoted little energy to attacking those who differed from her and instead built on the work of the past to construct something useful and new. The contributions of women teachers and scholars will remain invisible as long as the prevailing model of history focuses on individuals, exclusively male, battling each other.[16] Women and others without political power often choose strategies of resistance other than single combat, working instead through communities or networks. Members of the first and second generations of women college professors had little desire to battle the institutions that provided their jobs; Buck and her colleagues at Vassar emphasized harmony and cooperation to create an alternative environment for themselves and their students. Although Buck's conception of community could be criticized for ignoring lines of power and differences within the community, she had a clear sense of the college's civic responsibility and worked to create flexible, supportive communities of women during her tenure at Vassar. Her work and life were of one piece, and she offers academics today a model of harmonious, civic-minded scholarship passionately connected to the exigencies of teaching. Her classrooms were democratic arenas where students used the language skills and the interests they brought with them to grow and develop into thoughtful citizens. Such an educational environment was especially important for young women who entered universities amidst public debate over their health and the future of white civilization if they should study. What Gertrude Buck provided for her students at Vassar grew out of the community of her English department and her relationship with her partner, Laura Johnson Wylie. Her writing integrated theory and practice, spiritual and material concerns, and life inside and outside the academy. May her words inspire others to seek such connections in their lives as well.

16. Gerlach and Monseau, *Missing Chapters*, and Clifford, *Lone Voyagers*, are among the works that are beginning to recognize the contributions of women in the field.

I Theory of Organic Education

1 The Organic Curriculum

from *Organic Education*, coauthored with Harriet Scott
(Boston: Heath, 1899), 18–30, 96–105.

Harriet Scott was principal of the Detroit Normal School, a training school for teachers, where she had implemented a "culture epoch" theory based on the belief that "every child repeats in his own development the history of the race; therefore his education should follow, as closely as may be, the lines of progress drawn by the civilization of the race" (Buck, "Another Phase" 376). Buck learned of the school and, interested in this theory, lived with Harriet Scott, Fred Newton Scott's sister, observed at the school, and wrote a brief article describing her first visit to the school (published in 1896 in The Forum *).*

Organic Education was published as volume 35 in Heath's Pedagogical Library, subtitled "A Manual for Teachers in Primary and Grammar Grades." The first section of the book traces the influence of the European educational theorists Johann Heinrich Pestalozzi and Johann Friedrich Herbart on the authors' system, and the last section outlines the practical work of the course. Organic education was based on John Dewey's notion of the social individual who learns best when ideas are related and connected with life outside school. The program for elementary and secondary students proposed here follows a "progression" of civilizations through the grades, so that Eurocentric authors and artists are treated as more advanced or sophisticated and saved for later grades. For instance, first graders began their study with Hiawatha because supposedly children of five or six were as interested in the natural world as American Indians. After studying the story, appearance, and living conditions of Hiawatha, the children worked with materials that matched their own developmental stage. The Eurocentric determination of sophistication and development had the curriculum "advance" from indigenous American people, through the Greeks and Romans, to culminate with the Puritans.

The first excerpt, from chapter 3, sets out some of Buck's fundamental educational tenets which remained important throughout her career, such as reaching students' interests and letting them set the pace for learning. The second selection, from chapter 8, introduces Kablu, the Aryan boy, and suggests specific activities for the children.

The present status of popular thought upon matters educational is not altogether easy to define. In America for the most part we still retain our ancient conception of the public school system as somehow a thing in itself isolated, unique, understood in some vague way to "prepare for life," yet not, in any practical sense, responsible either to the individual child or to the social structure for its policy or its methods. Yet, in recent years, vigorous, though unorganized, revolt against this incoherent notion has raised the standard of individualism in education, declaring that here, as all elsewhere, the individual does not exist for the institution, but contrariwise.

And thus, of late, the old institutional conception of education may be said to contend with the newer theory of individualism. But out of the clash of these two conflicting notions, an ideal seems now to be rising, truer than either—the ideal of social individualism. Such an ideal has very recently come to expression in the aphorism of Professor John Dewey of the University of Chicago: "Education is not preparation for life: it *is* life;" and in that of Colonel Francis W. Parker, of the Chicago Training School: "The common school is the central means for preserving and perpetuating the true democracy."[1]

Such expressions as these recognize the fact that the individual is, indeed, the centre of every rational educational system, not however the individual as such, in the limited sense, but the whole individual in all his relations; that is, the social individual. They involve the philosophical conception of the individual as a specialized or focussed functioning of society, and, conversely, of society as the whole functioning of the individual. The individual is society acting in a certain direction. He is a focussed activity of the entire social organism, just as the eye is the whole body directed toward the end of seeing. Society for its part is the complete activity of each individual.

Such, then, being the essential interrelations of society and its individual members, it is idle to balance the one against the other as ends of education. The real advantage of society involves ultimately the advantage of the individual member of society. And, conversely, the real betterment of the individual must inevitably tend toward the betterment of society. The two are no more separable in practice than are faith and works, thought and feeling, capital and labor, or any of those delusive apparent dualisms whose unity is the life of each part.

With this point clearly in mind, that the latest word in education is social individualism, reconciling institutionalism on the one hand with private

1. The thought has come to pervade the best of modern educational literature. See, for example, Commissioner Harris's report on the Correlation of Studies in the Report of the Committee of Fifteen: "The branches to be studied and the extent to which they are studied, will be determined mainly by the demands of one's civilization. These will prescribe what is most useful to make the individual acquainted with physical nature and with human nature so as to fit him as an individual to perform his duties in the several institutions—family, civil society, the State and the Church."

individualism on the other, we shall proceed to compare the old curriculum with the new. From the standpoint of the older systems themselves, it is evident that the plan presented in this volume would familiarize the pupil with all the specific subjects now presented to his attention under the established order. He would study reading, spelling, grammar and composition, arithmetic, natural science, United States history, civil government, writing, drawing, and vocal music under the one as under the other system. But the new plan further provides him with systematic instruction in the history of civilization, sociology, literature, art, and ethics, which subjects are at present only incidentally and fragmentarily, if at all, touched upon in primary and grammar grades.

To this extension of the common-school curriculum two objections may be anticipated: (1) that the course is already overcrowded with subjects, so that the days are too short for their tasks, and both teachers and pupils are burdened beyond their strength, and (2) that such subjects as are here added are beyond the comprehension of primary-school pupils. To the first objection no disclaimer can be entered. The statement is literally true. The curriculum is overcrowded. But the difficulty inheres rather in lack of organization than in the mere number of subjects studied. There is a limit to the number of disconnected facts an individual can memorize. There is no limit to his grasp of organized, interrelated, and interdependent knowledge. In other words, while his stock of information may be finite, his knowing is infinite. And, thus, under a system of education whose methods both at large and in detail follow the ever-widening interests of the individual child in their natural development from a state of undifferentiated homogeneity to a more and more finely differentiated, and at the same time a more and more closely unified, organization,—under such a system, where the child is himself the leader, the rapidity of his mental development and the extent of his power of assimilation are fairly astonishing to teachers familiar only with the results of the old system. So far from being overcrowded, the children are perpetually a little in advance of the material provided. They feel the need of it before it is given. And, as a result, they are always mentally hungry. At times, indeed, this hunger seems keener than at others, but it never wholly abates, for it has never been choked up with undemanded material. Step by step their interest has gone before to guide the progress of the teaching, and every lesson, meeting this interest fairly, has contributed to widen and enrich it; so that, in the great majority of cases, it has gained, before school days are over, besides an enormous expansion and deepening, a certain capacity for conscious self-direction.

And, further upon this head, the overcrowding of the curriculum is greatly relieved by the continual use of every subject studied as a tool for further investigation. For instance: reading is no longer studied as an end in itself. The children spend no more time learning to read, but simply read for the sake of the subject-matter. The case is the same with spelling, writing, and composition. The technique of these arts once learned enables the child to use them as the carpenter uses his lathe or plane. He, indeed, by using, continually learns to use them better; but the period of mere learning to use them with no other immediate end, is exceedingly short as compared with the time devoted to the bare technique of reading and grammar, for instance, in our common schools. Under the organic system, an arithmetical process, as long division, is not taught as such, but as a means for determining, say, the amount of material needed for the new house of some child in the room. And the results of such methods of teaching would seem to justify the general answer to the objection of overcrowding the curriculum, that children thus taught cover the same ground in less time than under the old system, and with greater thoroughness.

By the statement that the child learns with "greater thoroughness" under the organic system is meant that since what he learns is here not an extraneous something imposed upon him from without, but the natural development of his own interests, it is his own, it is really himself. He cannot forget or lay it aside when school-hours are over for the day, or when school-days are over for life; for it is in a real literal sense his own self. This means thoroughness as a vital, not a mechanical, quality in education.

One further result of the organic system which contributes in no small degree to the rapidity and thoroughness of the pupils' mental assimilation, should be noted here. The logical presentation of each subject and each lesson may reasonably be expected so to habituate the children to coherent mental processes that the bearings of one fact upon another will be at once apparent to them. They would not then be compelled, in the study of any subject, to spend long hours groping blindly for some link of thought, vaguely felt, rather than perceived, to be missing; or to labor under chronic misconceptions due to perverted habits of thought. On the contrary, a subject would unfold itself to them in the first instance, logically proportioned and clearly articulated. They would thus be rendered capable of originating, as well as of following, a train of logical thought from beginning to end, moving from point to point with sure-footed ease. They would also be able often to detect and even to locate a fallacy in the reasoning of another, where many adults, whose logical instincts have been stultified rather than developed, are only dimly conscious of "a screw loose somewhere." The ethical bearings of such a capacity as this surely need not be elaborated. It may, however, be noted in passing, that without such capacity no rational self-determination of conduct is ever possible.

To return to the objections against the proposed extension of the school curriculum: as to the inability of children to comprehend the subjects of sociology, art, and ethics, it must be remembered that the child can grasp any subject whatever, if only it be unfolded to him in logical order in response to the demands of his own interest. This sole condition is satisfied by the organic system, so that if the ability of the child under this condition be admitted, the objection is met. No *a priori* argument, however, can be brought so convincing as the actual results of the teaching of these subjects by the organization method. The practicability of these subjects has been demonstrated to the entire satisfaction of experienced teachers at the outset incredulous. The children, it is true, do not know that they are studying art, ethics, and sociology, but they nevertheless are studying—or perhaps absorbing—these subjects from the first grade up, with a vital thoroughness such as no twenty weeks' course in college or university can possibly give. It is certainly fair to say that no college graduate, with but a year's or a half-year's "credit" in sociology, ethics, or art, is so saturated with the subject as is the child in the eighth grade, under the organic system. This is, of course, no discredit to the college or to the student. The case could not be otherwise. Appreciation of art and literature is not the product of a five months' gorging with the world's masterpieces. Nor do the text-book conclusions of ethics and sociology permeate the consciousness of the individual who is largely ignorant of the data from which they have been drawn, and who is justly satisfied with the philosophy which his experience has furnished him. Whatever may be true of other subjects, these three, at least, are a growth, or they are nothing.

Most of us are so well acquainted, either from observation or from experience, with the effects of the gorging process in one or all of these subjects, that this side of the contrast need not further be pursued. On the side of the slow assimilation plan, however, it may be said that while the results are not by any means startling, they are eminently sound and practical. The first crude artistic demands of the children are fed by equally crude artistic material. They see and use the bright Indian colors and the grotesque Indian picture-writing. From this point their taste continually expands and refines, through the exuberant sensuousness of Persian coloring, the pure severity of Greek outline, the multifarious richness of mediæval and Renaissance painting, absorbing the spirit of each of these, and becoming truly cosmopolitan. The extent to which the lives of the children are thus enriched is all but incredible to those unacquainted with the facts. Most adults when brought into direct daily contact with the masterpieces of Greek art, for instance, are thereby to a degree edified. But that children surrounded from an early age by the forms of art which precisely answer the demands of their own interest in each stage of its development,—that such children should not respond powerfully to such environment, would be more incredible than the fact. In truth, from grade to grade may be traced by the teacher the influence of the artistic environment of the child in the schoolroom. His dress, his manners, his moral character, his home, are all affected by it.

And the same facts are true as to the literature-teaching. The child's first instinctive desire for an expressive interpretation of the facts of life, in the beginning satisfied with animal stories and nature myths, grows with his growth until it demands a Goethe's, a Shakespeare's, and a Dante's master-pieces of poetic thought. And here also the ethical uplift is incontrovertible. This, however, has already been recognized far more universally than in the case of art, and many schools have discarded the "reader" pabulum for careful selections from the best literary material, both in poetry and prose. But the point will nevertheless bear further emphasizing, until an acquaintance with the world's highest literature shall be popularly regarded as the right of public-school children.

The study of sociology need not surely be defended to any believer in the doctrine of social individualism. The relationship between the individual and the social organism cannot be wholly effective until it has come to self-consciousness—of which self-consciousness sociology is the scientific expression. The social development of the individual is not complete without a knowledge of the science of society, and under the hypothesis of social individualism, the social development of the individual is the end proposed to education.

By those of us who believe that the moral nature is not something separated from the body or intellect, but that it is the whole man, it might indeed have been anticipated, that the ethical results of the organic system should be pronounced in proportion to those termed "intellectual." The prime advantage which the ethical teaching under the organization plan may be said to have over others, is that, instead of imposing upon the children in a certain stage of development an ideal wholly extraneous to themselves, the fruit of a different period in civilization, the ideals naturally growing out of their own mental status are simply allowed full fruition in their conduct, that these may, in turn, give place to further ideals. The natural ethical development of the child is furthered—that is all—not thwarted by the stamping out of his own ideals, nor by the imposition upon him of ideals remote from and incomprehensible to him. By this means, the individual child gains the invaluable habit of pursuing his ideals into the stage of conduct, reflecting upon that conduct, as its consequences return upon him, and thus modifying or reconstructing the old ideal in accordance with the new light. And it does not seem extravagant to say that if only this one habit were deposited from the tide of school life,—as it assuredly may be, under the organization plan,—the years of primary education would have been well spent; for it is this alone which renders possible a life at once morally free and morally responsible.

Some of the advantages afforded to the individual by the organization system have been discussed, its advantages to society being very largely implied in this. Let us, however, consider for a moment some changes which the new plan would of necessity bring about in the structure of the public-school system. Waiving details, it is evident that a degree of scholarship, practical efficiency, and enthusiasm hardly dreamed of before would be demanded of the teacher in the primary and intermediate grades. She must be at the outset, or must come to be in the course of her teaching, a wide and thorough student of psychology, ethics, sociology, economics, history, science, literature, and art. This at once sounds hopeless, but what the organization plan does for the pupil it also does for the teacher. Even the "average teacher," with fair capacity and some pluck, can do far better work with the organization system than under the old method. And as for the college graduate, to whom it seems that we are to look in the future for our teachers in secondary schools, such requirements should not lie beyond the scope of his ability.[2] And to him they will prove attractive as no stultifying routine under the old system could possibly be. There will be no reluctance on the part of men and women adequately educated to assume the task of primary education under these generous conditions. The law of supply and demand will hold here as

2. Professor Francis W. Kelsey, of the University of Michigan, in an article on "The Future of the High School," in the *Educational Review* for February, 1896, has this to say of the qualifications of the future teacher of the secondary school:—

"No one should now be encouraged to go into high-school teaching in any line without a range and quality of scholarship that may be fairly represented by the work of the master's degree; that is, the completion of the undergraduate course and a year of graduate work in an institution furnishing the best possible facilities. It will not be so very long before we shall see many positions in the larger high schools manned by those who have taken the doctor's degree."

If this prophecy as to the secondary schools be fulfilled, a corresponding rise may fairly be expected in the educational equipment of teachers for the primary and intermediate grades.

elsewhere. The kind of teachers wanted will be forthcoming. And the consequent advantage of wanting such teachers as are broadly educated is sufficiently obvious.

The transformation of the school under this system has been largely anticipated in the foregoing discussion. In general, it may be prophetically described as a treasure-house of the art, literature, science, and industry of the world, a laboratory of civilization, a busy cell or ganglion in the social system, a real segment of a real world.

For the particulars of the organic curriculum, the reader may be referred to the outline of study farther on in this work. At this point it will be sufficient to indicate in a general way the dominant interest for each grade, and the material which furnishes nutriment for the child at each stage of his development. These features may be exhibited in outline as follows:—

DOMINANT INTEREST.	MATERIAL.
To use senses (curiosity).	Nomadic period of history—Indian as type.
For possessions.	Pastoral and agricultural period—early Aryan as type.
For attention or notice.	Persian.
To imitate (suggestibility).	Greek.
To coöperate for sake of gain.	Roman.
For personal freedom.	Early German.
To serve (display power).	Feudalism and chivalry.
For adventure, experiment.	Renaissance—Columbus as type.
For what is true (incipient).	Puritan as type of reformation.
For activity, movement, affairs.	Story of America.
For the practical.	United States in its organic relations.
For what is personally practical.	Europe and its relations to the United States.
For authoritative knowledge.	Asia (past, present, future) in relation to the United States.
For explanation—how things came to be, or how they are done.	Africa, as showing nations crystallized (interpreted through their works), and as showing nations in the making. Its meaning to the United States.
For approval (extremes shown in diffidence and egotism).	The earth's history as a planet, its present physical conditions, and the evolution of industrial life. (Each individual, though but a small part, is seen to be organically related to the whole.)

For admiration and power.	Brief view of the history of the rise and decline of the great civilizations of the world (with causes), and special study of social life.
For a larger self, interest in community and national life.	Growth of the State as a larger self, as shown in United States history, and of the individual as a larger self, as shown in literature.
For the ideal.	Ideals of institutional life (particularly of the home), as shown through history, nature study, literature, and art.

The material indicated above is, in use, divided into the large natural units suggested by the dominant interest, and the direction which is given to that interest by the environment. Thus curiosity may be manifested toward the whole environment, or it may be restricted to nature, to institutional life, or to art. The extent to which these units are elaborated will of course depend upon the stage of development of the children. Certain material obviously cannot be employed in particular cases until the insight of the child has grown adequate to it. For example, the evolution of institutional life from the germinal ideas is a conception that must wait upon the growth of the child's powers of abstraction.

The material is in each case presented through the subject in the ordinary curriculum that will best disclose its meaning and value. The central thought, for instance, would be developed in the language lesson, the physical setting would appear in the geography lesson, the nature and function of the environment would be shown in the nature-study, and so on throughout the entire round of school work.

Kablu, the Aryan Boy
Grade A 1
Age of children, six years

A. ANALYSIS OF CHARACTER

For the child of this grade, the Hiawatha period of intense curiosity, imaginativeness, and contrivance has merged into the period represented by Kablu, a stage of curiosity somewhat less acute, of imagination somewhat less dominant, and of contrivance more complex and finished. In this stage the idea of possession is strong. The child is acquisitive, tenacious of his own rights, and not always regardful of the rights of others. But he soon learns that in order to retain his own possessions, he must respect the property-rights of others, and must even, when necessity arises, make common cause with them against a common foe. In this way he gets his first practical lesson in coöperation; and in much the same fashion he learns the necessity of obedience. This is the period in which the child, beginning to know more of danger, feels more keenly the need of protection. And thus family life, the shelter and protection of the home, mean more to him than they have done before or than they will for some time again. From this may be developed the idea of coöperation in the home, the duties of each member of the family, and of the child as a member of the family who is sheltered, nourished, and protected by it.

B. ETHICAL AIMS

The thought for this period is coöperation, with its corollaries of respect for the possessions of others, obedience, mutual helpfulness, and affection in the family. The school is regarded by the children as a larger family circle, or coöperative community, and all corrections and admonitions are made by the teacher upon the ground of community-interest.

C. MATERIAL

Kablu, the little Aryan boy, represents the agricultural period in civilization. As Hiawatha learned little by little to satisfy his needs for food, clothing, and shelter, new needs arose, which could be met only by a more settled mode of life. The first indication of these new needs is Hiawatha's fasting and prayer that his people might have more stable subsistence than that gained by hunting and fishing. His prayer was answered by the gift of Indian corn, which heralded the passing of the nomadic stage of civilization. At this point we begin the story of Kablu, and trace the growth of this embryo instinct for permanency and possession through the agricultural period.

Character stories should be told or read to the children as illustrative of family affection. As suggesting the advantages of coöperation, the teacher may tell some of Æsop's Fables, such as—

> The Blind Man and the Lame Man,
> The Two Travellers,
> The Two Goats,
> The Old Man and His Sons,
> The Bear and the Two Travellers,
> The Ant and the Dove,
> The Lion and the Mouse, etc.

As enforcing the duty of obedience in general may be used I Love You, Mother, and Obedience, by Phœbe Cary. The negative side of this enforcement may be emphasized by the story of Little Red Riding Hood, and of Adam and Eve as told by Adler in *Moral Instruction of Children*; the positive side, by the story of Tell's shooting the apple. For honesty, the story of Lincoln.

The stories originating in this period should be used whenever possible—those, for instance, of—

Cinderella,
Red Riding Hood,
Sleeping Beauty,
Jack and the Bean Stalk,
Jack the Giant-Killer,
The Seven-League Boots,
Toads and Diamonds, etc.

These are connected with the work of the grade, so as to bring out their significance, as in the story of Sleeping Beauty, cited under Kablu's House. The story of the Seven-League Boots may be used in connection with industrial life, as foreshadowing the railroads and fast ocean steamers of the present.

Songs: Three Robin Redbreasts, and Suppose.
The children read Obedience, by Phœbe Cary.

I. Kablu's Appearance

1. The Story.
Kablu was a fair child, with light hair and blue eyes. He was tall and stout for his age.

2. Comparison.
Compare Kablu with the children in the room, and with Hiawatha, as to size, color of eyes and hair, paying some attention to the distinction of shades.

In this grade color is constantly noticed and discriminated. Whether special mention of the fact is made or not, the teacher is supposed to call the children's attention to it in connection with every object studied. The children learn to select, match, sort, relate, and lay the spectrum colors to learn shades and tints.

3. Measure.
Each child measures some other child's height, girth, and length of limb. The teacher measures sight and hearing. The children compare their ages and

tell how many months there are in a year. They learn the names of the months in the different seasons, weeks and days in the month, and hours in a day.

4. Expression.

The children draw and color pictures of one child who looks most like Kablu and who poses for the rest. They sort colored papers, pieces of cloth or yarn, and weave paper mats, to show their discrimination of shades and tints.

READ: Where did you come from, Baby Dear? G. Macdonald.
Take Care.

II. Kablu's Clothing

1. The Story.

Kablu wore a tunic of sheep- or goat-skin in winter, of wool in summer, a cap and shoes made of sheep-skin.

The sheep is studied as the source of wool, and the dog as the protector of the sheep. The children learn the story-sequences of the spider (a weaver) and of the caterpillar (a spinner).

For stories may be used:—

Mary had a Little Lamb.
The Little Boy in our House, Wiltse.
The Boy and the Wolf, Æsop's Fables.
The Story of David tending his Sheep, Bible.
The Good Dog, from Victor Hugo's Tales to his Grandchildren, told by Brander Matthews, *Wide Awake*, November, 1896.
Cinderella.

SONGS: Little Bo-Peep, and Sleep, Baby, Sleep are appropriate.

Growing out of the study of clothing the children learn the principle of the processes of spinning and weaving. The children are shown pictures of the old Aryan spindle and loom. The children collect pieces of different kinds of material used for clothing, buttons, material or pictures that will show process of preparing material or making of clothing.

Kablu's clothing is compared, first with Hiawatha's, and then with that of the present child, as to material, color, shape, machinery for making, cost, difficulty of obtaining, and adaptation to the different seasons.

3. Measure.

The children learn how much material of all kinds it takes to make their dresses, coats, etc., how much each garment costs, and how much time it takes to make it. They add the time it takes to make their garments to the time it takes to make the clothing of the other members of the family, and find how much time the mother spends in sewing for them. The clothing of the dolls is made strictly by measurement and from patterns which they learn to cut. The children continue the work on the yard and its fractional parts, feet and inches, the dozen, the dollar and half-dollar as wholes, and the small pieces of money as wholes and with reference to their equivalents in smaller pieces of money.

4. Expression.

The children dress an Aryan doll, with tunic made of black or white woollen cloth, and shoes made of eiderdown flannel to represent sheepskin as nearly as may be. They also dress a modern doll. They make models of the old implements for weaving and spinning, and use them to make cloth. They tell or write the spinning and weaving sequences, illustrating them by drawings. They weave mats, learn to darn, and weave enough cloth on a weaving-machine to make a tunic for a doll. They draw pictures of sheep and illustrate stories about sheep. They make a balance; also they make the standards used in measuring extension.

> STORIES: The Wounded Daisy, in *Open Sesame*, Vol I.
> The Prettiest Doll in the World, by Charles Kingsley, in *Open Sesame*, Vol. I.

> READ: The Little Boy in our House, Wiltse.
> Mary had a Little Lamb.
> Sleep, Baby, Sleep. (Two stanzas.)

Murillo's Gentle Shepherd and Rosa Bonheur's sheep pictures should be hung in the schoolroom, and used to illustrate the study of the sheep. Other sheep pictures by good artists, and pictures of dogs by Landseer and other painters, should be shown.

III. Kablu's House

1. The Story.

Kablu lived in a house built of logs laid one upon another, the chinks between them filled with moss and clay. It leaned against a great rock, which formed the wall of the house at the back. In front, looking to the east, was the single door. Kablu's house consisted of but one room. Mats braided of rushes or of bark hung before the door to keep out the wind and rain. The family slept on the floor on beds of sheep- or goat-skin. Here were their clay-baked utensils for cooking, and the dishes from which they ate, also made of clay. About the house on every hand stood high mountains, on the slopes of which grew the wheat, barley, and beans that Kablu and his father planted, and the mountain grass, upon which the goats, sheep, and cattle grazed. Noisy little streams rushed down the mountains, clattering over the sharp edges of the rocks, and dropping here and there into cool still pools where the sheep and cattle might drink. Kablu got up every morning before the sun had risen, and helped his father gather the materials for the fire to the sun-god.

When their morning worship was over, he went out with the sheep upon the mountain side, kept the flock together, and drove them where there was the best pasturage. At night he brought them safely home into the fold, helped his father to hang the mats before the door of the house, and lay down to sleep. Sometimes he left the sheep for a little while, when they were quite safe, and helped his father plough the field, sow or reap the grain, or make some needed utensil for the house. And meanwhile Nema was helping her mother weave or spin the wool for their clothing, milking the goats and cows, cooking the food, or keeping the house tidy.

Kablu's family all loved one another very much, and for this reason each was glad to help the others in every way he could. Each tried his best to make the home a pleasant place for all of them to live in.

> READ: O tell me, Pretty Brooklet, from *Brooks and Brook-Basins*, Frye, p. 1.
> Wynken, Blynken, and Nod, Eugene Field.
>
> SONG: Home, Sweet Home.

The children study the physical environment of Kablu's home, and of their own, especially mountains, streams, the sun, the wind, and the rain.

> It may be hard, if there are no mountains in the vicinity, to give the children an idea of a mountain, but electric light towers, high buildings, etc., should be used for comparison, supplemented by pictures to show the proper proportion. Such questions as the following may aid in conveying an idea of the environment of Kablu's home:
>
> How much higher was the mountain than Kablu's house? Than some high building you have seen? How long would it take to reach the top? Do you think he would try to run to the top?
>
> Where did the stream come from?
>
> Did it run faster or slower than the river at home?
>
> Did the banks look like those of the same river?

Could you sail as many boats on it?

How many boats do you think Kablu saw?

Was Kablu glad or sorry to have the stream near?

Why? Was he glad on the night of the storm?

Why was the stream larger then?

Where did all the water come from?

Did Kablu watch the sun and moon very much?

Why? Where did the sun go at night?

Why did Kablu watch the moon?

In connection with the study of rain, the children should read: Rain, by Stevenson, *Child's Garden of Verses*, and Little White Lily, by George Macdonald.

As a basis for the study of winds, the children's attention should be called to the fact that neither Hiawatha nor Kablu had a chimney in his house, thence to the reason why we have chimneys in our houses, and the principle involved; this subject leading in higher grades into a discussion of the unequal heating of the earth as the cause of winds.

In this connection the children should read The Wind, by Stevenson, in *Child's Garden of Verses*.

In connection with the study of wind and rain, growing out of the story of the destruction of Kablu's home (told in *Ten Boys*), the children should be taught, if possible, not to fear storms, but to enjoy their grandeur and to recognize the fact that because of them we have the stable and comfortable homes of today.

For the sun, read: Summer Sun, and Night and Day, Stevenson's *Child's Garden of Verses*.

Kablu's food is studied. The life-stories of wheat and beans are used as the basis of the work on these subjects. The story of Sleeping Beauty is made an introduction to the wheat sequence, and the wheat seed compared to the Sleeping Princess. Other sleeping beauties are studied—cocoons, chrysalides, eggs, buds, minerals.

The wheat story is continued through the story of bread-making. This is followed by the study of the cow, and the sequences of butter and cheese making. The general subject of heat is considered from a practical standpoint—how it is secured and used, what it does. Clay pottery is studied in sequence.

STORIES: How the Indians learned to make clay dishes.
Wiltse, Grandmother Kaolin's Story.

Direction is taught. Copper, clay, and wood are studied, each in its proper sequence. Salt introduces the subject of crystallization. The homes of the birds and other animals previously studied are considered with reference to their adaptation to purposes of shelter and protection.

READ: A Chill, by Christina Rossetti, in *Open Sesame*, Vol. I.

Seed homes are also studied, and the care of the mother-plant observed in their shape, coloring, and provisions for the nourishment of the seeds.

All the nature-study for this grade lays especial stress upon the seasons as related to vegetable and animal life, clothing, industry, games, etc. The children learn the names and general characteristics of the various seasons, read poems appropriate to each, and bring into school all signs of an approaching or traces of a departing season.

STORIES: The Swallow is a Mason, Second Reader of *Normal Course in Reading*.
L. M. Child, Who Stole the Bird's Nest?
Jack and the Beanstalk (for the rainbow after the storm).
The Wind and the Sun, Æsop's Fables.
Alice Cary, Mother Faerie.
Jack the Giant-Killer.

SONGS: Sweet and Low.
The North Wind Doth Blow.
Home, Sweet Home.

READ: Fawcett, Two Kinds of Love.
The Child's World, *Lilliput Lectures*.
Alice Cary, Suppose.
Whittier, Barefoot Boy. (Second stanza.)

Industries studied are farming, building, sheep and cattle raising, making pottery, weaving mats; making bread, butter, cheese, salt, clothing.

2 The Religious Experience of a Skeptic

Reprinted in *The Vassar Miscellany Monthly*
9 (February 1923): 21–29.

A piece written when Buck was a student, this essay chronicles her spiritual journey from the Methodist church to Unitarianism and explains the principles upon which her faith was built. She here acknowledges the importance of strong women on her intellectual development and records several ideas that apply directly to her rhetorical teaching and practice; "the organic unity of all creation, and the evolution of the universe according to discernible laws," she writes, "were ideas which ultimately revolutionized my theological conceptions." Her statement of beliefs sounds at times like Walt Whitman's "Song of Myself" and incorporates many of the principles of "new thought" churches formed in the last quarter of the nineteenth century—Christian Scientist, Religious Science, and Unity.

Buck later became a Christian Scientist and in 1913 wrote to Fred Newton Scott about the Christian Science Monitor, *which she considered "the best daily newspaper in existence." Scott said the paper was "ill advised" in using that name, and Buck replied that "a great many people doubtless are so prejudiced by the name that they will not examine the publication, or judge it on its merits, but those who are willing to do so probably learn more about the practical application of the theory than they could in any other way" (letter to Scott, 24 January 1914).*

The second selection was originally published in the University of Michigan's literary magazine, The Inlander, *in 1893, when Buck was a junior in college.*

I accept the title "skeptic" as a designation of honor. I use the word in the only sense justified by its derivation, as meaning not primarily or necessarily a disbeliever, but essentially a looker-into, a searcher, an investigator. Indeed, I should define a skeptic as a person who habitually and without equivocation obeys St. Paul's injunction to "prove all things," with the single end in view of holding fast to that which is eventually proved to be good.

My religious consciousness began almost with the beginning of my life. My memory fails to reach a time when the thought of God was not with me a real and an ever-present thought. As I child I was nervously afraid of dogs, and would pray inaudibly when compelled to pass one on the street—"Dear God, don't let him hurt me!"

This practice of confident petition to a being stronger than myself and always willing to help me, extended to larger things as I grew older. I became as accustomed as many an older Christian to driving bargains with the Lord, and relying on Him to fulfill His part of the contract—in which expectation I cannot say that I was often disappointed. Whenever this did happen, however, I explained it to myself by assuming that my terms had perhaps not been wholly satisfactory to the divine respondent, and that He had consequently declined to accept them—as He had, of course, a perfect right to do. I only lamented that communication between us was so imperfect—He being always able to understand my position, while I could determine His only by the outcome, which sometimes made matters a little awkward for me. But I did not at all see how this could be helped, and accepted the situation philosophically.

I had considered myself a Christian almost from infancy, understanding by the term "a Child of God who recognizes his relationship," and, at twelve years of age, I joined the Methodist Church, as the custom of that denomination is, "on probation" for six months, at the expiration of which period I became a full-fledged member. There was a "revival" in progress in the church at the time when I presented myself for probationary membership. I attended only the "children's meetings," at one of which the pastor asked all who wished to join the church to give him their names. I accordingly did so, without consultation with anyone, not considering the step a particularly momentous one. I had always expected to join the church. Of course! Everybody who was respectable and respected did so! And I might as well do it now as later.

I was now entitled to attend the young people's prayer-meetings, a boon hitherto denied me on account of my extreme youth, and occasionally, urged on by a relentless sense of duty, I rose and repeated a Bible text, or announced in a trembling voice—"I am trying to be a Christian. Pray for me."

But I drifted into formalism from this point—though, in fact I do not know that I had ever been far from it. A little religion was altogether proper and commendable, but too much was as disreputable—almost—as none at all. "Revivals" and "revivalists," though generally approved in my circle, excited my pitying scorn. I considered the Bible a greatly over-rated book. I delighted to disparage and question it, to the horror of my namby-pamby Sunday School teachers, and to the corresponding joy of my less adventurous fellow-sufferers under their—shall I say instruction? The word is far too generous.

Still I conceived myself to be a Christian. I felt awed and pious at the communion table, or under an eloquent sermon, and in trouble turned to God for help without a thought of any other course as open to me.

When I was sixteen, the milk-and-water distributors of the gospel to me as a Sunday school scholar, were superseded by a woman of remarkably winning personality, and of the intensest piety. I fell in love; first with her, then with the religion which permeated—which *was*—her life. This was my first acquaintance with an individual in whom religion was at once a principle and a passion. I still felt myself to be a Christian, but somehow less completely a Christian than she. Perhaps she was "sanctified." I resolved to look up this distinctively Methodist doctrine. I read Hannah Whitall Smith's exposition of "The Christian's Secret of a Happy Life." I seized the idea—"Let Jesus speak and act through you. You be simply unhindering."

I gave the scheme a fair trial. When about to take part in an ordinary conversation, I was conscious of a holding back. I waited for Jesus to say for me what He would; and, hearing, would be conscious of no incongruity between His character and the words spoken through me. "I might have known what He would say," was my almost invariable reflection. I felt an aloofness from the things about me—a sort of disembodiment. I lived, yet not I, but Christ lived in me.

This very real possession of the human by the divine enabled me to testify to the "experience" in the weekly church prayer meeting, and led to its expression in verses not particularly original, as may be judged from the appended specimen, but very heart-felt.

I

Into Thy loving hands, dear Lord,
    I yield my life.
Thou art my Father, and through all
    Earth's sin and strife
Wilt guide my way.
    I ask for naught from Thy dear hands,
For Thou art mine.
    With Thee my soul shall ever walk
In light divine
    To perfect day.

II

I am all thine—my soul, my will,
    Myself, my all.

My time, my money and my strength,
    My talents small.
None are my own.
    All that I am and hope to be,
All that I do,
    Or think or say or win or own
My whole life through,
    Is Thine alone.

III

Help me, dear Lord, to do Thy will,
    Throughout each day,
And help me to show forth thy truth
    In all I say,
Till life shall end.
    To think Thy thoughts, till, lost in Thee,
Thy will is mine,
    And I am truly not my own
But wholly Thine,
    My Saviour-Friend!

This was published in the *Michigan Christian Advocate* under the title "Consecration" while the experience was at its meridian.

For nearly two months, I think sincerely that I performed no act and spoke no word without this mental hesitation for another's prompting, and without the consciousness, when it was over, that not I but another diviner being had spoken or acted in my stead.

I don't know how the spell was broken, but gradually I became less conscious of the divine indwelling, though I still recognized myself as a different being since the experience, and felt as truly "called" to a life of undivided service for God, as did any prophet of old.

I hardly "prayed" at all during this time—at least in the ordinary sense of the word. I felt with David Wasson:—

    "If I should pray
    I've naught to say
But this, that God should be
      God still.
    For Him to live
    Is still to give,

And sweeter than my wish
　　His will."

There was no cant about this. The words were borrowed, but the feeling was intensely my own.

So far my religious experiences had been largely of a subjective—not to say selfish—character. From this point, however, I became gradually, through association with a real humanity-lover, interested in people, as such—especially in the so-called "lower classes." I burned at first to preach to them, later just to live among and love them. My heart seemed bursting with love for all the loveless. I could scarcely restrain myself, passing on the street a gross and discontented-looking negro girl, or a bent, forlorn old day-laborer, from throwing my arms about them, holding my face to theirs and saying—"I love you! I love you with all my heart. And your Father loves you. Did you know that? And doesn't it make a difference?"

But just at this point occurred the secession of my favorite cousin, a woman some ten years older than myself, from the Methodist Church to the Unitarian ministry—an event which precipitated the intellectual stage in my religious life. It was an earthquake in my moral world,—though, up to this point, I had had really little concern about dogma. Nevertheless, to investigate the truth of the doctrine of the divinity of Christ I read, with minutest care, and with a poor attempt at disprejudice, the four gospels, finding in the transcendent wisdom of Jesus' words and the surpassing beauty of His deeds, the—for the present—sufficient proof of His super-human nature.

I went to college that year, and studied anew the life of Christ as found in Luke, by President Harper's inductive method, under a professor for whom I felt sincere reverence, and by this means only confirmed my former conclusions as to the main point at issue between Methodism and Unitarianism.

I began to formulate my views upon other theological questions, and found that, in my twentieth year, they stood somewhat like this.

I believed in the existence of an ultimate First Cause, since I could, in no other way, account for the universe itself, and in a personal First Cause, since I thought I discerned both wisdom and benevolence in the phenomena of the universe—which qualities are characteristic of personality alone—not of matter or of force. I believed in Jesus Christ as the divine Son of God, not being able otherwise to explain the superlative beauty and profundity of both His teachings and His character. I believed Him to be the Saviour from present sinfulness of as many as accepted His philosophy of life and took upon themselves the likeness of His character. The idea of vicarious atonement, however, seemed to me, then as now, wholly irrational, and hence absolutely repulsive. I believed in the Holy Spirit as man's consciousness of God, altogether rejecting the idea of a third person in the God-head. On grounds of justice to humanity, I predicated a future state of progressive development of the individual, denying, however, as immoral, and incompatible with a just conception of God, any notion of future rewards and punishments, the popular theories of heaven and hell.

So far my thought, unaided, had led me, when some fundamental studies in natural science and modern philosophy opened my eyes to see the universe as a single organism. It lay before me, one great, throbbing, living creature, of diverse organs and parts, yet one, like the fish, like the bird, or, better still, like myself. Like the fish, like the bird, like myself, the universe grows and changes, but always according to the laws of growth and change, as we know them in all life.

The organic unity of all creation, and the evolution of the universe according to discernible laws, were ideas which ultimately revolutionized my theological conceptions.

My God could not be less than all. He must then be the universe—this complex, highly developed organism, that is all we see or think or are—not immanent in, or working through the universe, since this excludes Him from the shell while making Him the core. The universe is one, and that one is the absolute, the unlimited—God. The grass under my feet, the air that touches my face, the blood that darts through my veins, the friend who walks by my side—all these are God. I, myself, in every common activity of life, am God. There is no limit, there is no incompleteness. God is all. The theologians are accustomed to say that God is in all space, knows and can do all things. But my God is a greater God than theirs; for He *is* all space, *is* all knowing and all doing.

It will be seen that thus God is not to me "a person" in the commonly accepted sense of the term. Not being such, prayer, as petition, becomes inadequate to the demands of the situation. The ultimate worship is simply action, in accordance with the laws of the universe. I stretch out my arm. The act is worship, because in it, as in every activity, I am one with God. The act is God. I go down town to my business. It is God. I rise in the morning and lay myself down to rest at evening. It is all God. The universe, then, is God.

But the universe is not a stable and unprogressive thing. The universe moves. The universe differentiates. As soon as any part of it ceases to change, it ceases to be, at all. Even a bit of matter is only a center of force, of motion. Heat is molecular motion. Chemical reaction is molecular or atomic motion.

The growing weed is protoplasmic, that is, molecular motion. My thought is molecular motion in the cells of my brain. Look where you will, motion is the fundamental law of the universe. Evolution is its history from Alpha to Omega,—save that evolution knows neither Alpha nor Omega. Every seemingly stationary existence or object is but a stage in the evolution of the whole. Nothing is finished. Nothing ever will be finished.

We, then, as temporary stages in the universe-life, shall never die out of the universe or cease to move. What ever does? We shall change form. We do so constantly. The carbon dioxide that exhales on my breath, the water that evaporates from the surface of my body, enters into the cell-structure of the vegetation about me, is eaten by the animal, which, in turn, becomes food for man, doing his day's work, thinking his evening thoughts, which work and thoughts again become activity, chemical, mental, spiritual, so that the chain is endless, and I live on, through countless transformations in the myriad life that surrounds me. That which was yesterday I, is to-day the grass at my feet, the bird that flies above my head, the neighbor that lives over the way. And, when I shall die, this transformation of force, which has been continuously going on from the cradle, is to be simply accelerated. I become, more completely than before, a part of all the physical universe. I live, then, as now, only more widely.

But immortality is not even thus circumscribed. It is of thought and character, as of physical and chemical constituents. My children perpetuate after my death, soul-elements that were temporarily mine. My words still are spoken, though it may be all-unconsciously, on the lips of those I knew and loved. My thoughts are by them made deathless in action. No smallest fraction of my being can ever die.

This, then, is the conception of immortality forced upon me by the analogy of scientific facts. Man, as man, must die, though man, as the universe, lives unendingly. Life is one, and never ceases, though it constantly passes into other forms. And in one form as in another, it is always God.

It will be useless to follow into further detail, the outlines of my present creed. I realize very fully that before the words have fairly grown cold upon my lips, they may come to represent what is, in some points, already an outgrown part of my past. And indeed if this were otherwise, I should feel myself unfaithful to my possibilities of mental growth. But, as my creed now stands, with all the clearness I can, I have stated it.

In conclusion, let me assert most firmly my conviction that my beliefs are still religious beliefs. Though accepting the title skeptic in the sense of power, I count myself among Christians, rather than with unbelievers—so far as unbelievers are, after all, ever such. I believe myself to be today far more truly Christian than I was ten years or even two years ago—not alone by my own standards of judgment, but, I am very sure, in accordance with His, who said, as the truest word of all ages, "By their fruits ye shall know them."

FROM *THE INLANDER*, MAY, 1893

It seems to me, always, a most unwarrantable, and—if I may venture to say so—an insulting act, to elect a woman for any office of service or of honor, simply because she is a woman. It is saying, with such cruel clearness—"You are called to this dignity, not because of any especial worth or fitness therefor, not because you have proved yourself to be, above all others, competent to fulfill just the duties involved in this position, but because, for certain reasons, we have decided to elect a woman—and you are a woman!" There is nothing more humiliating to the woman chosen and to womanhood at large, nothing more undignified in the voting constituency, than such an election.

In small matters, as in great ones, if a woman show peculiar qualifications for any office, it goes without saying, that she should be elected above any inferior person, male or female. In some cases her sex may constitute part of her peculiar qualification. If so, it should, of course, be regarded as such.

But the case in question, touching the election of women upon the editorial board of *The Inlander*, does not at all seem to me to be such a case. Women, as women, would have, in this position, little advantage over men. Their incumbency might, perhaps, slightly increase the circulation of the magazine among University women, by virtue of their more accurate knowledge as to what matter would especially appeal to the feminine constituency; but, as it is, the contributions from women are somewhat numerous, and serve sufficiently to furnish an element of femininity in the make up of each issue, if that be considered desirable. I do not see that to include women upon the board, would be, necessarily, to benefit *The Inlander*, in any considerable degree.

But to elect women editors, not as women, but as individuals possessing pre-eminent qualifications for such a position, in my estimation, could not fail to broaden the usefulness and to increase the attractiveness of the magazine to the same extent that the election of equally able men would tend toward the same result. A woman with good critical ability, literary taste and enterprise above other candidates should in all fairness be elected over them— but only if she thus excel. Nothing is gained, but much is lost by any attempt, however well meaning, to make some accident of birth co-ordinate with proved capacity, as qualification for office, in any sphere of activity.

The conclusion of the whole matter seems to me to be this. Women should, by every claim of common justice be declared eligible to election upon *The Inlander* board, but, by every law of common-sense, no woman should ever be elected to such position, who is not at once suggested for it by her own especial fitness, without a question of sex.

II A Social Rhetoric and Poetics

3   Genesis: Poetic Metaphor

from *The Metaphor: A Study in the Psychology of Rhetoric*,
Contributions to Rhetorical Theory 5 (Ann Arbor, Mich.: Inland Press, 1899), 26–33.

*Buck's interests in language theory, the history of rhetoric, and practical applications of
theory were combined in her dissertation on metaphor, an ambitious project that examines the function of figurative language from Plato to her present. Fred Newton Scott
published it in a series entitled "Contributions to Rhetorical Theory" that included*
Student Slang *by Willard C. Gore,* Two Problems in Composition Teaching *by Joseph
V. Denney, and* References on the Teaching of Rhetoric and Composition *by Scott.
Each sold for fifteen cents. The document has the markings of a dissertation, such as an
exhaustive review of previous treatments of the topic, including an appendix in which the
views are covered in greater detail, yet Buck demonstrates great skill in applying new
psychological theory to the topic and illustrating how this theoretical treatment has
relevance in classrooms. She argues that rhetoricians have "dissected the dead body of the
metaphor; but they have not told us how the living figure came to be, nor what it in
essence is" (2). This she sets out to do by systematically examining the theories explaining
metaphor, finding them lacking, and ultimately arguing for a psychological explanation
of metaphor as a development in speech and thought.*

*Metaphor was divided into three stages. Buck adopted Max Müller's term "radical
metaphor" to indicate the first metaphoric stage, where the user cannot distinguish
between two objects, such as teeth and pears, and therefore calls teeth pearls. Teeth and
pearls are equated until a closer inspection, further growth, or the development of
civilization shows the two to be different. The next stage then is poetic metaphor, where
the speaker sees the connection between the objects she once confused and creates a simile,
so that the connection is visible, the teeth are like pearls. Finally, the furthest development was plain statement, whereby the person clearly views the objects as two and states
them thus (42). Buck believed that too many textbook writers encouraged students to use
poetic metaphor to beautify or energize speech, and she used the work of John Dewey and
William James to point out the hedonistic fallacy: "One does not make a poetic metaphor
because he desires the pleasure which it will give him, but he makes it because he has to,
gaining pleasure therefrom, though he has not directly aimed at it" (23).*

*Buck believed that rhetoric had overemphasized the response of the hearer or reader,
which made people distrust rhetoric, for it implied that the speaker was not speaking to
express her or himself or to speak the truth, but solely to have a specific effect on the
listener. This use of poetic metaphor to achieve an effect was connected to rhetoric as
persuasion. Instead of viewing metaphor as persuasion, Buck wrote, "poetic metaphor,*

like radical, is a straightforward attempt to communicate to another person the maker's vision of an object as it appeared to him at the moment of expression, not at all to carry out a dark design of persuading the reader that this object is something which the writer knows it is not. The writer is simply taking a snap-shot at his own process of perception in one of its intermediate stages" (35). When the writer was concerned primarily with the reader, and only secondarily with self and subject, the metaphors became forced, mixed, or bad art. Buck called the consequences of this unnatural use of language "metaphoraphobia" to describe the readers' fears of the writer's designs.

Chapter 1, "Genesis: Radical Metaphor," discusses theories for the origin of metaphor based on the poverty of language. The introduction and a section of chapter 2, "Genesis: Poetic Metaphor," are included here. Chapter 3, "The Evolution into Plain Statement," argues that metaphor is only a beginning stage of perception. Chapter 4, "The Aesthetics of Metaphor," reveals Buck's rhetorical training, as she focuses on the reader's mind, what stimulates her, what happens after that stimulation, and how the process is evident in children's language development. Chapter 5, "Pathological Forms of Metaphor," evaluates mixed metaphor and other forms of "bad art" to determine how the labels reflect the reader's or writer's own thought process.

INTRODUCTION

The subject of metaphor bristles with problems. Is this figure a natural product or an artificial? How does it come to be? How does it die? How is it related to plain statement? How are "radical" metaphors different from "poetical"? Why does metaphor please the reader? How does it become "mixed"? These are questions which every serious consideration of the subject must at least attempt to answer.

Such solutions as have hitherto been furnished these problems have been rooted in the philosophy of an earlier generation, now discredited. The purpose of this study is to explain metaphor in terms of the contemporary psychology. In so doing it has, perhaps, been inevitable that a new face should be put up on this figure. From a mechanical structure it has become a biological organism. It has come to stand as the linguistic representative of a certain stage in the development of thought, and thus an expression perfectly natural and universal, rather than as a literary device, somewhat artificial and wholly unique, obedient to no laws save those empiric ones whose validity extends no farther than to itself.

In this conception of metaphor the present study differs from the rhetorical treatises as a class, though building upon their foundations. It also deviates from the practice of the rhetoricians in distinguishing carefully between the metaphor as viewed from the writer's and from the reader's standpoint. The fact of such a distinction has been often implied, but the essential difference between the activities set up in each case has not been explained and the one activity has often been confused with the other.

The doctrines that metaphor is invariably antecedent to plain statement, that radical and poetic metaphor differ only in representing different stages in the development of a perception, that metaphor is pleasurable to the reader because of the harmoniously differentiated activities which it sets up in his mind and body, are doctrines not formulated by the rhetoricians. They grow, however, directly from the fundamental conception that metaphor is the expression in language of a certain stage in the development of perception.

It has seemed natural to consider, first, the normal metaphor, and afterward some abnormal variation from the type. The term "pathology" in its application to rhetorical processes has been borrowed from Dr. Fred Newton Scott, Junior Professor of Rhetoric at the University of Michigan, who first used it in a paper entitled "Diseases of English Prose," read before the annual meeting of the Modern Language Association, in December, 1896.

To Dr. Scott I am also indebted for much stimulus and criticism in the preparation of this thesis; to Dr. John Dewey, now of the University of Chicago, for the fundamental philosophic conceptions embodied in it, to Professor Francis W. Kelsey of the University of Michigan, Professor Milton W. Humphreys of the University of Virginia, and Dr. Mary Gilmore Williams, now professor of Greek at Mt. Holyoke College, for a large number of classical metaphors which, though few of them appear upon these pages, have been of the greatest assistance to my own study of the subject.

CHAPTER 2
GENESIS: POETIC METAPHOR

It may, perhaps, be urged that the effect of the metaphor upon the hearer is regarded by the rhetoricians rather as a test for the metaphor, after it has been made, than as a statement of the end aimed at in making it. But it must be remembered that a test is meaningless except it refer, directly or indirectly, to the end for which the thing tested has been designed. Ultimate judgment must always be based upon the answer to the question, "Does this thing fulfill the purpose of its creation?" Such a test the rhetoricians are accustomed to apply to the metaphor when they say, "If it fails to produce a certain effect upon the reader, it is worthless. Discard it." The metaphor is designed, so these practical precepts may fairly be interpreted, to make the reader see the point more clearly than he could otherwise do, to give him a more vivid or forcible conception of the object presented, to stimulate his mind,—in brief, to produce upon him a certain effect. We may, then, conclude, both from the stated theories of the writers upon rhetoric, and from the implications lying in their practical precepts, that they, as a class, are fairly committed to the theory that a metaphor is made for the sake of inducing a certain effect upon the mind of the reader.[1]

We are asked to suppose that any writer who uses a figure of speech does so with a definite end in view, that of making the expression of his ideas more pleasurable[2] to the reader than it could be if plainly expressed. Suppose, for instance, that the writer wishes to speak of the sun. He might say "sun" without further ado, but that he desires to gain for his readers the pleasant sensation which he knows will result from the simple device of calling one thing by the name of another. Therefore he decides to call the sun something else—but what else? Here, as in the case of the radical metaphor, the fact of

1. One apparent exception to this statement should be noted. Mr. L. A. Sherman, in his *Analytics of Literature*, defines a metaphor as "seeing one thing spiritually identical with another thing," (notes, p. 399) and states explicitly that the writer in a particular case "saw mentally this same identity, and said or wrote the metaphor *because* he experienced it thus vividly in his mind." (p. 62.) Having made this most interesting statement, however, he at once proceeds to discredit it, by referring casually to metaphor as "the assignment of two objects to a new class by using it (resemblance) as the basis of classification" (p. 62) and hinting pretty broadly that the fact that this operation is "especially agreeable to the ego" (p. 62) bears a casual relation to the production of the metaphor. Here are certainly two widely different statements. The one shows the writer as having united two perfectly distinct objects into a single class because he wished the pleasure that the process would secure to him. The other makes the writer express directly his own vision of the identity of two objects. Sherman first adopts the latter hypothesis. According to this, the writer sees, at the height of the metaphor-process, not two objects at all, but one. Yet the one either had been two before this supreme moment of the writer's vision, or it became two after that moment had passed. Which belief does Sherman hold? His treatment of the subject clearly depends upon his faith in the first. "In metaphor it (the mind) perceives two objects, each with equal vividness, spiritually identified." (p. 399.) There were two objects. They have been fused into one. The process by which this fusion takes place now becomes the difficulty, and forces Sherman into a tacit acceptance of the hypothesis which regards two objects as being united in a single class by virtue of a resemblance existing between them, and, for the sake of giving pleasure to the author of the union. If Sherman had seen that psychologically the writer's vision must be single before it can be dual, he would not have predicated the existence of the two objects in consciousness as antecedent to the presence of the one, or their identity, and thus would not have been compelled to close up by artificial means a gap that did not actually exist. It may, then, be affirmed that while Mr. Sherman refuses, at first sight, to be classified with the rhetoricians in his understanding of the metaphor-process, in last analysis he is at one with them.

2. I include, for the present, under this term all the cognate expressions, "forcible," "vivacious," "economical," "stimulating," etc. The argument will attempt to disprove the theory that a metaphor is made for the sake of producing an effect upon the reader, pleasure standing as the representative of all these effects.

resemblance is the deus ex machina. The writer may be supposed to follow out in every direction from the object "sun" the radiating lines of its qualities or characteristics until one of these shall haply lead him to an object possessing the same quality or characteristic and thus connected with the original object, sun. Say, for instance, that he has in this way followed the line of the quality of roundness out from the round sun until he reached the round object ball. He can now call the sun a golden ball with perfect assurance that the reader cannot fail to receive therefrom the pleasure which has been designed for him.

It is difficult to avoid the ironical tone in discussing this explanation. It makes the act of metaphor so mechanical, so crude, so essentially cheap and tawdry that the sensitive reader of literature can hardly suffer serious consideration of its truthfulness. He revolts instinctively from the notion that Shakespeare, for instance, deliberately set about comparing the storm-whitened waves of the ocean to a culinary compound made foamy in the process of "rising," in order that he might tickle his reader's fancy by the phrase "the yesty waves."[3] Such an explanation virtually requires that Shakespeare, having one element in the metaphor—the storm-whitened sea—distinctly in mind, should consciously lay about him for an object which might serve as the other element. One must imagine him like the pedantic King Richard II, always studying how he might compare one thing to another. Or one must fancy the virile dramatist in the situation of a practiced conceit-monger, Thomas Sheridan, who thus owns to his poetic method:

"I often tried in vain to find
A simile for womankind,
A simile I mean to fit 'em,
In every circumstance to hit 'em.
Through every beast and bird I went,
I ransacked every element;
And after peeping through all nature,
To find so whimsical a creature,
A cloud presented to my view,
And strait this parable I drew."[4]

We are not surprised to learn that certain metaphors in our less naive and spontaneous poetry had their rise in such a process as this. Their flavor

---

3. *Macbeth*, IV, 53.
4. *New Simile for the Ladies. The Poetical Works* of Jonathan Swift, Vol. III, Aldine Ed.

suggests an origin no less mechanical. And few are the happy teachers of English composition who have not thus explained to themselves the existence of many a metaphor in student essays.[5] The boy who speaks of Hawthorne as "the queen-bee in American literature," and the girl who characterizes reading as "the indispensable nectar of existence" present us no insoluble problem as to the metaphorical process which has gone on in their minds. Clearly it was somewhat like this: A figure is necessary to any well-regulated composition. Therefore let us have a figure. Since we are writing about Hawthorne, we may as well say that Hawthorne was something besides what he really was. Hawthorne was . . . . . Hawthorne was . . . . . What was Hawthorne, anyhow? He was awfully important in American literature, the teacher said. Well, what else is important to something? Perhaps a bee wings across the field of vision just at the moment of despair and is frantically clutched at by the despairing mind. Oh I guess Hawthorne was the queen-bee in American literature. And the successful author beams with satisfaction over the way that expression will "hit" the teacher.

Not only, however, does the struggling student of composition thus manufacture his figures; but often the newspaper writer and compounder of dilute fiction seems to be conversant with the metaphor-recipe. Mr. A. S. Hill's incomparable illustrations,[6] "hair shot through with sunset spikes of yellow light," "and lips with musical curves" are in point.

Under the class of manufactured articles must also fall the following from Amélie Rives: "The stars had looked like great drops of trembling quicksilver, just ready to splash from the inverted pewter spoon of the sky."[7] We may be quite as certain as internal evidence can render us that the writer of this astonishing figure, moved by a keen desire to make a metaphor, looked wildly about her for some like object to which she could compare the stars and the sky of which she wished to speak. At this particular hour in the morning the

---

5. Such efforts as the following troop at once to mind: Margaret and Luke are reported as having at their first meeting seen "the juncture of two unfathomable revelations . . . . descend upon them like the downward flight of a soaring thing. Margaret felt the mist of a sudden indistinctness hurl her through infinite space, and a great gong seemed to beat a muffled distance of time and space across Luke's forehead."

"Liberty, powerful, just and equal, stands as the beacon light for this country, whose foundations were laid and cemented on the blood of the patriots who died in defense of it."

"Since that moment life has been a cesspool of malignity; an empty dream; a hollow mockery and a sham, totally unknown to the smiling face of pleasure, and only goaded along its labyrinthian highway to its everlasting doom, by the most despicable spirit of vengeance, despondency and immutable woe."

6. *Our English*, pp. 122–3.

7. *The Story of a Heart*, Amélie Rives. *Cosmopolitan*, July, 1897, p. 331.

stars resembled silver in color; but this comparison was far too common-place, and quicksilver was accordingly substituted as an equivalent. The sky was a dull, hard-looking gray. The use of quicksilver for the stars suggeted pewter for the sky: and the shape of the aerial dome furnished another analogy, that of a pewter spoon inverted. Nothing could be neater than this process; and nothing surer invariably to furnish a metaphor on demand.

Swinburne has evidently employed such a device in his stanza:

"Now the morning, faintlier risen,
    Seems no God come forth of prison,
  But a bird of plume-plucked wing
    Pale with thoughts of evening."[8]

Such a metaphor as this can hardly have been produced otherwise than by holding before the writer's consciousness the thought of the pale dawn and casting about for an object which might in some particular resemble it. The traditional God of day is discarded because too robust. The morning has been shorn of its usual glories, so Swinburne says it seems a plucked bird. But this comparison does not convey a sufficiently vivid idea of the pallor of the dawn, so that the statement must be added that the bird is "pale with thoughts of evening."

The figures cited are perhaps sufficiently absurd to demonstrate con-clusively the essential difference between "those metaphors which rise glow-ing from the heart, and those cold conceits which are engendered in the fancy."[9] We feel acutely that there is a real division here; that those metaphors which we can conceive to have been manufactured by a conscious effort of the mind directed to the recognized end of making a figure, for the sake, ultimately, of pleasing the reader,[10] inevitably fall into a class quite distinct from those fresh and vital figures which need no external witness to their spontaneous origin.

For the former class of metaphors we should not hesitate to adopt the hypothesis that they have come into being as the result of the writer's effort to produce a certain effect upon the reader. But we shrink instinctively from this theory as applied to the latter species—the genuine poetic metaphor. We feel

8. *Pastiche, Poems and Ballads*, Second Series.

9. Oliver Goldsmith, *Essay on the Use of Metaphors*. Cf. Emerson's distinction between imagination and fancy in the essay *Poetry and Imagination*. "Fancy is a willful, imagination a spontaneous action."

10. This process will be further analyzed under the head of the Pathology of Metaphor, Ch. V.

not only that it cannot account for these metaphors, but that it ought not to do so. Our half-conscious theories of literary art attribute to it a quality far less artificial—not to say meretricious—than that which characterizes the process of manufacturing a metaphor in the manner described. We feel assured that to substitute one word for another in order to produce a pleasant titillation of the reader's fancy is a shabby gallery-play, beneath the dignity of the real artist.

It is true that this is only a feeling, though a feeling so universal among people of literary sensibility that it might almost upon that ground be allowed in evidence. But if we trace this intuitional judgment to its source, we shall perhaps find that it roots in a philosophy of the literary process not the less true because so often unconscious. For the widespread feeling that metaphors made to produce a certain effect upon the reader fall below the level of real art, we find both source and justification in that philosophy of the literary process which regards it as having equal reference to two factors, the writer and the reader. This theory is that known as the communication theory of discourse, which has, in the later rhetorical systems, largely superseded the one-sided theories of discourse as persuasion and as self-expression. The theory that discourse is self-expression has reference only to the speaker; the hypothesis that it is persuasion makes the hearer all-important. When discourse is regarded as communication the two factors in the process are equally emphasized. In order that the writer's vision be communicated to the reader's eye, the one factor is as necessary as the other. Not the reader alone is concerned, nor yet the writer, but both equally have a part in the literary process. According to this standard a piece of writing which seeks only to lay bare the writer's thought, with no reference at all to the capacity or interests of the reader, is condemned as bad art; and no less is the work found wanting which looks only to its effect upon the reader, little caring to be true to the vision of him who writes. And of this last sort must be the metaphor which is made for the sake of pleasing the reader, if no real sight of the writer lies behind.

We find justification, then, in this conception of the normal literary process, for the instinctive feeling that such mechanical construction of the metaphor as is implied in the rhetorical explanation of its origin is bad art, because it leaves out of account one of the prime factors in the process of discourse. The dilemma then confronts us. Either we must accept the rhetorical explanation of the origin of metaphor, and bow to the conclusion that this figure lies outside the field of legitimate art; or we must deny the rhetorical explanation and hold to our instinctive faith in the artistic justification for a good metaphor.

The first of these alternatives has found the widest acceptance. Acquiescing in the theory of rhetoric that the metaphor is an expression not necessarily of the speaker's own vision of things, but of his desire to make other people see them in a certain way, the "practical man" is straightway seized with a distrust of the figure, amounting almost to fear. He regards metaphors much as the old saints regarded women—as charming snares, in which he may too easily be entangled. Tell a jury that your opponent's most telling argument is "only a beautiful metaphor," and you have at once wholly discredited it. You have by this means conveyed to the jury with more or less distinctness the idea that your opponent has been trying to cheat them; that, without seeing the matter in that light himself, he has deliberately set out to make them see it as he wished; in a word, to produce a certain effect upon them for his own ends.

Now this metaphoraphobia, if the term may be allowed, is only the logical consequence of the faith that metaphor arises from the desire of the writer to produce a certain effect upon the reader. We have a right to suppose that language will convey to us the speaker's thought, modified unconsciously perhaps by the speaker's knowledge of the hearer's capacities and predictions, but not wholly determined by them. When, however, we have learned to suspect any form of speech of occasionally mis-representing the thought it assumes to represent, we are bound to fear it as treacherous and misleading, and when we have finally become assured that this form of speech has no necessary reference to the speaker's thought, we can afford to scorn it. Having once determined its falsity, it can never deceive us again. We can safely snap our fingers at it and devote ourselves to warning other people against its deceptions. This last attitude is, as might be expected, that of the more vigorous and independent of straightforward minds. Philosophers, logicians and scientific men, it has often been observed, exhibit a healthy scorn for metaphor, evidently regarding it in the light of a meretricious device, a crude overreaching artifice, unworthy of the simplicity of truth. Locke seems to voice the opinions of this class, when he says: "If we would speak of things as they are, we must allow that all the art of rhetoric, besides order and clearness, all the artificial and figurative application of words eloquence hath invented, are for nothing else but to insinuate wrong ideas, move the passions, and thereby mislead the judgment, and so indeed are perfect cheats, and therefore, however laudable or allowable oratory may render them in harangues and popular addresses, they are certainly, in all discourses that pretend to inform or instruct, wholly to be avoided; and where truth and knowledge are concerned, cannot but be thought a great fault, either of the language or person that makes use of them."[11]

This is a point of view wholly self-consistent, if one hold with the faith that metaphor arises from the writer's desire to affect his reader in a certain predetermined fashion. One who shrinks from this doctrine may, however, seek another explanation of the genius of metaphor. And this search shall be our next task. Before entering upon it, we may, however, note a further reason for discrediting the accepted rhetorical theory, in that it makes no provision for the first poetic metaphor. This surely cannot be explained as the product of a desire for the reader's pleasure; for the writer had then no assurance, either from his own experience or observation, that pleasure would result to the reader from the device of substituting one word for another. We are compelled to one of two explanations. Perhaps the writer stumbled upon the device. He "just happened" by a lucky accident to substitute one word for another; and the pleasure resulting from it to the reader either encouraged the writer to make another metaphor on purpose to confer this pleasure, or incited the reader to make one himself for another person's delight. But granting this to be a possible explanation, the "accident" has still to be explained. There are psychological laws governing the metathesis of letters in rapid writing; there is always some reason why one misspeaks.[12] How did it happen that this original maker substituted one word for another? The fact that a certain resemblance or analogy existed between the two objects whose names were concerned may have made the substitution possible. But we cannot suppose an explicit recognition of this resemblance on the part of the maker of the metaphor; for, as soon as we do this, we are forced to assign a motive that led to the transfer; and we have promised that no motive existed. The maker of the metaphor "just happened" to substitute one name for another. In his haste he mis-spoke. As in the case of the radical metaphor, the resemblance existed but was not explicitly perceived by the speaker. Could it then have been a factor in the substitution which took place? Undoubtedly it could, precisely as with the radical metaphor, where that which is later perceived as resemblance or analogy is, at the time of

---

11. *Essay on the Human Understanding*, Bk. III, Ch. X § 34: "Figurative speech also an abuse of language." I find in *Blackwood* 18: 719 the statement: "It is said to have been a boast of Swift, or his friends, that 'he had hardly a metaphor in all his works.'"

12. There is a recent German treatise on this subject: *Versprechen und Verlesen*, by Rudolf Meringer and Karl Mayer, Stuttgart, 1895.

making the metaphor, seen but vaguely as complete identity between the two objects concerned in the figure. We can conceive that out of a primitive sensation of something fluffy white might spring into separate existence the two objects "cloud" and "snow." At the moment when the two were disentangling themselves from the first homogeneity, our metaphor-maker might express the starting differentiation by saying "snow" as he pointed to the clouds. When he had done so, doubtless he would feel a certain pleasure in the unity of which he was dimly conscious under the variety, and the impulse to a second metaphor-making would thus be strengthened. And from this point the story is easily told. But this explanation practically identifies the source of poetic with that of radical metaphor—in the speaker's homogeneous consciousness of a primitive sensation, out of which its constituent elements later separate themselves.

So much for the first explanation of the ultimate origin of poetic metaphor. The second, we shall see, brings us to this same point. It is that this first maker of the poetic metaphor was led to the making because he had noticed the pleasurable effect consequent upon his perception of the radical metaphor and resolved to create enjoyment for himself or for another person by the same method, consciously employed. Now it is quite unlikely, to say the least, that the maker of the first poetic metaphor had already arrived at a stage of reflection so advanced that he could recognize his pleasure in the radical metaphor, analyze its sources, and determine to use the same means to attain a like enjoyment. "Poetic metaphor" appeared in ages far too unsophisticate for such subtle ratiocination. But whether we grant or deny the possibility of this explanation, we are with equal promptness brought to the source of the radical metaphor as the ultimate spring also of the poetic.

We are, then, confronted at once by the question, "If the ultimate, why may not also the proximate source of the poetic metaphor be identical with that of the radical metaphor?[13] Is it not possible that the same psychological process of growing differentiation in perception may lie at the root of both phenomena?" Let us face this question fairly. We have seen that the radical metaphor is the single expression of an undeveloped perception which later divides into its elements, the division bringing to light an incongruity be-

13. Compare the following observation: "En effet, quand l'écrivain suivant le tour de sa pensée, exprime les choses de la façon particulière dont il les sent, ou les voit, il ne fait qu'obéir aux mêmes lois se l'esprit que le peuple. Il n'y a point de différence entre les figures du style d'un écrivain et celles de la langue populaire, sauf que chez l'écrivain ce sont des hardiesses individuelles, tandis que chez le peuple, si ces hardiesses sont individuelles à l'origine, elles ont été adoptées par tous, consacrées par l'usage, et sont devenues habitudes de langage.—Arsène Darmsteter, La Vie des Mots, pp. 45–46.

tween the dual character of the developed perception and the simplicity of the phrase which once represented it. Now this process by which perception develops from a vague unity into a more clearly defined duality or complexity is asserted by psychologists to be typical and universal. It must, then, go on in the modern as well as in the primitive consciousness. Civilization can only shorten the process, not do away with it. The savage who spoke of a nation that came "from so far off as the sun slept",[14] perhaps never in his life-time learned to distinguish clearly between the action of a man in withdrawing to sleep, and that of the sun in disappearing for the night. The child in a civilized nation, however, completes the process in a far shorter time. The lamp globe is a moon to him at first. He sees, both when he looks at the moon and when he looks at the globe, exactly the same thing, so far as his undeveloped perceptive powers can tell him. But not many months pass before the two have successfully separated themselves, and the one can no longer be mistaken for the other. In the case of the adult civilized man, the process is still more rapid. Although for the flash of a second he may see a curled stick as a snake, he cannot do so for long. The perception rapidly differentiates until the two elements, the stick and the snake, become perfectly distinct in his consciousness. The whole development of the perception from homogeneity to heterogeneity, to use the scientific phrase, may, in this instance, occupy but the fraction of a second, instead of the years or ages needed for the slower-moving mind of the savage, and the months required by the undeveloped intelligence of the child. But in all these cases the process is the same. The sophisticated modern, when he gives utterance to perception before it has developed out of the homogeneous stage, is making a radical metaphor just as truly as does the savage or the child. No two things are concerned in his thought, but only one. There is, in the ordinary sense of the word, no metaphor. The speaker has simply represented in words his own undifferentiate consciousness.

But so rapid is the process of differentiation, that often utterance takes place when the two elements in the perception are just emerging from the primitive mass, and both, therefore, appear in the figure. Emily Dickinson in her poem called "The Snake" represents exactly the development of a dim perception into definiteness. She says that she saw

.... "a whip-lash
Unbraiding in the sun,—

14. Barrett Wendell, *Eng. Comp.*, p. 249.

When, stooping to secure it,
It wrinkled, and was gone."

Her hazy impression of a something long, brown, slender and convolute had already separated out of its mass the idea of "whip-lash," with others, such as that of a snake, just stirring into consciousness, when, "stooping to secure it," of a sudden "it wrinkled and was gone," so that the dormant idea of "snake" sprang at once into full view and the figure was complete in which a snake is, according to the rhetorical dictum, "compared" to a whip-lash.

Similar readings of poetic metaphors might be multiplied indefinitely. When Tennyson says that "fear chalked her face,"[15] we can see that the thought has leaped to expression just at the instant when the first vague impression of a surface rapidly growing white was separating into the two yet half-conscious images of a surface being overlaid with chalk, and a face paling under the influence of fear. When he says again in the same poem, "I stole from court, cat-footed through the town," we are able to recognize the first nebulous perception as that of a stealthy, noiseless manner of walking, out of which were just emerging into consciousness the constituent image of the cautious tread of a cat and the hero's own sneaking footsteps. When Milton talks about "low-browed rocks,"[16] it is evident that the menacing effect of something dark and overhanging is but just resolving itself into the beetling rocks and the low brows of a human face. When Keats spoke of the "wings" of sweet peas, the vague perception of a rounded, half-pear-shaped outline was in the act of dividing itself into the form of the sweet-pea petals and the conventional shape of wings. Henry James says that "The gondolier's cry, carried over the quiet water, makes a kind of splash in the stillness,[17] thus showing the inchoate sensation of an interruption, a sharp difference in the ordinary course of things, as branching doubly into the two images of the sound produced by a cry breaking the stillness and that of a splash made in water.

Such an explanation as this for the origin of metaphor has two advantages over that propounded by the rhetoricians. It is psychologically defensible; and it avoids the artificiality of the rhetorical hypothesis. These two are of course, in the last resort, one, since the fact that metaphor is attributed to a normal and universal process of mind, which seeks only its natural expression in language, destroys at once the theory of an artificial origin.

---

15. *The Princess.*
16. *L'Allegro.*
17. *Venice, The Century*, Vol. XXV, p. 13.

We may say, then, in summary, that poetic metaphor, like radical, is a straightforward attempt to communicate to another person the maker's vision of an object as it appeared to him at the moment of expression, not at all to carry out a dark design of persuading the reader that this object is something which the writer knows it is not. The writer is simply taking a snap-shot at his own process of perception in one of its intermediate stages. This stage may be one not reached by the maker of a radical metaphor. To him, the constituents of his vague perception had not yet disclosed themselves; while often the poetic metaphor expresses this primitive perception in the act of differentiation, two or more images appearing side by side in the figure. The mistake of the rhetoricians lies in their failure to go back of the simultaneous presence of these two images in the metaphor, to the earlier stage of perception in which the two were seen as one. Failing thus to trace back the duality of the metaphor to a primitive unity of consciousness, they were forced to account in some way for the presence of the two images side by side in the figure. The resemblance which existed between them was accordingly made the connecting link, and the writer was conceived as making use of it for some purpose of his own to unite the two. Thus the whole artificial explanation of the rhetorical metaphor has been built up. The occasion for it, together with the hypothesis itself, tumbles to the ground when we touch the question of psychological genesis.

The old rhetorical hypothesis may be sharply contrasted with the psychological by saying that the former started with two objects and hitched them together to make the figure, while the latter begins with a single object or situation, out of which develop the two elements in the metaphor. The one explanation conceives of metaphor as a mechanical product, like a box, whose parts, gathered from different sources are put together to make the whole. The other regards it as the result of a vital process, more like a plant or an animal, whose members grow from the same source, out of a homogeneous mass into a clearly differentiated structure. The one represents the biological, the other the mechanical conception of the metaphor.

Metaphor, from this point of view, is vital. It is not compounded like a prescription with intent to produce a certain effect upon the person who swallows it; but it springs spontaneously out of a genuine thought-process and represents with exactness a certain stage of a growing perception. It is no artificial, manufactured product, but a real organism, living, growing and dying. We shall trace its further progress in the following chapter.

4 The Present Status of Rhetorical Theory

from *Modern Language Notes*
15 (March 1900): 84–87.

This is Buck's clearest statement of her rhetorical theory: discourse should aim for the further good of the social organism. Discourse aimed at persuading a hearer to the view of the speaker is individualistic and thus "socially irresponsible," and she likened such rhetoric to warfare. Her approach to argument as cooperation was a key component in her organic theory of language. Issues raised in this essay include the use of personal experience in student writing, the role of truth in rhetoric, and the definition of persuasion as violence. Buck subscribed to a traditional view of the Sophists, claiming they were immoral rhetors with designs solely on changing the hearers' minds to match their own preconceived ideas. Against this tradition Buck privileges Plato's epistemic views that discourse is "not an isolated phenomenon . . . cut off from all relations to the world in which it occurs, and exempt from the universal laws of justice and right" (85).

Two opposing conceptions of the nature of discourse bequeathed to us from classic times still struggle for dominance in our modern rhetorical theory—the social conception of Plato and the anti-social conception of the Sophists.[1] The latter, though known to us only fragmentarily from allusions and quotations in later treatises, can be, in its essential outlines, easily reconstructed. According to the sophistic teaching, discourse was simply a process of persuading the hearer to a conclusion which the speaker, for any reason, desired him to accept. Analyzed further, this familiar definition discloses certain significant features.

First of all it conveys, though somewhat indirectly, a notion of the ultimate end of the process of discourse. Why should discourse take place at all? Why should the hearer be persuaded? Because, answers the definition, the speaker wishes to persuade him. And, to pursue the inquiry still further, the speaker wishes to persuade the hearer to a certain belief presumably because he recognizes some advantage to himself in doing so. We should conclude,

---

1. The use of the term "social" in connection with rhetorical theory has been borrowed directly from Prof. F. N. Scott of the University of Michigan; though for the interpretation here put upon the word, he is not necessarily responsible.

therefore, from examination of the definition before us, that discourse is for the sake of the speaker.

Nor is this conclusion threatened by further investigation into the pre-Platonic philosophy of discourse. It is true that the practical precepts of the sophistic rhetoricians pay great deference to the hearer, even seeming, at first glance, to exalt him over the speaker. Every detail of the speech is to be sedulously "adapted" to the hearer. Nothing is to be done without reference to him. His tastes are to be studied, his prejudices regarded, his little jealousies and chagrins written down in a book;—but all this, be it remembered, in order simply that he may the more completely be subjugated to the speaker's will. As the definition has previously suggested, the hearer's ultimate importance to discourse is of the slightest. To his interests the process of discourse is quite indifferent.

But not only does persuasion, according to the sophistic notion, fail to consider the interests of the hearer; frequently it even assails them. In fact, the sophistic precepts bristle with implications that the hearer's part in discourse is virtually to be spoiled. The hearer is to be persuaded for the sake of some advantage to the speaker. If his own advantage should chance to lie in the same direction with that of the speaker, the utmost that the process of discourse could do would be merely to point out this fact to the hearer. In such a case little persuasive art is demanded. It is rather when the interests of the hearer, if rightly understood by him, oppose his acceptance of the conclusion urged by the speaker that real rhetorical skill comes into play. Then is the speaker confronted by a task worthy of his training—that of making the acceptance of this conclusion, which is really inimical to the hearer's interests, seem to him advantageous. In plainest statement, the speaker must by finesse assail the hearer's interests for the sake of his own.

This is a typical case of discourse, according to the sophistic conception. Its essentially anti-social character appears both in its conscious purpose and in its unrecognized issues. We have seen that the end it seeks is exclusively individual, sanctioned only by that primitive ethical principle of the dominance of the strong. The speaker through discourse secures his own advantage simply because he is able to do so. The meaning of his action to the hearer or to society as a whole, is purely a moral question with which rhetoric is not directly concerned. There is, in the rhetorical theory of the sophists, no test for the process of discourse larger than the success of the speaker in attaining his own end.

But further, the sophistic conception of discourse is anti-social in its outcome. Instead of levelling conditions between the two parties to the act, as we are told is the tendency in all true social functioning, discourse renders these conditions more unequal than they were before it took place. The speaker, superior at the outset, by virtue at least of a keener perception of the situation, through the process of discourse, comes still further to dominate the hearer. As in primitive warfare the stronger of two tribal organizations subdues and eventually enslaves the weaker, so in discourse the initial advantage of the speaker returns to him with usury.

This anti-social character of the sophistic discourse, as seen both in its purpose and in its outcome, may be finally traced to the fact that the process, as we have analyzed it, just fails of achieving complete communication between speaker and hearer. Some conclusion is, indeed, established in the mind of the hearer, but not necessarily the conclusion which the speaker himself has reached upon this subject. It may, in fact, oppose all his own experience and thought, and thus hold no organic relation to his own mind. But wishing the hearer to believe it, he picks it up somewhere and proceeds to insert it into the hearer's mind.

This absence of a vital relationship between the normal activities of the speaker's mind and the action by which he seeks to persuade the hearer, breaks the line of communication between the two persons concerned. Conditions at the ends of the circuit cannot be equalized, as in true social functioning, because the current is thus interrupted.

This conception of the process of discourse might be graphically represented in figure 1.

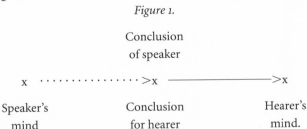

Figure 1.

Conclusion
of speaker

x ················>x ─────────────>x

Speaker's   Conclusion   Hearer's
mind   for hearer   mind.

The sophistic account of discourse, then, makes it a process essentially individualistic, and thus socially irresponsible. It secures the advantage of the speaker without regard to that of the hearer, or even in direct opposition to it. Because this conception leaves a gap in the chain of communication between the minds of speaker and hearer, it fails to equalize conditions between them. The speaker wins and the hearer loses continually. Discourse is purely predatory,—a primitive aggression of the strong upon the weak. The art of rhetoric is the art of war.

Against this essentially crude and anti-social conception of discourse, Plato seems to have raised the first articulate protest. Discourse is not an isolated phenomenon, he maintained, cut off from all relations to the world in which it occurs, and exempt from the universal laws of justice and right. The speaker has certain obligations, not perhaps directly to the hearer, but to the absolute truth of which he is but the mouthpiece, to the entire order of things which nowadays we are wont to call society. Discourse is, indeed, persuasion, but not persuasion to any belief the speaker pleases. Rather is it persuasion to the truth, knowledge of which, on the part of the hearer, ultimately advantages both himself and the speaker as well. The interests of both are equally furthered by legitimate discourse. In fact the interests of both are, when rightly understood, identical; hence there can be no antagonism between them.

In respect, then, to the advantage gained by each party to the act of discourse, speaker and hearer stand on a footing of at least approximate equality. In fact the ultimate end of discourse must be, from the Platonic premises, to establish equality between them. Before discourse takes place the speaker has a certain advantage over the hearer. He perceives a truth as yet hidden from the hearer, but necessary for him to know. Since the recognition of this truth on the part of the hearer must ultimately serve the speaker's interests as well, the speaker, through the act of discourse, communicates to the hearer his own vision. This done, the original inequality is removed, the interests of both speaker and hearer are furthered, and equilibrium is at this point restored to the social organism.

It is plain that the circuit of communication between speaker and hearer is in Plato's conception of discourse continuous. The speaker having himself come to a certain conclusion, does not set about establishing another in the hearer's mind, but simply transmits his own belief into the other's consciousness. The connection between the two minds is living and unbroken. The Platonic notion of the process of discourse may be thus illustrated as in figure 2.

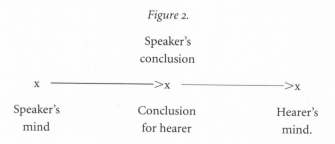

Figure 2.

Speaker's
conclusion

x ————————>x ——————————>x

Speaker's　　　　　Conclusion　　　　Hearer's
mind　　　　　　　for hearer　　　　mind.

Thus have been hastily reviewed the two opposing conceptions of discourse delivered to us by the earliest rhetoricians. The changes which they have suffered in the lapse of centuries are surprisingly slight. We find implicit in many of our modern text-books practically the same conception of discourse which was held by the pre-Platonic teachers of rhetoric,—a conception which regards discourse as an act performed by the speaker upon the hearer for the advantage of the speaker alone. It is true that the present-day sophists include in the end of discourse not persuasion alone, but the production of any desired effect upon the hearer. This fact does not, however, modify fundamentally the nature of the process itself. The hearer (or reader as he has now become) is to be interested or amused, or reduced to tears, or overborne with a sense of the sublime, not indeed because the writer himself has previously been interested or amused and, in obedience to the primal social instinct, would communicate his experience to another, but because,— well, because the writer wishes to produce this effect upon the reader. Thus wishing, and being able to gratify his desire, the act of discourse results,— an act still individualistic and one-sided, serving no ends but those of the speaker himself. The effect to be produced upon the hearer, being wholly external to the experience of the speaker, leaves unjoined the old break between speaker and hearer in the process of communication. We have again, in but slightly altered guise, the sophistic conception of discourse.

But in spite of the persistence of this outworn conception in even some recent text-books, there are not wanting many evidences that the Platonic theory of discourse is at last coming home to the modern consciousness. It is doubtless true that the later social theory of rhetoric would not venture to define the end of discourse as that of declaring to another the absolute and universal truth. There may be two reasons for this. In the first place we are not now-a-days on such joyfully intimate terms with the absolute truth as was Plato. And, again, the practical value of even a little relative and perhaps temporary truth has become clearer to us—such truth as touches us through our personal experiences and observations. Yet it must be remembered that Plato himself allowed the subject-matter of discourse to be the speaker's own vision of the absolute truth, thus individualizing the abstraction until we cannot regard it as fundamentally alien from our modern conception of experience, in the largest sense of the word.

Granting this substantial identity, then, we have only to prove that Plato's idea of personal experience as the subject-matter of discourse is a real factor in modern rhetorical theory. For this no long argument is required. We find this idea theoretically expressed in rhetorical treatises even as far back as

Quintilian, in the implied definition of discourse as self-expression, a conception recently popularized by such writers as Arnold and Pater. This notion of discourse, neglecting that part of the process of communication by which an experience is set up in the mind of the writer, emphasized exclusively that segment which develops the experience of the writer into articulate form. Being thus incomplete as was the sophistic theory of discourse, it served only to supplement that by bringing out into clear consciousness the Platonic truth that the subject-matter of discourse has a direct relation to the mental processes of the writer.

On the practical side this truth has appeared in the comparatively recent decay of formal instruction in rhetoric, and the correlative growth of composition work in our schools. This practical study of composition, in so far as it deserved its name, displaced the writing of biographical essays, largely drawn from encyclopedic sources, and of treatises on abstract subjects far removed from any natural interests of the student who wrote. Both these lines of effort proving relatively profitless, the experiment was tried of drawing the material for writing directly from the every-day experience, observation and thinking of the student,—an experiment whose results proved so successful that the practice has long been established in most of our schools. This is a piece of history so recent and so well-known that it need not be dwelt upon. Its import, however, is worth noting. It means the practical, though perhaps unconscious, acceptance of Plato's principle that the subject-matter of discourse bears a vital relation to the mind of the speaker. And by virtue of this, it means the complete closing of the circuit of communication between speaker and hearer.

So far, then, the rising modern rhetorical theory agrees with the doctrine of Plato. It may, perhaps, differ from him in making discourse a process somewhat less self-conscious than he seems to have conceived it, arising from the speaker's primitive social instinct for sympathy, or (to put it more technically) for closer relations with his environment, rather than from any explicit desire to communicate his own vision of the truth to another. But this modification affects neither the nature of the process itself nor its ultimate outcome. Both the Platonic and the modern theory of discourse make it not an individualistic and isolate process for the advantage of the speaker alone, but a real communication between speaker and hearer, to the equal advantage of both, and thus a real function of the social organism.

This conception of discourse is rich in implications which Plato never saw, and which no modern has yet formulated. To this formulation, however, our practical teaching of English with all its psychologic and sociological import, is daily bringing us nearer. It cannot be long before we shall recognize a modern theory of discourse as large in its outlines as Plato's and far better defined in its details; a theory which shall complete the social justification which rhetoric has so long been silently working out for itself.

5   What Does "Rhetoric" Mean?

from *Educational Review*
22 (September 1901): 197–200.

Buck had been teaching at Vassar for four years when this piece was written and had directed a few graduate students in advanced studies in rhetorical theory and literary criticism. This summary of a questionnaire from the Modern Language Association on graduate study in rhetoric reports that those who would admit the subject to the graduate curriculum define rhetoric as a science. As such, rhetoric need have no immediate "utilitarian" purpose. Buck believed that as composition instruction abandoned the "artificial process of manufacturing a composition, the scientific study of the normal writing-act becomes for the first time possible." In this essay Buck establishes her belief that theory always follows practice and distinguishes rhetoric from composition and literary criticism. Her comment that literary criticism has "never yet [been] deeply enough tilled for lack of the proper psychological implements" (199) foreshadows her later study, The Social Criticism of Literature.

The theory of English teaching, never more widely or more profoundly interesting than now, has received a notable contribution in the recent report of the pedagogical section of the Modern Language Association.[1] Ostensibly this report deals only—and that by the overworked *questionnaire* method—with the highly specialized subject of "graduate study in rhetoric." It consists of sixty-three answers from teachers of graduate courses in English at American colleges and universities[2] to the questions:

1. Is rhetoric, in your opinion, a proper subject for graduate work?

2. If so, what is the proper aim, what is the scope, and what are the leading problems of rhetoric as a graduate study?

---

1. The names of Professors F. N. Scott, president, and W. E. Mead, secretary, of the section are appended to the report.

2. It would be interesting to know at how many colleges and universities rhetoric is now pursued as a graduate study, but upon this point the report does not enlighten us. I believe that the University of Michigan was the first to sanction the graduate study of rhetoric. At Vassar College the development of rhetorical theory has been a minor subject with four or five graduate students during the past two years.

3. If rhetoric in your opinion should not be admitted to the list of graduate studies, what do you regard as the strongest reasons for excluding it?

The term "rhetoric" was "purposely"—so says the report—"left without interpretation or limitation," so that the definitions stated or implied by those answering the questions give us to know with some exactness what rhetoric actually means to-day in the vocabulary of experts. As might be expected, practically no one uses the word in its old sense of prescriptive rules for composition, tho the minority who regard rhetoric as not a proper subject for graduate study identify it with composition or theme-writing. The majority, however, who would admit it to the curriculum of graduate studies, define it, in varying terms, as the science or theory of the process of communication by language.

The significance of this definition is not trivial. From classic times the act of discourse has been subject to analysis, with a view to discovering its laws. The purpose of this analysis, at first purely utilitarian,—that is, for the sake of making the act more efficient,—seems now for the first time to be conceived as disinterestedly scientific. Like other scientific investigation, its results may ultimately serve some practical end, but the graduate study of the act of discourse need take no more account of any utilitarian purpose than does graduate study in physics or in pure mathematics. This is, indeed, a new word in the teaching of English, and one whose import cannot be lightly regarded.

The reports of those favoring graduate study in rhetoric indicate an all but unanimous disapproval of formal rhetoric as a subject for study, graduate or undergraduate, on the ground that it consists merely of a mass of empirical formulæ, unrelated to each other or to any principle of modern psychology, a dogmatic assumption where tentative scientific investigation is demanded.

Such investigation cannot, it is apparent, be carried on by undergraduates. To graduate students, then, we must look for the development of the new science of rhetoric. The unformulated condition of that science at present only enhances its value for purposes of advanced research. Rhetorical theory affords a field almost unworked by modern tools or with modern methods. It presents innumerable problems demanding solution on the basis of recently formulated psychological and æsthetic principles. A few of these problems suggested in the report may be mentioned as indicating the richness of the opportunity for investigation offered: "The nature and functions of discourse, its proper conditions and results, definition of the various kinds of discourse in psychological terms, determination of the æsthetic basis for certain rhetorical 'effects': the nature and function of figures of speech in general, of specific figures, prose rhythms, the theory of criticism, the fundamental theory of narration, the relations of argument to formal and to real logic, the exploration of a distinct and widespread form such as the short story, the analysis of a particular method, such as George Meredith's," and so forth.

Evidently many of these problems pass over into the field of literary criticism, so called, a field never yet deeply enough tilled, for lack of the proper psychological implements. One of the significant features of the report is the close relation evidently existing in the minds of English experts at the present time between literary criticism and rhetoric—subjects often set in different departments of our colleges and jealously depreciated each by the other. If the term rhetoric is once understood, however, in its new sense as a comprehensive study of communication by language, explanatory on psychologic grounds of all forms of written or spoken discourse, any sense of antagonism between it and literary criticism straightway becomes impossible, not to say absurd. Both in material and in method the two subjects find meeting ground and opportunity for mutual re-enforcement.

The relations of rhetoric as a graduate study to other departments of instruction are implied in the foregoing statements. On the side of method, affirms the report, rhetorical theory touches all the psychologic sciences, namely psychology itself, logic, æsthetics, sociology. On the side of material, it uses history, language, literature, all fine art.

Such a conception of rhetoric in its essential nature and relationships, when avowed by a majority of teachers of graduate courses in English throughout the country, shows, among other things, how far the recent reconstruction in practical English teaching has gone to leaven the theory of the subject. This reconstruction is familiar enough in its external features, at least, to demand only a sentence of recall. Within the memory almost of the youngest of English teachers, the precepts of formal rhetoric as a guide to writing have been discredited and abandoned, the act of composition in our schools has been conditioned more naturally by a real occasion for writing and a real audience to be addressed, such theory as must be involved in the criticism of the student's writing has grown steadily less complex and dogmatic because springing more directly from the writing itself. In short, the tendency of every recent reform in composition teaching has been to free the student's act of writing from all artificial conditions, and to substitute for these such conditions as accompany a genuine act of writing outside of the schoolroom. The purpose of this substitution has of course been purely practical; that, namely, of making the student's writing thereby fresher, directer, more spontaneously effective. And this practical purpose has unquestionably been fulfilled in precisely the degree to which the substitution of real for artificial conditions has actually been made. But more than this, once the normal writing-act comes to be clearly distinguished from the artificial process of manufacturing a composition, the scientific study of the normal writing-act becomes for the first time possible. Out of this distinction, then, painfully learned by the practical teacher of composition, arises the possibility for the modern science of rhetoric recognized in the report of the pedagogical section.

There is no doubt that this expert recognition of a pure theory of rhetoric following, not preceding, intelligent practice in composition, will go far to set the theory and the practice of writing in their proper relations to each other thruout the educational field. It cannot, perhaps, do more than rationalize, and therefore accelerate, the practical movement toward establishing this right relationship; but this will be regarded as a substantial service, leaving, as it does, the practical teacher of composition free to open up new fields for the theorist to occupy.

6   The Social Criticism of Literature

The Social Criticism of Literature
(New Haven, Conn.: Yale University Press, 1916).

On 17 December 1916, New York Times Book Review *advertised Buck's book as follows:*

> Gertrude Buck, Ph.D., a graduate of the University of Michigan, has been a beloved member of the English faculty of Vassar College for many years. In addition to her constructive work in creating a taste for good literature among her students, she has published a number of books and magazine articles. As she points out in her new volume, literary criticism has meant anything from an English teacher's red ink on a pupil's theme to anecdotes concerning Johnson's tea and the love affairs of Shelley. (561)

The volume sold for $1.00 and may be the earliest treatise in the tradition of reader-response criticism, preceding Louise Rosenblatt's Literature as Exploration *by twenty-two years. It weaves together Buck's rhetorical and literary interests and theory.*

Chapter 1, "The Muddle of Criticism," reviews the various types of criticism of the day; the second chapter, "Larger Criticism," advocates social criticism, which differs from other forms of literary criticism in that the critic views a book as an "activity," accounting for reader, writer, and the function of the literature. The third chapter, "Standards of Criticism," urges a social standard, not an eternal aesthetic housed within the book, and the final chapter, "The Function of the Critic," argues that the critic's purpose is to increase the reader's capacity to read rather than force some proclaimed classic on reluctant readers. To be considered literature, writing must be a sincere communication between the writer and reader; otherwise such "pseudo-communication . . . is properly speaking, not literature, but a commercial substitute for it, which the critic is bound to detect and expose" (45).

A reviewer in the 1916 English Journal *commented that "her book is a small one but full of meat" (715–16). The book was also favorably reviewed in the* New York Times Book Review *(12 November 1916), but a reviewer in* The Nation *balked at the transactional definition of reading and literature at its heart. Complaining that "her discussion of standards is extremely vague," the reviewer asserted that despite Buck's definition of the social definitions and functions of literature,* "Paradise Lost *exists, apart from its relations, fixed and the same amidst the flux of opinion. It has the essentials of a standard—it stands and is established; it can serve as a measure of its readers. The more one reflects on this point the more clear it becomes that what Professor Buck offers us is not a social criticism of literature, but a literary criticism of society" (18 January 1917, 80–81).*

THE SOCIAL CRITICISM OF LITERATURE

BY

GERTRUDE BUCK, Ph.D.

Professor of English in Vassar College

New Haven: Yale University Press
London: Humphrey Milford
Oxford University Press
MDCCCCXVI

PREFACE

The social criticism of literature has, no doubt, been practiced more widely than it has been recognized as a theory. With the more or less unconscious practice of such criticism, however, this book does not attempt to deal. It is concerned solely with the explicit theory of social criticism and with the development of the conception of literature underlying it, which has "come to consciousness" either partially or wholly in various writers about literature, since the time of Plato. Some of these writers have been noted in the following pages, but only such as seem best calculated to illustrate the conception or some phase of its development. A complete history of the genesis and evolution of the social theory of literature remains to be written, when the theory itself is more fully understood. As a contribution towards its fuller understanding, this little book is offered. Its purpose will be achieved, if it shall succeed in clearing the ground for further study of the social theory of literature, by presenting its relations to other critical theories and defining certain of its more obvious implications, both speculative and practical.

Grateful acknowledgment of my indebtedness for light upon this subject is due to Professor Fred Newton Scott, of the University of Michigan, whose courses, more than twenty years ago explicitly recognized the social significance of literature and inspired his students to further investigation of this significance; to Professor Laura Johnson Wylie, under whose leadership every course in English at Vassar College is animated by the social conception of literature; to Professor John Dewey, of Columbia University, whose philosophy of society has directed all my thinking about literature; and, finally, to my students in Literary Criticism, who for many years, attacking its problems with me, have stimulated and clarified my understanding of them.

G. B.

Vassar College, September 18, 1916.

CHAPTER I. THE MUDDLE OF CRITICISM

By simple folk in every age literary criticism has been accounted only a more pretentious name for finding fault with what one reads. All authorities, past and present, agree in ruling out of court this untutored definition; but when an accredited substitute for it is demanded, the hitherto unanimous voice of critical doctrine breaks into a jangle of dissonant statements. The flippant will have it that criticism consists chiefly in anecdotes concerning Johnson's tea and the love-affairs of Shelley. By no means, protest the philological.

Rather is it the textual emendation of Chaucer. It is nothing, urges the old-fashioned scholar, if it be not the principles of poetry delivered unto us by Aristotle. No doubt, asserts the pedagogue, criticism is the English teacher's use of red ink on a pupil's theme. The historian of literature finds his conception of criticism exemplified in Gilbert Murray's study of the folk-lore connected with the plot of Hamlet; the apostle of "general culture," in Arnold's cryptic enthusiasms over a passage from Homer or Dante.

Which of these diverse meanings is the bewildered reader to affix to the term "criticism" when it meets his eye in some literary essay? The writer may have had in mind any one of the foregoing conceptions of the term, or any one of a dozen others. Only the hard-worked context could possibly determine which, unless, indeed, a saving adjective has been prefixed to the general term. Accordingly such adjectives have been called to the rescue, and we read of scientific, and of historical literary criticism, of criticism deductive and inductive, comparative, appreciative, impressionistic, æsthetic and social.[1] But even these apparently definite terms refuse to yield immediate enlightenment. Mr. George Saintsbury, himself a distinguished advocate and exemplar of comparative criticism, protests, almost with tears, that while he has "gravely and strenuously endeavored to ascertain from the writings both of foreign critics . . . and of their disciples at home, what 'scientific' criticism means," in no case has he "been able to obtain any clear conception of its connotation in the mouths or minds of those who use the phrase."[2]

The case is not, however, for most of us, quite so hopeless as this. The fundamental distinction between judicial or deductive and scientific or inductive criticism has long since been broadly established on the lines suggested by their respective names, the former basing itself on accepted principles, the latter on tested facts. Deductive criticism, we are invariably told, both by its partisans and by its assailants, stands firmly upon some accredited canon of literature, such as, to take an extreme instance, the "three unities" of drama. Applying this canon to, say, *The Two Gentlemen of Verona*, a critic of the deductive school must conclude that the construction of this play is faulty. Inductive, historical or scientific criticism, on the contrary, turning its back upon all accepted principles, sets out to discover certain facts about this same play,—such facts, for instance, as its probable date, different printings and performances, changes in the text, the sources of various elements in the

1. Mr. R. G. Moulton, who gave currency to the term "inductive criticism," has also added "speculative criticism" to our nomenclature. See ch. x in his *Modern Study of Literature*.
2. *Essays in English Literature, 1780–1860*, pp. xi–xii.

plot. These facts must often lead to certain inferences, but not, it must be noted, inferences as to the value of the play. Scientific criticism, in its furthest recoil from judicial criticism, would confine itself to accounting for a given piece of literature, steadfastly refusing to evaluate it. In so doing it explicitly challenges the claim of judicial criticism that the literature of past ages, from which the latter's standards are necessarily drawn, should fix values for the literature of the present and of the future; and sets up a conception of literature as perpetually growing and changing, a creature of organic development, not of fixed, inorganic structure.

Out of such a conception, however, logically arises a new standard of judgment for particular pieces of literature. Those scientific critics who, like M. Brunetière, insist that the judgment of a work of art is an essential part of the process of criticism, imply, as a basis for this judgment, the accurate "placing" of the piece of literature in question in the development of a particular type or period. The ultimate question for such criticism is not: "Does this play follow the accredited literary traditions?" but "How does it further the observed development of literature?"

This observed development of literature, moreover, gives rise to a new conception of the laws of literature, which scientific criticism recognizes not as laws in the legal, mandatory sense of the word, but rather as "statements of the habits"[3] of ballads and essays, declaring not what ought to be, but what is. On these points, then—namely, the right starting point for the critical process, its proper method and conclusions, its underlying conceptions of the nature and the laws of literature,—scientific criticism stands, broadly speaking, in point-blank opposition to judicial criticism.

Comparative criticism is essentially scientific in its appeal to a wide reading of related literature rather than to a single accredited model or principle. Yet Mr. George Saintsbury's exposition[4] stresses its deductive affiliations, not merely in holding judgment of values to be a primary concern of the critic of literature (for, as we have seen, some scientific critics also profess this faith), but in making value apparently synonymous with conformity to accepted classic standards rather than with the furthering of literary evolution.

In this merry war of critical theories, the protagonists of scientific criticism, though largely outnumbering the defenders of the earlier faith, have not held the field unassailed. Mr. Irving Babbitt, in an article entitled *Impressionist versus Judicial Criticism*,[5] having roughly classified as either impres-

3. R. G. Moulton, *Shakespeare as a Dramatic Artist*, p. 33.
4. *Essays in English Literature, 1780–1860*, p. xxvi.
5. *Publications of the Modern Language Association*, 1906.

sionistic or scientific "nearly all recent criticism, so far as it is anything more than a form of gossip and small talk," asserts that neither of these types affords, as does judicial criticism, "any real means of escape from the quicksands of relativity to some firm ground of judgment." He neatly discriminates the types arraigned by declaring that for Taine, the scientific critic, a poem is the result of certain "prosaic facts of environment," while to the impressionist critic it is rather a cause of his own sensations. Impressionist criticism has no more concern with the process by which a book came into being than it has with a judgment of the book's value. It only revels in the unanalyzed effect produced by the book. When this effect is expressed in words for the benefit of other readers, we have a mere report of the critic's personal reactions to a work of literary art, a recital, in the overquoted phrase of M. Anatole France, of "les aventures de son âme au milieu des chefs-d'œuvre."[6] This recital may or may not be interesting reading; but neither it nor the report of the scientific critic can have any value as criticism, since neither affords any sure test of the quality of a given piece of writing. The scientific critic, declares Mr. Babbitt, fixes our attention "on precisely those features of a poem that are least poetical. The very prosaic facts he is looking for would be at least as visible in the writing of some mediocrity as in a work of the first order." Or, as Miss Ethel Puffer more picturesquely puts it, "the psychological process in the development of a dramatic idea . . . is, . . . from the point of view of such analysis, exactly the same for a Shakespeare and for the Hoyt of our American farces."[7]

And, as for impressionist criticism, Mr. Babbitt is quite sure that a "third-rate bit of contemporary sentimentality will 'suggest' more ineffable dreams to the young woman in the long chair than a play of Sophocles," and therefore must, by the premises of impressionistic criticism, be ranked as the better literature! Even the appreciative critic, most closely associated with the impressionist, has opened fire upon his shifting scale of values. "Can criticism," asks Mr. Lewis E. Gates, with portentous courtesy, "properly confine itself to the record of a momentary shiver across a single set of possibly degenerate nerves?"[8]

The alleged assumptions of impressionist criticism that the critic's reactions to a piece of literature are more important than the writer's process, and that these reactions are important as being individual, rather than as being typical or representative, have been repeatedly brought to light by its oppo-

6. *La Vie Littéraire*, 1 serie, p. iii.
7. *The Psychology of Beauty*, p. 17.
8. *Impressionism and Appreciation*, *The Atlantic Monthly*, July, 1900.

nents and set up as a plain target for ridicule. By its partisans they have, however, been as often disclaimed. The critic's reactions need not, they assert, be held more important than the writer's process in order to justify any presentation of them, nor does the critic of necessity regard his reactions as of importance primarily because they are his. A sensitive and cultivated mind, however rare, is not unique; and the record of its responses to any work of art must have value as the revelation of what this work of art may mean to other minds in some degrees capable of appreciating it.

The charge of relativity of judgment has never been disproved, because it could not be; but it is set aside by the fundamental conception of impressionist criticism, which it shares with the more radical body of scientific criticism, namely, that judgment of values in literature is no part of the critical process. Naturally this view is sustained by "appreciative criticism," which, as defined by Mr. Gates, seems to blend scientific and impressionist criticism in the fuller, deeper experience of appreciation. To appreciate a work of art, the critic must have regard to its historical setting and its psychological origin; but we note that his aim in so doing "is primarily not to explain (with the scientific critic) and not to judge or to dogmatize (as does the judicial critic) but to enjoy; to realize the manifold charms the work of art has gathered unto itself from all sources and to interpret this charm imaginatively to the men of his own day and generation."[9]

This statement suggests a sentence from the preface by Messrs. Gayley and Scott to their invaluable bibliography of literary criticism: "There are degrees of enjoyment, the highest of which is *criticism*; as there are of creation, the highest of which is *art*."[10] And such a conception seems to promise at once a freer and a richer development of the critical process than either facile impressionism or laborious fact-grubbing, taken each by itself.

Miss Puffer, however, finds even this larger notion of criticism incomplete.[11] It still lacks, as do its component elements, impressionist and scientific criticism, any standard of judgment. Through exact knowledge of the time, the writer, the language, other languages and literatures, one may reproduce mentally the process by which a work of art comes into being, yet have no idea whether it is beautiful or ugly or merely commonplace. One may enjoy a work of art without ever knowing "whence and why" its charm, be moved by it without understanding whether or to what degree one ought to be moved by it. There is need of a type of criticism, latterly styled "æsthe-

9. *Impressionism and Appreciation, The Atlantic Monthly*, July, 1900.
10. *Methods and Materials of Literary Criticism*, p. iv.
11. *The Psychology of Beauty*, ch. 1.

tic," a criticism which, disregarding the writer's end of the literary process, shall devote itself to explaining the effects produced by the play or poem upon the reader, and evaluating these effects by reference to established æsthetic laws.

This type of criticism, though newly named, is as old as Aristotle. The ancient critics, however inadequately from the modern point of view they were furnished for such inquiry, had a lively curiosity about the nature and cause of effects produced upon the reader by certain types of literature and certain "devices" of style. In fact the sophistic rhetoricians as represented in Plato's *Dialogues* and as followed too sedulously by Aristotle, tended to reduce the theory of discourse altogether to analyses of the means employed by the orator to bring about certain desired reactions in the hearer. Although ostensibly aiming to form the effective orator, they were actually so preoccupied with the auditor's thoughts and feelings that what the speaker thought and felt was largely left out of their account. In the *Poetics*, Aristotle, with no science of æsthetics at command, but with an unequalled power of using his self-made analytic instruments, essayed to discriminate and explain the peculiar effect upon the reader of tragedy, of metaphor, of "prose poetry" and of other phenomena of literature. Longinus, Cicero, Horace, Quintilian, Hegel, Lessing, Burke, Freytag, and many other critics have investigated similar phenomena to the end of accounting for the reader's reactions and disclosing the laws involved.

But a new reading of æsthetic criticism has been called forth by the development of modern æsthetic theory, which, even in its beginning, gives us glimpses of possible explanations at variance with those offered by the literary critics of two hundred or even fifty years ago. When Cicero tells us that metaphor gives pleasure because it "is directed immediately to our senses and principally to the sense of sight,"[12] we find the reason inadequate. Nor can Burke's assertion that we enjoy tragedy because "we have a degree of delight, and that no small one, in the real misfortunes and pains of others,"[13] bring conviction. In recent years, however, Miss Puffer's own dealings with *The Emotions of the Drama* and *The Beauty of Literature*, M. Bergson's chapters on *The Comic in Situations and in Words* and *The Comic in Character*, Miss Elizabeth Kemper Adams's *The Æsthetic Moment*, Mr. Fred N. Scott's *The Fundamental Differentia of Poetry and Prose* and *The Scansion of Prose Rhythm*, offer, for certain aspects or types of literature, explanations and

12. *De Oratore*, book III, ch. XL.
13. *On the Sublime and Beautiful*, part I, section XIV.

standards of valuation which modern psychology and æsthetics have not yet rendered obsolete.

Æsthetic criticism, then, as the latest claimant to the title of the one true criticism, stands, like all the others, in an attitude of opposition to every other type. Scientific criticism, as we have seen, condemns judicial criticism for judging literature solely by its conformity with accepted models or canons; and accuses it of blocking the progress of literature by this procedure. Judicial criticism, on the other hand, distrusts scientific criticism because it offers no fixed, external standards of judgment. Impressionist criticism holds both scientific and judicial criticism to be irrelevant to the one essential question: How does this piece of literature affect me, the reader? Scientific and judicial criticism, in their turn, ridicule impressionist criticism as superficial and egoistic. Appreciative criticism will accept the aid of scientific and of impressionist criticism, but sees both as inadequate to reach the final end of criticism, namely, the full experiencing of a piece of literature; while it finds judicial criticism incapable of even starting in the direction of this goal. Æsthetic criticism, rejecting all previous types, except deductive criticism, on the ground that they furnish no sure standard of judgment, discredits deductive criticism also, by the familiar declaration that it has only a traditional basis for its conclusions.

We have, thus, in the field of critical theory, at least six warring conceptions of what criticism really is. And to this confusion we must add the prevalent uncertainty as to whether criticism is an act (the act of judging or investigating or appreciating, or what-not), or whether it is rather the written product of this act (Pater's essay on *Coleridge* or Freytag's *Technique of the Drama*). These last illustrations, moreover, suggest still another source of confusion, which Mr. Saintsbury recognizes in distinguishing between Aristotle's "criticism" in the sense of critical judgments of particular writers or works, and his "critical theory"[14] as exemplified in the *Poetics*.[15]

Is it possible for the reader of current criticism to adjudicate the rival claims of these as yet unreconciled, though not irreconcilable, conceptions? Is there a central idea of criticism underlying them all, a single process of criticism to which each of the diverse types is contributory? If so, the discovery of this focal idea or larger process is surely incumbent upon students

14. *The History of Criticism*, vol. I, p. 35.

15. Professor Moulton follows this distinction (*The Modern Study of Literature*, ch. X) in separating "speculative criticism, working toward theory and philosophy of literature," from "inductive" and "judicial" criticism, which aim by different means at the interpretation, classification or assaying of particular pieces of literature.

of critical theory, to whom the hopeless muddle of critical conceptions exemplified by Mr. Saintsbury's omnibus definition of criticism has become intolerable.

> Criticism [he propounds] is pretty much the same thing as the reasoned exercise of Literary Taste—the attempt, by examination of literature, to find out what it is that makes literature pleasant, and therefore good,—the discovery, classification and, as far as possible, tracing to their sources, of the qualities of poetry and prose, of style and metre, the classification of literary kinds, the examination and "proving," as arms are proved, of literary means and weapons, not neglecting the observation of literary fashions and the like.[16]

Such a heterogeneous, unanalyzed mass of activities seems to have swept together most of the variant conceptions of criticism with which we started, making no attempt to inquire which are essential and what their relations to one another may be. Clear thinking demands that the literary anecdote and textual restoration alike, Aristotle's theory of tragedy and the English teacher's correction of faulty grammar, the tracing of *Hamlet* to spring-myths and the selection of "touch-stones of literature," be either "placed" in the one great activity of criticism or definitely excluded from it; that the essential, all-inclusive elements in this activity appear, freed from irrelevant and confusing detail; that starting-point, method and conclusion of the critical process be adequately distinguished from one another; that the writer's part in the production of literature and the reader's part in appreciating it be equally taken into account; that the various types of criticism be discriminated on a functional basis, the contribution of each type to a larger conception of criticism rightly understood, and the standards of literature implied in each fully recognized. When these things are done, and only then, will "the muddle of criticism" be resolved into rational order and the long war of critical theories end in the active peace of coöperation.

CHAPTER II.   THE LARGER CRITICISM

One must listen closely to hear, amid the jangle of conflicting theories as to what literary criticism really is, the still small voice of their harmonious relation to one another. Once heard, however, it cannot be disregarded.

Each type of criticism, arising to supplement the inadequacies of previous types, has enriched our conception of the critical process. Deductive criti-

16. *The History of Criticism*, vol. I, p. 4.

cism as first formulated could furnish no basis for its judgments save traditional authority or the arbitrary personal taste which had, though often unconsciously, been moulded by it. Recognizing the need of a broader and firmer grounding for the critic's conclusions, historic or scientific criticism offered to supply such a grounding in the thorough-going study of literary origins and development. This genetic study gave rise to a conception of literature which proved of immense importance to critical theory. In so far as any writing under examination was recognized as an outcome directly of the author's individual experience and training, indirectly of the political, social and industrial order in which he worked, in so far as the influence upon this writing of other writings in many languages both of this and of antecedent periods was taken into account, just so far did literature inevitably cease to be for criticism a mere static, rigidly limited thing-in-itself, and become an organic development, rooted deep in human history and complexly interfunctioning with it.

But though scientific criticism, so to speak, loosened the current conception of literature, and notably enlarged it at the writer's end, a corresponding extension in the direction of the reader took place only when impressionist criticism entered the field. As a result of the attention which this type of criticism directed upon the reader's reaction to a given piece of literature, the epic or drama in question ceased to be for criticism merely an outgrowth from the writer's mind, definitely conditioned by various historic, economic and literary elements in his environment, and came to include also the final flowering in the reader's mind of this deep-rooted growth.

Thus did scientific and impressionist criticism, each supplementing the work of the other, prepare a highway for appreciative criticism, which, not content to occupy merely one section of the great realm of literature thus opened to it, entered into possession of the whole. To the appreciative critic literature for the first time presented itself as properly inclusive of all the phenomena associated with it; and these phenomena were, moreover, for the first time explicitly recognized as constituting a continuous activity, comparable perhaps to that of an electric current. Literature, as thus conceived, might be generated immediately in the writer's consciousness and ultimately in the consciousness of his age, but it would complete itself only as it passed over into the reader's consciousness to enlighten or to stir it into action.

The entire literary activity, then, from writer to reader, has been preëmpted for criticism by the appreciative theory. Intensive research into its various stages or sections, however, belongs to those schools whose view of the critical field is more limited. Æsthetic criticism, for instance, has undertaken the closer analysis of the reader's reaction according to modern scientific method; and such a contribution can hardly be overvalued. Impressionist criticism had done a needed work in turning the critic's attention to the reader's end of the literary act. This attention could not, however, rest at the point of mere unanalyzed, personal impression; but, continually defining and universalizing every impression by the aid of known æsthetic principles, must finally evolve a genuine æsthetic criticism.

Æsthetic criticism points us to the future. It constitutes, however, an integral part of the continuous development of critical theory, by which a larger view of the field of criticism has been progressively gained and a conception of literature suggested which is at once inclusive and active. Each successive step in the history of criticism has brought us nearer to this conception of literature, until to the modern student, graduate of all the earlier critical schools, a book consists, not essentially of so many pages of printed paper bound between covers, but rather of certain activities, or, still more strictly speaking, of a single, continuous activity. This activity may, for purposes of analysis, be separated into the writer's action and the reader's reaction; but neither of these can in itself constitute a book. A book is, in philosophic terms, the writer's action transforming itself into the reader's reaction at the point of print. And the printed words thus reduce themselves to a mere sign of this transformation, not constituting literature but only making it possible. Literature as a social activity has not yet completely taken place when a book is printed and bound. It fulfills itself, becomes literature in any practical sense of the word, only in the act of reading.

The act of reading has thus taken on a new dignity, as literature, in the evolution of critical theories, has become a process rather than a product, something that takes place rather than something which has been made. Literature in this sense is no finished material object—a pill to be swallowed by the reader, or a sugar-plum to be eaten by him. Rather is it a great continuous activity, which goes on through and by the reader, his participation constituting its final stage, as organically related to it as the writer's function itself.

Thus defined, however, the act of reading suggests close relations with the act of criticism. Through criticism, at least of the appreciative type, the writer's activity is realized or fulfilled, as it is conceived to be through reading. We are, it is true, accustomed to think of reading as one of the simplest mental processes, of criticism as one of the most complex; and, while admitting that the child reads, we withhold the name critic from all but the highly trained scholar. But as the child may become the critic, so may the simple, unanalytic process of reading pass by imperceptible degrees into the furthest reaches of that extremely complex activity called criticism.

The essential character of reading, whether elementary or advanced in its type, is found in no mere perfunctory turning of leaves, but in active participation, however limited it may be, in the experience which the writer would communicate. One reads, in any real sense of the word, only in so far as he thinks the writer's thoughts after him under the stimulus of his words, sees what the writer saw, feels what the writer felt. Hence "the will to read," if one may paraphrase William James's title, an intelligent hospitality of mind, is the first condition of reading, as it is of criticism. Lacking this cooperative attitude, the preoccupied schoolboy can no more read than the critic, intent from the beginning on fault-finding, can criticise; while with it no limitations of knowledge or taste can prevent an infinite development of genuine reading and criticism.

Reading begins the process of criticism at the impressionistic stage. The reader cannot but be affected to some degree and in some manner by what he reads and by some means (not always formally "literary") he is bound to convey this impression to other persons. It is true that only in the degree of his training and sensitiveness has the reader's reaction value for anyone else. But this training and sensitiveness are by no means fixed quantities. They develop in and through the very act of reading. In some sense one must, as Ruskin says, in order to read at all, ascend to the writer's level. "If you will not rise to us, we cannot stoop to you."[17] One must approximate the writer's position in order even to begin to read him, but, once begun, the act of reading itself discloses its essential inadequacies. The active-minded reader finds that, in order to think the writer's thought after him, he must, for a time in very truth, be the writer. He must reconstruct the writer's *milieu*, social, industrial, political, and the writer's individual life as thus determined, or fail fully to apprehend the thought which grew out of and was modified by this particular set of conditions. And he must furthermore know the writer's literary tools, the form with which he worked, its limitations and its possibilities, how far it had been developed when he laid his hand upon it, or stop short of comprehending his view of life as it shaped itself in and through this form. Here it is evident that the gaining of an immediate impression from what one reads has passed into the realm of that "scientific" criticism which amasses data, brings to bear upon the printed page all relevant knowledge, historical, linguistic, psychological, æsthetic, that reading may be the more

17. *Sesame and Lilies: Of Kings' Treasuries.*

intelligent, the richer in content, that what the writer would convey may the more perfectly interpenetrate the reader's mind.

Such interpenetration, furthermore, is the indispensable condition of "appreciative criticism," that complete assimilation of the epic or the essay, with all its connotations, which Mr. Gates has painted for us in colors of delight.[18] And only such complete assimilation of any work of literature into the reader's mind enables him surely to "disengage" as Pater would say, its peculiar "virtue." Otherwise he is bound to miss some element in it, some essential tang or aroma, some fine distinction of tone. Thus qualified, however, his appreciation has the exquisite precision of line which we associate with masters of criticism such as Pater himself. Like them our reader can not only reproduce in his own imaginative experience the complex process by which a given poem through the ages came to be, but he can also realize in all its fullness of meaning the almost equally complex process by which it communicates itself to the reader's mind,—just what its peculiar individual effect is and how this effect has been produced. He is able, to quote Miss Puffer's words, descriptive of "æsthetic" criticism, "to tell us whence and why the charm of a work of art: to disengage, to explain, to measure, and to certify it."[19]

When he proceeds "to measure and to certify it," however, he has passed out of inductive into deductive or "judicial" criticism. He no longer merely receives, responds, assembles data, compares phenomena and investigates laws, but pronounces upon the quality of the work of literature under his hands. He understands not only how much and why and in what respects he likes it, but how and why and in what respects the intelligent reader ought to like it. And in so doing he has, either implicitly or openly, appealed to certain laws previously discovered in the examination of individual pieces of literature or works of art in other fields. By some body of æsthetic canons in general, or of literary canons in particular, he ranks and evaluates.

The discovery and formulation of these literary canons are a part of the process of criticism, but not necessarily a part of the process in reading, in which theory remains somewhat implicit. That point in the reading-act, then, at which some theory about what is read emerges into consciousness, may serve as the point of departure for criticism, in its more abstract stages, out of the concrete act of reading. A further point, at which this theory is definitely used as a basis for judging particular pieces of literature, may locate

18. *Impressionism and Appreciation, The Atlantic Monthly*, July, 1900.
19. *The Psychology of Beauty*, p. 25.

a boundary line between the theoretic and the judicial aspects of the critical process. Thus the critic's progress from naïve impression to formulated judgment seems, roughly speaking, to present three primary stages, the first of which coincides with reading, while the second and third ultimately derive from it. Criticism, as we have seen, begins with the reading of literature in the fullest sense of the term, including the gathering together of knowledge from all the various sources which might serve to enrich the understanding of what is read. In this reading certain theories of literature and of the specific types of literature read are bound to come to consciousness, resulting in a more or less formulated body of laws expressive of the modes in which literature has its rise under given conditions, takes particular forms, develops and changes these forms or invents new ones, acts in specific ways upon the reader and upon society as a whole. And finally, on the basis of these laws, particular pieces of literature are judged, ranked and classified.

In practice these three stages of the critical process are not rigidly separated from one another, and our nomenclature still leaves them undistinguished. The critical reading and interpretation of literature in the light of all relevant facts about it is criticism. The formulated body of laws derived from this reading is criticism. And the ranking of particular pieces of literature on the basis of these discovered laws is also criticism. This blanket-use of the term doubtless tends to confusion; and it seems desirable to adopt the self-explanatory names "critical reading," "critical theory" and "critical judgment" as a means of recognizing three important stages in the act of criticism without denying the essential unity of the act.

The logical order of these three stages is apparent. The term "critical reading" must be applied not alone to the exhaustive analyses of the highly trained and sensitive scholar, but to those simpler and less self-conscious acts of mental assimilation which by the law of their own nature tend continually to deepen and enrich themselves. In a very sober, literal sense it may be asserted that whoever sincerely reads anything—not perfunctorily running his eye over the pages but actually transforming the writer's experience into his own—has thereby started on the long path of criticism. Not only does such reading constantly improve itself, becoming more exact in its responses to the stimulus given by the writer, better informed on all points which full reaction to this stimulus involves, but eventually it yields a body of theory organically related to the literature read, not arbitrarily imposed upon it by some external authority.

It is such a body of theory, inductively derived, which all the protestants against deductive literary criticism, from Coleridge to Mr. J. E. Spingarn, explicitly demand. "We have done with all the old Rules," declares Mr. Spingarn;[20] and no doubt we have, in so far as these rules have become purely arbitrary, without vital connection with the works of literature to which they are applied. They can have validity for us today only as they come to consciousness anew in our reading of the more diversified body of literature known to our time, and as a result of the more exact psychological and æsthetic analysis for which we are now equipped. There is, of course, no doubt that an adequate theory of poetry, for instance, would ultimately be serviceable to the critical reading of poetry. This fact cannot, however, be allowed to obscure the more important principle that such a theory, in order to be thus serviceable, must presuppose an extended reading of poetry and arise out of it.

As for critical judgment, once apparently the sole interest of critics, it no longer both begins and ends the process of criticism. Instead of standing at the entrance of the critic's course, with an effect of blocking his progress, it follows upon a prolonged activity of critical reading and a tentative formulation of critical theory, so that it seems rather to reward his labors than to render them unnecessary. Built thus upon human study and reasoning, it loses its oracular quality, its unquestioned finality, and takes on the more useful aspect of a conclusion formulated for the present on the basis of what is now known, and serving merely as a stepping-stone to some further knowledge or understanding.

Such a conception of the process of criticism, far less authoritative than the old, but compensatingly richer and more organically related with the process of literary creation, must serve as basis for classifying the products of criticism. These, multitudinous though they may be, readily group themselves under the three headings, critical reading, critical theory, and critical judgment. Of these the second group is most obviously distinguished from the others. That stage of the critical process in which theories of literature come to consciousness leaves behind it systematic treatises such as Aristotle's *Poetics* and Freytag's *Technique of the Drama*. Critical reading, having collected historic and textual data to its own ends, may give them permanent, though usually unliterary, form in annotations, emendations, detailed comparisons and summaries of evidence upon disputed points. But critical reading in its less pedestrian realms, and critical judgment as growing out of it, yield the richest harvests of critical literature.

When Matthew Arnold declares that criticism consists in "a disinterested

20. *The New Criticism*, p. 20.

endeavor to learn and propagate the best that is known and thought in the world,"[21] the verb "to learn" suggests that vital assimilative activity of mind which we have termed "critical reading"; while its correlative "to propagate" lays hold of that creative product of the critical process which Arnold's own literary essays aptly represent. The writer who brings "a new piece of literature into being in some exquisitely happy characterization," creates "a lyric of criticism out of the unique pleasure of an æsthetic hour,"[22] propagates in other minds "the best that is known and thought in the world,"—merely carries over to these minds his own experience of that critical process which we have previously analyzed. Implicit or apparent in many of the literary essays of Arnold we find all the salient elements of the complete critical activity,—the inquiry after such data as may presumably enrich the act of reading, the full, vital interpenetration of the given book or writer with the critic's mind, the discovery, or at least the re-formulation, of certain laws of literature, the judgment of writer or book on the basis of these laws. Critical literature is, then, the final flowering in a creative literary act of the critical process, either in part or as a whole.

Through critical literature, critics of every school may contribute to the common stock their knowledge and understanding of literature in any of its aspects or relations. In an essay on *The Higher Study of English*, Mr. Albert S. Cook enumerates some of the possible activities of the scholarly critic:

According to the exigencies which circumstances create, or his own intuition perceives, he will edit dictionaries, like Johnson or Murray; make lexicons to individual authors, like Schmidt; compile concordances, like Bartlett or Ellis; investigate metre, like Sievers or Schipper; edit authors, as Skeat has edited Chaucer, Child the English and Scottish Ballads, and Furness Shakespeare; discourse on the laws of literature, like Sidney, or Ben Jonson, or Lewes, or Walter Pater; write literary biography, like Brandl or Dowden; or outline the features and progress of a national literature, like Ten Brink, or Stopford Brooke, or Taine.... Yet withal he must be content, if fortune, or his sense of a potential universe hidden in his apparently insignificant task, will have it so, merely to settle *hoti*'s business, properly base *oun*, or give us the doctrine of the enclitic *de*—sure that posterity, while it may ungratefully forget him, will at least have cause to bless his name, as that of one without whose strenuous and self-sacrificing exertions the poets, the orators, the historians, and the philoso-

---

21. *The Function of Criticism at the Present Time.*
22. *The Psychology of Beauty*, p. 3.

phers would have less completely yielded up their meaning, or communicated their inspiration, to an expectant and needy world.[23]

Plainly, as Mr. Saintsbury declares, "The life of Methuselah and the mind of Shakespeare together could hardly take the whole of critical knowledge to be their joint province."[24] But the many members are one body. To assign them relative values is not only an ungracious but an impossible task. "If they were all one member, where were the body?" Not the particular section of the critical field which is tilled, but the efficiency of its tilling determines the critic's value. Every type of critical activity is indispensable—one might almost say equally indispensable—to the great process of criticism. But each type can reach its highest effectiveness toward the ends of the process as a whole only in so far as it becomes intelligently aware of these ends. Sound perception of what criticism in its largest reaches aims to achieve makes even "*hoti*'s business" and "the doctrine of the enclitic *de*" a genuine help to our reading, instead of mere academic pottering, redeems impressionist rhapsodies from their accustomed trivial finality to fruitful suggestiveness, and teaches the critic of every school sincere gratitude to the many workers who in all ages have added even a little to our vital understanding of literature.

Recognition of the larger whole of criticism restores the seamless robe which partisanship and intolerance have rent to shreds. From the wars of critical theories, each too limited in its outlook to recognize its coöperative relation with all the others, the modern critic has emerged with one priceless possession—a vitalized, democratized conception of literature. To him a book can never again be a barren, finished product, a scholastic abstraction, but a living activity of more than writer and reader, a genuine function of the social body. This inconceivably precious idea he as yet hardly knows how to value or to use. Rightly used, it should solve, by its fundamental analysis of their factors, the age-old, baffling problems of criticism which previous partial or artificial conceptions of literature have succeeded only in restating. But such thoroughgoing solution awaits a more complete realization than has yet been generally attained of the length and breadth and depth and height of this epoch-making idea. When the modern critic knows, not as a mere formula, but with full realization of its as yet quite incredible implications, what literature as a social function may be, the larger criticism will also have

23. pp. 22–3.
24. *Essays in English Literature, 1780–1860*, p. xix.

become the deeper criticism, penetrating to the innermost meaning of our literature in its relations to our life.

Chapter III.   The Standards of Criticism

The practice of criticism has, in many directions, profited incalculably by the long development of theories of criticism throughout the ages of men's dealings with literature. One practical demand upon critical theory, however, yet remains unsatisfied,—the demand for a standard of judgment.

The standard of traditional authority which deductive criticism offers has been definitely rejected by modern critics. All but universally it is recognized that such a standard stultifies both criticism and literature. It substitutes a mechanical coercion for the living interconnections of criticism with literature, reduces the critic to an automaton while exalting him to a despot, and artificializes literature, by cutting it off from organic relation to its own time.

Scientific criticism, of the extreme "inductive" school, reacts, perhaps immoderately, from this tyranny of the deductive standard, by denying to judgment any place whatsoever in the act of criticism. This seems, indeed, to throw out the child with the bath. It should not be necessary to repudiate all measures of value, in order to do away with those arbitrary and external standards which have no vital relation with the writings to which they are applied. More penetrating thinkers, of the type of Coleridge, recognize this fact, and, as Miss Laura J. Wylie has pointed out in her *Evolution of English Criticism*,[25] stand with the romanticists not only in rejecting standards imposed from without upon art, but also in conceiving of the laws which have present validity for literature as essentially organic, because derived from the writings in question rather than from the classic models. Even Coleridge, however, fails to indicate precisely what laws or standards they are which may be thus derived from the work of literature itself. Nor do modern critics of Mr. J. E. Spingarn's way of thinking greatly further our search by insisting only that we apply to the writer "no other standard than that applied to any other creative artist: what has he tried to express, and how has he expressed it."[26] Such a test fixes for us what Mr. Gates rightly denominates the "intended value" of a book, but leaves undetermined its actual value, which may be quite outside the writer's calculation.

It seems plain that this actual value cannot be determined by standards

25. p. 184.
26. *The New Criticism*, p. 28.

derived from the book regarded merely in its relations to the writer or to the conditions under which it was produced, since the book, considered as a whole, involves relations to the reader as well. Miss Ethel Puffer implies this larger view of literature in her contention that the "placing" of a book in the process of literary development, which M. Brunetière insists upon as an essential part of historical or scientific criticism, does not necessarily involve any judgment as to the value of the book; since "the judgment of anything always means judgment with reference to the end for which it exists,"[27] and scientific criticism takes account only of the conditions under which literature arises.

Mr. Saintsbury vehemently reproaches scientific criticism for failing to supply us with an adequate standard for judging literature, but he himself suggests no such standard, nor apparently makes practical use of any except the traditional canons. In fact, it may be said that comparative criticism, in so far as it admits the conception of relative values, determines them by the old-fashioned rules, while in so far as it confines itself to "placing" a given piece of literature in the process of literary development, it is satisfied with the partial standards of scientific criticism.

Impressionist criticism cannot fairly be assailed for affording us no basis of judgment, since it joins with some scientific and most appreciative criticism in denying the need of any such basis. Mr. Gates, however, speaking for the appreciative critic, admits that even "in his search for the pleasure involved in a work of art," he "finds that he must go outside the work of art and beyond his own momentary state of consciousness; he must see the work of art in its relations to larger and larger groups of facts."[28] And such an admission seems significant not only because it decisively rejects the impressionist's purely personal and relative attitude toward literature; but because it suggests the possibility of seeing a work of art "in its relations to larger and larger groups of facts," until, at length, all its relations are taken into account and an adequate basis of judgment has thus been gained.

Æsthetic criticism stands with deductive criticism in definitely recognizing the obligation of critical theory to furnish a sure test of values. It stands with all the other types, however, in discrediting the deductive test. The æsthetic critic cannot as yet provide us with a usable standard in its place; but Miss Puffer gives us to understand that æsthetic theory will supply our need, once it has fully entered into its kingdom. The æsthetic critic is needed, she

27. *The Psychology of Beauty*, p. 8.
28. *Impressionism and Appreciation, The Atlantic Monthly*, July, 1900.

declares, to "teach us what great art means in literature," to tell us "what a novel ought to be," so that "we shall not always mingle the wheat and the chaff."[29]

This is the fairest promise we have had, and we may, I think, trust it, so far as the province of æsthetics covers the field of literature. Understood broadly the term æsthetics might include even those subtler intellectual and spiritual reverberations in the reader which Mr. Gates insists on taking into account. No scientific methods as yet devised, or in immediate prospect, can, it is true, measure them. But this is not to say that such measurement is inherently and ultimately impossible.

Modern criticism stands ready to welcome any achievement in this direction. But meanwhile it must make sure that the larger conception of literature is not reduced to such a conception as our present æsthetic science is qualified to deal with,—the conception (shall we say?) of literature as some piece of verbal apparatus, cleverly designed to produce certain reactions in the reader. This would be to renounce the spacious territory won by criticism through many generations, to drop out of account the writer's end of the literary process, to ignore our slowly clearing and strengthening sense of literature as a great social activity and institution.

This sense of literature we have seen evolving by gradual and chiefly unconscious stages as successive schools of criticism have perceived more clearly the great factors in their problem. But in a crude form the social conception of literature antedates all modern schools of criticism, since it was specifically implied in Plato's much-derided exclusion of the poets from his ideal state, on the ground that they indulge the feelings and enfeeble the reason of man.[30] Literature is a social institution, Plato in effect affirmed, and as such must be judged by social standards. That the nature and function of poetry were but imperfectly understood by Plato does not destroy the significance of this early suggestion, though it has often prevented modern critics from recognizing its significance. Nor can any later restrictions of the principle to crudely moralistic ends destroy its wider validity.

Mr. Arthur Ransome has lately reinterpreted the battle-cry, "Art for Art's sake," which was raised against the denomination of moralistic and naturalistic standards in art, into the theory of "Art for Life's sake."[31] But the second phrase merely substitutes a truer, that is, a more social, conception of moral-

29. *The Psychology of Beauty*, pp. 25–6.
30. *The Republic*, x.
31. *Portraits and Speculations*, p. 1.

ity for that implied in the *bourgeois* censure of art. Art exists not for its own sake, not for the sake of nature, or even for the sake of morals,—not, indeed, for any sake smaller than that of life itself. To heighten the poet's consciousness of life, and to "enrich the blood of the world" by offering to his readers "opportunities of conscious living," Mr. Ransome defines as the twofold function of poetry. And this is essentially a social function. The poet's intensified consciousness is transmitted to the reader, who receives from it an access of life, whether in the form of perception, emotion, or what-not. Wherever this transfer takes place society is at that point leveled up to the poet. The poet's individual gain in perception or emotion has been socialized.

Twenty years ago, Edward Rowland Sill, in an essay called *Principles of Criticism*, proposed as a test for literature its "life-giving power" and further analyzed this test, as follows:

> It is not enough that a picture or a novel or a poem should move us: the question is, *What* does it move in us? How much of the whole possible range of our inner life does it awaken? Nor is mere intensity of impression any sufficient test. For one must inquire, Whither does this tend,—toward further renewal of full existence, or toward reaction and stagnation? Some feelings are kindled only to smoulder away and leave dead ashes; . . . others tend to kindle on and on, awakening thought, rousing to vigorous action. Nor are the most easily moved activities always the most important ones in the effect of art and literature. . . . It is the great motive powers deep down in the soul that most contribute to abounding life, and whose awakening most surely proves the presence of genius.[32]

It is unlikely that Mr. Sill recognized the precise relation of this suggestion to previous theories of criticism or wholly perceived its social significance. But this relation and this significance are plain to the reader of today. Perhaps the fundamental conception had been drawn from Matthew Arnold's *Function of Criticism at the Present Time*, which in its recognition of the critic's duty to "propagate the best that is known and thought in the world" states by implication the social function of literature. The critic, in Arnold's theory, is the intellectual middleman of the social order, distributing ideas from producer to consumer; but with the ultimate purpose of transforming the capable consumer into a producer. The "current of true and fresh ideas" set in

32. *The Prose of E. R. Sill*, pp. 161–2.

motion by the critic swells the song of the poet, otherwise mute in a stifling atmosphere of practical life. From poet to critic, from critic to readers, from readers to new poets, passes the divine afflatus, in a self-perpetuating cycle. And thus society periodically catches up with its leaders, only to cast forward in the stream of its own progress new leaders whom it must overtake.

Literature, then, regarded from the social point of view, is a primary means by which the race advances. The critic's function is to further this advance by facilitating the interaction of literature with society. Wherever literature can directly and completely socialize its ideas, it does so. Where this is difficult, or delayed, the critic mediates. Having read a book, in the full meaning of the term, having gained some view of it or some knowledge about it which may conceivably enrich the reading of others, he communicates his experience to them, in order that the writer's thinking may the more completely interpenetrate their minds, and thus raise them to the writer's level.

Part of the critic's experience with the book has been his judgment of it as worthy of such communication, as in some respects and in some degree valuable to society. In this sense he may be said to regard it as "the best that is known and thought in the world"; the best, that is, not absolutely, but at this moment for himself and for the readers he addresses (who are presumably at approximately his own stage of development), the best calculated to satisfy their perhaps unrecognized needs, and to carry them a step beyond their present experience or powers. If it is too far in advance of them to draw them to its standing-ground, or if it is only abreast of them, to say nothing of lagging behind, it has no function to perform for them as individuals or as members of society, and it is not therefore for them the best, or even good, literature. Good literature, as judged by the social standard, is that which efficiently performs the function of literature for any individual or for any group of individuals, namely, the function of making common in society all peculiar advantages of mental endowment or experience.

Such a standard of literature will, it is apparent, yield us no immutable five-foot shelf of "the best books." Nor is this, I take it, what the reiterated demand in the history of criticism for an absolute standard of values means. A book that is "good literature" in the social sense for one reader or for one community may not be good for another. But it is good for each reader and for each community in the degree in which it furthers the development of each as part of the social whole. This means that, as Coleridge insisted, the standard by which we judge the book is inherent in the book itself; but not, we must remind ourselves, in the book as a thing printed on sheets of paper and enclosed between covers. The book, from which we are to derive its own standard of value, is the book regarded as a coöperative activity of writer and reader, to the end of the reader's heightened social consciousness. In so far as this activity (the book) achieves its end it is good literature. Like a social standard of value in expenditure, which would affix one value to opera tickets for a given person in a particular situation, and another for a different person in a different situation, but still remains the same standard, the social standard of value in literature marks what we roughly call the same book, high for one person at one time or in one set of conditions, low for another person at another time and in other conditions, while the standard itself fluctuates not at all. In the case of the high as of the low estimate, its unchanging basis of judgment is the social efficiency of this cooperative activity of writer and reader, whose visible symbol is the printed book.

For the measurement of this efficiency no methods have as yet been suggested, no instruments devised. The social values of literature cannot at present be stated in kilograms or in degrees Fahrenheit. But the frank recognition of such values, as legitimate material for critical judgment, and the open-minded investigation of them, must ultimately evolve an adequate procedure, which shall take account not of one section only of a literary act, but of the entire act, arising out of a given social situation, focusing itself, say, in a single poem of a single writer, communicating itself to the mind of a single reader in a different social situation, and thence throughout that social situation, modifying it both in obvious and in all but imperceptible ways. This view of literature as a living present activity, not the product of a past, finished act, is essential to any judgment of its social value. And the thoroughgoing acceptance of this view means to the criticism and to the creation of literature more than any of us can possibly imagine.

If the value of literature is first and last a social value, any writing which serves the social ends of literature must, in its degree, be accounted "good literature." The realm of good literature thus ceases to be an aristocratic preserve and becomes coextensive with all that is really literature. Even "our trashy, ephemeral, modern writing," to which the old-fashioned critic's resounding scorn would deny all value, may, however crude and unpleasing to him, have something to offer those whose thought and feeling are still more elementary.

But only if it be a sincere expression of the writer's mind. For without sincerity no writing can be good literature; it cannot, in the social sense, be literature at all,—as a counterfeit banknote is not really money. Literature, according to premise, is the thinking or feeling together of the writer and the reader through the agency of the written word. If, however, the word does not convey the writer's real thought and feeling, the reader cannot think and feel with him by its means, but will simply entertain a thought or a feeling which the writer for some reason wishes him to entertain.

The result of such pseudo-communication is, therefore, not to "level up" the reader with the writer, but to give the writer that advantage over the reader which his writing has, consciously or unconsciously, sought to gain. The process is as distinctly anti-social in its ends as the process of genuine communication is social. It is, properly speaking, not literature, but a commercial substitute for it, which the critic is bound to detect and to expose.

Given the indispensable quality of sincerity, then, any writing may for certain people at a certain stage of development, be good literature. As to the other rhetorical virtues, simplicity, elegance, restraint, vividness, force and the rest, it cannot yet be affirmed in how far any or all of them impart to a book the power of quickening and deepening the reader's conscious life. Doubtless one day we shall have a "new rhetoric" which will attempt to estimate in social terms the literary value of these qualities. But these have to do with degrees of excellence, and the social standard has not yet been applied beyond the first critical categories. For the present we must be content merely to substitute for the old personal distinction beween "good" literature and "poor," the new social distinction, and to know that degrees of excellence must ultimately be recognized on this same basis. Since literature, though the greatest among us, is as one that serveth it can be measured only by this service, never by the external signs of *editions de luxe* or a place "in every gentleman's library."

This social standard of criticism is the standard for which criticism throughout its long history has been searching, and for lack of which each type of criticism has been found inadequate. It is not a moral standard, in the narrow sense of the term; it is not an æsthetic standard in the superficial sense of the term: it is a social standard in the sense which deepens æsthetics and extends morality,—a sense best represented, perhaps, by the phrase, "Art for Life's sake."

Such a standard the criticism of two thousand years has slowly fashioned into crude and but half-apprehended form. For the criticism of the future remains the task of recognizing its unimagined implications, defining it more clearly, testing it at every point and applying it to the literature both of the past and of the present.

CHAPTER IV. THE FUNCTION OF THE CRITIC

No longer is the critic regarded as an oracle, enunciating infallible judgments of literature[33] by an easy comparison of any given book with certain accredited models or by an equally mechanical application to it of rules delivered unto us by Aristotle. We know him rather as a reader like ourselves, dealing with literature as we all deal with it, only carrying the process somewhat further. His dealings with it may be infinitely laborious and prolonged, but we are sure that they can be fruitful for himself and for others only as they are rooted in genuine reading and tend to make it continually more intelligent, more sensitive, more actively coöperative with the writer.

The critic's reading, then, like that of ordinary mortals, must be a process indefinitely progressive. It will continually arrive at valuations of particular books and authors, but must never regard these valuations as having, even for the critic himself, more than a present validity and a relative truth. His childish estimate of *The Swiss Family Robinson* probably differs widely from his grown-up verdict upon it. But his second judgment is not necessarily a truer judgment than the first, nor the first than the second. Each opinion, if indeed it is not a mere parroting of other people's ideas, but honestly his own, is as "true" as the other—and no truer; since each precisely records the value of the book to him at a given stage in his development.

Each opinion thus becomes to him, not a final truth in which to rest, but a point of departure for further reading and criticism. Any reader's ultimate capacity to appreciate literature depends far less on what he may think of a given piece of writing, than upon his really thinking something definite about it; for the recognition either of a book's value or of its lack of value for him increases his power of reading the next book intelligently; and this perpetual progress is essential, while one starting point or another is relatively immaterial. That he should reach a "right" conclusion, so-called, about a particular piece of literature, is, then, no such weighty matter as previous criticism would have us believe. Social criticism would insist only that he should honestly reach such a conclusion as he can reach, and then make each conclusion a stepping-stone to some further judgment, either of this book or of another. Value thus inheres, not in the judgment itself, but in the whole

---

33. Mr. John Galsworthy, in *Vague Thoughts about Art*, plays "with a light pen" about this ancient superstition of the infallibility of the critic. "I have not," he declares, "the firm soul of the critic. It is not my profession to know things for certain, and to make others feel that certainty. On the contrary I am often wrong—a luxury no critic can afford."

process of arriving at it and proceeding from it—that is, in the vital and continuous contact with literature which makes it literature indeed.

This continuous personal reaction upon literature, if supremely important for the critic, is no less essential to the general reader; and the critic can be of real use to such a reader, not by saving him all trouble of reading and of thinking about what he reads, but rather by furthering these activities of his in every possible way.

How the critic should proceed to this end is not at once evident, but it may perhaps appear more clearly once we have eliminated the time-honored method of imposing arbitrarily upon the reader the critic's opinions about books. On this point social criticism finds itself widely at variance with previous theories. For generations the schoolboy has been taught that *Paradise Lost* is good literature because all great critics have so rated it. The troublesome question, how we shall determine who the great critics are, by what standard we are to judge their claim to decide these matters for us, has been placidly put aside by the reiterated declaration that, "after all," those best fitted to fix values in literature must do so and every reader must recognize the values thus fixed.

This is the favorite and most persistent fallacy of criticism, but it is, none the less, a fallacy. Holding the critic's opinions to be obligatory upon other readers is very like "fiat money"—easy to issue but sometimes harder to realize upon. No power on earth can make a book really valuable to me if it is not so. Taking bodily over into my consciousness some critic's dictum that it is great literature gives it no fructifying power in my experience. Such a dictum can serve me only in so far as I use it to challenge or to clarify my own critical activity, which may ultimately lead me to a conclusion quite diverse.

Because literature is nothing at all to any individual if it does not become his personal experience, the criticism of literature cannot, in any sense or to any degree, be vicarious. Literary judgments are as essentially individual as the standard on which these judgments are based is universal. While it is true that a standard is no standard if it be not universal, it is equally true that a judgment is no judgment unless it is the culmination of an individual critical activity.

If the benevolent authority of the critic cannot legislate value for other readers into the books he chances to prefer, on the same principle it is powerless to deprive of value all writings which he, by an individual or by a class standard, must grade as "poor." Though these writings may have for him and for those who have reached his stage of development no gift of more abounding life, they are not therefore necessarily incapable of bestowing this gift upon any other human creature. From the social point of view a book which enables any person to see even a little more clearly than he has seen, to think more justly than he has thought, to feel more deeply than he has felt, thereby demonstrates its right to exist and to be read.

The critic's first duty is no doubt to be a good reader and thus to reach certain conclusions as to the value for him of the literature he reads. This duty has been abundantly recognized by all previous theories of criticism. But a new commandment has been given by social criticism, namely, that the critic, having reached these conclusions for himself, shall then hold them as essentially tentative and personal, not only refusing steadfastly to impose them upon other readers, but giving no sanction to their use by any reader as a substitute for his own critical activity. This is indeed a hard saying, for the critic as well as for the reader; and it can be fulfilled by the critic only as he definitely acknowledges his primary obligation to help, not hinder, the reading of others.

In admitting this obligation, however, the critic by no means abrogates all his powers and resigns all his responsibilities. As a matter of fact he gives up nothing that he ever really had. The critic who renounces every attempt to enforce his judgments of literature upon other people thereby parts only with the shadow, not with the substance, of authority. *Paradise Lost* never really became great literature to any schoolboy, merely because some critic had asserted its claim to the title. Such an assertion may, indeed, help one who has never cared to read the poem or one who has read it without interest to find some value in it for himself, but this can happen only if, refusing to accept the critic's dictum and to regard the case as by that dictum closed, he insists on submitting it to the test of an active-minded personal experience.

To make his expressed judgments of books thus provocative of genuine reading rather than in any degree a substitute for it is the aim of the modern critic. And to incite to an act of genuine reading is a great service, since such reading, as we have seen, tends continually to disclose and to supply its own inadequacies. But the critic may offer further aid in making the reader more acutely conscious of the defects in his own reading and of the means of remedying these defects, by presenting before him in the concrete form of critical essays a full, rich, personal experience with literature.

This full, rich, personal experience of literature may involve many distinct elements—not only a lively first-hand impression of what is read, but a patient accumulation of all the facts which can substantiate or refine this impression, a conscious recognition of whatever theories of literature or of particular types of literature may be involved, as well as a tentative judgment of the book in the light of these theories. The presentation to the reader of any or all of these elements should serve to stimulate and clarify his reactions to literature, should help to make him a better reader.

This, then, is the peculiar function of criticism, apart from its function as literature. Because the critic is a writer, he does, as Arnold declared, act as the middleman of ideas, disseminating throughout society "the best that is known and thought in the world," which might otherwise be inaccessible to many people. He gives ideas publicity, makes them more widely available. But this, it must be remembered, is the office of literature in general, not of criticism in particular.

Arnold's own definition of poetry as a "criticism of life" seems to justify the distinction that poetry (and thus perhaps all so-called "creative" litera-ture) deals with "life," that is, with the writer's experience outside of books, as criticism deals with his experience in the field of literature. But this distinc-tion is not clean-cut. The section of our experience which we call books so interpenetrates the section of our experience which we call "life" that a line of demarcation is extremely difficult to draw. What the poet may have read infallibly enters into his poetry, as what the critic has known of life at first hand invariably conditions his reaction to books.

The value of Arnold's definition perhaps lies rather in its suggestion of a unity of process underlying the two apparently diverse literary products, poetry and criticism. All literature, it would seem to say, communicates the writer's experience with something,—a book, a woman, a scientific observa-tion, the death of a dearly loved friend, a mountain peak at dawn, an abstract idea. It gives us, if you like, his "criticism" of that something, in the sense that poetry is a criticism of life. But this is only saying, after all, that poetry is literature, as Arnold's parallel statement that criticism distributes ideas throughout the social order declares only that criticism is also a form of literature.

In so far, then, as he is a writer, like the novelist or the poet, the critic's function is, no doubt, to heighten the reader's conscious life by sharing his reactions with him. But as peculiarly a critic, his function is something more specific,—namely, to heighten the reader's conscious life by increasing his capacity to read.

And this means that, in the measure of his success, he makes literature count for more in the lives of individuals, hence for more in the social order. He does not, in his specific function as critic, create the power of literature, but only multiplies it, by furthering the interaction of literature with society. He studies this interaction at various points as a biologist studies the interplay of an organism with its environment; and takes what means he can devise to increase the efficiency of the process.

One important means of increasing the efficiency of literature's interaction with society is to render this interaction more intelligent, better aware of its own ends. To promote in readers a truer conception of what literature is and does, thus becomes an essential part of the critic's work. A reader who understands the place of literature in the social economy cannot relegate it to the category either of private yachts or of ward politics, but must definitely take account of its relations to himself.

If he chance to be of the large class which prefers the current best seller to *Henry Esmond* or *The Egoist*, he need no longer apologize for his tastes to those who regard them as low. Once he clearly perceives the functional value of any genuine act of reading, with whatsoever book it may be connected, his dealing with the literature he can read in this way will cease to be a somewhat shamefaced playing with toys, and regain its rightful dignity, its wholeheartedness and, consequently, its power of development.

Such a reader will not feel it necessary either to pretend to share other people's preferences for the classic writers or to scorn these writers as "highbrow." Recognizing the fact that the great literature of past ages, like the popular writing of the present, belongs to readers whose conscious living it has power to quicken, and to such alone, he will not overlook the equally important truth that the real, that is, the social, value of literature depends primarily not on what is read, but on how it is read. He may thus venture to respect his own tastes, not, indeed, as representing any final attainment, but rather as the record of a constant advance in his powers of reading; and is thereby delivered both from the false shame and from the false pride which seem most effectually to bar this advance.

On the other hand, if our reader chance to be of those to whom the high qualities of our classic models are really precious, and who hold the democratic theory of literature responsible for the loss of these qualities from the popular, machine-made, commercialized writing of the present day, his relations both to ancient and to modern literature may be rendered more intelligent by applying to each the social standard of values. Such an application should not only increase his toleration for the modern books he may not care to read, but also distinguish for him the legitimately popular from the wholly commercial writings in this class. And it will assuredly enable him to read his ancient favorites with a fuller appreciation, because he will thus have gained a richer sense of their actual relation to the social order of their own time.

The censor of modern writing is often inclined to regard the critic's function at the present time as that of holding aloft a stainless banner of personal taste and dragooning all the world to follow where it leads. Apparently such a view fails to recognize the issue as educational rather than militant. The critic cannot coerce. Books which a cultivated taste considers deplorable are bound to multiply without permission from him, so long as they are read. And they must continue to be read while readers remain below the level of feeling and of thought which these books represent.

One practicable remedy, and only one, presents itself—the gradual education of readers through the very reading which now interests and satisfies them. In the genuine act of reading, we have not only a starting-point, but a continuous method of education. For progress is the law of mental life. The human mind is a developing organism: under normal conditions it neither stands still nor retrogrades. Under such conditions, if the literature adapted to further its progress is at hand, it tends to seize upon this literature in preference to that which either fails to quicken or actually stultifies it.

This fact has been repeatedly observed, where the experiment has been tried with individual readers or with a small group of them, as in settlement classes and in schools. The gradual disappearance, from situations so conditioned, of the books which are either palpably insincere or notably crude, at least suggests the possibility of making use of a similar procedure as a means of destroying over a wider area the demand for a type of literature which, though now socially useful, could not serve a more highly developed society.

To bring into the field of an individual reader's attention at the psychological moment the book which will then yield him most increase of capacity, is not always given to the writer-critic; but the teacher-critic finds this a most important part of his office. So far as experiment has been made on the point, a right sequence of books seems to be of itself an incredibly powerful agent in developing the reading-capacity of an individual. And if, in addition to this, teachers stand ready to further the reading-process by every other really efficient means, stimulating it by revealing some of its rich possibilities, defining it by bringing to light its social function and values, their students' progress from stage to stage must be even more rapid and assured.

Such a conception of the critic's function does, as a matter of fact, underlie our modern teaching of literature in the schools. It is, however, in many cases so imperfectly grasped and applied, that books which students cannot honestly read are untimely forced upon them, thus sacrificing the development of reading-capacity to the mere form of "doing" such and such writers or works; while the imposition of critical formulæ, emanating from text-book or teacher, too often seems to render unnecessary the pupil's personal experience with the literature prescribed. An abiding sense of what the student's own criticism of literature means to him, however crude and unsatisfactory it may be to others, and of the teacher's primary obligation to further his vital contact with any literature that can carry him a step beyond his present capacity, would serve to redeem English teaching from formality and barrenness, while developing a generation of readers who are bound to demand books on a constantly rising level of intelligence and taste.

The critic as teacher virtually chooses those whom he will teach by the progress he himself has made. And the critic as writer (whose office is equally, though less avowedly, preceptorial) chooses his readers by the same means. Those whose capacity to experience literature is fuller or finer than his will not care to listen to what he has to say; while those whose capacity is far below his cannot grasp it. Only those approximately, but not quite, at his own level, can he serve.

Having taken a step or two in advance of these, he constantly labors to close the gap between them by drawing the reader up to him. And so soon as he has done so, he must move beyond their common position, or the reader can no longer advance through him, but must find another helper.

To each reader, then, his own critic, and this critic often for only a limited period in his development. For the function of the critic is no empty honor, but a genuine utility, serving the sole end of the reader's limitless progress.

The terms writer and teacher by no means cover all possible phases of the critic's social activity. This activity may be carried on in an English classroom or on a lecture-platform; its results may be published in a popular magazine or in a learned review; it may take the form of club-work at a social settlement or of a dramatic experiment such as Professor George P. Baker's "Workshop"; it may involve copying manuscripts in the British Museum or taking down, as Professor John A. Lomax has done, the songs of cowboys on the Texas plains; but in all these and in many other guises, it seeks always the same end, namely, to further the activity of literature as an agent of social progress. And it reaches this end always by one means,—by applying to every concrete problem presented to it the principle that literature is not alone a creature but also a creator of the society it serves.

III. Composition Instruction with Purpose

7 Recent Tendencies in the Teaching of English Composition

from *Educational Review*
22 (November 1901): 371–82.

In this essay Buck formulates the primary problem in writing instruction: creating "natural conditions" in which students can write. Too often they concentrate on the rules of writing, which then become the ends rather than the means of communication. She discusses several approaches to criticizing student writing and concludes that the best criticism is actual response from a reader, so that criticism becomes "of vital participation in the developing of the act of writing." Best-selling rhetoric textbooks of Buck's day were largely didactic, emphasizing the "clearness," "force," "ease," and "unity" of a sentence (A. S. Hill) or the "unity, mass, and coherence" of a composition (Barrett Wendell). Buck's sarcastic description of a student with "no insatiable longing to compose a paragraph which shall have unity, coherence, and proportion" (376) questioned the foundation on which her competitors' work rested. She suggests in place of current "artificial" practices a rhetorical criticism that not only asks students to write for a genuine occasion but requests peers to respond with real questions to the composition.

The recent history of English composition-teaching seems at first glance made up of several distinct movements. Of these the revolt against the domination of the student's writing by formal rhetorical precepts was earliest and most conspicuous. Scarcely less marked, however, tho somewhat later in time, have been the tendencies to derive subjects for writing from the student's own experience, rather than from sources foreign to his knowledge or interest; to direct his writing toward some real audience; and, finally, to criticise his writing somewhat informally, in terms of the ultimate end of discourse, rather than by the direct application to it of prescriptive rules for composition.

Stated thus, no particular connection appears among these various movements. They are merely so many distinct efforts to better the teaching of English composition in our schools. Less superficially regarded, however, their common basis appears. Each aims at securing better writing from the student by furnishing more natural conditions for that writing. As early even as the time of Whately, "The cramped, meager, and feeble character of most of such essays, etc., as are avowedly composed according to the rules of any system"[1] of technical rhetoric, was noted, and the further observation made that "On the real occasions of after life (I mean when the object proposed is, not to fill up a sheet, a book, or an hour, but to communicate his thoughts to convince or persuade),—on these real occasions, he [the student] will find that he writes both better, and with more facility, than on the artificial occasion, as it may be called, of composing a declamation." From this dual discovery, so frequently made by the practical teacher of composition, the inference is plain. If the student writes both better and more easily when he has a real occasion for writing than when he composes an exercise to exemplify some rule for composition previously enjoined upon him, then let the teacher, so far as possible, replace this artificial situation by natural conditions for writing.

This general principle is rightly regarded as the foundation of our modern system of composition-teaching, as distinguished from the earlier teaching of formal rhetoric; but the practical problem, "How can natural conditions of writing be substituted in the schoolroom for artificial?" has found various answers. The first of these was inevitably negative; abolish all writing by rule.[2] Nowhere outside of composition classes does one write to conform with a certain rhetorical law. The condition is absurd. No wonder the student on whom it is imposed writes painfully and pretentiously; no wonder that continued exercises of this sort form "a habit of stringing together empty commonplaces and vapid declamations,—of multiplying words and spreading out the matter thin,—of composing in a stiff, artificial, and frigid manner."[3] No real literature, no genuine writing of any kind, was ever fashioned to the pattern of a rule. Let us, then, cast off the yoke of formal rhetoric, said the progressive teachers of an earlier decade. Let the student only write; the oftener the better. It is by writing that writing is learned. The process itself, if only it be normally conditioned, can work out its own perfection. And the first step toward securing normal conditions is to dispense with hampering rules.

Thus far the first reformers of the ancient régime. The difficulty in carrying out their program to its logical end was one quite inevitable at that stage in the development of the theory of composition-teaching. The deliberate

---

1. Whately, *Elements of rhetoric*, Introduction.
2. Among the influential colleges, Harvard was perhaps the first to insist upon this doctrine.
3. Again from Whately. The Introduction contains many other passages equally pertinent to present conditions and problems.

setting of a rule as a guide for writing could indeed be avoided, but so soon as the student became aware that his composition was later to be criticised by this rule, the knowledge could not but condition to some extent his present writing. He was not yet wholly emancipated from the "artificial condition." And even the boldest advocates of the "composition-without-rules" theory hesitated to dispense with all criticism, since it was plain that in this case every act of writing (and these acts were by hypothesis to be as frequent as possible) must only cut more deeply the grooves of such bad habits as negligence or the false methods of the old system had already worn. The necessity for criticism, and the lack of any other method of criticism than that of testing the writing by accepted rhetorical canons, made it impossible, therefore, at this stage for the student to achieve perfect freedom from any thought of rules during the process of composition. A long step had, however, been taken toward the substitution of natural for artificial conditions in writing, and the next movement in this direction had become possible.

This next movement might easily have been foretold—so logically inevitable was it. After doing away with the artificial motive for writing, that of exemplifying certain rules of discourse, it became necessary to substitute a real motive. The first that suggested itself was naturally that which impels one to write on any "genuine occasion"—the motive of having something to say which another person wishes or needs to hear. The acceptance of this motive as essential to any normal process of communication both initiated and justified the movements in composition-teaching which immediately succeeded it; namely, the derivation of subjects for writing from the student's own experience and the direction of his writing toward a definite audience. Upon subjects remote from his own experience or interests the student had no natural impulse to write. We are often reminded that the average schoolboy has nothing to say to anybody about "Pereunt et imputantur," "The vice of ambition" or "Autumn thoughts."[4] If left to himself, he would never voluntarily write a word on such a subject. Occasion would be wanting, since no observation or thought of his own presses for utterance, nor does any known interest on the part of another person in his ideas (if he had them) call forth their expression. Yet every schoolboy has interests, if one but knew them—interests which, however trivial they may be in the teacher's eyes, are for him and to his spiritual peers worth communicating. There is a real demand

4. That these particular subjects, and others similar to them, have actually been assigned to college preparatory students during the past year, by schools otherwise respectable, is a fact attested by documentary evidence in my possession.

somewhere for the experiences which he is eager to impart. And until this supply and this demand are brought into relations with each other, there can be no genuine writing. That the teacher's function is that of the middleman in this process of communicating ideas is a conviction clearly implied in the doctrines that the student should write for a definite audience and upon a subject which interests both this audience and himself.[5]

These doctrines, tho comparatively so recent in origin, have already established themselves both in the practical teaching of composition and in the formulated theories thereof. Such opposition as they still encounter consists chiefly in the indication of certain perils into which the recent convert to them may often fall—that, for instance, of accounting subjects interesting to the student merely because they are not abstract or profound, or that of resting content with the mere naming of an audience, without regard to its interest in the writer's message or its actual relations to himself. These dangers, however, obviously spring not from the doctrines of the real audience and the real subject, but from the spirit of formalism and artificiality in writing against which those doctrines are explicitly directed. If the ultimate purpose of insisting on a real subject and a real audience be kept in view, namely, that of replacing an artificial by a genuine occasion for writing, no subject can be assigned to a student for any reason save that he has something he wishes to say about it, nor a reader designated who has no natural desire to know the thing that the writer wishes to say.

So far the outlines of this history have the perspective of a certain lapse of time, tho only of a few years. In proceeding, however, to the fourth of the recent tendencies under discussion, we confront a movement in itself appreciably more complicated, and as yet but half-conscious of its own direction or significance.

It will be remembered that the question of criticism had been left practically untouched by the previous movements to normalize the writing process of the student. Logically inconsistent as it was with these movements, the old method of criticism yet persisted for a time in the midst of them. The

---

5. These doctrines were first practically exemplified in Scott and Denney's *Composition-rhetoric*, and later in Lewis's *First book in writing English*. A pamphlet by Mr. J. N. Denney, *Two problems in composition teaching* (published by J. V. Sheehan, Ann Arbor, Mich.), expounds the principles with many concrete illustrations, and an article in the *Technology review* (Massachusetts Institute of Technology), for October, 1899, by Mr. R. G. Valentine, on "Instruction in English at the Institute," reports them in active operation in the classroom. They have, perhaps, received their completest recognition and indorsement in Scott and Denney's recently issued *Elementary English composition*, in which the art of writing is consistently treated as a social function.

finished composition was estimated in terms of the formal rhetorical precepts from whose domination the writing act had but lately been freed. It soon became evident, however, that to say to the student "Write without a thought of the rules for unity, but I'll criticise your composition by them," was to demand of him the psychologically impossible. Under these circumstances he could not easily avoid thinking of the rules for unity and in effect writing to fulfill their requirements; the "artificial occasion" was restored, and the former sacrifice had become vain.

Nor did the case radically improve merely by reducing the number of rhetorical principles to which the student's writing must conform, by simplifying their phraseology or attuning it more kindly to the sensitive ear. Undoubtedly there is a real significance for the theory of composition-teaching in the practice of those professional critics who choose rather to say "Use short and simple sentences," than "Don't write such long and involved ones," and "This is a well-chosen word," than "That one is ill-chosen." Yet those who grant the palliative effect of this practice must yet recognize its failure to meet the main point of difficulty raised by the old method—the difficulty, once more, of the artificial occasion. The direct application to the student's composition of any rhetorical canon as such, however tactfully it may have been phrased, has invariably reached one result—that the student writes, consciously or unconsciously, to conform with this rule. This means, of course, that the end implied in the task assigned the student, that of sharing his own interesting experience with someone who wishes or needs to know it, has been displaced by another end, often quite unrelated to the first in the writer's mind, the end, namely, of fulfilling some injunction laid upon him by text-book, or teacher—to use figurative language, perhaps, or to alternate long with short sentences. The effect of such substitution may be briefly recalled.

In assigning a task in composition to the student, we have insisted, be it remembered, on a real occasion for his writing. He is not composing an essay to convince the teacher that he can observe all the laws of rhetoric which he has so far studied, but attempts to convey to the mind of a friend something which that friend is for some reason interested to know. If, therefore, it occurs to him at all to question his own performance of this task, he will naturally do so in terms of the end which he has proposed to himself. He will ask of himself, not "Are there enough figures of speech to satisfy the teacher?" "Have I written short sentences interspersed with long ones, as the text-book says to do?" "Did I make correct use of the method of obverse iteration?" but rather, "Have I told the thing so that Fred or Jim will know just how it happened?" "Will he see it as I did?" "Will he understand what I mean?" Even if thoroly indoctrinated with rhetorical formulæ, the average student is conscious of no particular desire to "produce an effect of vivacity" on some unspecified and unimagined audience. He feels no insatiable longing to compose a paragraph which shall have unity, coherence, and proportion. Hence, when his work is estimated by these alien standards, he feels much as would any intelligent youth to whom, when making a kite, some insane elder should remark in passing—"That will never spin in the world." The reply, "Well, who wants it to? This isn't a top!" embodies emotions of mingled contempt, derision, and indignation no more acute than the unexpressed sensations of many a schoolboy reading the penciled criticisms on his returned theme.

But if the rhetorical standard be maintained by the teacher as the basis for criticism, that which the "real occasion" has suggested to the student's mind comes rapidly to be regarded by him as a mere pretense, and consequently to be ignored in his writing. His compositions are fashioned, so far as possible, with a view to sustaining the teacher's peculiar tests. Not that he sees any reason in them, but, being the teacher's, a due regard for marks constrains him. This perfunctory and external conformity is probably far from satisfying his taskmaster, who feels that the real occasion has here proved itself a failure; but surely this is not the student's fault. He is doing his best to fulfill all requirements, so far as he understands them, and the woodenly vacuous result should, he feels, be highly approved by his over-lord, for there is not a loose sentence in it!—or perhaps a mixed metaphor, if this chance to be the fault for which his last production fell under condemnation. Such are the cross-purposes inevitably consequent upon the attempt to pour the new wine of the genuine occasion into the old bottles of formal criticism.

Not finally convinced of the futility of this attempt, but keenly alive to the danger of allowing the rhetorical standard to coexist independently with the practical, and hence ultimately to dominate it in the student's mind, some ingenious teachers have undertaken to reconcile the two by translating the former into terms of the latter. Thus the student, altho holding in mind the injunction to use concrete words, shall yet understand that he is to do this, not finally because the textbook enjoins it, but because only by so doing can he succeed in flashing before the eyes of his reader the picture he himself has once seen.

There is no doubt that many of the accredited rhetorical precepts may be interpreted in this way, with reference to the normal writing process whence originally they were derived. And when this interpretation has been successfully made, the printed rule forthwith ceases to be merely the arbitrary enactment of some unknown authority and gains for the student a real meaning in terms of the end which his writing seeks. He must, indeed, still write to conform with a certain requirement made by his text-book, but no longer with a requirement which is for him intellectually a *cul-de-sac*. It has now an outlet, leading him to a further end, that of the writing process itself. For the time, at least, conformity with the rhetorical law has taken its right position toward the ultimate end of communication, as a means thereto. In aiming at the means, the student's attention may be for an instant withdrawn from the final end of his spontaneous writing, namely, the communication of a certain content to the mind of another person, yet returns to it again thru the acknowledged relation of the means to this end.

This method of reconciling the proximate with the ultimate standards for criticism assuredly marks an advance upon that crude system which allows mere conformity with rhetorical canons, as such, to seem to the student the end of his writing. Its difficulties are, however, considerable. It requires at least a fair amount of psychological training, as well as native acuteness of mind, to perceive in all cases the exact relation between the somewhat abstract formulæ of the text-book and the practical aim of discourse; hence, some not unskillful teachers have abandoned the undertaking as impracticable. Furthermore, the critics of the method have not failed to point out its tendency to revert by imperceptible degrees to the more primitive type. Little by little, they assert, the rhetorical standard comes in the student's mind to take on, as before, an independent existence. Satisfied that it can be translated into terms of the ultimate end of the writing process, the student ceases thus to translate it except on explicit demand of the teacher. As a matter of fact he again writes to use concrete terms, instead of using concrete terms in order to write—that is, the real occasion has once more been displaced by the artificial.

Recognition of the failure of this method has perhaps closed the long list of attempts to tinker the old formal criticism into a practical consistency with the new theory of composition-teaching. Henceforth it becomes clearly evident that one of three courses must be followed: to turn back the previous movements to normalize the writing process, and restore the ancient order of composition-by-rules, in which case criticism-by-rules could logically be retained; or, rejecting formal criticism under all its disguises, and unable to conceive any other effective method, to discard all criticism, trusting to the normally conditioned writing process, unaided, to develop ultimately its highest efficiency; or, finally, to displace formal criticism by a method which should be both logically and practically consistent with the free and natural act of writing.

The first of these proposed courses has been mentioned only to exhaust the theoretic possibilities. While some few individuals may have solved the problem for themselves in this way, a general reversion to the old order has long been almost as inconceivable as the restoration of pre-laboratory methods in the teaching of natural science.

Nor has the second program met with general acceptance. So far as I am aware, there has been, even in these latter days, no visible tendency among teachers of composition to abolish entirely the article of criticism.[6] Against this last sacrifice for the freedom of the writing process practical considerations have always successfully protested. Granting that the normal act of writing has within itself the all-sufficient germ of its ultimate perfection, it is still maintained that such gradual, unassisted evolution requires a period of time far exceeding that set aside for the teaching of English in our schools or colleges; and further, that the entire hypothesis can very rarely be fulfilled, since, after the first year of a child's school life, composition has all but invariably become to him an artificial rule-regarding process, hence one has to deal not with the normal writing act which needs development only, but with an unnatural, perverted function which cannot develop rightly until it first has been restored to health.

Theoretically, also, criticism is commonly held essential to the highest efficiency of the writing act, however natural, even instinctive, we may allow that act in its origin to be. Without its bumps and falls—assuredly an objective criticism of its methods of locomotion—the child would hardly learn to walk. For psychology, as well as for ethics, it has become a truism that every intelligent act is in its freedom responsible—not, indeed, to an arbitrary rule, externally imposed, but to the inner law of its own nature, as defined by the end it seeks to reach. From its success or failure in reaching this end arises that practical criticism thru which alone it gradually gains a higher and yet

---

6. In making this statement I do not ignore such recent declarations as those of Mr. Robert Herrick (in the pamphlet entitled *Methods of teaching rhetoric*, by Scott, Foresman & Co., Chicago), and at least one other writer, to the effect that when a pupil's writing is peculiarly anemic and artificial, it is often desirable to omit criticism entirely for a time. The intention here is very evidently not to discard criticism altogether, but merely to postpone it until the writing-process has thereby gained a freedom and vigor which can defy its paralyzing effect. The question is not between criticism and no criticism, but solely as to the time when criticism will be most advantageous—or least injurious—to the student.

higher efficiency. Such criticism, then, is essential to the intelligent act of writing.

The third program[7] has thus been reached by successive rejections of the other two. Those teachers who have been forced to it, along this path or another, found its larger outlines already sketched for them. The genuine occasion for writing, like that for the child's walking, furnishes its own practical standard for criticism. Did I succeed in reproducing my experience exactly in my friend's mind? Did he receive from me the sensation I had previously felt? Did he see each event as it had passed before my eyes? Did he think my thought after me? Did he reach my conclusion as I had earlier reached it? Questions such as these furnish the starting point for all that new order of criticism which is held by its advocates to be both practically and theoretically consistent with genuine writing. The more objective and impersonal the answers given to these questions, the more likely is the criticism to be vital—the student's judgment of his own writing, not the teacher's externally imposed estimate of it. Hence the devices of some ingenious teachers[8] for returning directly to the writer, for comparison with the original experience, the experience which he has actually transmitted to the reader's mind. For instance, some outdoor scene is described to a friend skillful with the brush, whereupon he paints for the writer a sketch of the same scene as it flashed before his eyes while reading the description. Or, a fellow-student, taking the point of view of the reader addressed, gives back to the writer in other language, and possibly in further detail, a verbal account of the image transmitted to his consciousness. Thus the writer may know of a surety

7. On the way to this program some have been deflected, in the blindness of their first reaction against the old formal methods, to that naive expression of untutored personal preference sometimes dignified by the name of criticism. "I like that description," "That story somehow didn't appeal to me," are comments which, tho scornfully tabooed in the formalist's classroom, can yet be admitted as ultimate critical judgments only by those anti-conventional teachers who fail to recognize under this mask a standard at least equal in artificiality to that which they have once rightly repudiated. Such informal comments, tempting as they are to the protestant against rigid criticism by rules, must too frequently set before the student's mind a goal no less abnormal than mere conformity with some rhetorical law—the goal, namely, of approbation from a group of auditors to whom the writing is not actually addressed. A specious habit of writing "to the galleries"—briefly "rhetoric," in one of the most obnoxious senses of the term—must be the price for this kind of criticism, unless, indeed, the critic be invariably required to take the point of view of the person or persons actually addressed, and to trace his avowed pleasure or displeasure in the writing to an otherwise formulated sense of its success or failure as an act of communication.

8. All emanating, I believe, from Professor F. N. Scott of the University of Michigan.

whether or not his communication reached home; and, more than this, often in the process of comparison the source of its failure or success becomes evident. Here we have, it is urged, the living germ of criticism. Not technically formulated, it yet serves to render the student vitally conscious of the adequacy or inadequacy of his communication to reach its end, with at least the grosser reasons therefor, while never for an instant deflecting his eyes from the thing he is saying and the person to whom he says it—those primary elements in the genuine occasion for writing.

That such criticism, altho at present but a rough-and-ready practical judgment of any piece of writing, such as the reader addressed by it could instantly give, is yet the original plasm of all the finer critical judgments, and hence capable of ultimate differentiation into them, is well maintained and certainly cannot at present be disproved. That it must finally yield a body of practical formulæ for conveying a given content most directly or vividly under specified conditions is unquestionable. There is, however, no immediate cause for alarm in this prospect, even to the most uncompromising anti-formalist. So long as the student discovers in reaching the end certain means most effective for reaching it, these means never having been presented to his attention as ends in themselves, nor indeed having received undue emphasis by separation from the final aim of his writing,[9] the chances of his composing to rules are slight.

We have thus traced the evolution of the functon of criticism in the teaching of English composition out of its early formalism and externality, thru many fruitless experiments, half-understood failures and unrecognized successes, into its present estate, of vital participation in the development of the act of writing. This transformation is clearly a corollary of the large movement whose various aspects have been successively discussed in this paper. The trend of every recent reform in composition-teaching has been toward a responsible freedom for the process of writing—a freedom from laws apparently arbitrary and externally imposed, a responsibility to the law of its own nature as a process of communication. Thus free and thus responsible, composition becomes for the first time a normal act, capable of development practically unlimited. The initial movement has been made toward teaching the student, in any genuine sense of the words, to write.

9. The description will be recognized as that of the laboratory, or inductive, or psychological method of composition-teaching, as it has variously been characterized.

8 The Basis of Exposition

from *A Course in Expository Writing*,
co-authored with Elisabeth Woodbridge
(New York: Henry Holt, 1899), iii–viii, 1–8.

Buck co-authored this book with her Vassar colleague Elisabeth Woodbridge, publishing it two years after she began teaching the first-year writing course. One of the first to focus on only one mode of writing (description, narration, argumentation, or exposition), this text relied primarily on canonical literature, available in inexpensive classroom editions, for readings. We may assume that much of the material came from the course she designed and piloted, and the book, used for fifteen years, brought uniformity to the various sections. Robert Connors notes that Buck's single-mode textbooks, A Course in Argumentative Writing, A Course in Narrative Writing, *and* A Course in Expository Writing, *along with George Pierce Baker's* The Principles of Argumentation *(1895) and Carrol L. Maxcy's* The Rhetorical Principles of Narration *(1911), indicate that "the modes were accepted almost absolutely [as] the controlling classification" in composition instruction ("Rise and Fall of the Modes" 448).*

Although this book went through three editions, it is difficult to ascertain how widely Buck's texts were used, which schools adopted them, and whether they appealed to secondary as well as postsecondary audiences. One study that documents textbook use around the turn of the century reports that Buck and Woodbridge's text was used one year at Williams between 1910 and 1920 (Wozniak 277), but few women's colleges are included in the survey. Records indicate that Smith College used A Course in Expository Writing *in 1902–03, and Mount Holyoke based its theme writing course in 1905 and 1906 on the text.*

The three main sections of the textbook detail Buck's epistemology and her belief that language conveyed thought only if the writer accurately related how she perceived objects in the world. Such an approach differed from the prescriptivist approach of John Genung or A. S. Hill, whose books were widely used at other institutions. The book moved from the process of description to its relation to exposition, and the concluding section was "definition in its relation to exposition." Each section contained six to eight lessons which included prose selections and writing exercises for the students. Included here are the preface and chapter 1, "The Basis of Exposition."

PREFACE

The English teacher, more perhaps than any other, is consciously aiming, not to give his students information, but to make them acquire capacity,—capacity, in this case, for expressing their thoughts to others. But it is only by writing that the student can learn to write well, though much writing may not teach this, and one of the difficulties which an English teacher has to meet is a no less fundamental one than the difficulty of getting his students to write at all—to write, that is, not perfunctorily, but spontaneously, for this is the only kind of writing that counts.

This difficulty has its source, at least very largely, in the student's sense of the artificial character of his work. What is the use, he thinks, of writing about the birthplace of Hawthorne, or the character of Lady Macbeth? His teacher knows all about them beforehand, and besides, he isn't writing to his teacher, he isn't writing to anybody, he is just "writing a composition" that is to be corrected for spelling, punctuation, paragraphing; or for its lack of certain qualities, such as "clearness," "precision," and "unity." No wonder he finds it hard to write. We ourselves, when alone, do not usually talk aloud about the things around us, describe the picture before us, or the desk, or the view. We should feel "silly" to be talking to nobody. Why should we expect a child to talk to nobody on paper? He feels "silly" too, or at least uncomfortable. But give him somebody to talk to, a real audience, and a subject that his audience is interested in, and his whole attitude will change. Tell him to "describe a game of basket-ball," and he will be lifeless enough; but find some classmates who like football better, and tell him to describe the game to them so as to convert them, or let each side try to convert the other, with the class as judge,—then he has something worth doing. Evidently it is the subject, as well as the audience, that has been wrong; give a boy or girl something that he—not we—calls "interesting," and give him somebody who is interested, or whom he must make interested, and he will write for you. Not that "the character of Lady Macbeth" is in itself an unfit subject. Take a class studying Macbeth for college preparatory work and set them talking about the characters. Some will pity Macbeth and despise his lady, others will feel differently; discussion will arise, sides will be taken. Before they have reached a decision, tell each student to defend his opinion in writing; the results will be spirited, and the effect of the writing, when read to the class, will be eagerly watched, while if a little argument creeps into the exposition, no harm is done.

All sorts of such devices can be found to provide the students with an audience, and of course it will be best of all if they feel that the teacher himself

A COURSE IN

EXPOSITORY WRITING

BY

GERTRUDE BUCK, Ph.D.
(University of Michigan)

AND

ELISABETH WOODBRIDGE, Ph.D.
(Yale)

Instructors in English at Vassar College

NEW YORK
HENRY HOLT AND COMPANY
1899

is a real, not a sham, audience; that he is listening for what they have to say, as well as holding himself ready to correct the way they say it. And when the students have got a little out of the old rut of "writing compositions" addressed to nobody, and have had some experience in writing to real readers, they will be able to imagine audiences for themselves, and write with vigor to these hypothetical hearers. They will describe a football game "to a boy who was on the team last year," or "to a gentleman who doesn't want his son to play, but may be persuaded to let him," etc., etc. In the following pages the subjects suggested for writing have not always had their specific audience thus defined, because this can often be better done by the teacher himself so as to appeal most successfully to the particular students he is dealing with.

Supposing, then, that by various means the teacher has got some spirited writing from his students; this writing must be criticised, and how shall it be done without dampening their ardor and losing everything that has been gained?

This problem, which is indeed a hard one, has been partly solved in supplying a real audience. For the test of writing is its effect on the audience. If the student knows his audience, and can measure the effect he produces, he has a means not merely of knowing, in a general way, that his writing is "weak" or "ineffective," but of discovering just what is the difference between the kind of effect it actually produces and the kind he meant it to produce; and he will be ready and able to go back to his writing and find the causes of his failure. If his account of basket-ball is not convincing, the question naturally comes up, "why?" and he is directed back to his writing to find out the trouble.

The more the students can thus be made to supply their own criticism, the better will be the results; and to this end, all kinds of devices will be of use— exchange of papers between students, descriptions read aloud where the class does not know the subject but must recognize it from the account there given, and so on. Any means whatever is worth using which may make the student himself understand the effectiveness or ineffectiveness of his work. For example, the description of the rose, cited on pages 16–17 of this book, was criticised by making some rough water-color sketches from it, representing the successive images that actually came to the teacher's mind as she read the paragraph. Again, some descriptions, written by the students, of the main entrance to a building, were sent away to an architect who made sketches from them. The results gave the clearest possible evidence as to just how far the descriptions had been successful and in what way they had failed.

When this kind of thing cannot be done, verbal sketches may be substituted, where the teacher or a fellow-student tries to give back in other words the impression he has received. For example, a college student wrote a description of a summer lake which was, as the Scotch say, "throughither." But how make the writer not only see this, but do it better? The teacher said: "Now, I am going to tell you what you have made me see. This is the picture I get as I read: first I see a narrow lake, etc.,—and houses over there, etc.;" but after a few sentences she was interrupted by the astonished student,—"But it isn't narrow, it's wide; and the houses aren't that way, they're—" and she went on with a really intelligible account. The realization of how completely she had been misunderstood, gained in this way, did not discourage her, it stimulated her into immediate and more intelligent effort. Her audience was before her, she had seen the effect she produced, and this gave her the power to do better.

Furthermore, criticism is apt to be discouraging because it considers too many things at once. The student has a hopeless feeling that he is all wrong, and he does not know which of his numberless vices to reform first. Usually, in grades of work where this book would be used, the simpler principles of punctuation and the rules of spelling ought to be observed as a matter of course, although a case is conceivable where it would be better to let even spelling go to the winds for a while, until other things had been gained. Taking these for granted, criticism will do well to attend to one thing at a time, and the rational order of progress would be, of course, from the large questions to details, from the fundamental matters of structure or plan, the developing of the main possibilities in a subject, to the details of finish, questions of emphasis needing delicate discrimination and shading. It is best to begin with paragraphs, and come later on to sentences and phrases and words. Beginning with the big things, the little things will many of them right themselves, and those that do not, can wait.

And in general it may be suggested that it is always best, not first to tell a student how to write a thing, and then bid him do it, but first to get him to do it, and afterwards to let him see how it was done. Take, for example, the various forms of the paragraph,—the paragraph "by method of specific instance" or by "method of contrast." These forms have arisen because they were the best ones for the treatment of a given subject; give the student such a subject and he is more than likely to drop naturally into this form. Tell him to write a paper about the intelligence of his dog or cat or parrot, and if he does not do it by the method of "specific instance" he is a remarkable boy. Or tell him to discuss the comparative merits of setters and collies; he cannot help doing it by the method of "contrast." Having dropped into the form, he will be interested in seeing how better writers than he have used it, and will get hints from them as to ways of making his own work more effective, while at the same time he will come to realize that writing is not made from rules, but rules are discovered in writing.

In the following lessons, few explicit directions are given for detailed work on paragraphs and sentences. For such work Scott and Denney's *Composition-Rhetoric* may profitably be used as a guide.[1]

CHAPTER I   THE BASIS OF EXPOSITION

All language, written or spoken, has one object: to put the person addressed in possession of certain ideas, to make him possess those ideas as firmly as though he had arrived at them independently. We have seen a beautiful orchid, our friend has not seen it, and we try to make language take the place of experience for him; in common parlance, we "try to make him see it." Or, there is a practical issue before us; our friend wants to go trout-fishing, and we know a certain pool that has not been fished out. We could take him there, but that is not feasible, and we fall back upon language to put him in possession of the ideas he needs to have. Perhaps, however, he has never been trout-fishing, and does not know a trout when he sees it. "How can I tell one when I catch him?" he asks, and we try to tell him how.

In making these attempts to substitute something else in place of actual experience, we usually feel that a certain degree of success is attainable,—that if we do not succeed, it is not because the thing cannot be done, but because we do not know how to do it. That is, we have considerable faith in the power of language as a medium of communication. The word "trout" may not mean to our friend what it does to us, but the word "speckled" may, and by choosing such words as we both understand to explain those we do not, we can quickly increase our stock of trustworthy terms.

But why do we believe that any terms are trustworthy? We have reached this belief by a process of experience, begun long before we began to talk, whose basis is a belief that fundamentally other people are like ourselves.

1. The same text-book, it should be said, makes practical use of the principles laid down in this preface, as to the furnishing of an audience for the students' writing. A pamphlet by Mr. Joseph V. Denney, entitled "Two Problems of Composition-Teaching" (in the series of Contributions to Rhetorical Theory, edited by Prof. F. N. Scott), embodies similar suggestions. Mr. Robert Herrick's "Method of Teaching Rhetoric in Schools" (Scott, Foresman & Co., 378–388 Wabash Avenue, Chicago) has also been largely drawn upon by the writers.

The idea of using pictorial material as subject-matter of expository writing had been borrowed from the Practice of Professor F. N. Scott in his classes at the University of Michigan.

Some one points out a red pillow and says "red! red!" We look at the pillow and are conscious of a peculiar color-sensation, and soon we not only associate the word with this sensation, but we also believe that other people will do the same, and that when they say "red" they have the same sensation that we have. That is, we believe that they see things as we do, and think about them as we do. So strong does this conviction become, that where it does not seem to be justified we usually conclude that the difficulty has arisen either because we are not really talking about the same thing, or else because we are not really speaking the same language.

And so, when we have seen the orchid that our friend has not, we believe that we can really help him to see it,—that we can by means of certain words really call up to his mind certain perceptions of form and color which the flower itself would have called up if he had seen it. We have the same confidence when we set about telling our fisherman how he can know a trout when he sees it. The problem is, to be sure, a little different from that of the orchid, because instead of describing some one trout, we must give him an account that will fit any trout he may catch, and so we must mention only such traits as all trout, in distinction from all other fish, are sure to possess. We may say: "They're six to ten inches long, with roundish bodies—not flat like sunfish—and rather long for their breadth; and they have a smooth skin—no scales that you can see—pale gray, and speckled along the sides with pretty pink and silver dots, but the color varies a good deal, some are brighter than others; and they're gamey!"

Here, we are not exactly trying to call up a definite image such as would be called up by any particular trout, for each trout would call up an image distinct from every other; it would not be "six to twelve inches long," but say, seven and a quarter, or nine and a half. But though we are giving a general, rather than a specific description, still we are recalling and using the phrases of sense-experience, we are going back to impressions of form and color.

One word used, however, "gamey," is rather more remote from these impressions, and it may bring us into difficulty. Our hearer looks a bit incredulous: "Gamey! In a brook three feet wide! Guess you don't mean what I mean by gamey. *Bluefish* are gamey." "Well," we may answer, "I don't know what *you* mean by gamey, and I've never caught bluefish, but the other day I got a ten-inch trout in that pool who bent my pole double—" and we go on to tell our experience. What have we done this time? We found a difficulty with what is called an "abstract term," indicating an "abstract" quality—gaminess—and we met the difficulty by going back to a concrete experience—one of many through which we ourselves got our perception of this "abstract" quality. Here, being back in the realm of immediate, concrete, experience, we felt ourselves once more on firm ground; quickly and confidently we put the skeptic in possession of this experience, trusting that it would mean to him what it did to us.

For all our own convictions have been gained through sense-experience, and we unconsciously recognize this when we revert to experience in communicating with others. The farther removed we are from the direct testimony of the senses, the more liability there is to misunderstandings, and these can best be cleared up by reverting again to sense-experience. When this cannot be done, we are lost indeed. Suppose that in discussing some question of beauty or taste, I find myself differing with my companion; to settle the trouble, we resort to a concrete instance, and at once I discover that my companion is partially color-blind. Instantly I realize that no matter how long I talk, I can never really communicate to him certain ideas whose foundation is in our color-sense, for there is nothing more fundamental, where we can find a common meeting-ground, and from which we can attempt an explanation. I may discover that his sense of hearing agrees with mine, and perhaps I may appeal to that and tell him that "red is like the sound of a trumpet," or I may appeal to his sense of temperature, and tell him that red is "hot" and green is "cool," but so long as he cannot practically tell green from red, what use is it? And how can I hope that the line,

The multitudinous seas incarnadine,

will ever have for him the associative meaning that it has for me? Such difference in sense-perception is fundamental and insurmountable.

Aside from differences of this sort, which probably exist among us all, though not to this extent, there are secondary differences in people, which while they do not preclude an ultimate understanding, do condition the way in which it can be reached. Two sportsmen, for instance, who have hunted through the same kind of country, do not need to get back to primitive sensations to establish their starting-point—they have had many common experiences, have therefore reached similar convictions in regard to things, and can talk to one another by short cuts of suggestion, assuming much that to a layman would have to be elaborately explained. Imagine one of these congenial spirits talking to a society girl, who says, "Do tell me about your hunting." Where shall he begin? Evidently, "at first principles," that is, with such sense-appeal as he judges she can understand, though indeed he may feel that she has as much need of a "sixth sense" as our color-blind person had need of a fifth. The two cases might be represented thus:

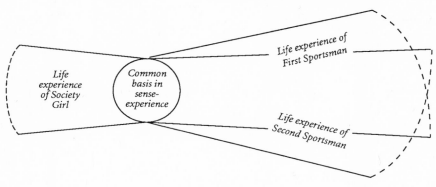

Fig. 1

The case is supposed, simply to emphasize the necessity, if we really wish not merely to talk but to communicate ideas, that we shall know whom we are talking to, what his experience has been, and how far it has been parallel with ours.

In the following discussion, therefore, one thing has been taken for granted: namely, that the impressions of our eyes and ears and other sense-organs are the basis of our knowledge; rightly understood, they are our knowledge. Hence, although expository writing aims to communicate to others our interpretation of sense-experience,—which we may call knowledge or opinion according to the degree of our conviction,—yet we shall understand its principles best if we approach it through a study of description, which is the communication of our immediate sense-experience itself.

Lesson I

1. Cite one or two instances in which you have tried to convey an idea to some one else, and try to account for your success or failure.[2]

2. Recall cases in which other people have tried to convey ideas to you, and explain their success or failure. In some given case where they failed, how do you think they ought to have appealed to you to have been successful?

3. In any of these cases, how would the way of going to work have been modified if the person addressed had been different? (e.g., if, instead of a fellow-student, he had been a day-laborer, or a newsboy, or a shop-girl, etc.)?

4. The following passages occur near the beginning of an address on

2. This should of course be narrowed by the teacher, so that it may not seem vague and unsuggestive. Either the audience should be specified—the idea was to be conveyed to one's father, or little brother, or a schoolmate; or the idea—you were talking about golf, or a lesson, or the last school examination; or both subject and idea may be defined.

"Technical Education" delivered by Huxley to a working men's club. What is their value to the exposition that is to follow?

"Technical education" ... is, in fact, a fine Greco-Latin equivalent for what in good vernacular English would be called "the teaching of handicrafts." ...

"I am, and have been, any time these thirty years, a man who works with his hands,—a handicrafts-man. I do not say this in the broadly metaphorical sense in which fine gentlemen, with all the delicacy of Agag about them, trip to the hustings about election time, and protest that they too are working men. I really mean my words to be taken in their direct, literal, and straight-forward sense. In fact, if the most nimble-fingered watchmaker among you will come to my workshop, he may set me to put a watch together, and I will set him to dissect, say, a blackbeetle's nerves. I do not wish to vaunt, but I am inclined to think that I shall manage my job to his satisfaction sooner than he will do his piece of work to mine.

"In truth, anatomy, which is my handicraft, is one of the most difficult kinds of mechanical labor, involving, as it does, not only lightness and dexterity of hand, but sharp eyes and endless patience.

. . . .

"Now, let me apply the lessons I have learned from my handicraft to yours. If any of you were obliged to take an apprentice, I suppose you would like to get a good healthy lad, ready and willing to learn, handy, and with his fingers not all thumbs, as the saying goes. You would like that he should read, write, and cipher well; and if you were an intelligent master, and your trade involved the application of scientific principles, as so many trades do, you would like him to know enough of the elementary principles of science to understand what was going on. I suppose that in nine trades out of ten, it would be useful if he could draw; and many of you must have lamented your inability to find out for yourself what foreigners are doing or have done. So that some knowledge of French and German might, in many cases, be very desirable."[3]

In these passages, how are the words and phrases adapted to convey the lecturer's ideas to his audience?

5. If Huxley had been addressing an audience of college seniors, what difference would it have made in his procedure?

6. Read in Shakespeare's *Julius Cæsar* the speeches made by Brutus and Antony to the Roman mob (Act III, Scene 2). Brutus' purpose is to justify the murder of Cæsar, that is, to make the populace look at it as he does. How does he go to work to put the people in possession of his ideas? He seems to be

3. Huxley, *Science and Culture, and Other Essays.*

successful. Is he really so? What is the difference between his method and Huxley's? Antony's purpose is to convey to the people certain ideas about the murder quite contrary to those of Brutus. What means does he use? Why do the ideas conveyed by him to the people so easily efface those conveyed by Brutus? Were Brutus' ideas really conveyed?

9 Argumentation

from *A Course in Argumentative Writing*
(New York: Henry Holt, 1899), iii–viii, 1–9.

Early in this book Buck defines argument as "the act of establishing in the mind of another person a conclusion which has become fixed in your own, by means of setting up in the other person's mind the train of thought or reasoning which has previously led you to this conclusion" (3). After introducing the inductive nature of her approach, she includes exercises in each chapter designed to help the student argue along certain lines. Buck's definition differed from others in that she emphasized helping the speaker arrive at the conclusions to then establish in the reader's mind.

This textbook competed with George Baker's and G. R. Carpenter's for the college market, but it included more references to women student writers. The chapter on a priori reasoning concludes with an exercise to write an argument leading to any of the following conclusions: "A certain rule will soon be abolished in [a] school or college. Women will be allowed to vote on all questions in all states. Capital punishment will ultimately be abolished throughout the civilized world. A satisfactory flying machine will some day be invented" (125–26). The chapter on argument from analogy suggests the following conclusions: "The ability to write well can be acquired. Every woman should be able to earn her own living. Women who desire to do so should enter the profession of medicine. Eight hours of daily work should be the maximum for a college student" (150–51). These selections, the preface and chapter 1, establish the theory upon which the book is based.

PREFACE

This book arises out of certain beliefs concerning the study of argumentation, which, though perhaps not wholly novel, have as yet found no recognition in the literature of the subject. The first of these beliefs is that the principles of argumentation should be derived by the student from its practice before the practice is made to conform to the principles. In short—one may as well acknowledge it—a firm faith in the so-called "inductive method" as applied to argumentation lies at the root of this treatise. Such a faith implies, of course, that the student should be asked to dissect out logical formulæ for himself from his own unconscious reasonings, using them,

A COURSE IN

ARGUMENTATIVE WRITING

BY

GERTRUDE BUCK, Ph.D.

Instructor in English in Vassar College

NEW YORK

HENRY HOLT AND COMPANY

1899

when discovered, to render those reasonings more exact. The construction and the rough analysis of arguments would, similarly, precede the formulation of any principles of persuasion.

Such a plan as this, it will be noted, assigns to the student a task at once more difficult and more stimulating than that which the usual methods require. He is not asked simply to accept certain logical formulæ on the authority of text-book or teacher and apply them to his own writing; but first to quarry out these formulæ from his own writing and then to use them for such modification of that writing as may seem necessary. His duty is thus doubled; but it is also enlivened by the zest of discovery. He deals not with the dead products of other people's labor, but with the fruits of his own first-hand observation and thought. In his study of the processes of reasoning he reasons himself, inductively as well as deductively,—an issue by no means inevitable under the old system.

From the conviction that the student should formulate his own principles of argumentation follows the second article of faith: that the subjects set for argument and the material used for analysis should be not remote from the student's natural interests, but interwoven with his daily experiences. If the student is to gain his principles from his unconscious practice, it follows that he will, for a time at least, be concerned with arguments about the probable score of the coming football game or the fairness of a certain examination rather than the desirability of a high protective tariff for the United States or the iniquity of free silver. Whenever these latter topics come to have a real and first-hand interest, they may well be used; but simpler and more intimate questions will usually serve better to disclose the typical processes of reasoning and argument, not obscuring them by needless bulk and complexity in the subject-matter. When once these typical processes have become thoroughly familiar in their simpler aspects, they may easily be traced through the mazes of an intricate and voluminous argument in politics or sociology. Work of this more ambitious type, however, properly follows the elementary style of the principles of argumentation with which we are here concerned.[1]

The third canon of which this book is exponent is also involved, though somewhat indirectly, in the first. This is the conviction that the logical basis of argumentation should be ultimately referred to psychology. This is an old word in philosophy, but it has not yet found place in treatises on argumenta-

1. The sketch found in Appendix C of a course given conjointly by the departments of Economics and of English at Vassar College will furnish some suggestions for more advanced work in argumentation.

tion. The logical substructure of arguments is universally recognized, but seldom is the psychological stratum beneath that pointed out, and thus, cut off from its deepest roots, logic has come to seem rather like a dead tool than like a living expression of thought. Beginning, however, as this study of argumentation does, with the unconscious reasonings of the student, it is bound to see them as they are, not compositions carefully planned to exhibit logical principles, but natural outputs of typical mental processes. Each argument is referred not only to its logical but to its psychological antecedent, so that the maxims and formulæ, usually regarded by the learner as malign inventions of Aristotle, represent to our student rather the ways in which real people really think. In fact, he himself thinks and argues in these ways—he has often caught himself doing so; and from this fact the abstract logical equations acquire a distinct flavor of personal interest. Knowing them thus inwardly, not as a mere external imposition upon his memory, he has them better in hand as a tool. He uses them not gingerly, but with the dash of intimacy.

Some explanation or defense of the syllogistic brief as used in the text may be demanded. The adoption of this form of analysis is due to the fact that it brings into clear relief the actual structure of an argument, which the ordinary brief so often allows to be forgotten. The syllogistic brief insists, more strenuously than does any other form, upon an exact representation of the entire reasoning process which underlies the argument, with all the relationships and interrelationships among its various parts. What is needed, at least for the beginner, is a brief that first represents the argument as a unit, and then shows with precision how every point in the proof leads directly or indirectly to the single conclusion. This the syllogistic brief accomplishes. It reveals the comparative rank of all arguments and sifts out those which are irrelevant by virtue of its insistence upon the exact bearing of each point upon the main conclusion. This the ordinary form may also be compelled to do, if skillfully handled, and the more advanced student can safely be trusted to use it, having recourse to the syllogistic brief only in cases of doubt. But for the immature analyst of argument the more explicit and detailed method commends itself.

The emphasis laid by the exercises upon the exact analysis of trains of reasoning and arguments should perhaps be still further heightened by an explicit statement of its purpose. No part of the study of argumentation seems to the student more difficult than the correct analysis of his own arguments and of those of other people. But nothing is more indispensable than this to a mastery of argumentation as a practical art. The rapid unfailing insight into the core of an argument, the swift separation of the essential from the non-essential, the sure recognition of major and minor points in the proof of any question, these are the marks of a master logician, or one might say of a trained mind in any field. And it is to such mastery of argument and of thinking that exact analysis tends. The student should be trained to it by every means, analyzing first the simplest arguments, next those with one subsidiary train of reasoning supporting the first, later those containing not only a secondary but a tertiary grade, and so on until the complexest arguments may be resolved at once into their ultimate elements. It may be added that the teacher should by all means supplement the arguments set for analysis in the various exercises by many others drawn from current reading and conversation. The study of argumentation is perhaps most effectually quickened by a judicious selection of arguments and subjects for argument with reference to topics of current interest. The daily newspapers and the magazines furnish always abundant supplies of timely material for a class in argumentation. Toward the close of a course, if the students are sufficiently mature, the complete analysis of such popular arguments as those involved in books like Bellamy's *Looking Backward* or Kidd's *Social Evolution* may safely be attempted.

A considerable amount of oral debating is found to be useful as complementary to the writng. Often an impromptu debate may be held upon a subject before it is assigned for written argument. The question is then talked over as well as thought out, new points of view are suggested and objections raised, so that the written argument becomes better digested than is usually the case when put to paper without such preliminary working over. The writer's own belief in the efficacy of debating as an aid to the study of argumentation may appear from an account of the arrangement of the course as given in Vassar College. The class meets three times a week, twice in separate sections for quiz on the text, for writing and criticism, once for an exercise in which the whole class participates, usually a debate, either formal or impromptu. These debates are not only regarded by the students as the most interesting feature of the course, but they seem fully to have justified their institution by the impetus they have given to the written work.

The course as here laid down is intended to occupy the work of one semester, the class meeting three times a week. It might, however, by the multiplication of exercises and the study of logical principles not discussed at all in this book, be indefinitely expanded.

CHAPTER 1   ARGUMENTATION

We often find ourselves attempting to convince another person that something is or is not true, that a certain course of conduct ought or ought not to
be pursued, or that a certain result will follow a certain action. Only yesterday, it may be, you persuaded another member of your class that Fred Ostrander ought not to be elected class treasurer, or tried to prove to your father
that geometry is a useless branch of study.

If you recall the process by which you induced your classmate not to vote
for Fred Ostrander for treasurer, you will remember that it was something
like this. You told him that Fred was unbusinesslike in his methods, never
paying his class dues till the last minute, not because he hadn't the money, but
because he just forgot to. And then he never wanted a receipt for them, and
never could remember whether he had paid them or not. He was the most
absent-minded member of the class and didn't come to the meetings half the
time. Of course he was popular, but what was wanted for a treasurer was a
good, prompt, wide-awake business-man, who would collect all the dues on
time, keep the books ship-shape, be on hand at every meeting, and know to a
cent just how the class stood financially. No man who couldn't do these
things ought to be treasurer. And it was plain as day that Fred couldn't do one
of them. So your classmate agreed that Fred assuredly ought not to be elected
treasurer of the class.

This was what you had been working for—to make your classmate believe
the thing that you believed, namely, that Fred Ostrander ought not to be
elected treasurer. You wanted to transplant your conviction into his mind.
But you knew at once that it was impossible to do this simply by expressing
your own belief. You might have said to your classmate a dozen times that
Fred Ostrander ought not to be elected, without making him accept that
statement. He would be likely to inquire at once "Why?" and until you
could answer that question satisfactorily, he would refuse to believe in your
conclusion.

But you knew he would want your reasons, so you gave them at once
without even being asked for them. You had come to believe that Fred ought
not to be elected because you had noticed in him certain unbusinesslike
habits and characteristics. In other words you had made these observations
before you came to the conclusion that Fred ought not to be elected. They
had formed part of a process of thinking which ultimately led you to the
belief you desired your classmate to accept. They were the first step in the

path that induced you to the conclusion. Hence, when you wished some one else to reach this belief or conclusion, you naturally conducted him over this same path until he arrived at its goal. He might perhaps have reached it by another road, but you were familiar with this one, having just traversed it yourself, and knew that it would issue in the desired conclusion, hence you naturally guided the steps of your friend into it.

This is perhaps a typical instance of the process called argumentation. It is the act of establishing in the mind of another person a conclusion which has become fixed in your own, by means of setting up in the other person's mind the train of thought or reasoning which has previously led you to this conclusion.[2] Here we have a statement both of the end and of the means employed for attaining the end. The goal is the establishment of a certain belief or conclusion in the mind of the hearer or reader. But as soon as this goal is clearly recognized the question arises—How is it to be attained? How can this conclusion be implanted in the mind of the reader or hearer? It is evident at first glance that no conclusion of a process of thought can be introduced bodily into any person's mind without the train of reasoning which naturally leads to it. A conclusion is not an isolated thing, which can be thrown into another mind from without. A belief is not accepted by one who sees no justification for it. To convince any person of the truth of a proposition requires that he reach that proposition himself as the logical outcome of some process of thought. Hence it is necessary, if one wish to persuade another person to a certain conclusion, that he set up in that person's mind a train of reasoning which is bound to issue in this conclusion.

This, then, is the problem of argumentation: given the conclusion which is to be established in the mind of the hearer or reader, to find the train of ideas which is bound to lead to this conclusion. The solution which at once pre-

---

2. In its statement of the end to be attained this definition agrees substantially with such as the following: "Argumentation is the art of producing in the mind of some one else a belief in the ideas which the speaker or writer wishes the hearer to accept." (Baker, *Principles of Argumentation*, p. 1). "Argumentation is the process of proving or disproving a proposition." (MacEwan, *Essentials of Argumentation*, p. 1.) In both of these definitions, however, the means to attain the ends remains unspecified.

It may further be noted that these definitions do not insist upon the speaker's having previously arrived at the conclusion he would establish in the hearer's mind. It is, however, manifestly impossible that a speaker should be able to conduct his hearer to a goal which he himself has not, at least in imagination, reached. Even when he wishes to convince another person of the truth of a proposition which he himself does not believe, he must imagine himself as having come to belief in it, and trace out the route thereto, in order that he may be able to act as guide.

sents itself is that of using the train of ideas which, in the speaker's mind, has already served to establish the conclusion in question. Let us say, for instance, that the speaker has come to the conclusion that teachers in the primary schools of this country receive very small salaries. If he wishes to convince another person of the truth of this judgment, he will naturally cite the various cases in which such teachers are poorly paid, which, coming to his knowledge, have induced him to this belief. Or if he has become convinced, as in the previous illustration, that Fred Ostrander ought not to be elected treasurer of the class, he will doubtless attempt to bring another person to this view by alleging the reasons which have moved himself, namely, Fred's careless habits, his unpunctuality and irregularity in attendance, with perhaps still other disqualifications of this sort.

This is the most obvious way of finding a train of reasoning pretty certain to issue in the conclusion to be established,—looking into one's own mind and noting the series of ideas which there have actually established the conclusion for one's self. One feels assured that this series should lead to the desired conclusion in another person's mind simply because in his own it has already done so. And, in view of the fact that the mental processes of all normal people follow the same general laws, this assurance is by no means unreasonable. Certain difficulties should, however, be at once noted.

In the first place there is the difficulty of exact knowledge about one's own mental processes. One may think he can tell exactly what train of thought has preceded his arrival at a certain conclusion; but can he be sure that he has not overlooked his real starting-point or included considerations which might indeed be expected to influence him, but which actually had no weight, ignoring the points which were the true determinants of his conclusion? Can he assert with absolute assurance that he has followed the order in which his ideas moved to the conclusion, not transposing or omitting or interpolating any? It is a ticklish matter to determine without other aid than that of one's own impressions. Further assistance may, however, be derived from a knowledge of the typical ways in which other people come to conclusions. Granting that one's fundamental thought-processes do not differ essentially from those of his kind, it is possible to clarify and correct one's impressions of his own trains of reasoning by a knowledge of those typical activities of mind common to all thinking people. The science of these typical activities of mind, commonly called logic, must, then, be detailed to supplement introspection in our search for the train of reasoning which shall lead another person to a given conclusion.

A second difficulty in the process of argumentation is also solved by the assistance of logical principles. Granting that the writer's train of reasoning is clearly and correctly perceived by him, can he be in any way assured that it is not exceptional, different from the thought-processes of other people, and hence not warranted to bring about in another's mind the conclusion it yielded to the writer? Our general postulate that the essential modes of thinking are common to all normal minds renders this belief unlikely, indeed, but still not impossible. It can be absolutely proved or completely discredited only by a comparison of this particular reasoning process of the writer with the typical reasoning processes of other people. And such comparison implies, again, that knowledge of the laws of thought which we call logic.

If, then, the writer is enabled, by familiarity with the typical logical processes, not only to recognize what the train of thought has been which has brought him to a certain conclusion, but to determine whether or not it is so universal in character as to be reasonably certain in another mind to issue in the same conclusion, he is ready to set up his own train of thought in the mind of the reader. But just here a third difficulty may arise. Perhaps this train of reasoning, however clearly and exactly perceived, however normal and universal it may be, yet, because of some peculiar circumstances, refuses to be reproduced in the mind of the other person. Suppose, to take an extreme instance, the case in which a priest wishes to induce a criminal to confess his crime, that an innocent person falsely accused may go free. The priest believes that the criminal ought to do this on the general principle that one ought to do whatever will prevent injustice. But it is impossible to introduce into the mind of the criminal any chain of reasoning in which this principle constitutes the first link. If the priest's only resource is to reproduce the train of thought which originally led him to the conclusion, his case is hopeless; for this train of thought refuses to enter the mind of the criminal, whose conclusion, that he ought to keep still about his crime, is founded upon the accepted principle that one ought to do whatever will save one's skin, or, more broadly, whatever it is for one's interest to do. Under such circumstances, the priest's course is perfectly plain. He must put himself imaginatively in the place of the person he addresses, and then come, by any way he logically can, to the conclusion he desires to establish. Perhaps he can do this by such a thought-process as the following: One ought to do whatever will be best for himself. It will be best for me to confess because the crime is likely to be discovered, and if it is, my sentence may be more severe than if I confess, and at any rate by confession I shall escape the greatest danger of all—that of going to hell ultimately. Having followed such a path of reasoning in imagination, the priest is able to reproduce it in the mind of the criminal and thus establish the conclusion.

We may say, then, that the best way to find a train of reasoning which, if set up in the reader's mind, will establish the conclusion desired by the writer, is for the writer to note carefully the train of reasoning which has led him previously, either in his own proper person, or imaginatively in that of another person, to this same conclusion; his observation of his own reasoning being tested and assured by a knowledge of the typical logical processes of other people.

The three divisions of the process of argumentation reflect themselves in our study of the subject. We shall learn first to examine our own reasoning processes with a view to determine precisely what they are; second, to define and either confirm or correct these observations by a knowledge of the typical reasoning processes of other people; and, third, to reproduce in other minds our own trains of reasoning as thus determined.

EXERCISES

1. Write a list of all the conclusions which you have tried recently to induce some one else to accept. Did you believe the conclusion yourself? What did you do to make your hearer believe it? Did you succeed in making him accept it? Do you know why you succeeded or why you failed? In case you did not succeed, do you think you could have done so by a different method?

2. Write a similar list of all the conclusions to which other people have recently tried to lead you. (Recall sermons and public addresses of any kind as well as private conversations.) Did you accept the conclusion in each case? If so, why? If not, why not? Would you have accepted it if the speaker had given you different reasons? Or if he had presented his reasons in a different order or form?

3. Of the three stages or divisions of the process of argumentation, which is the end and which are means? Distinguish the relative importance of the three as determined by their respective distances from the ultimate end, that of implanting the conclusion in the mind of another person.

4. Write an account, as exact in its details as you can make it, of the way in which you as a child came from your own experiences to believe any or all of the following facts:

(a) Dark corners are not dangerous. (Or, there is nothing to be afraid of in the dark.)

(b) All large children go to school.

(c) Flowers bloom in the spring.

(d) Cats scratch if you squeeze them hard.

(e) Everybody has to pay to ride on the railroad train (or street-car).

(f) Birds sing.

(g) Roses have a sweet smell.

10   Marks in Freshman English

from *The Vassar Miscellany News*,
11 and 21 February 1920.

This exchange, between Buck and a student who complained of unfair grading practices, was published in the Vassar student newspaper. In her response, Buck explains the criteria used in grading compositions and the method of consulting with other instructors, and she urges the student to examine her own complaint. She writes here as an administrator rather than as a theorist of a student-centered curriculum. By 1920 Buck's writing and publishing energies were devoted to theater, both with the Vassar Dramatic Workshop and the Poughkeepsie Community Theatre, and she was publishing relatively little on the subject of composition. Although she does acknowledge the possibility that a student's perception of her work may legitimately differ from her teacher's, Buck assures the readers that the English Department does everything in its power to avoid any unfairness. Buck seems to advocate a single, Platonic standard against which student papers are measured and does not challenge the issue of grading per se. But note how her understanding of a student's originality takes on a decidedly more social nature.

THE INJUSTICE OF MARKS

To the Editors of the *News*:

Marks are a measure of academic work. They are the standard by which our scholarship, our mental capacity is judged among family and fellow students. To a great degree they indicate our success in college. Yet how are they given! One teacher emphasizes one phase of a subject to the exclusion of the phase another stresses. One gives lessons double the length of another's. One is a high marker, another a low marker. No consideration is taken of natural gifts, of natural handicaps. Effort is too often disregarded. In examinations one type of mind only is provided for,—the quick working mind. Speed instead of being but one part of the examination is greater than the whole. The slow plodder who arrives with flying colors at the end has her natural handicap increased. Too many English teachers make form their criterion. To it must ideas, originality, independence of thought, imagination, breadth, quality of reading bow in subjection. Form without ideas is futile and ineffectual. Ideas without form are still a dynamic force. Yet how many "d"s are given for lack of form, how many "b"s for its presence with an entire absence of ideas!

What are marks for? To shock into increased effort, to discourage faults, to boost upward? So unjustly given they count for nought. A course into which the most has been put, the greatest gotten out, receives a low mark. Of what use is the mark! Cast it aside. Disregard it. It is not a measure of intellectual ability, of mental effort, of gain received. It neither discourages nor encourages, for it is valueless. It is a symbol of injustice inciting to rebellion.

Upon marks thus unfairly given depends our right to stay in college. Personality, strength of character, personal magnetism, superlative honesty and determination—have they no part? Breadth of mind, sanity, balance, ideals, capacity for appreciation, are they to count for nothing? These are no more the gifts of the gods than pure mental ability. They can be developed. Is not the purpose of college to fashion well-balanced efficient women who shall take their place in life with profit and gain to the world and the race and happiness to themselves? Is its aim only the development of mental ability and intellectual interest? It is the only acknowledged, recognized one. Strong personalities whose impress is left at every point of contact are forced to leave while weak ineffectual nonentities remain.

H.C. '23

Marks in Freshman English

To the Editors of the *News*:

"H.C. 1923" evidently does not know what the basis of marking in freshman English is, although Miss Wylie, in her lecture to the whole class in October, explained very definitely what kind of training the course is designed to give and what constitutes good work in it.

The required course in English attempts to increase every student's ability to read and write English,—her ability, that is, to gain precisely ideas or experiences from the literature written in her mother-tongue and to convey ideas or experiences clearly to others through her own writing.

Each of these ends is equally important and indispensable. Marked ability in reading, as evidenced either by its wide range or by an unusual accuracy and fullness of understanding of what is read, would not secure an *a*, without a corresponding degree of skill in conveying ideas to others through language. Nor would a considerable power in writing counter balance, (if the two could ever be associated), slipshod habits of reading, or an incapacity to grasp any but the simplest of unrelated ideas as presented in print.

The degree of the student's skill in using this two-fold art of communication is, then, the measure of her mark in freshman English. But since the art is twofold, involving both the gaining of other people's ideas or experiences and the transmitting to others of our own ideas or experiences, and since each of these processes involves many different activities, no one point of excellence, such as "form," can possibly overshadow all others in the reckoning of grades. "Form" is, indeed, important,—not, however, as a mere convention arbitrarily imposed from without, but as the flexible, ever-changing means by which our speech is adjusted to convey our ideas effectively. A student who cannot intelligently adjust means to ends in the process of "getting over" her relatively simple ideas to a particular reader has not yet attained such control of the writing act as the freshman course is designed to give. And a marked incapacity in this direction, indicated by habitual incorrectness of technique, would, like an equally undeveloped power of reading, classify a student as below passing grade.

So much for "form". As for "originality", and "ideas", if by these terms is meant such thinking as the student evolves solely from her inner consciousness, it does not constitute a large factor in the practical situation. Most of our thinking, whether we know it or not, is rooted in some suggestion we have gained from talk or reading. It is the constructive use which we make of these suggestions which tests our thinking-power. And we do not fully "get" other people's ideas (i.e. do not read with complete understanding) until we have done something with these ideas—corroborated, challenged, tested, refuted or modified them, compared them with our previous ideas or experience, applied them in some new quarter, in a word, carried them a step beyond the point where the writer had left them. Even when we read a description, we do not fully "realize" the experience it represents, until we have in some measure squared it with similar experiences of our own, or recognized its differences from them. Such reconstruction of the writer's material in terms of our own mental life may or may not involve "originality". That depends on one's definition of the term. But in any case, we must carry our reading to this point, if we would get all that the writer can give us, and if we would have anything worth conveying to anyone else. For only as we relate other people's experiences and ideas to our own are we able to see what we have to contribute, however small it may be, to the sum of human consciousness.

This evaluation of the experiences or ideas gained from reading, is then, an intermediate stage between reading and writing, and the student's ability at this point is taken into account in grading her work. Her "critical ability" is also estimated. But this, again, is involved in such practical understanding of the process of communication, as the course is designed to give. Only as the student knows, both in theory and in practice, what makes communication successful or unsuccessful, is she able to recognize excellencies and defects either in her own writing or in that of others.

Four points, then, enter into the reckoning of a student's mark in freshman English: (1) her ability to get other people's experiences or ideas precisely through reading, (2) to make some constructive use of this material, (3) to transmit effectively the results of this mental activity to others by means of language, and (4) to judge her own efforts at communication, as well as other people's, to the end of making her own writing steadily more effective. The last examination in freshman English was designed to test these four points. Its results merely supplemented those of the semester's writing and class-work, and counted for not more than one-third. If the evidence presented by both the semester's work and the examination showed that the student had gained an exceptionally high degree of power in all four of these respects, she would, of course, receive an *a*; if her achievement at all four points was regarded as well above the average, but not exceptional, she would have *b*; and so on, down to *f.* The foregoing statements, however, cover only the cases in which the student's ability at all four points is approximately equal. In such cases, the difficulty of assigning a just mark is relatively small. But where excellence at one pont must be balanced against only average ability (or less) at another, the problem is more difficult. Its difficulty is not, however, unrecognized by those who assign the marks, and every effort is made to take into account at its full value each of the constituent factors. The various permutations and combinations involved in these estimates are too complicated to work out in the space at hand, but their application to any given case will be made by any instructor upon the request of the student concerned.

An estimate of a student's skill in any process is, of course, more difficult to make and more open to question, than a judgment as to her mere knowledge of particular facts. Ratings of proficiency in an art must obviously vary with the judge's understanding of that art. The mark assigned to a given student in English might therefore be expected to vary less among different teachers, who are about equally skilled in the arts of reading and writing, than between a teacher and a student who is relatively unskilled in them. This may, in some degree, account for the occasional divergences in judgment between the teacher of an English course and her students. If the students understood the art of communication by language as thoroughly as the teacher presumably does, their judgments of a particular student's ability in it might accord better with hers. It is, in fact, to gain a better understanding of what constitutes intelligent reading and effective writing that they are taking the course. This does not mean that a student's estimate of her own or of her classmate's attainment is necessarily wrong and the teacher's necessarily right; but in cases of marked divergence it furnishes a possible alternative to the more usual explanations of favoritism or injustice. It should also be remembered that the student often measures her own work and that of her class-mates by a relative standard. The best work done in a section of a low grade of ability or training, may deserve no more than a *d* or at most a *c*; while, if ranked on the basis of this section alone, it might seem to be of *a* quality. A comparison of the writing done in less advanced sections with that published in *The Sampler*, might often serve to rectify such partial judgments.

The danger of a teacher's marking her students either too low or too high because she is estimating their work in terms of an advanced or of a backward section rather than in terms of the class as a whole is a real danger, but one that is guarded against at every point, both by the comparison of papers and marks among teachers of sections of different grades, and by the practice of assigning sections so that each teacher deals with students of all the different grades in the same year if possible, or at any rate in consecutive years. The fact that sections in freshman English are graded explains, by the way, the fact sometimes cited as evidence of Miss So-and-So's unfairness, that "about half of her section got *d!*"

In order to standardize individual judgments, the teachers of freshman English meet after each semester's examination and exchange papers. Doubtful papers are often read and marked independently by three or four teachers. When the readers do not agree in the marks given to a paper, this paper is fully discussed, the reasons for each mark compared and a final evaluation jointly reached. Thus a semester mark, instead of being the irresponsible expression of a single teacher's personal prejudice in favor of one quality, such as "form", in a student's work, is rather a balanced complex of several judgments, often of more than one person, and always upon evidence presented by class-recitations, themes and examination, as to the student's mastery of at least four distinct processes involved in the practical arts of reading and writing English.

The recent questioning of the basis on which marks are assigned is a promising indication of a more or less general consciousness on the part of students that their standards are not always as those of the faculty. Let it go on!—not in a spirit of resentment or accusation on the one side, or of self-justification on the other, but with an honest desire on both sides to compare and evaluate our bases of judgment. Only thus will every student come to understand clearly what each course is for and how she can intelligently avail herself of the utmost it offers. And only thus can the faculty, testing their own standards anew, be sure that they are working with the students on a foundation of mutual understanding and confidence.

Gertrude Buck

IV Holistic Grammar Instruction

11   The Sentence-Diagram

from *Educational Review*
13 (March 1897): 250–60.

This essay, written while Buck was still at Michigan, continues the argument of psycholog-
ical development elaborated in her dissertation on metaphor. In the place of the diagram
first presented by Alonzo Reed and Brainerd Kellogg in Higher Lessons in English *(1878),*
Buck proposes amoebalike figures that reflect the growth of thought; she argues that
ultimately something like a tree will be needed to accurately reflect the complexity of both
thought and sentence. What Gerald Mulderig has called Buck's "admittedly quaint
amoeba and tree diagrams" (97) illustrated what she believed to be the true psychological
origins of language and emphasized an organic rather than a mechanical orientation to
grammar instruction.

Those who attempt to justify the use of the sentence-diagram in the teaching of grammar commonly do so upon one of two grounds. Either the
diagram represents the actual structure of the sentence, but fleshless, articulated, so that the student may see plainly its anatomy as he cannot do in the
living body; or the diagram, though not in any real sense representing the
actual structure of the sentence, yet serves as an arbitrary mechanical device
for expressing visually the parts of speech contained in the sentence, with
their relations to each other, as the science of grammar has ordained them.
The use of the diagram implied in the first defense may be termed logical,
that in the second formal.

Let us examine the first of these conceptions of the diagram. We shall all
agree that a diagram which truly represents to the eye the actual logical or
psychological structure of the sentence is a desideratum. An X-ray photo-
graph of the sentence is needed. Such the diagram purports to be, but can its
claims be allowed? If we assume that the horizontal, straight-line diagram
represents with any degree of accuracy the structure of the sentence, what
must we conclude as to that structure? First, that the sentence is a definitely
fixed and bounded thing, about which we have no concern save to know that
it now is, and that it can be chopped up into small pieces for rearrangement
in a set pattern called the diagram. Any sense of its origin in the mental
processes of one individual, or its destination in the mind of another, is

excluded. It is enough to know that the sentence is here, printed in a book, and that it may be broken up by him who has the skill to do it into minuter fragments. But, in the second place, the very coexistence of these separately named fragments in the sentence implies the problem, How did they come to be here together? Did they develop successively out of the inchoate sentence, as a psychological fire-mist? Is the history of the sentence that of the solar system—first, a nebulous whole, out of which, one by one in the process of development, emerged the various members? That is, does the sentence, psychologically, precede the separate words? Or do the separate words pre-exist in their isolation, these being gathered up by the speaker and joined each to each to form the sentence? The latter conception is that which has always been held by our grammarians, and which underlies our use of the straight-line diagram. The teacher, and at least the brighter pupils, under-stand that in diagramming we are but undoing the work of our hands, in order that we may the more clearly see just how we have done it.

This, then, is our conclusion from the premise that the diagram accurately represents the structure of the sentence—that the sentence comes into being not as the natural outcome of psychological or social conditions, growing and differentiating according to biological laws, but that it is more or less an arbitrary thing, once consisting of separate words, which were selected, per-haps, from a dictionary, and laboriously tacked together by someone who set out to make a sentence—it may be even with the malign intention of printing it in a book, to be diagrammed! More briefly, the structure of the sentence is mechanic rather than organic. It has not grown, but has been manufactured. Stated so baldly as this, the conclusion is manifestly absurd. Yet we have been so long accustomed to regard the sentence from the standpoint of formal grammar—that is, as a thing dead and static, a manufacture instead of a growth—that it will not be superfluous to discuss briefly what the living sentence actually is.

Let us say, in the first place, that the sentence is any form of words which conveys an idea from one person to another. It may, then, not be more than one word—such a word, for instance, as an interjection. We often hear a boy who cuts his fingers while whittling say, "Ouch!" "Cracky!" "Jiminy!" or use some other favorite exclamation of surprise and pain. He may, very likely, in another instant add, "I tell you, that hurt!" but we do not need to be told that. His exclamation has already conveyed his thought to us. And, in the same way, the girl who comes unexpectedly upon one of her companions says "Good gracious!" or "Mercy sakes!" adding, as soon as she gets her breath, "How you scared me!" But in this case, as before, we do not really need this added sentence to tell us that the girl is frightened. That we know from the first exclamation. The interjection has, in both cases, conveyed an idea, complete, though primitive. We gain from it the speaker's half-formulated sense of a certain state of things, felt in the one case as pain and in the other as fright.

That the interjection does represent a state of things dimly perceived by the speaker will become more evident if we try to determine, in so far as we can, just what is this thought of the boy and the girl that the exclamation has conveyed to us. And perhaps we can best do that by going back to memory for it. If you can remember just what you thought at a certain time when you were hurt, and cried out with some exclamation such as our whittling boy used, you will find that at first, just as you cried out, you did not think anything distinctly. You had a confused feeling of pain that made you say "Ouch!" but for the shortest possible time you didn't know what had made it, or how. Then, in another instant, you had realized that you yourself had caused it by cutting yourself with your knife. In this way your thought grew out of the confused feeling of pain. It has two parts now, yourself and the cutting, while before there was only one—the confused feeling of pain. These two parts were in the one feeling all the time, but you could not see them at first. Only as your thought grew did it divide so that you could see its two sides or aspects.

So a child's thought grows, by successive differentiations from a homogeneous whole. A very young child knows only that it is comfortable or uncomfortable. If it is uncomfortable it cries, but it does not know that the sun hurts its eyes or that a pin is pricking it. Its thought has not divided into the sun and its mode of acting on its eyes, nor into the pain and its mode of acting on its flesh. The child's thought is hardly yet a thought at all, but a vague, undifferentiated feeling. But by successive experiences of comfort and discomfort, it learns, as we say, to distinguish—that is, to separate out of this jelly-like mass of feeling the chief agent of the feeling and the way in which it has acted to produce that feeling. The thought has grown, and divided as it has grown.

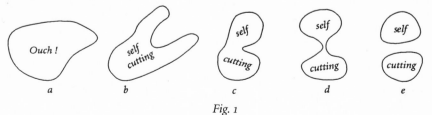

Fig. 1

The first nebulous idea of a state of things is like the seed in which lies folded, yet indistinguishable, the entire tree. Unless you are a scientist, you cannot tell by looking at the acorn which part will be the trunk of the tree, which the roots, and which the leaves. When it begins to grow, you see a green shoot rising from the ground. This, too, is one, like the seed; but after a while it unfolds into two leaves; its stem grows and finally becomes the trunk of the tree, which divides into two main branches, these each into two again, and so on until, as you look up into the tree, you find its smallest twigs have divided off two and two from the next larger, and so on to the trunk itself. The tree has divided as it has grown. And so with every thought. It is at first one and undivided; a confused sense, perhaps of pain, which, as it grows, sends off its two main branches—the thought of the chief agent in producing the state of things felt as pain, and the thought of the way in which this agent acted to produce that pain.

If thoughts divide as they grow, we should expect to find also that sentences, which convey thoughts, do the same thing; for otherwise, how could a thought that had begun to divide be communicated to another person? It would need to be expressed just as if it were still undivided. But we know that we do express, by means of sentences, thoughts that have already divided. You say "Ouch!" at the moment when the knife slips, and you feel the pain of the cut without thinking clearly what has happened or what has caused it; but

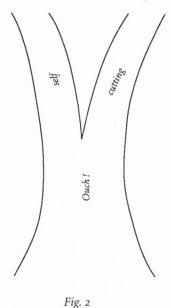

self *cutting*

Ouch!

Fig. 2

when someone asks, "What's the matter?" your thought has had time to grow and divide; you realize you are hurt, and by a cut from your knife, and answer, "I cut myself with my knife." Your thought has by this time divided into the two thoughts: yourself that has been hurt on the one side, and the way in which you have been hurt on the other; and so the sentence also divides. Anyone who heard you say "Ouch!" knew at once that you had been hurt; but, as your thought grew, it divided more distinctly until you could say plainly: "I cut myself with my knife." The "Ouch!" has grown and divided into a sentence with two parts. Let us consider another dividing sentence. Let us suppose, for instance, that you are a child set to take care of your younger brother, and have let him play in the yard while you tried to read and watch him at the same time, and suddenly you looked up to see that he was nowhere in sight. Your first sentence, if you stopped to say anything at all, would probably be something like this: "Why! Fred's run away!" When you said "Why!" you did not think anything clearly, but were shocked, startled. Something had happened. But in an instant this vague sense of something wrong had divided itself into the thought of the person who had caused the shock and the way in which he had done it. That is, you thought "Fred" on the one hand, and "has run away" on the other. Or, if you went home from school some afternoon and found the corn all trampled down, and cattle tracks on the ground, you would probably exclaim in dismay: "Oh, my! The cows have been in the corn!" Your first "Oh, my!" meant dismayed surprise at the state in which you found things; but in an instant you realized that this state of things was occasioned by the cows, and that they had done the damage by being in the corn. And so your sentence split up, as your thought had done, into two parts—"the cows" and "have been in the corn." It is not so easy to see that all sentences develop like these from a nebulous, ill-defined consciousness of a state of things into a two-branched thought of the agent of that state of things and its method of action; but if there were time to analyze each variety of sentence separately, we should be convinced that the same fundamental method of growth is characteristic of all those expressed judgments which we call sentences. Let us pause to analyze just one variety—such as is represented by the sentences, "The knife is sharp," "The milk is sour," "That chimney is hot," "My ankle is lame." This is the kind of sentence with the analysis of which formal logic is wont to begin; hence its fallacious conception of the copula as a coupling pin. When once we come

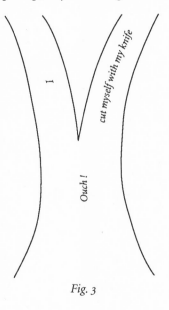

Fig. 3

to study sentences as live, growing things, warm from the speaker's mind, we must see that the copula-sentence is a shorthand reduction from some earlier, livelier saying. It is a petrifaction, or a desiccation of the verbal sentence. This will, however, become more apparent in the course of the analysis.

The whittling boy, of whom we have previously spoken, would say "Ouch! That knife's sharp!" for precisely the same reason that he said "Ouch! I tell you that hurt!" He has cut his finger with the knife, and, in saying "This knife is sharp," he says "This knife acts sharp," This knife acts as sharp things do," that is, "This knife acts in such a way as to show that it has a good edge." These facts he expresses in short form by saying, "The knife is sharp." The pain of which he is conscious in his cut finger divides itself into that, on the one hand, which had most to do in producing the pain, "The knife," and, on the other, the way in which the knife produced it, "is (acts) sharp."

In the same manner, if you touch the chimney on a lighted lamp, you will at once draw back your hand with the exclamation, "Whew! that's hot!" But by this you evidently mean that the chimney has burned you, or has acted upon your hand as hot things do. You are conscious, in exclaiming "Whew!" of a state of things, a pain, which divides straightway into the chimney as the thing most active in bringing about this pain, and the way in which it acted to bring

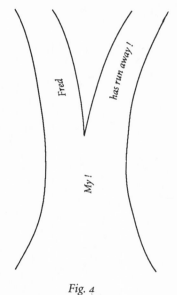

about the pain. It acts as if it were hot, it acts as hot things do, it is hot. We continually reduce in this way a verbal to a copula-sentence. The first time John comes to a decision without due deliberation, we say charitably, "John acted hastily in that matter." But when John has acted hastily, not once, but half a dozen times, to our personal knowledge, we shorten the judgment process by affirming not, "John acts as hasty persons do," or "in a hasty manner," but "John is hasty," "John's a hasty fellow."

In the same way we learn to say, "The report of the gun was loud," rather than "It jarred the ground under our feet and deafened our ears"; "My medicine is bitter," instead of "It puckers up my face," and "The sun is bright," and "It dazzles my eyes."

Fig. 4

We have become so accustomed to this shorthand method of expression that we do not realize that it was ever anything else with us. We find it difficult to get back into the habit of the savage and the child, who naturally think of persons and things as always acting in some way, as always doing something. Here, however, the scientific attitude will help us. It is our scientist who now habitually thinks of every object in the natural world as somehow acting upon every other. He recognizes that things are said by us to be round, green, or smooth because they act in a certain way upon our eyes; that a ribbon is declared to be red because it acts in such a way (that is, by stopping all the yellow, green, blue, and violet rays of the sun, and allowing only the red ones to pass to us) that it produces a state of things recognized as red.

When we can put ourselves back in our own experience, or in that of the race, to a period in which the copula-sentence was fluid, we find it, like the verbal sentence, a doubly branching development out of a single state of things dimly perceived by the speaker.

If there were time, it might be shown that the various kinds of sentence—declarative, interrogative, exclamatory, and imperative— grow in the same manner; their differences being matters of the extent of their growth rather than of its method. We should also find, as we might indeed expect, that the sentence does not stop growing when once it has divided into two main branches, any more than

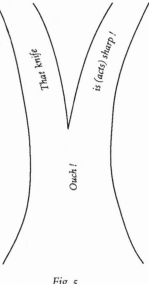

Fig. 5

the tree does. As the two main limbs of the tree keep dividing into smaller branches, then into twigs and leaves, so does the sentence. The subject and the predicate divide and subdivide into clauses, phrases, and finally into words.

Now it is clear that if we are to represent adequately the vital structure of sentences regarded as products of growth, we shall need some device other than the straight-line diagram. This diagram will of necessity convey the notion that the subject and the predicate have been taken from different quarters and set arbitrarily alongside each other ready for adjectives, adverbs, phrases, and clauses to be successively tacked to them. But this is, as we know, very far from the truth of the matter. The interjection has expressed for us in a single word the whole sentence, albeit yet undeveloped. We have almost seen it grow before our eyes. Putting ourselves imaginatively in the place of the speaker, we have traced the twofold branchings of this embryo thought, and have seen the subject and the

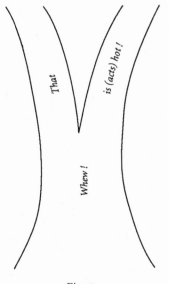

Fig. 6

predicate unfold almost simultaneously out of the sentence-germ. This unfolding we may, if we choose, represent by such a figure as the amœba, with its tentative outreachings. A blackboard full of amœbas, while perhaps somewhat shocking to the sensibilities of the old-fashioned grammarian, is yet several degrees less absurd, and infinitely less misleading than the network of prim straight lines in which we are wont to encase the several members of the sentence. The amœba diagram would not, however, carry us very far. As the subject branches, and the predicate in its turn begins to divide, the amœba must be abandoned for a more highly developed structure, such as that of the tree. This, with its ramifications, is capable of figuring the most complex sentence likely to grow from a human mind. But it is not necessary to insist on the tree. The active-minded teacher may use a hundred diagrams, the more the better, if only they be true to the thing they claim to represent. They will not, however, be truthful representations of sentence-structure unless, like the amœba- or the tree-diagram, they take account of the growth of the sentence, figuring it as a natural development rather than as a mechanical construction.

It is surely high time that this idea of growth, now dominant in other fields of investigation, dawn upon the darkness of grammar. We have been too long bound by the mechanical notions of an earlier and a cruder philosophy. Before the evolutionary hypothesis gained credence in biology, and while the animal was still regarded as a compound of his various members, these being joined each to each in some little-understood way, then logic, using the conceptions furnished by science, held the judgment to be a hitching together of the particular and the universal, and grammar had no theory to account for the sentence except that it was a similar tacking of predicate to subject. But biology has long since discarded the notion of a mechanical splicing of part to part as the genesis of the animal structure, to adopt the theory of successive differentiations of the various members from one homogeneous jelly-like mass of protoplasm, wherein lay the promise and potency of the developed creature. Logic, following this cue, has, in our own day, substituted for the notion of the judgment as particular plus universal, or percept plus concept, that of the vague, nebulous feeling of a state of things which divides, on the one side, into the agent of that state of things, and, on the other, into that agent's method of action. And grammar, which has hitherto embodied the conceptions of the old logic, may now fairly be expected to follow the later philosophy in its less artificial notions of the structure of thought, thus breathing new life into the traditional forms of syntax. The new point of view is inevitable. As it has come to prevail in science and philosophy, so must it in the study of language. And of its advent we surely need seek no further sign than the widespread revolt against the use of the old diagram in the teaching of grammar.

To conclude the argument: The old diagram does not represent the actual structure of the sentence, as our best psychology has it. Therefore it cannot be justified as the visual representation of sentence-anatomy. And still less can it be justified as a mechanical device, convenient though inexact. For, far as we must with all our best efforts come from imparting to our pupils right conceptions of any subject, we dare not willfully mislead them by the use of any "device," however temptingly "convenient," that does not truthfully represent, so far as we can judge, the reality which it symbolizes.[1]

1. The organic character and growth of the sentence is suggested by scattered observations of Romanes' *Mental evolution in man*, and, more explicitly, in Jespersen's *Progress in language*. The last paragraph of the preface to Bosanquet's *Logic* hints at this conception, but the body of the work develops it no further. The foregoing suggestions have, however, been for me *ex post facto*. But I am genuinely indebted, for my fundamental notions of the logic of the sentence, to certain implications in unpublished lectures on the Logic of Ethics, delivered by Professor John Dewey at the University of Chicago, October to December, 1895, and to some investigations into the psychology of the judgment-process made at the time by Dr. A. F. McLennan, the Fellow in Philosophy at the University of Chicago. Finally, in rhetoric, a parallel conception is found in the just-issued *Composition-Rhetoric* of Professor Fred Newton Scott of the University of Michigan, the lessons entitled, "How paragraphs grow."

12   The Psychology of the Diagram

from *School Review*
5 (April 1897): 240–42, 470–72.

The two letters reprinted here grew out of a discussion by the Michigan Schoolmasters'
Club of a paper delivered by Buck. F. A. Barbour elaborates on that discussion, and Buck
briefly responds from Indianapolis, where she taught high school for a year. The most
important argument for Buck is whether or not the diagram reflects the way sentences
actually form. According to psychological theories, the linear sentence diagram does not,
and Buck writes that "no conceivable advantages could neutralize the tremendous disad-
vantage of untruthfulness." This exchange illustrates the disciplinary debate on a popular
pedagogical method for teaching language. Buck wrote about grammar instruction on
several occasions. See, for instance, "The Foundations of English Grammar Teach-
ing" and "Some Preliminary Considerations in Planning the Revision of Grammatical
Terminology."

*E*ditor of the School Review.
In the report of the proceedings of the Michigan Schoolmasters Club in
the February number of the SCHOOL REVIEW my own discussion of the paper
upon The Psychology of the Diagram is limited to a single sentence. I requested that this brief report be given in the expectation that the paper would
appear in full in the REVIEW and that I should then have an opportunity to
discuss it and the remarks made upon it somewhat at length. As it is, this
brief letter must suffice.

We are told that the diagram is faulty because it does not represent the
psychological genesis of the sentence from a single undifferentiated word like
the interjection. But what, pray, has English grammar, as taught in the public
schools, to do with this genesis of the sentence? "I have cut my finger with my
knife." Such a sentence, it is said, is an outgrowth psychologically of a sensation of pain which expressed itself at first in a simple exclamation. Very well,
if that be so, it may be an interesting fact to the student of the origin of
language, but what has it to do with the teaching of grammar in the seventh
and eighth grades or in the ordinary high school?

If we are to get any disciplinary value from the study of grammar, any real
knowledge of syntax; indeed, if we are to teach grammar at all, it must be

done through analysis. We must consider the sentence as a living product, as an organism made up of a subject and its modifiers and a predicate verb and its modifiers. We must take the organism apart and we must put it together again. In fact, if we teach grammar pedagogically, we shall make the sentence our point of departure.

We shall develop from it the idea of noun, pronoun, inflection, agreement, word, phrase, clause, etc. Of course, analysis may be overdone, but as a method it is absolutely indispensable to any sound progress whatsoever. But how about the "genesis of the sentence psychologically from a single undifferentiated word?" How about involving the false conception of the nature of a sentence, the conception that it is a machine like a watch, for instance, to be taken to pieces and put together again in order to learn its structure?" The entire argument of our philosophic objectors to the diagram holds its validity just as truly against oral analysis as it does against the diagram, and we should have been somewhat relieved if they had condescended to notice method long enough to tell us *how* they would teach grammar. Have they some scheme by which they purpose to inject the psychologic genesis of the sentence into the minds of our boys and girls in the public schools; or, if some diagram is useful, as they admit, how will they project some retinal image of this interesting origin of the sentence into the field of external vision? We are anxious about it.

Now the fact of the matter is that the diagram as an instrument or aid in teaching grammar in the public schools has both its advantages and its disadvantages. Had we space at our disposal, we should be glad to discuss these somewhat in detail. Our point, however, is that the "conservative thinking" which our critic calls for demands a judicial consideration of both the advantages and the disadvantages, not a prejudiced emphasis of the disadvantages alone, not the scant courtesy of declaring that the "systems of diagramming now in vogue rest upon superficial and arbitrary knowledge, and that the use made of them smacks very generally of charlatanism!"

In conclusion we wish to notice one or two statements of our critic: "There are a thousand variations that no system yet devised can exhibit," he says; "the diagram as a method of recitation or examination must remain hopelessly deficient." The first statement is an exaggeration. There are a few constructions which we have not been able to find symbols for in any system of diagram; but they are few in number, and we are no more disturbed by them than we are by unparsable idioms or constructions whose history is difficult to trace. We do not discard all parsing and analysis on account of these idioms and constructions. The second statement is a mistake, and is made without the writer ever having studied the system of diagram in detail; not a commendable *method*, certainly of settling a pedagogic problem.

Concerning the advantages of the diagram, a final statement or two, which space will not permit us to elaborate. (1) The diagram does, in a general way, fairly well represent the grammatical structure of the English sentence. (2) With young pupils, the understanding of grammatical relations in English is especially difficult because of our lack of inflections; in this respect, the diagram, appealing to the eye, is a sort of substitute for the inflections of foreign languages. This is its chief psychologic value, rendered in no respect invalid because it does not portray the historical development of the sentence. Basing our opinion upon some twenty years of observation and experience, we reiterate the statement of Superintendent Perry of Ann Arbor, that "It is not too much to say that grammar as a productive study has been made possible in the seventh and eighth grades by the diagram." (3) In high schools, and in normal schools with large classes, the diagram is an indispensable aid in the rapid conduct of recitation; and to the teacher overburdened with much manuscript it is a sort of god-send as a system of stenography.

That we may not seem to have overlooked the disadvantages, which we have not space to discuss, allow us, as a final word, to say that before the County Commissioners of the state, as well as the Schoolmasters' Club, we frankly admit that owing to the abuses of the diagram arising from faulty teaching, it is a fair question whether as an instrument of instruction it has not done quite as much harm as good in the public schools of the state. We are convinced, however, that the disadvantages are not inherent in the system itself, but that they are due rather to abuses which it is the duty of sound pedagogy to correct.

Very truly yours,

F. A. Barbour

MICHIGAN STATE NORMAL SCHOOL

The gist of Professor Barbour's contribution (in the April number of the SCHOOL REVIEW) to the discussion of the psychology of the diagram seems to be the time-honored objection of the pedagogue to every innovation in education—"it cannot be adjusted to fit our methods." Doubtless it is true that the psychological genesis of the sentence will not avail to teach the subject of grammar as that subject is today commonly understood—that is, accounting it to be the science of crystallized or fossilized thought-structure, the anatomy not the physiology, of sentential expression. If that is the grammar we want to teach now, as we have done in the past, let be. The straight-line Reed and Kellogg diagram will adequately serve us.

But those who still insist upon this diagram, and thus upon the outworn conception of grammar which it implies, seem not to realize that they are fighting the flood of irresistible progress in education. The all but universal disfavor into which the subject of grammar has fallen, not alone in the higher circles of pedagogical thought, but among the practical and progressive teachers of our primary and secondary schools, bears witness to the fact that this subject is going the way of botany and zoölogy, of psychology and logic, whose conversion from formal to biological sciences is a matter of comparatively recent history. The advocates of the straight-line diagram are playing today the rôle of objectors fifty years ago to the study of plant physiology. "How does the embryology, the physiological development, of the plant structure, help us to classify a buttercup in the genus ranunculaceæ?" they inquired scornfully. But we have found that there are things more vital in the science of botany than the Linnæan classification. It is now somewhat late in the day for protest against the dominant tendency in education to view all structures from the standpoint of growth, of evolution. This tendency has been unsuccessfully resisted in science and in philosophy. Can we hope that even the stern encasements of grammar will be able to prevail against it?

It is true that the new psychology of the sentence has not yet been digested into a detailed method of teaching grammar. But patience. No genuine "system" of teaching any subject springs full-grown into birth, but forms itself slowly out of a new point of view, such as in grammar the later theory of sentence-structure affords. And certainly the suggestion that the organic constitution of the sentence be represented by the growing diagram, such as that of the tree, the amœba, or the solar system, rather than by the static diagram of crossing straight lines, is nothing unless it be a practical suggestion looking toward the pedagogy of the new grammar. The whole point of the paper read at the English conference in Ann Arbor, and later published in the *Educational Review*, was the recommendation that a diagram be used in teaching grammar, which represents truly the biological development of the sentence-thought. This the tree diagram does. This the straight-line diagram does not. And, since it is complained that certain "advantages" accruing from the use of the straight-line diagram have been ignored, let it be said that both these advantages (those of representing sentence-structure to the eye of the pupil and of serving as a stenographic device for the teacher) are secured equally well by the use of the biological diagram; and, furthermore, if this were not so, no conceivable advantages could neutralize the tremendous disadvantage of untruthfulness. If the straight-line diagram is not true to the structure of the sentence, its supporters have no arguments for it strong enough to overbear that fact. The whole matter lies here. There is only one question to settle, and that is the question, "Does the straight-line diagram truthfully represent the actual structure of the sentence?" And for the answer to this question we have no appeal but to modern psychology, which at once and emphatically negatives Professor Barbour's statement that "the straight-line diagram does in a general way fairly represent the grammatical structure of the English sentence." The straight-line diagram unqualifiedly *mis*represents that structure, as it is understood by the accredited psychology of the present day; and in the face of this fact all minor contentions fade into the background.

Allow me to correct a misapprehension on the part of Professor Barbour. The genesis of the sentence is not of historical interest alone, or even chiefly, since such genesis takes place in the mind of every child who utters a sentence. It is the development in the speaker's mind of the inchoate thought into clearly differentiate utterance that concerns us. I should not care to affirm that the interjection was historically the earliest form of speech, though from psychological considerations I might be inclined to that view. That puzzle has, I believe, been relinquished by philologists, and I am not so rash as to attempt its solution offhand. What I do assert is only that the interjection represents adequately the first vague stage of a thought in the mind of the person who afterwards utters from it a somewhat primitive sentence. From interjection to developed sentence is the progress of a single thought in a single human brain. Beyond that we need not for our purposes go.

Professor Barbour rightly says: "If we teach grammar pedagogically we shall make the sentence our point of departure." I would not only indorse this statement, but go a step further still, and say that the sentence must be our point of departure and also of return. It is at once the starting point and goal. It is, rightly understood, the whole subject of grammar. And it is for this reason that I must again urge the fundamental necessity of regarding the sentence from the psychological point of view, not as the mathematical formula, "subject + predicate = sentence," but as a living and growing organism, which has developed from a simple to a complexer unity. Let us have done, as speedily as may be, with the mechanical *e pluribus unum* conception of the sentence, and read the development of expression as we have come to read that of life and of thought, in terms of biological growth.

Gertrude Buck

INDIANAPOLIS, IND.

13   Make-Believe Grammar

from *School Review*
17 (January 1909): 21–33.

This essay (originally read before the Michigan Schoolmasters' Club in Ann Arbor, Michigan, April 2, 1908) justifies teaching grammar and suggests the ways such instruction should be handled. If grammar instruction does not acknowledge language as a means of communication first and foremost it seems "make-believe," and the purpose of the work seems to be to meet a requirement or to show off. Given formulaic instruction (e.g., to mix a predicate from one column with a subject from another), students learn to think of language itself as mechanical rather than as a living, changing thing "of unrivaled importance to the social order." The argument might be heard today as advocates for "whole language" and "academic writing" identify real contexts as crucial for student learning.

Richard Grant White's statement that "nearly all of our so-called English grammar is mere make-believe grammar"[1] has recently been quoted with approval by Professor Tolman, of the University of Chicago, in his interesting account of "The Revival of English Grammar."[2] By "make-believe grammar" both writers mean, as Professor Tolman states, the application of rules modeled upon those of the highly inflected Latin language to the facts of the English tongue, which is almost wholly uninflected. As conspicuous examples of such unwarranted borrowings from Latin grammar are cited the objective case of nouns and the agreement of finite verbs with their subjects. In both these instances we have in English no modification of form to correspond with the Latin nomenclature; yet the nomenclature persists, with the necessary result that insensibly the pupil comes to regard the English tongue as falling short at many points of the accepted standard. Any well regulated language will, it is assumed, modify the form of a noun when it serves as direct object of a verb and that of a finite verb to agree with its subject in person and number. Since English does neither of these things, so much the worse for English. And from such entirely reasonable inferences the pupil cannot but derive an essentially false conception of his mother-tongue, a

1. *Words and Their Uses*, p. 304.
2. *School Review*, February, 1902.

conception undefined, unacknowledged, but no less real and permanent, that the English language is a kind of inferior or degenerate Latin.

This species of "make-believe grammar," however, is pretty generally recognized and need not detain us long. Professor Barbour in his admirable "History of English Grammar Teaching"[3] has indicated its source in the Latinistic conceptions of English held by our earliest grammarians and has traced at least the beginnings of its decline under the influence of the wider linguistic knowledge of their successors. Professor Tolman cites Jespersen's *Progress in Language, with Especial Reference to English*, as competent authority for regarding the relatively uninflected English tongue as a stage, not in the deterioration or decay, but in the progressive evolution of language-structure. We are all theoretically at one upon this matter, it would seem, and though some details of reform demanded by the protestants may not be at once yielded by the practical teacher of grammar, the direction of our advance lies clear before us. English grammar must be presented as the formulated laws of *English* speech.

This essentially scientific attitude toward the facts of the English language is already exemplified to a marked degree in our modern treatment of questions of usage. Professors Brander Matthews and G. R. Carpenter, of Columbia University, Professor Scott, of the University of Michigan, and Professor Lounsbury, of Yale, have taught us that the old fashioned dogmatism of grammarians as to how people "ought" to speak is too commonly based on ignorance of the idiomatic peculiarities of our own language, of the past history of certain forms, or of present customs of speech outside a very limited circle. The more a man knows about any language the more clearly he sees it as a living, growing, changing thing; and the less willing is he to impose upon it an arbitrary legislation drawn from the usages of other tongues, from past usages of its own, or even from present usages not widely representative.

Both theoretically, then, and in at least one notable point of practice, "make-believe grammar" of the type so far discussed in this paper has fallen into disrepute. There seems little room for doubt that it will eventually, and at no remote period, be superseded in every detail by a grammar which bases itself unequivocally upon the facts of the English tongue as English.

But the term "make-believe grammar" need not be confined to this fictitious structure of laws, terms, and definitions built up by analogy from another language and without firm foundation in the facts of English speech. There is another species, no less figmentary than this, and in my judgment far

3. *Educational Review*, December, 1896.

more fundamentally misleading to the pupil; that grammar, I mean, which is derived not only from speech that is not English, but from speech that is not, in any genuine sense, speech at all. Our early grammarians, we allege, turned away their eyes from the facts of English speech and gave us rules drawn by analogy from the usages of the Latin tongue. But have not grammarians of all languages and all times, too frequently turned away their eyes from the facts of speech itself, from the language process as we understand it today, and given us laws from the dead and detached product of that process? If this be true, we have a fictitious construction in English grammar considerably more important as it is both deeper-lying and farther-reaching than the mere Latinizing of English.

Is it, however, true? Almost infallibly one is assured upon the first page of every textbook on English grammar that "language is a means of communication." And from this indubitable, though somewhat shadowy declaration, we should naturally expect to proceed by observing certain cases in which an idea is conveyed from one mind to another and analyzing the process as reflected in the language used. The office of various elements involved in this communication would then presumably be noted, and the elements defined on this basis. That is, one would analyze a sentence as the unit of language, to discover the parts of speech. But instead of this the accredited procedure up to a very recent date, both for textbook and for teacher, has been first to define the parts of speech in turn and then proceed to join certain of them together in such fashion as to make what was called a sentence. A noun, that is a word, representing a person or thing was prefixed to a verb, that is, a word standing for an action or a state of being, and behold a sentence! Thirty years ago pupils were not infrequently required to manufacture sentences after this method, of which a *reductio ad absurdum* appears in the following "direction" taken from Reed and Kellogg's *Higher Lessons in English*.[4] "Unite the words in columns 2 and 3 below [auxilliaries appear in column 2, past participles in column 3] and append the verbs thus formed to the nouns and pronouns in column 1 so as to make good sentences." And the implication that this is the typical sentence-structure, that language is a mechanical aggregation of separate elements, appears continually in the definitions and rules current during this period. In his *Essentials of English Grammar*,[5] Whitney assures us that the parts of speech must be "joined" together, "in order to make a whole, in order to be speech." "For a sentence," he declares further,

4. Lesson II.
5. Chap. ii.

"there must be not only words of more than one kind, but words of certain kinds, *fitted together in certain ways.*" (The italics are, of course, mine.) Nor can we "make a complete sentence without *joining together* a subject and a predicate."

There could be no more unequivocal statement of the conception of language as a mechanical aggregation of separate words. And I might quote interminably from Whitney's contemporaries, even, I regret to say, from some modern textbooks also, equally direct implications of this conception.

It is doubtless true that to the grammarian of an older generation there was no apparent inconsistency between this *e pluribus unum* conception of sentence-structure and the statement that language communicates the speaker's thought, since to the crude psychology which he has inherited from a still earlier time thought itself was "a thing of shreds and patches." One was, indeed, supposed to think first "house" and then "burning" and then put these two thoughts together before he could think—or say—"the house is burning." Granting this as a true account of the structure of thought, language might with entire consistency be described as a similar adding of word to word.

But we all know now, that whatever else this splicing of "percept" to "concept" may be, it is not in the genuine sense of the term "thought," any more than a leaf, a stem and a root tied together are a plant. The leaf, the stem and the root are found in the plant as the ideas of house and burning are found in the thought that the house is on fire; but as the plant is a living growth, which has put out root, stem, and leaf, so the thought is an organic structure out of which its constituent ideas have developed. From a confused sense of something wrong perhaps as one suddenly wakes out of sleep, grows the single thought of the whole situation, namely, the house's being on fire, in which neither the house as such nor the act of burning as such have any separate existence. The thought is, in truth, one before it is many. The growing plant or animal is its fair analogy, not the mosaic or the stone wall.

This organic conception of thought the present generation of English grammar teachers have gained from psychology and from real logic. And further, all that we know of the structure of language from modern philologists and students of literature goes to show that it, too, is a living, growing thing, not in any sentimental or remotely analogical sense, but as sober, scientific fact. The sentence which is spliced together out of the "parts of speech" is, in truth, no sentence at all. It is not language any more than a company drill is fighting, or a scarecrow a man. Thought which is living, growing, organic in structure, cannot be conveyed or represented by a lifeless, static, artificial construction. Nor are we studying language by studying such a construction. The sentences which grammar presents to us have in very truth ceased to be language, once they have been cut off from all reference to the various acts of thought-communication which gave rise to them, so that they seem to exist in and for themselves, mere mechanical congeries of words, brought together only to fulfil certain arbitrary requirements of the sentence form as such.

That an artificial conception of the sentence similar to this, and directly at variance with our best knowledge of its nature and structure at the present time, has conditioned much teaching of English grammar in the past, seems to be indubitable. And that this false conception has actually been conveyed to pupils through their study of English grammar I also believe. A priori we should, indeed, expect it to be so. The mind of the child is extraordinarily sensitive to the images latent in our phrases. Professor Scott's paper on the "Figurative Element in Grammatical Terminology"[6] discloses some quite unforeseen conclusions drawn by the young pupil from the uses in grammar of such supposably abstract and wholly technical terms as "case," "agree," "govern," "decline." And it is hardly conceivable that he should be insensitive to the suggestions of mechanical aggregation offered by such words as "joined with," "fitted together," "added to," "put with," "put together with," or "put along with," which in the older textbook are continually applied to the relations of words with one another in the sentence.

The expectation, moreover, that images of sentence-structure, as mechanical rather than organic, must inevitably be carried by language of this sort, has been abundantly confirmed by such data upon the subject as I have been able to gather for myself. From time to time during the past few years I have taken occasion to inquire into the ideas of language-structure and function actually carried away by children from their study of English grammar. Students in both high school and college have written for me at various times answers to the following questions: "What image (or picture) stood for the sentence in your mind after you had first studied grammar in school? What did you then think a sentence was for?" Though many pupils were of course conscious of no definite image, and many saw the sentence always in terms of the formal diagram they had been taught to use, the remaining answers all but invariably indicated both an artificial conception of sentence structure and a complete dissociation of the sentence from any purpose other than that of serving as a grammatical exercise. The picture suggested might be a string

6. *Leaflet No. 36*, published by the New England Association of Teachers of English.

of beads, a line of wooden blocks, a train of cars, a card-house, a square of crazy patchwork; but it was almost invariably a whole made up of separate things put together in a certain way. And these things were put together, not in order to express an idea to someone else, but simply to—why, to make a sentence! "It was built up by somebody," says one student, "just as a block house might have been—for no purpose but to pull it down again." "I never thought a sentence was for anything but to study," sadly remarks another; while a third volunteers the admission that, though "a sentence in grammar" seemed to her as a child, like a square of patchwork, she does not think of "a real sentence" in this way—"one that comes in my reading, I mean." This pointed distinction between "a real sentence" and "a sentence in grammar," has been repeatedly implied in the statements of different pupils, and seems to me worthy of serious consideration.

Such inquiries as this are no doubt relatively unimpressive to anyone who receives them at second hand; but I believe that any teacher who, without prejudice, undertakes a similar line of investigation for himself, will come upon some astonishing and not insignificant revelations as to the vestigia left in the child's mind from his study of English grammar. Most convincing of all, to me, upon this point, however, are the unconscious betrayals to the teacher of literature or composition of a pupil's unrecognized sense of language as dissociated from the living thought process, an artificial structure of mere words for no end save that of meeting a requirement or "showing off" one's skill. Sometimes in such cases the source of this idea of language seems to lie back of any larger study of writing or literature in some obscure but persistent image, finally traced to the pages of the grammar textbook or to the lips of the grammar teacher, an image of the sentence as a "made-up" thing, consisting of words put together to form a certain pattern or to exemplify a given rule. Such a deep-lying, inwoven conception, as many of us know, goes not out by prayer or fasting. Only the expulsive power of a new and truer image will avail; and upon the task of making an entrance for such an image into the preoccupied mind, presenting it again and again, etching it deeper and deeper over the lines of the old picture—upon this task, sometimes seemingly hopeless, many teachers of composition and literature are today expending their best efforts. No real writing, no real reading can be done by the student until works become to him direct and genuine expressions of thought. But surely all this labor to restore a vital significance which need never have been lost, is an indefensible waste in education.

It is only fair to say, however, that year by year such cases as this become fewer, in my own experience at least. And they would reach the vanishing-point within a college generation or so, if only our growing sense of the fatuity of teaching a pupil in English grammar ideas of language which must be with infinite difficulty unlearned when he studies composition and litera- ture could be reinforced by an unerring choice of means for imparting to him the truer and more permanent conception of language as organic. This last is, indeed, the crux of the practical situation. Since the reign of W. D. Whitney and of Reed and Kellogg in the field of English grammar we have unquestionably advanced several steps in the direction of teaching the actual structure of language; but the tale is not yet fully told. Many of our recent textbooks strive, with varying success, to keep the "real sentence" and the sentence of grammar from invidious separation in the pupil's mind. They forbear to require the manufacture of imitation sentences, according to a formula furnished by them. Instead of "building" sentences to order after this fashion, they rather study such sentences as grow naturally out of the student's own thought or such as easily communicate to him the thought of another person, and hence become vicariously his own. These sentences are not mere puzzles, combinations of words in a certain pattern. They exist to convey thought, and do convey it to the pupil, since it is thought of a type which either is already or readily may become his. And at least the vanguard of our grammar teachers at the present time see that whether the pupil himself actually makes the sentence or whether it is suggested to him, he does not study its structure until it is to him a living sentence, a real expression of thought.

The modern textbook and the modern teacher, moreover, insist upon studying the parts of speech as derived from the sentence, not the sentence as made up from the parts of speech. They attempt, at least, to define each part of speech by the actual service it renders in conveying the thought of the sentence as a whole, rather than as merely representing some particular class of things in the world. This is a little fire, but it kindles a great matter. Verbs do, no doubt, in the realm of words, roughly correspond to actions or "states of being" in the world of things, nouns to persons or things, adjectives to the qualities of persons or things, prepositions to relations between persons and things, and so on. But to define a verb, a noun, an adjective, and a preposition in this way is certainly to give color to the mechanical conception of sentence- structure. Join a person or thing to an action, a quality to the person or thing, a relation to another thing, and the two to the action, and you have a thought. In the same fashion unite a noun with a verb, an adjective with a noun, a preposition with another noun, and the two with the verb, and behold the language-structure corresponding to the thought. Such is the implication of these definitions. If, however, the subject as a whole has been first distinguished from the predicate as a whole, on the basis of the different function each performs in conveying the thought of the whole sentence, if then each part of speech is similarly discriminated from every other on the basis of its office in developing further any element of the thought, the adjective, for instance, being defined by virtue of its function as particularizing in various ways the meaning of a noun or pronoun, an adverb as discriminating the precise manner or conditions of the action indicated by the verb—if, in short, a vivid sense of the *activity* of the whole sentence and of all its parts in the communication of thought underlies every definition and rule, we have at least an honest effort to deal with real language and to represent it as it is.

Attempts of this sort are certain to be faulty in detail until we have become more completely interpenetrated than any of us can be as yet with the functional conception of the sentence. But they serve at least to point the way of our advance in the rational and scientific teaching of English grammar.

We know that the study of English grammar has long since ceased to justify itself as a practical art. It has been pretty thoroughly demonstrated in experience that by parsing words and memorizing rules children do not learn to speak and write correctly. There remains, then, to the subject, only such justification as it may fairly claim on grounds of being a science, the theoretic formulation of the laws of the English language within the limits of the sentence-form. But this justification is surely imperiled by the charge of unscientific method and conclusion brought against it by students of comparative philology, in their contention that English grammar treats and represents the English language not as English but as a hybrid or deteriorated Latin. And still more conclusively we must admit does English grammar forfeit its justification to a place in the curriculum of studies as the science or theory of the English sentence, if it continues to treat its subject-matter in a fashion essentially unscientific, averting the eyes from the facts of genuine speech and writing, to analyze instead a fictitious construction of its own; if it studies and presents to pupils, in lieu of the living language, an artificial substitute manufactured by the grammarian and without real existence or usefulness in the world; if it holds and conveys to students false conceptions of the English language not only as English but also as language itself. This is "make-believe grammar" in its deadliest aspect. Until we have done with it entirely we cannot begin to enter into the possibilities which real grammar offers to education in these present days.

A word only in conclusion as to these possibilities. If we pass in review the great tendencies and achievements in education for the past half-century, we may note one principle as common to them all—the principle, namely, of displacing a formula by an activity, second-hand by first-hand knowledge. The laboratory method in natural science thus substitutes the pupil's own drawing of inferences and formulation of laws for his acceptance of them ready-made as the products of other people's observations and induction. He sees, traces out, controls, and analyzes the processes giving rise to the formulae which once he merely memorized from the pages of a book. And wherever the experimental method has obtained, even in subjects once regarded as insusceptible of scientific treatment, such as psychology and history, the observation of activities has supplanted the mere learning of the results of these activities.

In manual training we have a further instance of the transmutation of dead fact into living action. Those facts and principles of measurement, calculation, physical properties, which were once given directly to the student as rules or formulae to be learned, are now encountered by him as he follows step by step some active process in which they are involved. He thus grasps them more readily and retains them more easily, since they represent to him the living conditions or results of an activity which he has himself witnessed or carried on.

Of similar significance is that interesting type of primary education which uses the primitive industrial processes, such as pottery making, weaving, iron and metal work, not only to train the eye, the hand, and the mind of the pupil, but to afford him some insight into the complex social organization of which he is a part. By following out these processes from their crude beginnings to their complicated development in the present industrial order, the child is believed to gain not only a vital and thorough knowledge of the facts and principles incident to them throughout their evolution, but also some comprehension of those infinitely tangled and multitudinous activities which constitute the world's life, but which to those of us not thus initiated are usually little more than a "big blooming buzzing Confusion."

With the relative values of these various educational movements we are not now concerned. Our interest is wholly in the coincidence of their animating ideas, a coincidence which can hardly be regarded as purely accidental. Beneath innumerable differences of superficial aspect, these three noteworthy tendencies in modern education are rooted in the same elementary principle, namely that the products or results of an active process can be rightly understood and strongly seized upon by the human mind only in connection with that process.

Within the field of language-study, moreover, this principle has to some extent already obtained. The historical and the comparative study of languages and literature is in fact built upon it. Our teaching of English composition has for several years paid tribute to it. In English grammar, last of all, we are beginning to recognize it. In this subject, therefore, we have yet to receive the returns which its completer acceptance and more consistent carrying out have elsewhere yielded.

These returns are so far conceded that I need only enumerate them. The laboratory method, manual training, the study of social and industrial activities, the organic or functional study of languages, of literature, of English composition, restore to dead forms, detached facts, meaningless laws, the color, the life, the significance which they have lost through separation from the activities which gave them birth. Such restoration will assuredly take place in grammar—has indeed already taken place wherever the organic conception of language has entered into it.

When we have at length dismissed entirely from our teaching that artificial product of the grammarian's ingenuity which I cannot forbear characterizing as "near-language," and set our pupils in earnest to studying the language process by direct analysis of the sentence-activity, we shall find this subject richer in its opportunities than any of us has conceived. In the first place the language process is not, like weaving or pottery making, obsolete in our modern households. It is at hand whenever and wherever one wants it. It is carried on by every child without self-consciousness as an essential activity in his daily life. It may be studied without elaborate apparatus of any kind. Since it involves abstract relations, without that actual manipulation of material substance characteristic of the industrial processes, it should doubtless not be the earliest activity studied by the child; but we must not on the other hand forget that when every language relation is consistently referred to the concrete reality behind the words, intelligent dealing with it becomes comparatively easy even for pupils in the lower grades.

But beyond its extraordinary availability, the language process has a second and quite incommensurable advantage over any other process as a subject for study, in its unrivaled importance to the social order. If it is held advisable that the young student should understand certain industrial processes, that he may thereby gain some insight into this complicated modern world of ours, he should assuredly to this same end apply himself to that great process of communication by language between man and man, through which alone the individual can put his knowledge and thought at the service of his fellows, through which alone society can profit by the achievements of its members.

It is with this act, rightly understood, that grammar has to deal, not with mere words printed on the page. And in so far as it studies this act at first hand, observing and analyzing it as communication, as the living transference of thought from mind to mind, creating thus and shaping to its ends the sentence form—in so far may it be accounted real grammar.

V   Poetry, Plays, and Feminist Fiction

14   Preface to *Poems and Plays*

from *Poems and Plays*,
edited by Laura Johnson Wylie (New York: Duffield, 1922).

Poems and Plays *was posthumously published, edited by Buck's life partner, Laura Wylie. In her preface, which serves as an introduction to this section, Wylie indicates that Buck wrote poetry and fiction only during the spare moments of her teaching life. George Pierce Baker, whose playwriting workshop she attended at Harvard, wondered what it meant to Buck to "put aside her own play writing, when she had had as much success as that, and give out richly to the people who wanted to write. When you know, or think you know that you can do something in art, and then spend your life in giving to people who hope they can do something in art, there must be a memorable moment. Such a moment must have been hers, because she was already coming to understand the handling of a longer play when she returned [to Vassar] and began what she created, the Vassar Workshop" ("Address" 11–12).*

Buck wrote poetry primarily to express the beauty she found in natural settings, the joy she felt with animals, and the depth of her love and friendships. The six poems included here represent the subjects and the forms she most frequently employed. She also published two limericks about suffrage (see the introduction) and wrote a hymn for Vassar College which she shared with President Henry MacCracken, writing that "the problem of 'setting' words to music has always interested me greatly" (letter, 7 May 1916).

PREFACE

An introduction to such a volume as this may seem an impertinence; what the author has to say must speak for itself and to its fitting audience. Yet the editor cannot let the book go out without a word as to the life-long interest of Gertrude Buck in imaginative writing and the part played by this interest in her intellectual and practical life. She was, even to her friends, primarily the teacher, the thinker, the administrator, remarkable for constant and energetic advance towards new ends or for unflagging zeal in working out new experiments. But, however apparently absorbed in such tasks, she lived always to a surprising degree outside and beyond them; was from first to last, as artist and poet, most deeply concerned with shaping into form some mood or character, some situation or idea, that had touched her imagination. This creative impulse, moreover, grew with her growth, gave tone and character to everything she did, and in turn changed direction as she gained in maturity and in intellectual and emotional experience.

There was never a time when Miss Buck was not directly occupied with some piece of imaginative writing. Her literary experiments began in her school days. Before she was graduated from college, she was recognized as a successful newspaper writer and a poet remarkable among her contemporaries for delicacy of technique and range and depth of emotion. Throughout her professional years, she found in the writing of verse or novel or play not only illumination of literary theory, but a counterpoise to the distracting demands of practical life. Almost her last definite plan was the completion of a novel dealing with contemporary social and academic conditions, laid aside a few years before in the stress of a developing interest in drama. The strength of her imaginative bent showed itself throughout her life in the use she made of such scanty leisure as came to her. A few days of vacation were prized less that she might hear or see some new thing than because in them her imagination, released from daily service, could work out some one of the many themes always revolving in her mind.

This persistence of the artistic impulse in her was the more remarkable because she responded whole-heartedly to calls, individual and social, that might easily have absorbed all her energy. She began her career as a teacher just when the rapidly increasing number of students in Vassar was rendering the faculty acutely conscious of the need to reconstruct its educational theory and practice. The practical grasp of the issues involved and the thorough training in philosophy which she brought to this work of reconstruction were rare indeed among her colleagues; and to these gifts she added a genuine passion for teaching and an administrative ability that forced her into the very center of the struggle between old and new conceptions of education. The tasks she set herself were the more arduous because she made no compromise with her ideal of perfection; was as indefatigable in doing the kind of teaching in which she believed as in establishing fundamental educational theories. When the vantage ground for which she had long striven was attained, and real and vital order realized, at least approximately, in English teaching at Vassar, she was ready for the next step and at once enlarged her departmental activities by initiating and organizing two cooperative educational ventures, the Vassar Workshop and the Community Theatre of Poughkeepsie. Her work, from beginning to end of her professional career, was thus that of the pioneer; and, like that of the pioneer in every field, pressed all her faculties into its service.

POEMS AND PLAYS

BY
GERTRUDE BUCK

Edited by
LAURA JOHNSON WYLIE

NEW YORK
DUFFIELD & COMPANY
1922

The creative power that showed itself in her work as a teacher, was no less characteristic of her as a critic. Her intellectual gifts were in large part those of the poet. Perhaps most conspicuous among them was a vivid realization of individuality, whether in character, idea, or physical object. Her range of interests was singularly wide; her mind explored many fields, her response to forward-looking movements, whether social or literary, was immediate, her large circle of friends included people of all ages and condition. But although she ranged far, her thought was never weakened by diffusion, or paled into abstractness. Ideas took on with her the sharpness of individual existences; when most far-reaching they were seen in relation to the real life of real people. In even casual meetings, she was quick to recognize the unique qualities of personality. The generalization thus embodied to her the richness of concrete experience: the concrete experience was illumined with the ideas it visualized or illustrated. With this vividness of perception she combined an exceptional power to trace out the relationship between objects and to recognize the laws operating in them. Conclusions never remained in her mind as mere conclusions, but became at once vital and active realities, living forces working for the discovery of ever-new truths. Her indefatigable challenge of every element in idea or term or fact might seem to the formally-minded meaningless repetition; but her thought was fruitful precisely because of the Socratic temper with which in dealing with any subject she suffered nothing to remain that was not essential and operative, because observation and generalization were alike but means for the attainment of a fuller and richer concept.

The simplicity she inexorably demanded was the necessary consequence of all her intellectual processes. It was based on concrete experience made significant by the fullest understanding. The isolated, the irrelevant, the confused—welcomed as first steps in the intellectual life—were tolerated for but a moment; in the end lucidity, significance, simplicity, were exacted of every thought or perception or emotion. Search for this fine clarity revealed itself in her every characteristic and in all aspects of her life. Her tastes, refined to asceticism, were yet instruments of exquisite discernment; her friendships were companionships in strenuous and discriminating pursuit of some excellence. The truth she prized shone in the "white light" of clearest vision; experience she valued only as the whole energy was focused in the activity of the moment. Thought found its place in the intellectual life in so far as by simplifying and organizing knowledge, it made possible still further advance; criticism was justified among the intellectual activities as it led to an idea informed with something of a Platonic vitality as well as a Platonic richness of content.

The fact that Miss Buck was peculiarly at home in the world of imaginative creation or that the core of her activity in all fields was an imaginative power that habitually led her beyond the analysis of her experiences to their reconstruction and expression, has of course nothing to do with the value of these writings themselves. Yet the editor stresses these points in view of their relation to the more obvious aspects of her life and work. There was nothing on which as thinker and teacher she insisted more energetically than on the general educational value of imaginative discipline. But the characteristic intellectual bias that both conditioned this conviction and was reinforced by it was in great part concealed by the fact that her mind acted to an unusual degree as a whole, that her various faculties worked together if they worked at all. In this volume, therefore, we have a key to much that, though implicit in everything she did, was not always evident to those who knew her chiefly as teacher or critic. Her imaginative writings were, in a very real sense, intellectual by-products, the avocations of a mind habitually preoccupied with thought and practice; but they were none the less signs of her constant return to those elemental and primary impulses which gave unmistakable character to everything she did and thought.

Laura Johnson Wylie

NOVEMBER, 1922.

POEMS

The Road to Nowhere

The road to Nowhere is white and still;
It slopes up softly, then dips from sight;
Blue over its shoulder peers the hill,
And brambles guard it to left and right.

A Maine Road

A glint of birches in the dusky pines,
A sudden scent of balsam and sweet fern,

Long starry plumes of wild blackberry vines,
A flash of ocean at the roadway's turn.

Fishing

The wash of waters against the prow,
The guttural grunt of the frog's bassoon,
The far light laughter of the loon—,
A hush of hopeful waiting—now
A twitch on the line as if to say
"Are the folks at home?" then the rascal turns
And runs till the reel 'gainst your fingers burns.
You jerk in answer "Yes, home today,"
Pull in the mischief with steady hand,
Hold hard, no slack,—see his armor flash
All silver green through the foaming splash!
An instant more and he's brought to land—
The devil! he's spewed the hook clean out
And dived 'neath the boat with a leer and a flout!

Berlin
His Epitaph Written by Himself

In life I was a sporty dog: I never took a dare.
I always leaped before I looked, and landed—God knows where.

Into a bath-tub, down a drain, upon a blazing fire,—
'Twas one to me, who hurled myself straight at my heart's desire.

I climbed back fences after cats, and scaled our own Dutch door,
To greet my mistress home returned from journeys long and sore.

But motor-cars my passion were. When one would gently glide
Along the curb, I'd make a dash and boldly leap inside.

If mistress had but followed me, and not been such a muff,
We two had had some glorious spins; but women lack the stuff.

Whene'er a car came sweeping on directly in my track
I sat me down and scratched my ear, until it changed its tack.

My mistress chid me sternly, but you know what women are—
I wonder what my life had been under another star.

If I had had a master, and he a sporting gent,
Black Johnson, say, or Jefferies—but I do not lament.

My days knew scant excitement, save that I did create,
But my dear mistress would for ills e'en greater compensate.

And in that heaven where she holds we shall together be,
Perhaps she'll lose her sole defect, and be a man like me.

An Epitaph
A. B. B.

Of sun and fields and every joy of sight
A simple lover—Christ her spirit keep!—
She toiled and prayed beneath a fading light;
The room was darkened and she fell asleep.

The Return

By night my mother heard me sobbing, calling on her name,
And from the blessed heights of death to comfort me she came.

I flung myself once more upon my mother's gentle breast
And sobbed out all the thorny griefs against my heart long pressed,—

The hours I might have spent with her, the words I never said,
The love I drank so carelessly till she who loved was dead.

What I would say she knew, although my words were choked and wild;
We sat close-locked; my years slipped off; naught was I but her child.

Into my breast a healing came; black grief did from me part.
I woke to peace; though death was king, my mother knew my heart.

By night my mother heard me sobbing, calling on her name,
And from the blessed heights of death to comfort me she came.

from *Poems and Plays,*
edited by Laura Johnson Wylie (New York: Duffield, 1922), 57–85.

Buck wrote this one-act play in George P. Baker's English 47 class at Harvard/Radcliffe in 1915–1916. Its central character is Maggie Ross, a dressmaker and the unmarried care-taker of her mother and older, mentally disabled sister. Maggie's brother Jim left years ago, yet her mother waits for his return, keeping his room, hoarding money to go to him, and otherwise ignoring the emotional and material needs of her two daughters. As the title indicates, Buck challenges sex stereotypes, such as maternal "instinct" and society's privileging of males.

At Buck's memorial service, Baker commented that although she was much older than the other students, she had "such admirable poise that you never would have suspected for a moment that she had behind her all those years of extremely successful teaching." Although Baker and the performers initially had doubts that such a "very disagreeable play" might succeed, it was performed and they "found that Miss Buck had given to the actors in those two parts material such that when they handled it rightly the play became one of infinite pathos. I myself have seldom seen a more pathetic figure than this little, demented gray-haired woman. . . . It touched the audience profoundly" ("Address" 11–12).

In the late nineteenth century, Buck and many other college graduates of her genera-tion did not marry or have children, which alarmed opponents of higher education for women, who feared for the future of the race. In an 1895 article in The Century Maga-zine, *a University of California graduate, Millicent Washburn Shinn, analyzed data from the 1,805 members of the Association of Collegiate Alumnae and reported that 28.2 percent were married, compared with 80 percent of the women over age twenty in the country in general. Even excluding the youngest classes, only 54.5 percent of college women over the age of forty had married, compared to about 90 percent of the nation's female population. Shinn noted a slightly lower marriage rate for alumnae of women's colleges, which she attributed to the "pretty elaborate and pleasant social life constructed out of purely feminine materials, [that] left a woman less disposed and less fitted after-ward for informal friendships and cooperations with men" (947). The financial indepen-dence a college degree afforded kept some women out of mercenary marriages, and several sources comment that college marriages were happier ones. Shinn wrote that the "college woman is not only more exacting in her standards of marriage, but under less pressure to accept what falls below her standard than the average woman, because she can better support and occupy herself alone" (948). As for childbearing rates, Rosenberg* reports that "[w]hile 92 percent of all married women bore three to four children each, only 68 percent of married college graduates bore any children, and most of them bore only one or two" (23). These statistics were not much different from the upper middle class women's child-bearing rates, however, regardless of college education.

Maggie Ross, however, has less freedom than a college-educated woman who chose not to marry. At the conclusion of the play, she seems to give her own life up to the caretaking of her sister, telling her mother: "You can do anything to me, but you mustn't hurt Lura." This willingness to sacrifice herself for her mentally disabled sister is likened to the mythical fierceness of a mother's love in her next line: "I'll—I'll kill you, if you do" (82). The twists in allegiances, the plays on the nature of love, and the deconstruction of motherhood make Buck's playwriting an early feminist effort in twentieth-century theater.

Characters

MAGGIE ROSS, a dressmaker
MRS. ROSS, her mother
JIM ROSS, her brother
LURA ROSS, her sister

It is an evening in mid-December. Maggie's sewing-room is a low-ceiled, shabbily furnished room, with an outside door in the back. Another door at the right opens into the kitchen. A third door at the left leads upstairs. There is a window in the back wall. A small door-bell, connected by a visible wire with the outside door, hangs from the ceiling in the corner of the room. An old-fashioned haircloth-covered sofa stands against the wall, with a small table at its head. A high chest of drawers is at the back of the room and a large round table with a lamp on it is in the center. A small, brightly-glowing coal-stove is at the right front, a folding screen covered with gay cretonne back of it, opened against the right wall. A figure for fitting dresses, standing at one side, has on it an ugly, unfinished dress of wide-striped black and red silk. The bright-colored, well-worn ingrain carpet is strewn with snippets of cloth and bits of basting cotton. Paper patterns and fashion-plates from magazines are pinned to the coarse lace window curtains and the flower-papered walls. Maggie is standing over the sofa on which Mother is lying, propped up high on a pile of cretonne-covered pillows, with a knitted afghan spread over her. Maggie is a middle-aged woman with a delicate-featured face which, though worn and sometimes anxious in expression, seems to be lighted from within by an absorbing happiness. She wears a shabby serge dress and a white apron, with a red pin-cushion full of pins hanging from her belt. Mother is attired in a tumbled lavender kimono trimmed lavishly with cheap machine-made lace. Her white hair falls untidily about her sleek self-indulgent, self-satisfied face.

MAGGIE [*cheerfully*]: It's a little better, isn't it Mother? Just a little?

MOTHER [*in a feeble but irritable voice*]: Maggie, how often have I told you not to ask me questions when I have a headache? You always make it worse.

MAGGIE [*arrested by contrition in the act of dropping the cloth into the basin*]: Oh, I *hope* I haven't this time, Mumsie dear! I thought it must be nearly well.

MOTHER [*petulantly*]: No, it isn't. And it won't be if you act like this. [*She sighs deeply and closes her eyes. Maggie dips the cloth in the water, wrings it out, and lays it on Mother's head. Mother snatches it off.—In a voice of intense exasperation*]: Don't put that thing on me again.

MAGGIE [*surprised*]: Oh, I thought—

MOTHER [*plaintively, recovering her feeble tone*]: It doesn't do me a speck of good. Nothing does. [*With a yawn, followed by a heavy sigh.*] I might as well go to bed I s'pose. But of course I can't sleep.

MAGGIE [*takes the cloth from Mother, drops it into the basin, and wipes her hands on the towel lying beside it*]: Yes, do go, Mumsie. Lura has got your bed open for you and she's going to bathe your head with cologne, till you drop off.

MOTHER [*pettishly, with half closed eyes*]: I'd rather have you.

MAGGIE [*imploringly*]: Oh Mumsie, *do* let her do it. She loves to take care of people. And I could just about finish her doll, while she's upstairs. [*She takes half-dressed doll out of the chest of drawers and displays it admiringly.*] Isn't her little hat sweet? Lura will be tickled to pieces when she sees that blue-jay feather on it.

MOTHER [*opening her eyes wide, and sitting up*]: Maggie Ross, are you going to give her that doll—after all I've said?

MAGGIE [*takes her work-basket, and sits down to sew on the doll's dress*]: Why, Mother dear, that's what she *wants*. I can't give her grown-up things, you know. She'd be so disappointed.

MOTHER [*fiercely*]: Well, if *you* like to see a gray-headed woman messing 'round with dolls and picture-books, other people don't. It makes *me* so sick I can hardly *live*. You might think once in a while of *my* feelings.

MAGGIE [*laying aside the doll, jumps up from her chair and sits beside Mother on the sofa*]: Oh, Mother dear, I do. But Lura isn't a gray-headed woman to me, you know. I guess I see her the way she sees herself—just a little girl eight years old. [*Tenderly.*] And we must make her happy, mustn't we? It's all we *can* do for her.

MOTHER [*acidly*]: Oh, of course, if *she's* only happy. Nobody cares about me. It's all Lura with you. [*With rising anger.*] I guess I know what is best for my own child, Maggie Ross, but you never listen to me. Anybody'd think she was your child, instead of mine.

MAGGIE: Why, no, Mother. But it's for her Christmas.

MOTHER: Christmas! Don't talk about Christmas to me. What kind of a Christmas will it be for me, I'd like to know, with my boy at the ends of the earth, or maybe lying in his grave?

MAGGIE [*trying to put her arms around Mother*]: Oh, Mumsie, dear, I know. But couldn't you—just for Lura and me—

MOTHER [*putting her away*]: No, I couldn't. And I don't want any presents from either of you. Just remember that.

MAGGIE: Oh, Mother, not anything at all?

MOTHER: No. You can give me the money you were going to spend for me, if you want to. But I won't have anything else.

MAGGIE: But, Mother, we're only *making* some little things for you. They don't cost anything much. But they give us the Christmas feeling.

MOTHER: Well, if they don't cost but a nickel, I'd rather have that than anything you'd buy with it and fuss up. There's no Christmas feeling for me till my boy comes home, and I ain't going to pretend there is.

[*Lura's voice is heard from above.*]

LURA: Maggie.

MAGGIE [*going to stair door and opening it*]: Yes, dear.

LURA [*accusingly*]: I'm waiting an' *waiting*.

MAGGIE: Mother's coming—just a minute.

MOTHER [*fretfully*]: Where's my handkerchief, Maggie?

MAGGIE: It must be on the sofa. [*She looks for it behind Mother, finds and shakes it out. It is seen to be full of holes.*]

MAGGIE [*giving it to her*]: Oh, Mother, dear, haven't you any better handkerchiefs than this?

MOTHER [*with conscious heroism*]: It doesn't matter.

MAGGIE: Didn't you buy some new ones with the money I gave you? [*Mother purses her lips and looks complacently mysterious, but does not answer.*] I guess she embezzled it again, the bad Mumsie, and put it in her secret drawer. Well, I might have known she would. [*She sighs involuntarily.*]

MOTHER [*rising indignantly and looking down on Maggie with an outraged expression*]: Embezzle, Miss Maggie? That is a strange word for a daughter to use about her mother.

MAGGIE [*rising and attempting to take Mother's hands, which Mother im-*

patiently withdraws]: Oh, Mumsie, dear, I'm only joking, of course. But I can't *bear* to have you go without things so.

MOTHER [*with sad dignity*]: It is for my boy, Maggie. I want nothing for myself.

MAGGIE [*with a sigh*]: Take some of my handkerchiefs, dear, till I can buy a few new ones. We're nearly out of coal, and Lura's shoes—

MOTHER: I am used to doing without things. It is a mother's lot to sacrifice for her children.

LURA [*from above*]: Maggie, hurry up!

MAGGIE: Yes, dearie, coming right away. Want your novel, Mother? [*She picks up a volume from the sofa.*]

MOTHER [*languidly*]: I've finished that. Lura must go to the library for me, tomorrow.

MAGGIE: All right. Good-night, Mumsie. Pleasant dreams!

MOTHER [*ascending the stairs*]: I don't expect to sleep at all. Good-night.

[*Maggie folds the afghan and lays it smoothly over the foot of the sofa, sets the pillows in order, and takes the basin from the table into the kitchen. The door-bell rings softly and she re-enters hastily, smoothing her apron with her hands as she goes to the outside door and opens it wide.*]

MAGGIE: Good evening.

JIM [*outside*]: Good evening. Is this Miss Ross?

MAGGIE: Yes. Is there something—?

JIM: Can I see you a few minutes? A little matter of business.

MAGGIE: Why certainly. Won't you come in?

[*Jim enters with a jaunty yet somewhat uncertain air. Removing his hat, he shows a bald head with a fringe of gray hair about it, a gray Van Dyke beard and pointed moustache, perched incongruously on a fat red face. Heavy glasses almost conceal his eyes, but he looks easy-going, impressionable, sympathetic. His overcoat is worn but of a stylish cut. At first glance one might place him in a higher social class than Maggie's. Maggie offers him a chair by the table.*] Please sit down.

[*Jim pulls off his overcoat and lays it with his hat on the chair Maggie indicates, turns another with its back to the lamp and sits down. Maggie sits near him, facing the light. Jim devours with his eyes her face and every detail of the room, but she seems wholly unconscious of his scrutiny, absorbed in the business in hand.*]

JIM: I'm looking for a room, and a lady up the street told me maybe I could rent one here.

MAGGIE [*surprised*]: Oh, no, I'm afraid not. We haven't any room. That is. . [*She stops abruptly, as if struck by a new idea, and clasps and unclasps her hands, looking from Jim to the stairway door with alternate eager desire and despondency. With an almost imperceptible shake of the head, she drops her hands quietly into her lap.*]

JIM [*regretfully*]: I wish you had. I'd like to stay here first-rate.

MAGGIE [*glancing again toward the stairs*]: There *is* a room that we don't use now for anyone, but Mother wouldn't hear of it, I'm sure.

JIM [*in a hushed, sympathetic tone*]: Belonged to some one who's dead?

MAGGIE: It's my brother's room. He's been away twenty-eight years now, and it's sixteen years this Christmas since we heard from him.

JIM: Well, that don't look as if he'd be wanting to use his room right away, does it?

MAGGIE: No. And I wish we *could* let you have it. [*Again clasping and unclasping her hands and leaning forward eagerly.*] I wonder—do you believe in prayer?

JIM [*kindly, but with an embarrassed chuckle*]: Well, I don't know as I do, much. There might be something in it.

MAGGIE: I do wish I *knew*. I've been asking God to show me some way to earn a little money, and it seems as if He *must* have sent you.

JIM [*with another chuckle, half-tender, half-amused*]: Well, 'sposin' He did?

MAGGIE [*with conviction*]: He *must* have done it. I never even *thought* of that room. But I don't know what Mother will say?

JIM: Will she mind awfully?

MAGGIE [*in an awed tone*]: You don't know what it means to her. [*With intensity.*] But we've *got* to have a new roof. The old one can't be mended any more. And it costs almost a hundred dollars! [*She looks at Jim for sympathy.*]

JIM [*feelingly*]: That's a terrible price!

MAGGIE [*with a stifled sigh, looking toward the figure*]: And I can't do very much dressmaking, what with the housework and all, though Lura's a wonderful help, for a child, so—

JIM [*startled*]: A child?

MAGGIE [*with a low, tender laugh*]: She isn't really a child, she's my older sister, but she had an awful sickness when she was eight years old and her brain never grew after that, so she's always stayed just the way she was then.

JIM [*thoughtfully*]: I see. Well, I should think you'd *have* to rent a room, if you've got one *to* rent.

MAGGIE [*desperately*]: Yes, I *must*. But I don't believe Mother *will*. If you take it, you won't mind, will you, if she tells you to go?

JIM [*chuckling*]: No, I won't mind. Shall I stay right on till she begins throwing the flatirons?

MAGGIE [*reproachfully*]: Oh you *mustn't* laugh. That room—well, it's really sacred to her, because it was Jim's. She's never let *anybody* sleep in it—not even Lura or me. Lura sleeps with me and she'd like a room all her own. But Mother *couldn't* do it. Oh, I'm *sure* she won't let you stay in it!

JIM: But if you need money so much—

MAGGIE: Mother doesn't think much about money, only for Jim.

JIM: For Jim? Why, she doesn't know where he is.

MAGGIE: No, but she thinks Jim will ask her to come and live with him some day, and she wants to have money to go with. Or she thinks maybe he will fall sick and she must go where he is and have something to help him with. She thinks *everything* of Jim.

JIM [*with half-smothered irritation*]: Well, why should she? What's he ever done for her? Did he use to send her money before he quit writing?

MAGGIE [*reluctantly*]: Well, no. But he couldn't really. He didn't get on very well, I guess. And it's hard for a man to economize, don't you think so? They don't know how, the way a woman does, That's what Mother always says.

JIM [*with a snort of contempt*]: I know *his* sort, all right.

MAGGIE [*really hurt*]: You don't know Jim. You couldn't help liking him, if you did.

JIM [*with an obstinate wag of the head*]: You bet I could! But I'll tell you what I'll do, if you want me to. I'm going west myself, in a month or so, and, if you'll tell me where your brother was when he wrote you the last letter, I'll look him up.

MAGGIE [*in a flutter of delight*]: Oh, would you, really? He was in Phoenix, Arizona. It seems too much for you to do, for strangers, so. But if you *could* find him, it would be more to Mother than anything else in the world.

JIM [*gruffly*]: 'Twouldn't be much to you, I s'pose, and I don't blame you.

MAGGIE: Oh, yes, it *would*. But he's all Mother has, you know. And I've got Lura. [*Her face lights at Lura's name.*]

JIM [*exasperated*]: Say, your Mother's got you, hasn't she, and Lura, too?

MAGGIE: Oh, but daughters *can't* be like a son, you know—an only son. She thinks about him all the time, I guess, but Christmas and her birthday are the worst of all. She always used to get a letter on those days, and when she doesn't, we can't do *anything* to make her happy. She just sits and grieves over Jim. It's awful to see her.

JIM: Must be pretty tough.

MAGGIE: Yes, sometimes we can't get her to speak to either of us for days and days. I feel so bad for Lura, you know. She ought to have a happy childhood, don't you think so? even if it *is* an extra long one. Seems, if that's all we *can* do for her, just make her happy.

JIM [*in a choked voice*]: Say, I guess *you're* Lura's mother, all right.

MAGGIE [*shocked at the idea*]: Oh, no. I couldn't be that. Mother says if you're not really a mother, you can't know how a mother feels; and I'm not, you know. I'm not married.

JIM [*indignantly*]: What's that got to do with it? I've seen women runnin' over with kids that was no more mothers than I am. An' some ole maids— why, Good Lord! They mothered everything in sight.

MAGGIE [*softly, her face kindling*]: I wish I *was* her mother.

JIM [*looking at her speculatively*]: I don't see why you *didn't* get married.

MAGGIE [*surprised*]: Why, I couldn't. What would Mother and Lura do?

JIM: Sure enough. What would they? Well, if I get hold of that brother of yours, I'll make him come home and look after his family if I have to kick him all the way from Arizona.

MAGGIE [*sternly*]: If you're going to talk like that to him, you needn't look him up at all. None of us feels that way about Jim.

JIM: Well, you have a good right to.

MAGGIE: Say, I wish you'd put yourself in Jim's place, once. Things were hard for him here. I see just how it was, now.

JIM: The deuce you do!

MAGGIE: I couldn't help seeing. It isn't natural for a boy to be loving his mother all the time, I 'spose; and Mother is a great one for petting and love-talk. Jim couldn't bear to disappoint her—he has the *kindest* heart—so he had to go off some place where he wouldn't feel like a brute.

JIM [*with great satisfaction*]: That's it. He had to. [*In sudden revulsion.*] But he was a dirty quitter, just the same. [*Maggie does not notice his words. Steps are heard on the stair. Maggie's eyes turn toward the door; her face lights with gentle happiness. She rises hastily, puts the doll into a drawer, and turns for an instant toward Jim.*]

MAGGIE: Here's my little girl.

[*The stair-door is pushed softly open and Lura enters. Her figure is that of a small, slight, elderly woman. She wears steel-bowed spectacles, but her face is unlined, and her expression is wistfully appealing, like that of a child. Her iron-*

gray hair is held back by a child's circle-comb and tied with a red-ribbon top-
knot. Her short, red and blue plaid, woolen dress is made in a child's fashion.
Her movements are timid, yet without the self-consciousness of an adult. Maggie
goes to meet Lura, who hesitates at sight of Jim, puts her arm around her and
leads her forward.]

MAGGIE: Come in, dear. This is my sister Lura. This gentleman has come
to see about renting a room, but I'm afraid we haven't got any for him. [*Jim*
rises and offers his hand. His expression is wholly kind and pitiful.]

JIM: How do you do—Lura?

LURA [*shakes hands, looking solemnly into Jim's face, and turning to Mag-*
gie]: Is it brother Jim?

MAGGIE: Oh, no dear. [*To Jim.*] She asks God every night to send
brother Jim home to us, so whenever any man comes to the house on an
errand she thinks it must be Jim. I don't wonder; it's been a long time. [*To*
Lura.] But God hasn't sent him yet, dear.

LURA [*decisively*]: I think it's time He did, don't you, Maggie? [*She fon-*
dles Maggie's hand, swinging her arm by it and looking shyly at Jim.]

JIM [*steps forward with an air of sudden decision and takes Lura's other*
hand]: Lura, you tell sister Maggie you guessed it, first time. It *is* brother Jim!

LURA [*jumps up and down, chanting ecstatically*]: He's come home for
Christmas! 'n brought me some presents!

MAGGIE [*incredulously, putting out a hand to still Lura*]: Jim? No, 'tisn't.

JIM [*gently*]: Yes, it is. I thought you wouldn't know me. I've got so fat and
bald. And these glasses. [*He takes them off. Maggie moves toward him as if in*
a dream, and suddenly flings herself into his arms.]

MAGGIE [*in a sobbing voice*]: Oh, Jim, *why* didn't you tell me? Here I went
on talking like a great zany, telling you all the things you knew—

JIM: You told me lots I didn't know, too.

LURA [*charging upon his pockets*]: What'd you bring me? A doll an'—

MAGGIE [*pulling Lura's hands away*]: Lura, *dear*. You mustn't. That's rude.
Let me talk to brother Jim a minute. [*She keeps an arm around Lura as she*
turns again to Jim.] Did you come clear from Arizona, Jim? I can't believe it.

JIM [*laughing in some embarrassment*]: Oh, I ain't been in Arizona for
fifteen years. I just happened to be down to the races at Galesburg an' so I
thought mebbe I'd run over an'—an' take a look at things here.

MAGGIE [*looking earnestly into his face*]: Oh, Jim, didn't you *mean* to
come home?

JIM [*uneasily*]: Oh, well, I didn't know *what* I was goin' to do. Thought I'd
prospect 'round a little an' see. An' it came to me I'd get the laugh on you,

askin' for a room an' makin' you talk some about *me*, if I could. That went slick, didn't it? You're an easy mark, Magsie.

MAGGIE: I don't care.

JIM: Well, I guess the laugh's on me, all right. You've put me wise what a low-lived scoundrel I've been, leavin' you to hold up the house all these years. But I'm goin' to give you a lift now—you just watch me.

MAGGIE: Oh, that's all right, Jim. The only thing is—I do wish you'd written to Mother.

JIM: I ought to have, Maggie, I know. If I'd only struck it rich, I could of sent some money home; but all I could scrape up seemed to go, somehow, 'n Mother kep' teasin' me to send for her till I just dreaded to get a letter. I couldn't cook up anything more to put her off with—so then I had to stop writin'.

MAGGIE: Why—Mother doesn't know yet! I must tell her, this minute. Oh, Jim, I'm so glad!

[*She flings her arms around his neck and kisses him rapturously, then goes upstairs. Lura makes another charge upon Jim's pockets and in spite of his efforts to defend them pulls out first a much soiled handkerchief, then a very flat leather purse, and a cigar case.*]

LURA [*with disappointment as each article is disclosed*]: Oh, a handkerchief! A purse! What's that? [*Jim opens it for her.*]

JIM: It's a case for cigars, Sis, but not a blame one left in it. Want to smell? [*He holds it to her nose. She wrinkles it in disgust.*]

LURA: Ugh! It's a nasty smell. I can feel what's in this pocket. [*She traces the outline of some object with her hands, while Jim holds the opening so that she cannot get into it.*] Just a bottle. A medicine bottle. Do you have to take medicine?

JIM [*with a grimace*]: Sometimes. But look here, little one. Christmas is quite a ways down the road, yet. And children that pry don't get any presents at all, you know.

LURA: Well, I won't then. [*Jim sits down and she perches on the arm of his chair, rubbing her head against his sleeve as she talks. Jim takes her hands in his and fondles them.*] Do you eat an egg for your breakfast?

JIM: Yes, if I can get it.

LURA [*warningly*]: It makes you fat. Mother does, but Maggie and I don't. We don't want to be fat. I want to fly, 'n you can't fly if you're fat. Maybe *you're* too fat. I shouldn't wonder . . . I don't want to fly like an angel, you know. They can't fly till they're dead. I want to fly like a bird. They fly all around while they're alive. I 'most flew once, but then I fell down.

JIM [*with a laugh*]: Where d'you learn so much about angels. In Sunday School?

LURA: Yes, but I don't go any more. Maggie won't let me. I think it's mean. But there are some boys that aren't very nice. Maggie doesn't want me to play with them. We have a Sunday School at home Sunday afternoons, but it isn't as nice as the real one. We can't sing, 'cause Mother is taking a nap. Shall I sing you a song I learned in the real Sunday School?

JIM: Yes.

[*Lura snuggles up closer to him and sings in a breathy, somewhat uncertain old voice, which still has something in it of the child-like quality.*]

LURA: "I think when I re-ad that sweet sto-ory of o-old,
When Je-sus was he-ere a-mong men,
How He ca-alled little chil-drun like la-ambs to his fold,
I would like to uv be-en with him then."
—Don't you think that's a nice song?

JIM [*swallowing*]: Yes, very nice, dear. You can sing it again for me, some-time.

LURA: Yes, and I know another—But I guess I'd ruther play face-tag. [*She darts her face toward his, shouting, "Face-tag!" then averts it and runs across the room, keeping her face to the wall.*]

JIM [*strides across the room to her, takes her by the shoulder and turns her face around to him*]: Face-tag. I see your face.

LURA [*beating him with her fists*]: No fair, no fair. Face-tag, I see yours. [*She darts to the other side of the room, with her face averted. The stair-door opens and Mother plunges into the room. Her hair has been roughly combed back into an approximation of tidiness. She rushes upon Jim with arms outstretched.*]

JIM: Hullo, Mother.

MOTHER: My son! My son! [*She folds him in her arms and lays her head on his shoulder. Jim kisses her and puts his arms around her.*]

JIM [*in a cooing, caressing voice*]: Guess the little Mumsie is pretty glad to see her big boy, isn't she?

MOTHER [*in a choked, hysterical voice*]: Glad! Oh, Jim, you don't *know* what I've suffered.

JIM [*patting her arm soothingly*]: Been lonesome for her big boy, has she? Well, it's all over now. Come and tell him all about it. [*He leads her to an easy chair and sits on the floor beside her, his head leaning against her knee. She strokes his hair and frequently bends down to kiss his forehead or his ear. Lura brings a little hassock, and a battered, old picture-book and seats herself near the stove where the light from it falls on her book. She looks up from time to time, listening to what is said.*]

MOTHER: Oh, Jim, my darling, *why* didn't you write to your Mother?

JIM: Why, Mumsie dear, I couldn't write any more till I had some good news for you. I thought every year I was going to make a haul, but I didn't—and—well, what was the use, saying the same old things and never making good?

MOTHER: I could have sent you some money, Jim, to make a start with, if I'd only known where to send it. Not much, of course, but I've been saving it for you all these years.

JIM: Dear little Mumsie! But I guess you and Maggie need it worse than I do.

MOTHER: I don't need anything but you, Jim. Oh, you *will* stay with me, won't you—as long as I can be with you? It won't be many years now—[*She breaks into a sob and weeps into her handkerchief for a moment, then heroically smiles through her tears. Jim rises and puts his arms around her, laying his cheek against hers.*] You will, won't you, my boy?

JIM [*fervently*]: I will, Mumsie, darling. I'll never leave you again.

MOTHER [*solemnly*]: This is the happiest moment of my life. If you only knew what I have gone through in these thirty years, shut up day after day with a human sewing-machine and an everlasting baby!

[*Lura looks up from her book.*]

JIM [*quickly*]: Lura, dear, don't you want to go upstairs and help Maggie? I guess she's getting my room ready for me.

LURA [*pouting*]: It's cold upstairs, 'xcept in Mother's room.

MOTHER: Don't bother about her. She doesn't understand.

LURA [*indignantly*]: I do, too. I understand every word you say, so there now.

MOTHER [*shrugging her shoulders and turning wearily to Jim*]: There, you see what I've had to endure. I wonder I have kept my own senses.

JIM: If it's cold upstairs, Lura, please tell sister Maggie to come down. We don't want her to catch cold, do we?

LURA: Well. [*She drops her book on the hassock and goes upstairs. Jim sits on the arm of Mother's chair.*]

MOTHER: She ought to be put in an institution. There are places enough for such people. I think it's a crime to let them live with us, don't you? You'll find my ideas very modern on all such questions. But I can't do a thing with Maggie. I'm positively afraid to speak to her again about it. You don't know how fierce she can be if anyone says a word about Lura. And I felt so helpless here all alone with her. [*Her voice hints at tears.*]

JIM: Why, Mother, you wouldn't separate Lura from Maggie, would you? She'd be miserable, and I guess Maggie would too.

MOTHER [*acridly*]: I don't know why I should be the only one to bear things.

JIM: But there's nothing repulsive about Lura. She just hasn't grown up. I don't see anything so dreadful in that.

MOTHER: Of course *you* can take it lightly, Jim. It's nothing to *you*. But just suppose you were— Oh, I can hardly say it—her mother? Oh, it's too horrible! I think I should have gone mad pretty soon, if you hadn't come. You have no idea what I've been through! Many a day I've had to sit from early morning till far into the night reading some exciting book that would keep these dreadful thoughts away. I didn't know *what* I might do. And I wanted my boy to find his mother, when he came home. [*She lowers her voice on the last sentence and buries her face on Jim's shoulder.*]

JIM [*caressing her hair*]: I wish you wouldn't feel that way about it, Mother. Poor little Lura! It's worse for her than it is for any of us.

MOTHER [*firmly, raising her head in protest*]: I don't think so at all. *She* is happy enough. And Maggie doesn't mind. *I* have all the suffering. But that seems to be a mother's lot.

JIM: Ssh.

[*Maggie enters, followed by Lura.*]

MAGGIE: Your room's all ready, Jim. It's not very warm, I'm afraid, but you must pop into bed as quick as you can.

JIM [*rising and stretching himself*]: Well, that sounds good. But I'm going to talk to you a while, Sis, before I turn in.

MOTHER [*jealously*]: Why you've been visiting with Maggie all the evening! I must have my boy now. Come up to my room, dearest, and we'll have one of our old bedtime talks. [*Sentimentally.*] I wonder if you remember them as I do.

JIM [*grimly*]: Yes, I remember them. But I guess I'll make a bee line for my room tonight. I'm fair dopey for sleep. Haven't had much lately.

MOTHER: Come right up with me, then, and after we've had our little talk I'll tuck you in, just as I always used to. [*Jim makes an involuntary grimace, which Mother catches.*] What is it, Jim, dear? Are you in pain anywhere?

JIM: A grumble in a tooth once in a while, that's all.

MOTHER: You poor, dear boy! And you never said a word about it. I shall give you a tooth-plaster to put on it.

JIM: No, thanks, Mother. The toothache for mine. Well good-night, Maggie-girl. [*Aside, as he kisses her.*] See you later—if I can work it. [*He takes Lura's face between his hands and kisses her on both cheeks.*] Good-night. Sleep tight.

LURA [*giggling delightedly*]: Good-night. Sleep tight. [*Mother advances to Lura with an air of nerving herself to do a beautiful act, and kisses her kindly on the forehead.*]

MOTHER: Good-night, Lura.

LURA [*a little mystified*]: Goo'-night.

[*Mother goes to Maggie and prints a kiss on her cheek. Maggie returns the kiss warmly, her arms about Mother.*]

MAGGIE: Good-night, Mother. I'm *so* glad. You must sleep well tonight.

[*Jim opens the stair-door for Mother. Mother draws Jim to her, and stands with an effect of tableau, at the door, as she speaks with sad sweetness.*]

MOTHER: *I* am far too happy to sleep, but I hope my children will.

[*Mother and Jim go upstairs.*]

MAGGIE: Come here, dear, and let me unfasten your dress. [*She sits down and Lura backs up to her, while Maggie unbuttons her dress, unties her hair ribbon, takes out her comb, and braids her hair loosely for the night.*]

LURA: I don't have to ask God any more to send brother Jim home, do I? 'Cause he's here. [*She laughs.*]

MAGGIE: No, dear, but you might thank God for sending him.

LURA: Aw ri'. Will he play with me in the morning after I've taken Mother's breakfast up?

MAGGIE: Maybe for a little while, dear. But he'll probably have to go to his work pretty soon.

LURA [*disappointedly*]: Oh, is *he* going to work every day, too?

MAGGIE: I hope so, dear. [*Giving her a little push as she finishes braiding her hair.*] There, go and get on your nightie. Hang your clothes neatly over the chair, so you can dress fast in the morning. [*Lura goes behind the screen. She calls.*]

LURA: He eats an egg for his breakfast—when he can get one.

MAGGIE: Well, I'm afraid he can't have one tomorrow morning. There's only one for Mother. [*She looks toward the stairway door from which Jim enters noiselessly, shoes in hand. He shuts the door without a sound, makes a gesture of silence to Maggie, hastily pulls on his shoes, picks up his overcoat and hat from the chair and puts them on.*]

MAGGIE [*fearfully*]: Oh, Jim, where are you going?

JIM: Damned if I know. I've got to get out. That's all.

MAGGIE [*as if stunned*]: Are you going away—tonight?

JIM: You bet I am. The quicker the sooner. Before she gets her claws in me, the old vampire. What the hell I ever came back for— [*He lifts his hands and drops them, shaking his head, in a gesture of hopeless incomprehension.*]

MAGGIE [*breathlessly*]: But Jim, you *mustn't*—it will *kill* her to have you go off like this.

JIM: If she stood in that door now, I'd shoot her to get out. That's how I feel.

MAGGIE: Oh, no, Jim. Don't say that. How can you mind *anything* she does, when you know how she loves you?

JIM [*disgustedly*]: Loves me! Aw, Maggie, you've got too much sense to swallow all the talk she hands out. Do you s'pose I'd mind the kissin'-matches, an' tears leaked all over me or any of the rest of it, if there was anything *to* it, really? But you know there ain't. What'd you s'pose Mother cares about *me*—what I'm thinkin' about, or whether I'm square an' decent, or anything like that, just so as the pettin' and play-actin' goes right along? That's all *she* wants. But I'm damned if I'll play up to it any more. It makes me too sick.

[*Maggie sits looking at him, wide-eyed, clasping and unclasping her hands, then rising, she throws her arms about him in an anguish of entreaty.*]

MAGGIE: Oh, Jim dear, I know she didn't bring you up right. But can't you bring yourself up, now? Oh, do stay and help make things comfy for Lura. *Can't* you, Jim?

[*As she speaks Lura emerges from behind the screen with a red woolen wrapper over her nightgown, and red knitted slippers on her feet. Neither Maggie nor Jim notices her. She hesitates a moment, looking at them, then goes over to a chair near Maggie, draws it to the stove and puts her feet on the fender.*]

JIM [*gently detaching her arms and holding both her hands in his*]: Magsie, dear, I wish I could. You don't know how I hate to sneak off like this and leave you to carry everything. But you see yourself I couldn't stand it—not if I was paid to! And I bet you couldn't yourself, if you was in my place.

MAGGIE: But Jim—

JIM [*warmly*]: I tell you, I want to, bad enough. And I need to, if it comes to that. I haven't got a nickel. But I'd get pinched and sent up before I'd stay in this house. I feel just like I'm in jail every minute.

MAGGIE: I know, Jim, dear, but couldn't you *make* yourself stay—just till after Christmas? Oh, if you only *could*!

[*A sound on the stair brings Jim to his feet, he makes for the outer door, but Mother bursts into the room, flings her arms about him, and breaks into hysterical sobs.*]

MOTHER: Oh, my son! My son! Are you going to leave me? Are you going to leave your Mother?

JIM [*soothingly*]: No, no, Mother, of course not. Can't I go out and buy a cigar without—

MOTHER [*shrieking*]: No! No! Don't deceive me, Jim. You were going to leave me. You might as well kill me now. It would be kinder.

JIM [*impatiently*]: Mother, won't you listen to me? I tell you I'm only going out to buy a cigar.

MOTHER: Maggie, tell me the truth. Is he going to leave me?

[*Maggie is silent. Mother looks from her downcast face to Jim and falls into a chair, moaning piteously.*]

MOTHER: My son, my only son! I might have known this cup of joy would be dashed from my lips. Oh, God, let me die!

[*Lura retreats to the open door of the stairway, watching her mother, with fascinated, terror-filled eyes. She makes several futile moves toward Maggie, but Mother and Jim are between and she does not venture. After a moment Maggie sees her, goes over to her and puts her arm around her.*]

MAGGIE: Go right up to bed now, Lura, dear.

LURA [*shaking her off*]: I don't want to. Is brother Jim going away? [*A muffled shriek from Mother.*]

JIM [*under his breath*]: Damnation! [*Louder.*] Mother, I do have to go away for a few days, and you see why I was afraid to tell you—you cut up so rough. It isn't exactly pleasant for me. And there's no need of making such a fuss. I'll come back to spend Christmas with you—

[*Mother rises and with a heart-broken wail again flings herself upon him.*]

MOTHER: Oh, my son, take me with you. No matter where you are going! I'll live in a cellar with you—or anywhere—or tramp the streets. Other people are nothing to me. I only want you. Think how—all these years— [*Her voice trails off and is choked in sobs.*]

JIM [*moved in spite of himself*]: There, there, Mother, don't cry so. You can't go with me till I get a place to take you to, of course, but just as soon as I find one, I'll send for you.

MOTHER [*breaking from him and taking a stand against the door*]: You must trample over your mother's dead body, if you leave this house without her!

MAGGIE [*springing to her in terror and trying to drag her from the door*]: Oh, Mother, don't say that. Don't stand there!

[*Mother pushes her aside. Lura runs to Maggie and clings to her speechlessly.*]

JIM: Don't be afraid, Maggie. I won't hurt her. [*He turns to Mother with an air of decision.*] Well, Mother, all right. If you've got to go, get your togs together. But remember I've warned you. Don't blame me for what you get into.

MOTHER [*kissing him rapturously*]: Oh, my darling boy! I don't *care* what I get into. I can endure *anything* if I'm only with you. [*In lowered voice.*] And you know I have some money—a little—for us both.

JIM [*flinching from her*]: Aw, cut that out.

MOTHER [*bravely wiping her eyes*]: Well, I'll be ready in five minutes.

JIM: All right. [*Mother starts toward the stairway, but stops, casts a suspicious glance on Jim and Maggie, goes back to the door, locks it, and takes the key with a defiant air.*]

JIM [*disgustedly*]: Oh, I say, Mother!

MOTHER [*with dignity*]: My life's happiness is at stake, Jim. I cannot afford to risk it. [*She goes out.*]

JIM: Well, isn't that the limit? Good-bye, Maggie, I'll send you the first money I can lay hands on. Sure, I will. Good-bye, Lura. Be a good girl.

[*He runs up the shade, opens the window, and vaults out of it. A shriek is heard from above, and Mother rushing down the stairs precipitates herself toward the window. Maggie intervenes, and prevents her jumping out of it. Lura looks at them in wide-eyed terror and screams shrilly as Maggie's words give her the clue to what is happening.*]

MAGGIE: Mother, you'll kill yourself!

MOTHER: Kill myself! Yes, I will. And you shan't stop me—you double-faced hypocrite, you! You drove him away, I know you did! My only son! [*She pushes Maggie from her in a fury. Maggie totters against the chest of drawers. Lura, shrinking against the wall, begins to cry.*]

MAGGIE: Oh, Lura, dear, *don't. Please* go upstairs. It's so cold here, too. [*She closes the window, takes Lura in her arms and tries to hush her crying.*]

MOTHER [*spitefully*]: Yes, it *would* be too bad if that fifty-year old cry-baby should take cold. But you can drive my only son out of the house, the only comfort of my last years, and kill me with loneliness and grief—[*sobbing*]—and *that's* all right. You don't care anything about *that*. Oh, my son, my son! The only creature I ever loved has been driven from me. And I am alone.

MAGGIE [*sharply*]: Why do you say I have driven him away? I did everything I could to keep him.

MOTHER [*sneeringly*]: Yes, you did! I know well enough what *you* did. You tried to pull me away from the door, so he could go and leave me. And why did he *want* to leave me? I never spoke a word of blame to him. I was all love and tenderness. But you made him feel he wasn't welcome here. I know all about you, Miss Maggie.

MAGGIE: But I didn't—I didn't at all.

MOTHER: You needn't tell me. That's why he went away the first time. I saw it all then, but I was powerless. All my life long you have separated me from my son, my only son. Perhaps God will forgive you, but I never shall. Never. [*Lura sobs louder.*]

MAGGIE: Mother, *please* don't talk so before Lura. She'll go upstairs in a minute, but it frightens her so.

MOTHER [*with shrill hysterical laughter*]: Lura! There's another attraction for our happy home! An idiot as well as a Pharisee! No wonder he didn't care to stay.

MAGGIE [*putting Lura aside and advancing upon Mother with a threatening aspect*]: Never let me hear that word from you again! Never as long as you live!

MOTHER [*cowering against the wall, but essaying a weak defense*]: I shall say just what I please, Miss Maggie—

MAGGIE [*seizing her by the shoulders and shaking her slightly to emphasize her words*]: *You will not. Do* you *hear* me? *Never* as long as you *live.*

MOTHER [*in a quavering voice of abject terror*]: No—no—I won't. Let me go, Maggie. [*She tries to twist herself out of Maggie's grasp.*]

MAGGIE [*sternly, with a parting shake*]: See that you don't, then.

MOTHER [*throwing herself upon Maggie with a burst of tears*]: Oh, Maggie, don't *you* turn against me, too! I'm a poor, broken old woman, and my only son has cast me off.

MAGGIE [*taking Mother in her arms*]: I'll *never* turn against you, Mother, dear. You can do *anything* to me, but you mustn't hurt Lura. [*With a sudden fierceness, holding Mother off by the shoulders and looking her squarely in the eyes.*] I'll—I'll *kill* you, if you do.

MOTHER [*sobbing wildly*]: Oh, I won't, I won't. But you love her best and *nobody* cares about me.

MAGGIE [*patting her shoulder tenderly*]: I love you too, dear. But I've *got* to make Lura happy. I used to think that maybe things would be different when Jim came home, but she has no one but me to look to now.

MOTHER [*with muffled sobs*]: But *I* have no one but you either. I want you to take care of *me*.

MAGGIE: I will, dear. I'll take care of you both—my two children. [*She smiles half-whimsically at Mother, and keeping one arm about her, holds out the other to Lura, who timidly slips into it.*]

LURA [*in a quavering voice, clinging to Maggie*]: Doesn't brother Jim *like* me, Maggie?

MAGGIE: Of course he does, darling. Mother didn't understand. And Maggie loves you, *hard.*

[*Lura snuggles closer and heaves a long, fluttering sigh of relief.*]

LURA [*almost inaudibly*]: I'm not an idiot, am I, Maggie?

MAGGIE: Indeed you're not. And I'm not a Pharisee either. Mother didn't know *what* she was saying—she was so disappointed. Did you, Mother?

MOTHER [*dramatically*]: I was *crazed* with grief. My only son had forsaken me, had trampled under foot the love of the mother who had watched and wept for him thirty years. No wonder I was— [*Her voice trails off in sobs. Lura shrinks from her, still holding to Maggie.*]

MAGGIE: I guess Jim couldn't help it, Mother. He's never learned to do hard things. But maybe he will, sometime, and then—

MOTHER: He will *never* come back to me. [*Thrusting her hand into her bosom and bringing out a packet.*] Here, Maggie, this is the money I had saved for him by the self-denial of years. I can never help him with it, now. Take it and spend it for yourself and Lura— [*She breaks into uncontrollable weeping.*]

MAGGIE [*taking the packet and glancing at it with some surprise*]: Oh, thank you, Mumsie, dear. Why, what a lot of bills. I believe there's enough to pay for the roof! [*Embracing Mother ecstatically.*] Just think how snug and tight we'll be all next winter!

MOTHER [*striking a tragic attitude*]: The lid of my coffin will cover me then. I shall not burden you long. Some morning you will find me cold and stiff in my bed—

[*Lura shudders and shrinks from her.*]

MAGGIE [*putting her hand over Mother's mouth*]: Hush, dear, I can't allow my children to say things like that.

MOTHER [*after a visible struggle*]: All right, [*she swallows hard*] —Mother. I'll try to be a good girl.

MAGGIE [*kissing her warmly*]: That's right, dear. Then will you go straight upstairs to bed, now? It's after ten. I'll come and tuck you up in a minute.

MOTHER [*in a dull, hopeless tone*]: I might as well.

MAGGIE: Good-night, dear.

MOTHER: Good-night. [*She goes out, closing the stair-door behind her.*]

MAGGIE [*pulling a chair close to the stove*]: Warm your feet a minute, darling, before you run up to bed. [*Lura sits with her feet on the fender. Maggie moves about the room, setting it in order.*]

LURA [*in wondering tones*]: Is Mother going to play being a little girl now?

MAGGIE [*wearily*]: I guess so.

LURA [*sagely*]: Maybe she's tired playing Mother. Is she going to be a good little girl or a bad little girl?

MAGGIE [*with a sigh which she turns into a laugh*]: We aren't any of us good all the time, are we? The Wicked Fairy sometimes lays a spell on us, you know.

LURA [*eagerly*]: And somebody must take it off again—like little Bright-Eyes. Oh, Magsie! [*She jumps up from her seat and runs over to hug Maggie, ecstatically.*]

MAGGIE [*putting her arm about Lura*]: What is it, dearie?

LURA [*excitedly*]: I'll be little Bright-Eyes, an' Mother can be the Dragon, an' you can be the Good Fairy that tells me what to do. An' when it comes summer, I'll bring her every kind of flower to smell of, and the smell of one of them will take off the spell!

MAGGIE [*heartily*]: Sure enough! That's a game we can play all by ourselves, isn't it? Nobody else will know. [*She kisses Lura with lingering tenderness.*] Now you're good and warm, aren't you, sweetheart? Jump into bed fast, and Maggie will come, right away.

LURA: All right. [*She kisses Maggie and gives her two "bear hugs." Standing by the stair-door, she swings it thoughtfully to and fro.*]

LURA: I'm not going to ask God to send brother Jim home again.

MAGGIE: He won't, dear. Now scamper upstairs.

[*Lura goes upstairs. Maggie locks the window and puts coal on the fire. She picks up Lura's picture-book from the hassock, clasps it passionately to her breast, and lays her cheek against it for a moment before replacing it on the table. The tender brooding smile of a mother lights her face. She extinguishes the lamp, and, in the darkness, is heard wearily ascending the stairs.*]

16 The Girl from the Marsh Croft

from *Poems and Plays*,
edited by Laura Johnson Wylie (New York: Duffield, 1922), 86–166.

This adaptation of Selma Lagerlöf's story, featuring a peasant girl of great integrity and goodness of heart, challenges conventions of social class. Lagerlöf, a native of Sweden, was the first woman to be awarded the Nobel prize in literature (1909) and her feminist story lent itself to Buck's talent at playwriting. It was performed by the Poughkeepsie Community Theatre with the following dedication to its founder, Gertrude Buck, printed on the program: "The Community Theatre has striven to express in some small measure the deep indebtedness it bears to her. Not for her work alone do we feel gratitude, but rather for the spirit with which she imbued the Theatre, a spirit so enduring that it continues to manifest itself as a living memorial to her life work."

Buck was deeply involved with the Community Theatre until her death, and in 1928 Ruth Benedict wrote a letter to the New York Times *protesting that Buck's "name has dropped out from mention of the theatre's present activities, and at Vassar College incoming freshmen plunge into dramatics, which take on an increasingly cheerful professionalism, with no idea that there ever existed the person who struggled years to hatch this condition and only succeeded just before she died" (3 October 1928).*

Characters

HELGA, the girl from the Marsh Croft
PER MARTENSSON, her betrayer
THE JUDGE
GUDMUND ERLANDSSON, a young farmer, heir of Närlunda
ERLAND ERLANDSSON, Gudmund's father
INGEBORG, Gudmund's mother
HILDUR, Gudmund's fiancee
THE COUNCILMAN, Hildur's father
THE COUNCILMAN'S WIFE, Hildur's mother
KARIN, Hildur's sister
THORWALD LARSSON, a young poet ⎫ friends of Gudmund
HUGO ANDERSSON, a student at Upsala ⎭
INGRID, a housemaid

OLGA, a barmaid
A Swiss Pedlar
A Constable
Spectators in the Courtroom
Riders
Musicians

PROLOGUE

The Courtroom of a rural district in Sweden. The Judge, a middle-aged man, with a cynical expression and an irritable manner, sits at a heavy table strewn with papers, right front. Deal benches run from front to back of the stage. Half a dozen spectators, mostly farmers, occupy the benches further from the table. The Judge and the spectators, in common with all other characters except the pedlar, wear the peasant costumes of Varmland.

Gudmund Erlandsson sits nearest the audience. He is dressed smartly in a short hunting jacket, a small gray felt hat and top boots into which his trousers are tucked. He looks honest and kindly. At first, he, like the other spectators, glances at Helga somewhat contemptuously; but as the case proceeds, he leans forward to look at her with an expression of unconcealed admiration.

On the bench in front, nearest the Judge's table, but sitting far from one another, are Per Martensson, a prosperous farmer of about forty, with a bold and dashing appearance, and Helga, a young servant girl, not more than eighteen years of age, with an oval face, delicate features, and pale brown hair curling softly about her head. She wears a Swedish peasant costume consisting of a skirt of dark blue wool reaching to the ankle, and a yellow apron tied with leather strings from whose ends dangle little tassels, a bodice of red cloth over a white waist, red stockings, low shoes and a red cap. Her eyes are swollen with weeping. She twists a drenched handkerchief nervously in her hands.

JUDGE [*in a loud voice*]: Next case. [*Fussing with papers on the desk, finally fishing out one, adjusting his eye glasses, and reading from it in a loud voice.*] Helga Nilsdotter, plaintiff, against Per Martensson, defendant. Are the parties here? [*He glances at Helga and Martensson. Martensson nods easily and Helga bows her head into her handkerchief in a fresh burst of tears.*]

JUDGE [*impatiently*]: Helga Nilsdotter, stand up. [*Helga rises with an attempt to wipe away her tears. She looks steadily down at the Judge's table, twisting her handkerchief in her hands. The spectators nudge each other and smile knowingly.*]

JUDGE [*irritably pounding the table with his fists, as he notes these glances*]: Order in the court! What is your name?

HELGA [*in a trembling voice*]: Helga Nilsdotter.

JUDGE [*writing down each answer before he asks the next*]: Your age?

HELGA: Eighteen last April.

JUDGE: Residence?

HELGA: The Marsh Croft.

JUDGE: Occupation?

HELGA: General servant,—that is, I was. [*She breaks into silent weeping.*]

JUDGE: Do you know Per Martensson?

HELGA: Yes, sir,—I worked in his family.

JUDGE: When?

HELGA: From January to August last year.

JUDGE: What are you bringing suit against him for?

HELGA [*with bowed head, in a low, tremulous voice*]: He is the father of my child and I cannot support it. No one wants me in service now, and the child will starve.

JUDGE: You want an order from the Court to compel Per Martensson to support this child?

HELGA: Yes, sir.

JUDGE: You say Per Martensson is the father of the child?

HELGA: Yes, sir.

JUDGE: Are you quite sure?

HELGA [*with surprise*]: Yes, sir. [*Snickers from the spectators.*]

JUDGE [*pounding the desk again*]: Order in the Court. [*with an access of severity in his manner.*] You know what an oath is?

HELGA: Yes, sir.

JUDGE: Will you swear, on this Bible, that Per Martensson is the father of your child?

HELGA: Yes, sir.

JUDGE [*severely*]: Do you know that if you swear falsely on a Bible, your soul is lost forever? There is no salvation for the perjurer in this world or the next.

HELGA [*shuddering*]: Yes, I know.

JUDGE: Think well, then, before you swear that Per Martensson is the father of your child.

HELGA: It is the truth.

JUDGE: Step nearer. Lay your hand on the Bible—so—now repeat after me. I swear before God—

HELGA: I swear before God—

JUDGE: That Per Martensson—

HELGA: That Per Martensson—

JUDGE: Is the father of my child—

HELGA: Is the father of my child.

JUDGE [*leaning back in his chair and surveying her sternly*]: So you want me to compel Per Martensson to support this child. Why cannot your parents take care of it?

HELGA: Oh sir, they are so poor—The Marsh Croft gives them scant food for themselves alone. And I am a burden on them now. We shall all starve together unless Per— [*Her voice is choked with sobs.*]

JUDGE [*sternly*]: That is the misery that sin brings, Helga Nilsdotter. You cannot expect decent people to employ you in their houses now.

HELGA [*weeping*]: No, sir. But the child has done no wrong.

JUDGE: He suffers for the sins of his parents. You have applied to Per Martensson for aid?

HELGA: He will not see me. Three times I have been to the farm, but the door was closed against me. I waited by the road to speak to him, but he cast me off and would not listen. Indeed, I would not bring disgrace upon him if I could help it, but I have nowhere else to turn.

JUDGE: No man can be compelled to support a child merely because some woman chooses to say it is his. That will do for you, Helga Nilsdotter. Per Martensson, stand up. [*Martensson rises.*] What is your name?

MARTENSSON: Per Martensson.

JUDGE: Residence?

MARTENSSON: The old Martensson farmstead.

JUDGE: Occupation?

MARTENSSON: Farmer.

JUDGE: Do you know Helga Nilsdotter?

MARTENSSON [*carelessly*]: Yes. She was employed for a time as servant in my household.

JUDGE: Are you the father of her child?

MARTENSSON: I am not. [*Helga starts in amazement and looks at him. He looks straight at the judge.*]

JUDGE: Did you ever carry on an intrigue with her?

MARTENSSON: Never. [*Helga stares at him in undisguised astonishment.*]

JUDGE: Will you swear to these statements?

MARTENSSON: I will. [*The handkerchief Helga has been twisting in her hands falls to the floor. An expression of doubt and perplexity crosses her face as if she cannot believe what she has heard.*]

JUDGE: Place your hand upon the Bible. So. [*Helga half rises from her seat and sinks back again.*] Now repeat after me. I swear before God—

MARTENSSON [*in a low stumbling voice*]: I swear before God—

HELGA [*rising in terror*]: Oh stop! [*She sweeps Martensson's hand off the Bible and seizing the book, holds it close to her breast in a defensive attitude. The Judge pounds the table furiously.*]

JUDGE: What are you doing, woman? Put the Bible down.

HELGA [*bursting into tears*]: He shall not take the oath. He shall not.

JUDGE: What is the matter with you? What business have you with the Bible?

HELGA: He must not take the oath.

JUDGE [*sharply*]: Are you so determined to win your suit?

HELGA [*in a high, agitated voice*]: No. No. I want to withdraw the suit. I don't want to force him to swear falsely. He mustn't lose his soul.

JUDGE: Are you out of your mind?

HELGA [*slowly and earnestly looking into the Judge's face*]: Let me withdraw the suit. He is the father of my child. I am still fond of him. I don't want him to be lost forever. [*The Judge looks at her almost incredulously, then with a sudden irradiation of his stern face. The spectators breathe a quick sigh of relief and satisfaction. They gaze at Helga with something approaching reverence in their expression.*]

JUDGE [*after an instant's silence*]: It shall be as you wish, my child. The case shall be stricken from the calendar. [*He starts to draw a line through his paper.*]

MARTENSSON [*starting forward*]: But I—

JUDGE: Well, what is it? Have you anything to say?

MARTENSSON [*hanging his head and speaking almost inaudibly*]: Well— no. I dare say it is best to let it go that way.

JUDGE [*looking contemptuously at him*]: The hearing is adjourned. [*He rises, walks around the table and offers his hand to Helga.*] Thank you! [*She shakes hands with him in some bewilderment, looking wonderingly up into his face. Per Martensson slinks out of the door, and the spectators follow him, casting glances of respect and admiration back at Helga, who sinks down again listlessly upon the bench. The Judge leaves the room, and after a moment she rises to go, but stops halfway to the door overcome with another gust of tears.*]

[*Gudmund, who, as one of the spectators, has been visibly moved by Helga's action, returns to the room just as she abandons herself to her grief, and stands for an instant irresolute in the doorway. He comes in a few steps, but she does not hear him. He listens to her inarticulate bursts of grief and makes as if to go, but finally shuffles slightly with his feet so that she hears and springs up, choking down her sobs and standing all aquiver in pose of flight.*]

GUDMUND [*in a soothing voice*]: Don't be afraid, Helga. I want to speak to you.

HELGA: It is not best for any honest young man to be seen speaking to me, Gudmund Erlandsson.

GUDMUND [*with conscious pride*]: It will not hurt me. Tell me, what can you do now, Helga? How will you live—and your child?

HELGA [*choking down a sob*]: I do not know.

GUDMUND: I will ask my mother to employ you at the farm. Since she was ill she needs some one to be feet for her—to run errands for her and to wheel her about in her chair.

HELGA [*clasping her hands in an ecstasy of gratitude*]: It is a kind thought, Gudmund, and God will bless you for it. But [*sadly*] Mother Ingeborg will not want me in her house.

GUDMUND: Nonsense, Helga. Of course, she will. I will tell her what you have done today, and she will see that you are not a bad girl.

HELGA: I am not a bad girl. But I did wrong. And it will not be forgotten.

GUDMUND: You wait and see. Why you were only seventeen! And you've got fifty years more to make it right in!

HELGA [*sobbing and wringing her hands*]: Oh Gudmund, don't. I can't make it right, *ever.* There is only one thing to do now, and I shall do it.

GUDMUND: One thing, Helga? And what is it?

HELGA [*in a low voice*]: Do not ask me, Gudmund. It concerns me only.

GUDMUND: Do you mean—What *do* you mean, Helga?

HELGA: I will not tell you. It is nothing to you, nor to anyone.

GUDMUND: It is something to me, and to all of us, Helga, after today. You have given us something that we may remember when there seems to be no goodness in the world.

HELGA [*surprised*]: I?

GUDMUND: Did you not see how the Judge wished to shake your hand?

HELGA: It was kind of him. And you, too, have been kind to me. But there is not enough for the four of us on the Marsh Croft, and I cannot tell my father and mother that Per Martensson will not help us— [*She breaks off with a sob.*]

GUDMUND [*moving a step toward her and patting her hand soothingly*]: Poor little Helga!

HELGA [*snatching her hand away, covering her face and breaking into a flood of tears*]: I must go away where—I can never—come back again. Then little Nils can have enough to eat.

GUDMUND: Helga! Are you thinking of the Marsh? [*Helga nods vehemently without uncovering her face.*]

GUDMUND [*seizing both hands from her face and holding them tight in his*]: Don't you *dare*, Helga Nilsdotter!

HELGA [*struggling to free her hands*]: Let me alone, Gudmund. I know very well what is best for all of us.

GUDMUND [*shaking her gently*]: You are a wicked girl, Helga. Do you want to lose your soul? You would not let Per Martensson throw his away today, and I will not let you, either.

HELGA [*still sobbing*]: It can't be a sin, Gudmund, to go out of the world when there is no place for you in it.

GUDMUND: But there *is* a place. I will talk with my mother and bring you word in the morning. Promise that you will wait till I come.

HELGA [*after a pause, putting out both her hands to him in a gesture of impulsive gratitude*]: I will wait, Gudmund.

GUDMUND [*clasping her hands and looking solicitously into her eyes*]: You will not be afraid to go home now, will you, Helga?

HELGA: No, I shall tell my parents that you will speak to Mother Ingeborg for me; and perhaps they will not be so angry, because I am to have no help from Per Martensson. [*She drops her hands from his and turns away, as if to go.*]

GUDMUND [*taking a step toward her*]: It is a long walk for you, Helga. You can ride with me as far as the Crossroads.

HELGA: Oh no, Gudmund, I thank you with all my heart, but I will not ride with you.

GUDMUND [*brusquely*]: Nonsense, Helga. Why not?

HELGA: It is not fitting that I should ride with you, Gudmund, and you understand this quite well. I will not repay your kindness by leading anyone to think less of you.

GUDMUND: What do I care what low-minded fools think? Come along, Helga. I'll drive my horse up to the door. [*Starts to go.*]

HELGA: Forgive me, Gudmund, but I cannot ride with you. Good-bye. [*Sits down resolutely and begins to loosen her shoes.*]

GUDMUND: What are you doing?

HELGA: I shall carry my shoes. They are new and it is a long walk.

GUDMUND [*with a tender, teasing note in his voice*]: You are a headstrong girl, Helga. I must tell my mother that you are one to take your own way, and perhaps she will not want to employ you.

HELGA [*sorrowfully, but resolutely, slipping off her shoes and stockings*]: You must tell her what you will, Gudmund, but I will never do you an injury. Good-bye to you.

GUDMUND [*half annoyed, but indulgent*]: Good-bye, Helga Headstrong. I shall speak only good of you to my mother. But you must be more docile when you are under her rule. [*He stands in the door for a moment, smiling protectingly down at her. She smiles up at him with complete trustfulness.*]

HELGA: I will try, Gudmund. [*Exit Gudmund.*

Helga rapidly stuffs her stockings into her shoes, ties the shoes together and hangs them about her neck, pins her skirt up around the bottom, opens the door a crack and peers out to make sure that no one is outside, then goes quietly out.]

CURTAIN

ACT I

Six weeks later. The living room at Närlunda: a spacious room with an immense fireplace occupying nearly all the right wall. Above the fireplace hangs a pole which passes through the holes of countless loaves of ring-bread, big as the wheel of a wheelbarrow, but thin as a wafer. Wide windows and a glass door at back, showing a garden in full bloom. The ceiling has massive beams and the floor is strewn with green twigs. Benches of heavy oak stand near the fireplace and against the walls. A heavy oak table covered with books and magazines is in the center of the room. A loom stands in one corner, and two spinning wheels near by. A door at left leads to the kitchen and bedrooms.

Helga is discovered, in Swedish costume as before, her yellow apron filled with fresh green twigs which she scatters on the newly scrubbed floor. As she works, she hums joyously a Swedish folk-song. When she talks, she is full of eager, unconscious gestures; her bubbling, childish laughter is frequently heard: and she seems altogether transformed from the despairing creature of the Prologue. She has covered all but a small section of the floor at the front of the stage, and finishes this as Gudmund enters, bearing a basket of cones for the fire. He sets it down by the hearth, after laying a few on the logs. Helga, meanwhile, tosses the last twigs from her apron, glances critically at a tall vase of wild appleblossoms on the table, loosens the branches from one another so that they stand out in graceful lines, and surveys the result with immense satisfaction.

HELGA [*gazing rapturously at the apple-blossoms*]: Aren't they beautiful, Gudmund? Do you think Hildur will notice them?

GUDMUND: No doubt she will. And she will thank you, when I tell her that you gathered them for her.

HELGA: They are from the wild trees by the road. I could not get many,— the twigs were so gnarly and hard to break. Will you lend me your knife, Gudmund? I want to cut an armful of them and strew the driveway before her.

GUDMUND [*handing her a knife from his pocket, with an indulgent smile*]: But Hildur is not a queen, little one.

HELGA [*slipping the knife into the pocket of her apron*]: She will be queen of Närlunda,—after tomorrow. Then we shall dress the house with birch boughs for the bride. But we would do that for anyone you married, these are for Hildur herself. [*As the talk goes on, she deftly puts the finishing touches to the room, dusting the furniture, setting the books and magazines in order upon the table, etc. Gudmund standing by the fire, watches her.*]

GUDMUND: So Hildur is fond of apple-blossoms?

HELGA: I don't know. But they are like her. Don't you think so, Gudmund?—only too pink. She is whiter,—more like the orchard blossoms. Oh, Gudmund! [*She claps her hands in an ecstasy of appeal.*]

GUDMUND: What is it, little one?

HELGA: May I not cut branches from the orchard,—armfuls to strew before Hildur?

GUDMUND: Why, little Vandal! If you did that, we should have but a short crop of apples in the fall.

HELGA: But Hildur would rather have the blossoms now, than the apples next winter!

GUDMUND [*doubtfully*]: Would she? But what would the Councilman say? No doubt he would take back his word, even on the day before the wedding, and forbid his daughter to marry the poor farmer, who had no more sense than wealth. Since I am not so rich as the Councilman, Helga, I must try to be as prudent.

HELGA: But no one is as rich as the Councilman,—except, perhaps, the King himself.

GUDMUND [*laughing*]: Except the King. Very true, little Helga.

HELGA: But the King himself has no more beautiful home than you have, Gudmund. [*Looking about with affectionate admiration.*]

GUDMUND: You think so, Helga? Are you content then, to be here with us?

HELGA: Indeed, I am! Mother Ingeborg and all of you have been as kind as angels to me.

GUDMUND: Have you not been homesick for the forest? I have heard that one who belongs to the forest cannot help yearning for it.

HELGA: Oh yes, in the beginning, I was homesick; but not now, any more. At first,—but you mustn't speak of this to your mother.

GUDMUND: I will be silent, if you wish me to.

HELGA: I understood, of course, all the time, how well it was for me to be here; but there was something that took hold of me and wanted to draw me back to the forest. I felt as if I were deserting and betraying someone who had a right to me.

GUDMUND: It was, perhaps—[*He checks himself.*]

HELGA: No, it was not the boy I longed for. My mother had made him her own and he had no more need of me. It was nothing in particular. I felt as though I were a wild bird that had been caged and I thought I should die if I were not let out.

GUDMUND [*smiling*]: To think that you had such a hard time of it!

HELGA [*smiling back at him*]: I didn't sleep a single night. As soon as I went to bed, the tears began to flow, and when I got up of a morning, the pillow was wet through.

GUDMUND: You have wept much in your time. But you are not homesick now?

HELGA: No, I have been cured. Shall I tell you how?

GUDMUND: Yes. Tell me.

HELGA: When I was the most unhappy, I asked Mother Ingeborg to let me go home on a Saturday evening, and remain over Sunday. I meant to tell my mother and father that I could never, no never, go back to Närlunda. But they were so happy because I had found service with good and respectable people, that I didn't dare to tell them.

GUDMUND [*softly*]: Poor little Helga!

HELGA: But I didn't need to tell them. For on Monday morning as I awoke and lay crying and fretting, because I knew I must return to the farm,—suddenly I remembered hearing that if one took some ashes from the hearth in one's home and strewed them on the fire in the strange place, one would be rid of homesickness.

GUDMUND: That was a remedy easy to take.

HELGA: Yes, but it has this effect also. Afterwards one can never be content in any other place. So, if one were to go away—

GUDMUND: Couldn't one carry ashes along to every place one moved to?

HELGA: No. It can't be done more than once. So it was a great risk to try anything like that.

GUDMUND [*laughing*]: I shouldn't have taken such a chance.

HELGA: But I did. It was better than having to seem an ingrate in your mother's eyes and in yours, when you had tried to help me. So I brought a little ashes from home, and when no one was in, I scattered them over the hearth— [*She makes a gesture of scattering them over the hearth.*]

GUDMUND: And you believe this is what helped you?

HELGA: You shall judge. I thought no more about the ashes all that day. There was much to be done, and I went about the house grieving, exactly as before, until the fire was lighted on this hearth in the evening. After the milking was done, when I entered this room—

GUDMUND [*encouragingly*]: What then?

HELGA: As I lifted the latch, it flashed across my mind that I was going into our own cabin and that mother would be sitting by the hearth. This flew past like a dream, but when I came in, it seemed really good to enter,—it had not been so before. Your mother and the rest of you had never appeared so pleasant as you did in the firelight. You were no longer strangers to me, and I could talk to you about all sorts of things. I was so astonished that I could hardly keep from clapping my hands and shouting. I wondered if I had been bewitched; and then I remembered the ashes. [*She claps her hands in joyous recollection and looks up at him triumphantly.*]

GUDMUND [*teasingly*]: This is indeed marvelous. But what if sometime you had to leave Närlunda?

HELGA [*in a quivering voice, dropping her hands apart*]: Then I must long to come back again all my life.

GUDMUND [*laughing, but warmly*]: Well, I shall not be the one to drive you away. [*He stoops to put more cones on the fire. A sound is heard at the door on the left and Helga springs to open it. A wheel-chair, in which sits Mother Ingeborg, a kindly, strong faced, gray haired woman of fifty, is propelled into the room by Erland Erlandsson, a man about the same age, partly bald and wearing a black skull cap. They both wear the peasant costumes of Varmland. Mother Ingeborg's manner is authoritative but benevolent, Erland's quiet and full of humorous understanding.*]

HELGA [*joyously*]: Will you look at the room, Mother Ingeborg? Is all as you would have it here? [*She takes the chair from Erland and, as the following talk goes on, wheels Mother Ingeborg about the room, until Mother Ingeborg smiles and nods approval. Gudmund and his father meanwhile confer in low tones near the fireplace.*]

MOTHER INGEBORG: It is very well, my child. You have done all that I could, were my legs strong to bear me about. The Councilman's wife can find little amiss, I fancy, in our housekeeping. Eh, Erland?

ERLAND: There is no better housekeeper in all Sweden than Mother Ingeborg. Did not the Councilman's wife say so herself, when she first visited our home?

MOTHER INGEBORG: But that may have been a compliment. Today we shall know what she really thinks. If she hints that this and that should be altered, to make Närlunda a fit place for her daughter—

ERLAND: I want nothing altered here.

MOTHER INGEBORG: Nor I. But when Hildur, out of love for our Gudmund, leaves the wealth of Alvakra for our humble farmhouse, we surely can do whatever she or her mother may wish. It is but little after all.—Is the table spread, Helga?

HELGA: Yes, Mother Ingeborg.

MOTHER INGEBORG: And fresh linen laid in all the bedrooms?

HELGA: Yes, Mother Ingeborg. Would you like to see all for yourself before they come?

MOTHER INGEBORG: I trust you as I would trust myself. There is no more then to do anywhere in the house?

HELGA: Only to cut the wild apple branches, which I would strew in the driveway. Shall I bring them in, now?

MOTHER INGEBORG: Go now, and be ready to show our guests in when they arrive.

[*During the last two speeches, Helga has moved Mother Ingeborg's chair nearer the fireplace. Now she adjusts one of the blinds so that the light does not shine directly in her face and smoothes the kerchief over one shoulder. Exit Helga. Mother Ingeborg looks after her fondly.*]

MOTHER INGEBORG: It was a good thought, Gudmund, to bring Helga here. I could hardly do without her now.

GUDMUND: She tries to please you,—one can see that.

MOTHER INGEBORG: And she is able to please me. Our house is kept as it used to be when I could be busy in it from morning to night. And I have had no care in all the preparations for the wedding. Everything is in readiness as if the fairies' hands had been at work here.

ERLAND: Helga is a good girl. It is well that she is with us, who will protect her, rather than with some Per Martensson.

[*Helga is seen without, opening the door wide for the Councilman, Mother Anna, and their daughters, Hildur and Karin. The Councilman is a pompous, aldermanic personage; his wife a stately, somewhat supercilious, but determinedly gracious Great Lady; Hildur a tall, beautiful girl of twenty, with a graceful assurance of manner that pleases rather than wins; Karin, two or three years younger than Hildur, has a round, boyish-looking face, with a lively, good-humored expression. All wear the costumes of Varmland.*]

ERLAND [*advancing*]: Welcome to Närlunda, friends.

MOTHER INGEBORG: Thanks for the last time, honored guests.

THE COUNCILMAN: I thank you, Erland Erlandsson, and you, Mother Ingeborg. [*They shake hands with Erland and Mother Ingeborg and Gudmund. Helga closes the door, and stands near the Councilman's wife, ready to assist her in removing her cloak. Gudmund goes at once to Hildur and they talk apart, he holding her hands in his.*]

MOTHER ANNA: How is it with you, Mother Ingeborg? No worse than usual, I hope!

MOTHER INGEBORG: No worse than usual, I thank you, Mother Anna. Are you also well,—and Hildur?—and Karin?

MOTHER ANNA: Very well, I thank you. [*Hildur and Karin curtsy.*] A thousand pardons Mother Ingeborg, for entering your respected house, with our outer wraps. But we could not resist the approach through your beautiful garden.

MOTHER INGEBORG: You are fully pardoned, Mother Anna. Helga will take your cloaks. [*As Helga offers to remove her cloak, the Councilman's Wife surveys her coldly through a lorgnette.*]

MOTHER ANNA [*dropping her lorgnette but without lowering her voice*]: Is that the Marsh Croft girl? [*Hildur looks up keenly at Helga and, with a slight shrug of the shoulders, turns back to Gudmund.*]

MOTHER INGEBORG [*glancing apprehensively at Helga*]: Yes. Leave the cloaks in the west bedroom, Helga.

[*As Helga offers to take Hildur's cloak from her, the Councilman's wife intervenes, takes the cloak from her daughter and hands it to Helga without looking at her. She would do the same for Karin, but Karin makes her cloak into a roll and tosses it to Helga with a boyish, "Catch, Helga." Helga flashes a grateful smile at her as she catches the cloak. The Councilman's wife pushes determinedly between Karin and Helga, speaking to Karin in a low tone, with*] *evident displeasure. As Mother Ingeborg addresses the Councilman's wife, Karin pirouettes over to Erland and engages him in animated talk.*]

MOTHER INGEBORG: Once more let me thank you, Mother Anna, for your courtesy in permitting us to have the wedding here. Otherwise my infirmity would have prevented me from seeing my only son married. And that would have been hard to bear, I assure you.

MOTHER ANNA: Do not mention it, my dear Mother Ingeborg. The Councilman and I were happy to oblige you in so small a matter. Were we not, my dear?

THE COUNCILMAN: Delighted, I assure you.

KARIN: We get the best of that bargain, I think,—All the solemn, tiresome part here, then a jolly canter to Alväkra for the dancing and fun. Indeed it suits us very well, Mother Ingeborg.

MOTHER ANNA: My dear Karin!

MOTHER INGEBORG [*smiling indulgently at her*]: Then I am glad for you as well as for myself. Shall we go into the garden now, my friends? Erland cannot wait until after dinner to show you his young plum trees.

THE COUNCILMAN [*after glancing at his wife*]: We shall be charmed.

MOTHER ANNA: Delighted.

KARIN [*mischievously*]: I'll stay with Hildur. [*She casts a glance at Hildur and pretends to stagger against the wall, transfixed by the cold stare of disapproval which she gets in return.*]

MOTHER INGEBORG: You can wheel me, Erland. The young people will join us when they wish. [*Exeunt all but Gudmund and Hildur. Gudmund holds the door open and closes it after Karin, giving her a playful shake, as, shielding her eyes with her arm, she affects to escape through it. Then he returns to take Hildur in his arms.*]

GUDMUND: Hildur! Dearest! [*He kisses her passionately again and again. She yields herself to him for a moment and then pushes him away with a coquettish gesture.*]

HILDUR: That will do, Gudmund. You must not smother me, you know.

GUDMUND [*thickly*]: I could kiss you to death. You were made to be kissed, Hildur,—and by me. [*He tries to kiss her again.*]

HILDUR [*smiling, but keeping him at a distance*]: No doubt. But I do not care to be kissed to death even by you. We shall be married many years, Gudmund, if God will. Do not let us take a pace we can't keep up.

GUDMUND: But,—but Hildur!—I can't be as sensible as you.

HILDUR [*calmly*]: Then I will be sensible for both. A wife must be so, often. And we have many things to settle today.

GUDMUND: Let the old folks settle them. While you are here, I shall think of nothing but you.

HILDUR: Mother will speak to Mother Ingeborg about that girl. Of course I cannot come to Närlunda while she is here.

GUDMUND [thunderstruck]: What girl?

HILDUR [with a contemptuous smile]: The girl from the Marsh Croft, naturally. You did not suppose I meant old Ingrid?

GUDMUND: You cannot come here if Helga—?

HILDUR: You would hardly expect me to, would you?

GUDMUND: Why, of course I should. Mother could not get on without her.

HILDUR: She will not need her when I am here. And everyone knows it is not right to keep a girl of such character in a respectable house.

GUDMUND [earnestly]: But she is not a bad girl. She was very young when she first went out to service, and it was not strange that things went badly when she came across such a dastardly brute as Per Martensson.

HILDUR: That may be. But when a girl has once gone wrong, one never knows.

GUDMUND: But if we should push her out, she might meet with misfortune again, through no fault of her own.

HILDUR: Misfortune of that kind doesn't come without fault.

GUDMUND: How hard you are, Hildur. Surely you don't want to deprive Helga of her chance to live a good life?

HILDUR [with a shrug of the shoulders]: If that girl is to remain at Närlunda, I will never come here. I cannot tolerate a person of that kind in my house.

GUDMUND: You don't know what you are doing. No one understands so well as Helga how to care for mother. We have all been happier since she came. And I have given her my word that she should stay.

HILDUR: I shall not compel you to send her away.

GUDMUND: But you make it a condition of your marrying me. Hildur, do you want a husband who has broken his word?

HILDUR [coldly]: I want nothing at all. You shall please yourself in this matter.

GUDMUND [hotly]: Please myself! Yes, to be sure. I can please myself by breaking my word to Helga, pushing her out of the one refuge she has found, and marrying you. Or I can please myself by keeping my word to her and losing you. I shall be very happy, no doubt, either way! [He flings himself away from her, and sees through the window his mother's wheelchair approaching, pushed by Erland. He goes to the door and opens it.]

MOTHER INGEBORG [*cheerfully*]: Well, my children, are you not ready to go to the garden now? I have asked to be excused, Hildur, from making the rounds of the farm. I tire so easily. But I will wait you here. Send Helga to me, will you not, Erland?

ERLAND: Certainly, my dear.

GUDMUND: I will call Helga, mother. Will you excuse me, Hildur? Father will take you to your mother, I must speak with Mother Ingeborg before I join you. [*Exit Gudmund.*]

ERLAND [*offering his arm to Hildur with courtly courtesy and chattering volubly to cover the awkwardness of the moment*]: Will you come with me, gracious Hildur, and intercede with your worthy parents for my kitchen garden? I left them arguing about the potato patch. Mother Anna was for making it larger, by rooting up all my lettuce, radishes and chives; while the Councilman would plant fewer potatoes and more cucumbers. You will tell them, will you not, that when I want a baked potato I cannot be put off with a raw cucumber? And that when a salad is to be dressed, it cannot be done with rutabaga?

HILDUR [*smiling pleasantly at him and taking his arm*]: But you should tell them yourself, Erland Erlandsson. You can put it much more eloquently than I.

ERLAND: I will tell them the story of my father. He ordered a dish of black-berries once at a hotel in Stockholm, but the waiter said they had no black-berries, "No blackberries," said my father, much annoyed, "Well, then, bring me a couple of boiled eggs!" [*He laughs expectantly. Hildur looks puzzled.*]

HILDUR: How very singular! And boiled eggs in the city are so seldom fresh.

ERLAND [*opening the door for her*]: Very true, my dear Hildur. The old gentleman should have known better. On the whole, I think I won't tell your honored parents about him. Probably they would not approve of him, either. [*Exeunt, as Gudmund enters.*]

GUDMUND: I have asked Helga to come to you, Mother. Has the Council-man's wife told you to send her away?

MOTHER INGEBORG: We shall have trouble about Helga, I fear, Gud-mund. I will ask her not to appear again while they are here. Ingrid can serve the dinner.

GUDMUND [*grimly*]: It is as well the poor girl should not be insulted again. What did Mother Anna say to you?

MOTHER INGEBORG: She thinks it wrong for us to have Helga in service here; and impossible for her to remain after Hildur comes.

GUDMUND: Hildur said the same to me. They are well agreed. But I do not mean to send Helga away.

MOTHER INGEBORG: But Gudmund,—if you should lose Hildur?

GUDMUND: Then I must lose her. You could not get on without Helga, now.

MOTHER INGEBORG: Oh, my son, I would get on somehow, if only you were married to Hildur. It has been my dream for so many years!

GUDMUND: But what about my promise?

MOTHER INGEBORG: Did you promise Helga that she should stay here?

GUDMUND: This morning, just before they came I said to her,—"I shall never be the one to drive you away."

MOTHER INGEBORG: Oh, Gudmund, why did you say that? But she will not hold you to it, I am sure she won't.

GUDMUND: I shall hold myself to it. It is not best, mother, that I should give way to Hildur in this. She will think to rule me in all things and there will be unhappiness between us continually.

MOTHER INGEBORG: But you love her, Gudmund, do you not?

GUDMUND: Twenty minutes ago, I loved her to distraction; and no doubt I shall again, when this has blown over. But just now I should like to shake her!

MOTHER INGEBORG [*with a sigh*]: No doubt men often feel so. But you must be patient with her, Gudmund. Girls like her are brought up to think that way about girls like Helga. I was, too. But, perhaps, when you are married—.

[*Gudmund shrugs his shoulders doubtfully. Enter Helga. She is grave and has evidently been weeping.*]

MOTHER INGEBORG [*kindly*]: Helga, my child, you have tired yourself with all these preparations. Now will you do me still another kindness? Take Ingrid's place in the kitchen, so that all may be done well there. She is apt to be careless at the last. Let her serve dinner in your place, and after dinner, you may have a holiday for the afternoon.

HELGA: I understand, Mother Ingeborg. And after dinner, I will go to my home. It is best that I should leave you, now.

MOTHER INGEBORG: Leave us, Helga?

HELGA: Yes, Mother Ingeborg. You gave me shelter when there was no one to open a door to me, and I will never leave you while you want me to stay. But it will be easier for all of you now, if I am no longer here.

GUDMUND: No, Helga. We do not wish you to go. You have made a place for yourself here, and you shall not be driven from it.

HELGA: I thank you, Gudmund. But I will not repay kindness with injury. Mother Ingeborg knows that it is best for me to go.

MOTHER INGEBORG: You are more generous than we, Helga. We do not want you to go,—any of us,—but, perhaps—for a time—there will be some way later, I am sure, for you to return to us.

HELGA: Good bye, Mother Ingeborg. Good bye, Gudmund. [*She shakes hands with Mother Ingeborg and offers her hand to Gudmund, who refuses to shake it.*]

GUDMUND [*hotly*]: I won't have it so, I tell you. Mother, why don't you tell her she must stay?

HELGA [*quietly*]: I will not stay, Gudmund, not even if Mother Ingeborg should bid me to. Good bye. [*She turns, as if to go.*]

MOTHER INGEBORG: Do not go now, my child. You must not walk all that long way. The master will drive you home this afternoon, after our guests have gone. And he will pay you your wages for the month.

HELGA: It is kind of you, but I am well able to walk.

MOTHER INGEBORG: Let him drive you, Helga. It is so little we can do—he will carry with him flax enough for six tablecloths and six dozen napkins, which you must weave for me.

HELGA: I thank you, Mother Ingeborg. The work will make us all happy.

MOTHER INGEBORG: Besides he will explain to your parents that we are parting with you now only because after Hildur comes, we shall not need so much help. And that when the weaving is finished, I will find you another good situation, where you will be safe and happy as you have been with us.

HELGA: I am very grateful to you, Mother Ingeborg, and my parents will be proud that I have pleased you. [*Exit Helga, as Erland and the guests are seen approaching through the garden. They enter with a confused babble of thanks and compliments.*]

MOTHER ANNA: I am enchanted, Mother Ingeborg. Your dairy— [*She throws up her hands in an ecstacy of admiration.*]

THE COUNCILMAN: A fine herd of Holsteins you have, Gudmund.

GUDMUND [*as if aroused from a dream*]: Hol— Oh, yes. Very fine indeed.

ERLAND [*hastily*]: The Councilman greatly admires our prize bull.

THE COUNCILMAN: A magnificent creature. I have no finer on my farm.

MOTHER INGEBORG: Did you drink a gourd of new milk, Hildur, as you did before?

HILDUR: We all did. It was delicious—so cool and sweet-smelling.

MOTHER ANNA: Quite a farmer's wife, already, is she not, Mother Ingeborg? [*They all laugh and Hildur pretends to a pretty confusion. Enter*

Thorwald and Hugo, two young men of about Gudmund's age. Thorwald is slender and flaxen-haired, with large, lustrous, abstracted eyes. He carries a fiddle under his arm. Hugo is shorter and sturdier of build, with a shock of brown hair. He wears spectacles and looks like the typical University student.]

MOTHER INGEBORG: Here are our other guests!

[*Gudmund springs to the door and flings it open, greeting them both with an obvious appearance of relief on their arrival. The two young men bow low over the hand of Mother Ingeborg and each of the other ladies, during the following speeches. Erland and the Councilman nod to them in friendly fashion.*]

GUDMUND [*heartily*]: Come in, old chaps, come in.

ERLAND: Welcome, my friends.

MOTHER INGEBORG: Thanks for the last time.

HUGO: I thank you, Erland Erlandsson, and you, Mother Ingeborg.

[*Thorwald only bows in acknowledgment of these greetings. After bending over Hildur's hand, he forgets altogether to salute Karin and retires to a corner whence he can stare unobserved at Hildur, while playing imaginary tunes in the air on the strings of his fiddle.*]

MOTHER ANNA [*patronizingly to Hugo as he bends over her hand*]: So here is our University student! What honors have you brought home to us, in Värmland, Hugo Andersson?

HUGO [*somewhat embarrassed*]: Nothing, as yet, Mother Anna, I am sorry to say. But I have not spent my time in idleness.

MOTHER ANNA: I am glad to hear that, indeed. The young men of these days have so little sense of responsibility. And what are you doing for yourself, Thorwald Larsson?

HILDUR [*reproachfully*]: Thorwald is a poet, mother. We do not expect poets to work for money like other men.

THORWALD [*gazing at Hildur gratefully*]: I thank you, Hildur Ericsdotter. Everyone expects it but you, I think.

GUDMUND: But your father has let you off, now, Thorwald, hasn't he?— since you nearly killed yourself in the forest.

THORWALD: Yes. He'd rather my head were a little cracked than broken outright.

HILDUR: How was it you were nearly killed, Thorwald Larsson?

THORWALD [*with a laugh*]: I tried my best to go into my father's business, as he wanted me to. But I could not tell one kind of lumber from another. And in the forest I would sometimes take a book of poems from my pocket and read it as I walked.

GUDMUND [*laughing uproariously*]: So one day he ran into a tree and broke his head open and lay unconscious till a searching party found him. Poor old Thorwald! [*All laugh.*]

MOTHER INGEBORG: Then your father has given up all hopes of making a timber merchant of you?

THORWALD: Yes. And what is more, he has given up a good income to me while he lives and has willed the business to me, under trustees, so I can go on forever writing poetry and playing the fiddle. What do you think of that for a man who hates poetry and music?

THE COUNCILMAN: Very extraordinary, upon my word!

THORWALD [*with feeling, speaking as if to Hildur alone*]: If I could make myself into the kind of a son he really wants by chopping myself into small pieces and putting them together some other way I'd do it in a minute. But I've got to disappoint him always.

HILDUR [*gravely*]: But someone must always be disappointed. And no doubt it is better to disappoint another than oneself.

THORWALD [*deeply impressed*]: How true that is! Not to disappoint one-self—I shall remember that.

KARIN [*irrepressibly*]: I'm so glad you've brought your fiddle, Thorwald. Now we can dance the crown off the bride's head.

MOTHER ANNA: By no means, Karin—What are you thinking of?

THE COUNCILMAN [*shaking his head wisely*]: That would be unlucky. It should never be done until after the wedding.

KARIN [*exuberantly*]: Fiddlesticks! Bother! She isn't going to wear her wedding dress, is she? That's the only thing that's really unlucky. I've got to practice catching her crown.

MOTHER INGEBORG: Little madcap! Do you want to wear the bride's crown so soon?

KARIN: Indeed I do—I never get my own way at home. Please, Hildur! Strike up a dance, Thorwald. [*She pulls Hugo and Erland, who stand near her, to the other side of the room and, standing between them, and holding each by the hand, begins to skip up and down like an impatient child.*]

KARIN: Come, Hildur. Hurry up, Thorwald. [*Thorwald looks at Hildur for permission to play, but she does not give it.*]

HILDUR [*coldly*]: I have no crown.

KARIN [*dropping the hands of Hugo and Erland and looking about the room*]: Oh, I forgot that,—here, this will do. [*She runs hastily to the vase of wild apple branches, and detaches two or three small sprays, pulling the rest impatiently out and dropping them on the table. She twists the small sprays with a few deft movements into a circle and puts it on Hildur's head.*]

KARIN [*stepping back and viewing her handiwork*]: Behold the bride! I believe it's more becoming than the golden one will be. [*Hildur takes the crown from her head and tosses it contemptuously away. Karin dexterously catches it.*]

KARIN [*with bubbling laughter*]: Aha! I caught it that time. Little Karin may be your next bride after all!

HUGO [*adventurously*]: After all—what? Who is more likely? [*Karin drops him a curtsy.*]

KARIN: We must have more room. May we push back the table, Mother Ingeborg?

MOTHER INGEBORG: Surely, my child,—whatever you wish. [*Gudmund and Erland push back the table. While they are doing so, Karin turns to Hugo.*]

KARIN: Have you got a clean pocket handkerchief, Hugo? [*Hugo produces it.*] You can blindfold her, then. [*Laughingly Hugo advances towards Hildur, but Thorwald, as if impelled by a force he cannot resist, interposes between them.*]

THORWALD [*breathlessly*]: Oh, let Gudmund do it! [*Amazed, Hugo, Karin, and Hildur stare at him for an instant, then look at Gudmund, who stands apart from the group, moodily abstracted, hearing nothing that has been said, and even unconscious of the attention suddenly focused upon him.*]

KARIN [*teasingly*]: Listen to the poet! Such fine feelings for our Gudmund, who never even thought of them himself! [*Hugo, Erland and Karin laugh loudly. Thorwald shrinks back in confusion. Hildur frowns and tosses her head slightly. Gudmund wakes up from his abstraction at the sound of his name.*]

GUDMUND [*with a forced laugh*]: What's the joke?

KARIN: Will your Highness, the Prince Consort, graciously allow your gentleman in waiting, Hugo, to bind the eyes of your fair Princess for the dance?

GUDMUND [*carelessly*]: Go ahead, old man.

HILDUR [*turning with a swiftly gracious movement to Thorwald and bending her head to him*]: Thorwald, will you, please? [*Thorwald, in an agony of embarrassment, draws out his handkerchief, and binds it about Hildur's eyes. Karin sets the apple blossom crown again upon Hildur's head, seizes upon her mother and forms with her, Erland, Gudmund and Hugo a ring about Hildur. The Councilman remains seated by Mother Ingeborg.*]

KARIN: Mother, you must chaperone me. But don't you dare catch the crown! You're excused, Father, to talk with Mother Ingeborg. I know you'd lots rather.

THE COUNCILMAN [*gratefully*]: Thank you, my dear, I would.

MOTHER ANNA: But my dear Karin—

KARIN [*dragging her along*]: Oh, be a sport, Mother! Your dancing days aren't quite over!

MOTHER ANNA [*bridling*]: Not at all, my dear. Why should they be?

KARIN: Come along then. Strike up, Thorwald.

[*Thorwald glances at Hildur, who smiles slightly in assent. He plays the Varmland polska, and all dance around Hildur, three or four times, when she takes the crown from her head and flings it before her. Gudmund catches it, as if mechanically. There is a burst of laughter, the music stops suddenly, and Karin flies at him in mock fury. She snatches the crown from him and beats him with it.*]

KARIN: Beast! Numbskull! You'd take my chance from me, would you? A sweet, pretty bride, isn't he? [*She puts the crown on his head and they all shout at his foolish appearance.*]

GUDMUND [*humbly, removing the crown and handing it to her with a low bow*]: I'm very sorry, Karin.

KARIN [*severely*]: Don't you know that this is a ladies' game? You men are in the ring to fill up space—that's all. I'll do the catching.

ERLAND [*apologetically*]: Gudmund was asleep, I believe.

GUDMUND: I believe I was. Try it again, Karin. I promise not to catch.

KARIN: We'll try it until *I* catch,—I warn you.

HILDUR [*pettishly*]: That's all very well for you; but I'd like to dance myself—and get this blindfold off my eyes. [*She pulls impatiently at it. Karin springs to her in alarmed entreaty, straightens the blindfold, and places the crown upon her head.*]

KARIN: Oh, Hildur *dear*, just till I catch once! Oh, *please*.

HILDUR [*reluctantly*]: Well, catch it quick, then.

KARIN [*hopefully*]: I'll wave my handkerchief toward you, and, when you smell heliotrope, you throw the crown. [*All laugh.*]

HILDUR [*stiffly*]: I shall play fair, if I play at all. [*Music strikes up and they all circle about Hildur again. Karin waves her handkerchief violently as she comes in front of Hildur, Hildur flings the crown and Karin catches it. The music stops. Laughter and applause from the dancers.*]

KARIN [*rapturously*]: I'm getting the knack. Just watch me pull it in tomorrow. [*The Councilman's Wife sinks breathlessly into a chair. Erland stands beside her and fans her. Hildur starts to pull off her blindfold and Thorwald springs to loosen it for her. They consult together in low tones during the following speeches.*]

MOTHER INGEBORG [*to Karin*]: Well done, my child. But tomorrow do not try to catch the crown. Your parents will not wish to lose a second daughter so soon.

KARIN [*confidentially*]: The fact is, Mother Ingeborg, I'm going to lock my hands tight behind me, if it comes my way tomorrow. But today doesn't count. And everybody was so glum, I had to do something.

MOTHER INGEBORG [*laughing softly and patting Karin's hand*]: We are all your debtors, little Karin.

[*Thorwald drawing a few sharp notes from his fiddle by way of attracting attention, strikes up the well known music for the dance called "Reaping Oats." Hildur beckons to Karin, who springs to her side, dragging the Councilman's wife with her.*]

KARIN [*joyously*]: Oh, we're going to reap the oats! Come, boys! [*Erland, Gudmund and Hugo range themselves opposite the women.*]

GUDMUND: Hugo will lead us.

KARIN: Hildur for us. [*The two lines dance toward one another, interweave and separate, waving their arms with the motion of a sower, singing as they move. Each verse of the women is sung first by Hildur, then repeated by the three women in unison; each verse of the men, first by Hugo, then by the three men in unison.*]

WOMEN: Grow, grain, long as our flowing locks.

MEN: Sun warm the seed, rain swell it to bursting.

WOMEN: Leap from the ground, light as we leap in the dance.

Sway in the wind, free as our bodies, giving themselves to the music.

MEN: Gleam in the life-giving sun, darken in life-giving showers.

Give to us as freely as we give the seed to the earth.

[*The music changes and the dance imitates motions of cutting the grain with a long scythe and binding it into sheaves.*]

MEN: Deep stand we in waves of the yellow grain.

WOMEN: Swing we the long bright blades that shine in the sun.

MEN: Hosts fall before us as proudly we advance.

WOMEN: Tenderly we lift the drooping grain and bind it.

[*Again a change in the music, which becomes martial and triumphant. The dancers seem to beat out the grain with flails, then join hands and circle round and round in a dizzying whirl of exultation.*]

WOMEN: Yield us the yellow grain, strength for our children.

MEN: Hold not a kernel back, for we have given all our strength to you.

MEN AND WOMEN together: Rich is our harvest, earth hath been bountiful. Full are our granaries, great our hearts with gladness. [*Music stops and there is a patter of applause from Mother Ingeborg and the Councilman.*]

MOTHER INGEBORG [*beaming with happiness*]: Thank you, my children. It was a kind thought to bring to me the games I cannot see tomorrow.

THE COUNCILMAN: We shall have all the old dances tomorrow, Mother Ingeborg. I insisted upon it. To be sure, the youngsters can't dance them as we did,—Nor sing them, either. But—

[*There is a chorus of disgusted groans from the young people, in the midst of which Ingrid appears at the door.*]

KARIN: All right, Father. Show us how, then. Do the weaving dance,—you and mother.

INGRID: Dinner is served.

KARIN: Oh bother. Well, after dinner then. Don't eat too much, Father, so you can't sing.

MOTHER INGEBORG: Eric Sigurdsson, will you wheel me to the table? [*The Councilman bows and takes his place behind her chair.*] Erland, give Mother Anna your arm. You young people may follow as you choose. [*Gudmund takes Hildur's arm and detains her a moment as the others, laughing and talking, go out.*]

GUDMUND: Just a minute, Hildur. I must speak to you.

HILDUR [*with tolerant kindness*]: What is it, Gudmund?

GUDMUND: You have got your way about Helga. She is going this afternoon. But it is against my will. I begged her to stay, but she would not, because she did not wish me to lose you.

HILDUR [*quite unmoved*]: Well?

GUDMUND [*passionately*]: But I *have* lost you. We do not feel the same about things. Do you think we can be happy together?

HILDUR [*surprised and a little piqued*]: What do you mean, Gudmund?

GUDMUND: Do you think we can? [*With sudden resolution.*] Perhaps,— perhaps it would be better if you did not give yourself to me tomorrow.

HILDUR [*startled*]: I don't know what you mean.

GUDMUND [*not looking at her*]: We are so far apart—

HILDUR [*sharply*]: What are you thinking of? Would you shame me tomorrow before all the countryside?

GUDMUND [*earnestly*]: How could I shame you, Hildur? I am not your equal in this marriage. There would be few to blame you if you should take back your promise.

HILDUR [*proudly*]: I am not one to take back promises.—But if you— [*Suddenly softening.*]—Has anything changed between us, Gudmund?

GUDMUND [*miserably*]: It seems to me that everything is changed.

HILDUR [*with growing tenderness*]: I have not changed. You said you had lost me. But this is not true.

GUDMUND [*devouring her with his eyes*]: Isn't it true?

HILDUR: No, indeed. There is nothing to separate us, now that Helga has had the good sense to go away.

GUDMUND [*with a harsh laugh*]: Good sense! [*More quietly.*] Yes, that was it, no doubt.

HILDUR: Assuredly. She saw herself that it was not right for her to be here. And we can do much for her in her own home,—afterwards. Do not think me hardhearted, Gudmund, or unkind.

GUDMUND [*looking at her dreamily*]: Surely you cannot be so, with that face. [*Unconsciously he moves towards her.*] Oh, Hildur— [*She puts her hands against his breast and holds him at a little distance.*]

HILDUR [*playfully*]: How is it, then, Gudmund? Shall I take back my promise to you? Or do you still want me to come to you tomorrow,—that you may—do with me—as you will— [*She holds him with full gaze for an instant, then, on the last words drops her eyes and yields herself into his arms. Gudmund catches her hotly to his breast and kisses her hungrily.*]

GUDMUND [*thickly*]: Hildur! Do you love me after all? Do you *want* to belong to me?

HILDUR [*gently disengaging herself from his arms*]: Of course I do, silly boy.—Why else should I—? But what will they think of us? [*She glances toward the dining room.*] Dinner will be waiting.

GUDMUND [*kissing her rapturously*]: Who wants dinner?

HILDUR [*pushing him from her with a playful but decisive movement*]: That is enough now, Gudmund. They'll be sending someone for us. Come.

[*They go out, arms entwined about each other. Gudmund stoops to kiss her again in the doorway as the curtain falls.*]

ACT II

Scene 1

Near midnight of the same day. The village tavern. A low room with heavy oak beams and scanty, rough furnishings. A rude bar runs along most of the back wall facing the audience. Kegs of beer and a few bottles of wine stand behind the bar. In the back wall left is the outer door. Door in left wall leads to other rooms of the tavern. A high Swiss clock points to ten minutes before twelve. Two or three heavy deal tables with chairs at them stand about the room. At the one furthest right and close to the front of the stage, sit Gudmund, Thorwald and Hugo, beer mugs and cards before them. One candle burns on this table. Olga stands behind the bar. She is of the large, blonde, impassive Swedish type, with slow-moving, wide blue eyes and a full, well moulded figure. The men drink incessantly during the scene.

GUDMUND: Fill the mugs, Olga, and we'll have one more game. Your deal, Hugo.

[*Hugo shuffles the cards unsteadily. Olga draws a great flagon of beer and moves in stately fashion toward the table, setting the flagon in the center after she has filled the mugs.*]

HUGO: All I shay is, it's too pointed—hic—not invitin' him to th' weddin'. Makesh talk—hic—

THORWALD: Talk! I should think it had!

GUDMUND: That's what I want. Talk's the only thing Martensson minds. He'd do any dirty thing in a corner; but people's whispering about it and pointing the finger at him is what he can't stand.

THORWALD: You've made him the most unpopular fellow in Värmland, Gudmund.

HUGO: He mi' do you a mischief, ole chap. He's an ugly brute w'en you corner him.

GUDMUND: Let him, then. If he'd give me a chance, I'd stamp on him like a spider. When I think of the way he treated Helga—

HUGO [*sentimentally*]: Yesh, poor lil Helga—

THORWALD: Did Hildur and her mother object to leaving him out?

GUDMUND: No doubt they thought I was carrying things a bit too far; but they agreed. I said I wouldn't be there, if he was.

HUGO: Ha! ha! ha! ha! That shettled it, I should think. Haha.

THORWALD: Hildur agreed with you, I am sure, Gudmund, and admired you. She is one who must admire where she loves—I don't know whether I love you, or not—what is love between men?—but I too admire you.—And there's something else—trust, I think. That's it—I trust you, Gudmund.

HUGO [*snivelling*]: So do I—I trusht you, Gudmund. Who says I don't trusht you? We all trusht you. Hildur trushts you. Lil' Shelma trushts you. Her muzzer trushts—

GUDMUND: Oh don't mention it, ole chap. We'll take your word for it. Let's start something else.

THORWALD [*dreamily*]: At times like this—

GUDMUND: When you're about half-fuddled, do you mean?

THORWALD: I'm not fuddled—I'm clarified. Something—the stimulus of

drink or of happy companionship—has sharpened and cleared my vision, till
I seem to catch now and again faint, cloud-hung glimpses of—

HUGO: Wha'sh he talkin' 'bout, Gu'mun'?

GUDMUND: Glimpses of what?

THORWALD [*dreamily*]: Of what—what the love of man for man really is.

GUDMUND: What is it, then?

THORWALD: It comes in flashes. I can't see it clearly. But I know that it is
something fairer than the love of man for woman. It is of the spirit, not of the
flesh, and so it will endure.

GUDMUND: Oh bosh! [*Drinks a long draught.*]

HUGO: Ha! ha! the shpirit, he shays—the shpirit in thish beer—thash
what he meansh. [*Pounds on the table with his mug and laughs loudly.*]

GUDMUND: Shut up, Hugo. Go on, Thorwald.

THORWALD: I shall love many women, I suppose—many, because it is
never a woman herself that I love but the spirit of beauty and of power that
she wakens in me. I love the greater self that I become in her presence.

GUDMUND [*wonderingly*]: Izh that it? Then—

THORWALD: But does the passion to possess her enlarge me? No. The
possessive instinct is small, dwarfing. I shrink to a lesser man when I try to
seize upon something, appropriate it to myself. I expand only as I rejoice in
its limitless beauty, absorb myself in its infinite calm and goodness.—

HUGO [*drunkenly, pounding the table*]: Hear! Hear! Good ole Thorwald.

[*While Thorwald is speaking the outer door opens and the Swiss pedlar
shuffles in. He is dressed in European costume, a nondescript and dirty combination of brown trousers, gray coat and black waistcoat, with a visored, shape-
less cap on his head, a huge pack on his shoulders.*]

PEDLAR [*at the door*]: Goot efening, all. [*No one answers, and with no
sign of expecting this courtesy, he sets his pack in the corner behind the door, and
cap in hand, bowing incessantly, advances to the bar.*]

PEDLAR: A mug of stout, if you blease, my tear. [*Olga pours him the
stout.*]

GUDMUND: Go on, Thorwald. Thish izh our—hic—party. Don' min'
the—hic—greasy Outlander—hic—

THORWALD [*peevishly*]: The scarecrow has frightened away all my darting, wheeling thoughts.

HUGO [*belligerently*]: Who zat, Olga? Sen' 'im away. I don' want 'im here.

GUDMUND: More beer, Olga,—hic— [*She fills the mugs and the flagon.*]

THORWALD: See that you wash the mug well, Olga, after that fellow has
drunk from it.

HUGO: Give him—hic—the shpittoon. [*He kicks it toward her and slides off his chair, recovering himself with some difficulty.*]

OLGA [*with a contemptuous glance at the pedlar*]: One must serve them all.

GUDMUND [*hilariously*]: But not all alike, Olga, my girl. We've notished that—hic—

[*Sings*] To shweeten Carl's glash with a kish
She thought it wash nussin' amissh—
But when Larsh craved the shame
She called a new game—hic—
And poured his good beer
Down hish ear—hic— Ha! ha! ha!

[*Thorwald and Hugo join in his laughter.*]

HUGO [*pulling Olga down to him*]: A kish for lil Hugo, pleash. [*He kisses her and she cuffs his ear perfunctorily.*]

OLGA: Let me alone. You'd best go home now. Your legs won't carry you if you drink any more.

GUDMUND: We'll shee him home. My legsh are shteady. Shee— [*He executes a few shuffling dance steps and sits down suddenly on the floor.*] Ha!ha! Thorwald, ole boy, mus' take us bosh home, Hugo'n me.

HUGO: Less shtay here, aw'night. W'y not? On th' floor. [*He looks vacantly at the floor and settles down in his chair in a drunken stupor.*]

GUDMUND [*rising from the floor and reseating himself clumsily in his chair*]: Olga! Give—hic—dthat dam' Outlander—hic—a flagonful on my 'count an' then—hic—turn—'im out. We want—hic—th' plasch to ourshelves—hic—. [*Olga goes behind bar.*]

PEDLAR [*bowing very low to Gudmund*]: T'ank you a t'ousant time, your honor. [*To Olga.*] Gif me the flagon. I vill serf myself at that dable. [*He indicates the table next Gudmund's.*]

GUDMUND [*belligerently*]: Not that table—hic—Keep your distansh, Ishaac. I can shmell you—hic—from here—hic.

[*Per Martensson enters in time to hear Gudmund's last two speeches. He pauses at the door long enough to exchange a glance of secret understanding with Olga, then moves toward the bar.*]

PEDLAR: Very well, Meester, I vill dake dhis dable, den. [*Moving to one in the corner nearest the door and sitting at it.*] It is all vun to me.

[*As Per Martensson passes near Gudmund's table, he nods curtly to the three friends. Gudmund and Thorwald stare at him with hostile expressions, not acknowledging his salutation. Hugo, however, opens his eyes, gazes at him*] *stupidly for an instant and then bursts into exuberant drunken greetings, half rising from his chair.*]

HUGO: Well, if it ishn't Per Martensshon! Good ole boy! Come an' have a—hic—dhrink—hic—with ush. We're dhrinking the ole year out—hic—yeh know.—

THORWALD: Shut up, Hugo.

GUDMUND [*pulling him down into his chair*]: Si' down. You're drunk.

HUGO [*with outraged virtue*]: Coursh I'm drunk—hic—I'm dhrinking th' ole year—hic—out.

GUDMUND: Keep still.

HUGO: Keep still, yerself—hic—I'm tellin' Per, Gudmun's gettin' married t'morrah, Per,—poor ole boy.—Sho we're drinkin' th' ole—I mean th' new year in. Thass it. Si' down, Per. Get chair for ole Per, Thorwal'. All frien's here. [*While Hugo talks, Martensson stands by the table, surveying the group with a malicious smile. He lights a cigarette and puffs nonchalantly at it, waiting to see what Gudmund will do.*]

GUDMUND: Si' down yourself. [*He pushes Hugo into his chair with no gentle hand.*] That fellow shall never drink at my table. I'd ask Ishaac here first.—hic—Come, Ishaac,—hic—bring your bottle. You may not be honest, but you're decent—hic—for all I know. Come along. [*He rises unsteadily and pulls the pedlar by the arm to the larger table, drags up a chair and pushes him into it. The pedlar holds fast to his flagon. Martensson, with a contemptuous shrug of his shoulders, moves to the bar and stands, leaning over it, blowing smoke from his cigarette into Olga's neck and bosom. She pretends to resent this but is evidently flattered and pleased.*]

PEDLAR [*bowing low to the three friends*]: T'anks, your honors. I vill, mit mooch playsure, make vun in your liddle pardy. [*Hugo's head gradually sinks down on the table and he seems to have fallen asleep. Gudmund pours drinks all around and drains his mug.*]

MARTENSSON: A glass of cordial, please— [*Olga pours and he drinks, leaning over the bar. Setting down his glass, he fondles Olga's arm, slipping his hand up her sleeve, and saying something to her in a low tone, which makes her look at Gudmund, apparently fearful lest he has heard. Martensson jerks his head contemptuously in Gudmund's direction and laughs harshly.*]

THORWALD [*disgustedly*]: But Gudmund, why should you ask *him*? [*Jerking his thumb toward the pedlar.*]

GUDMUND [*boisterously, with evident intention to be heard by Martensson*]: His shtench ish better—hic—than the othersh—hic.

THORWALD [*seeing that Martensson has heard this*]: Keep shtill, Gudmun', can't you? You talk too much. [*Gudmund gathers up the cards and begins to shuffle them, not looking at Martensson.*]

GUDMUND [*loudly*]: More beer, Olga. [*Olga starts to fetch it, but Martensson holds her by the arm, looking up into her face with a cool, calculating, provocative smile.*]

THORWALD: Less take Hugo home.

GUDMUND [*calls*]: Give us shome beer, I shay—quick. We're goin' home. Thish comp'ny here—hic—ish not to our tashte.

MARTENSSON [*again detaining Olga and speaking in a smooth, cutting voice*]: Another glass of cordial, Olga. [*Olga mechanically pours it out and offers it to him. Still holding Olga's arm, he raises the glass as if drinking her health, then turns and surveys Gudmund wtih insolent satisfaction.*]

MARTENSSON: When I am quite done with Olga, you can have her. It won't be the first time you've taken my leavings.

GUDMUND [*stupidly*]: Wha'sh that?

THORWALD: [*sharply, after a pause*]: Look oud! Are you shpeakin' of—of Gudmund's bride?

MARTENSSON [*smoothly, with a mocking smile*]: By no means. Do not excite yourself unnecessarily, Thorwald Larsson.

GUDMUND [*vacantly*]: Hildur? Leavingsh? What! [*He leaps from his chair, steadying himself with his hands on the table. His voice clears, and the drunken stupor seems to slip off him like a garment.*] Is it Helga you mean? You—you dirty liar! [*He hurls himself at Martensson in one agile spring.*]

THORWALD [*jumping in between them*]: Stop! Stop! Hugo—Isaac, pull him off!

HUGO [*waking partly*]: Wha—wha's the madder? [*He lurches toward the group and apparently without much consciousness of what he is doing, helps the pedlar pull Gudmund from behind.*]

PEDLAR: In Gott's name, sir— [*Gudmund has Martensson down, but Thorwald and the pedlar pull him off and draw him away to a safe distance. During the next two speeches Olga goes to Martensson, helps him to rise and dusts off his clothing.*]

GUDMUND [*trying to pull loose from Thorwald and the pedlar*]: Let me alone, can't you?

THORWALD: Don't be a fool. You can't get married, if you kill him—

PEDLAR: Or if he should kill you, young sir— See—he has a knife! [*Martensson has pulled a clasp knife from his pocket, opened it, and, as Gudmund speaks, lunges toward him, knife in hand.*]

GUDMUND: Killing's too good for such a swine! [*He makes for Martens-*

son again, but is stopped by Thorwald and the pedlar, while Olga catches Martensson's arm and steps between the two men.]

OLGA: You must go outside, gentlemen, if you're for breaking the peace. The master is a constable now, and he will have a quiet house.

THORWALD [*to Martensson, holding Gudmund back*]: Get out, quick. And you'd best hold your tongue, after this.

GUDMUND [*advancing upon Martensson menacingly*]: Say it was a dirty lie, you cur, or I'll finish you now. [*Martensson hesitates.*]

THORWALD [*warningly, still holding Gudmund*]: Say it, and get out. He means business.

HUGO: Yesh, he meansh bushinesh.

MARTENSSON [*blackly*]: So do I— [*Gudmund makes a spring at him and catches him by the throat. His knife falls to the floor.*]

THORWALD: Quick, Hugo. [*Hugo and Thorwald pull Gudmund off until he turns savagely upon them. They hold him firmly while the pedlar picks up the knife.*]

THORWALD [*to Martensson*]: Have you had enough? Say what he wants or he'll murder you.

GUDMUND: Say you lied, you dirty scoundrel.

MARTENSSON [*sullenly, after a pause*]: If he denies it, of course I accept [*sneeringly*] the word of a gentleman. [*Gudmund starts as if to lay hands on him again, but Thorwald and Hugo restrain him.*]

THORWALD: That's enough from him. Let him go, Gudmund.

[*The pedlar returns his knife to Martensson with a low bow and Martensson slinks toward the door.*]

GUDMUND [*thickly*]: But our account isn't settled yet—remember that.

MARTENSSON [*in the doorway*]: No. It is not settled yet.

[*EXIT Martensson. Gudmund reseats himself at the table and the others follow his example.*]

OLGA: It is time to close, gentlemen. [*She indicates the clock.*]

GUDMUND: After one more drink, Olga. I must wash the taste of that carrion out of my mouth. Faugh! [*He spits and drinks the remainder of his mug, holding it out for more.*]

THORWALD: You've had enough, Gudmund, and so have we.—

GUDMUND [*obstinately*]: One more, old chap. Then we'll go home. My head is clear as sunrise now.

OLGA [*bringing another flagon of beer, fills mugs and sets flagon on table. She gathers up all the candles except that on Gudmund's table and blows them out.*] I'll leave you one candle. Good night, gentlemen.

ALL IN CHORUS: Goo' night, Olga.

[*EXIT Olga.*]

PEDLAR [*rising as door closes behind her*]: Gen'lemen, I gif you Olga—the mos' peautiful mait oudsite of Swisserlant. [*He raises his mug, and Gudmund and Thorwald raising their mugs drink.*]

GUDMUND ⎤ [*drinking*]: Olga! [*The outside door opens softly and Mar-*
THORWALD ⎬ *tensson slips in, unobserved by anyone on the stage. He drops*
HUGO ⎦ *on his hands and knees and crawls to the nearest table, con-*
cealing himself beneath it.]

GUDMUND [*aggressively*]: See here, Isaac, I've seen your Swiss girls— they're not so much.

PEDLAR [*raising his hands to heaven*]: Gott im Himmel! The Swiss maitens are the mos' peautiful in all the worldt. This is by all men known—

THORWALD ⎱ :Ha! ha! ha! ha! [*Hugo slides down in his chair again and*
GUDMUND ⎰ *lays his head on the table.*]

PEDLAR [*excitedly*]: As far as Swisserlant is the mos' peautiful of lants, so are her maitens the mos' peautiful of maitens. I gif you Swisserlant,—mit her mountains so vite, mit her fir trees so plack, mit— [*his voice has risen to a drunken, oratorical, sing-song.*]

THORWALD: Oh, shut up, Ishaac. Go back to Shwitzerland, if you want to—hic— Don't let ush keep you.

[*Thorwald and Gudmund laugh boisterously, winking at each other.*]

THORWALD [*shaking Hugo by the shoulder*]: Wake up, Hugo. We're going home. [*Hugo does not stir.*]

PEDLAR [*knowingly*]: I can vake the shentleman—So— [*He dashes the contents of his mug into Hugo's face. Hugo starts and splutters, opening his eyes wonderingly.*]

GUDMUND [*springing to his feet*]: You stinking Outlander! Here, Thorwald, put him out! [*Gudmund seizes one of the pedlar's arms, Thorwald a leg, throwing him down. They both shake Hugo, and pull him from his chair.*]

PEDLAR [*struggling*]: But, shentlemen, vait a minute.

THORWALD: Take his other leg, Hugo. [*Hugo stupidly obeys.*]

GUDMUND: Now, heave him out.

[*As they move toward the door in a lurching, swaying mass, the pedlar struggling to free himself, the three friends hardly able to keep their feet, Martensson slips noiselessly out from under the table. When the group is half way to the door, he seizes upon and extinguishes the one candle. There are startled exclamations from Gudmund and Thorwald, a rush across the floor, the sound of a body precipitating itself upon the four men, a scuffling thud as the mass of*

intertwined men fall, "Mein Gott" in the pedlar's voice, breaking into a hoarse
scream which is suddenly checked, a few faint, choking groans, then the sound of
someone scrambling to his feet, the scrape of the outer door opening and running
footsteps outside. Meanwhile—]

GUDMUND [*in a stupid, dazed voice*]: Is—is anybody hurt?

THORWALD: What's up? Where's the candle?

GUDMUND: Hugo, where are you? Hugo!—

THORWALD: Here, I've got a match. [*Strikes it, showing a huddle of two*
dark figures on the floor. Gudmund strikes another match, finds a candle and
lights it, as the door in the left wall is thrown violently open and the Constable
walks in, lantern in hand.]

CONSTABLE [*Gruffly, swinging his lantern in all directions*]: What's this?
What's this? Who's disturbing the peace in my house?

GUDMUND: Bring your light here. I'm afraid somebody's hurt.

CONSTABLE [*bringing light*]: Hurt? If there's mischief done, some of you
shall smart for it. Who's here? [*peering into his face*] Gudmund Erlandsson,
as I'm a sinner! And Thorwald Larsson! And—

THORWALD [*pulling Hugo out from under the pedlar*]: Wake up, old man.
[*Shakes him gently.*]

CONSTABLE: Hugo Anderson, too! Young gentlemen, I'm the guardian of
the law, and if there's been mischief done here—

GUDMUND [*kneeling by Hugo, who is beginning to open his eyes*]: You're all
right, aren't you, old boy?

HUGO [*stupidly*]: Aw' ri'. 'Course, I'm aw' ri'. [*They assist him to rise and*
he stands staring round-eyed at the pedlar, who still lies on the floor.]

CONSTABLE: And who's this? [*Bending over the pedlar.*]

GUDMUND: The pedlar. Is he hurt?

CONSTABLE [*setting down his lantern and putting his ear to the man's*
heart]: He's dead.

GUDMUND
THORWALD } : Dead?

CONSTABLE: Look at this! A knife in him. Blade broken off— He's done for.

HUGO: He's dead?

GUDMUND: A knife?

THORWALD: Why, why—how could—?

CONSTABLE [*sternly, withdrawing from the dazed group about the pedlar*]:
That is what we must find out. [*Raising his hand authoritatively.*] Gentlemen,
you are under arrest.

CURTAIN

ACT II

Scene 2

Same as Act I.—the living room at Närlunda, as in Act I., but trimmed with garlands of young birch leaves. Early the next morning. Mother Ingeborg in her wheel-chair is discovered sitting by the fireplace, and Erland reading a news-paper by the table, which is spread for breakfast.

ERLAND [*throwing down his newspaper*]: Well, my dear, I want my break-fast.

MOTHER INGEBORG: Go and see if Gudmund is not ready. I can't bear to sit down without Gudmund.

ERLAND [*looking hungrily at the table*]: I can. But he'd better sleep as long as he will. He must have come in very late last night.

MOTHER INGEBORG: I didn't hear him at all.

ERLAND: Nor I. Sometime after midnight, I heard wheels on the road and looked out, but it was that fellow Martensson. Then I went sound asleep till morning.

MOTHER INGEBORG: I wish he would come. It is our last meal with him before—

ERLAND: But I expect to have several with him—*after.*

MOTHER INGEBORG: It will not be the same when he is married, Erland. You know that very well. Now he is here with us just as he has been for twenty-two years. Tomorrow there will be Hildur.

ERLAND [*densely*]: But you want Hildur to be here, don't you? Was it not your idea in the first place,—this marriage?

MOTHER INGEBORG: Of course I want her here. She is just the wife for Gudmund. I have always said so. But I never would have urged him to marry her,—for all her money,—if he hadn't been in love with her.

ERLAND: Well, he *is* in love with her. So why are you faint-hearted now?— when your victorious army is just marching into the city?

MOTHER INGEBORG: Nonsense, Erland. It's not *my* army. And I'm not faint-hearted, exactly. Only it is a great change for her. And suppose she shouldn't like being a farmer's wife, after all?

ERLAND [*cheerfully*]: Well then, I suppose she won't like it. But no doubt she's fond of Gudmund, and they'll manage to worry through somehow, as others have before them.

MOTHER INGEBORG: Have we worried through, Erland? Is that what you'd call it?

ERLAND: Well, my dear, there have been some—some adjustments. I've made most of them, but no doubt you've made a few yourself!

MOTHER INGEBORG: A few!— Well, if he's as happy as we've been,— Go and knock at the door, Erland. Tell him to dress quickly.

[*Gudmund is seen approaching through the garden with the Constable.*]

ERLAND [*rising and seeing Gudmund*]: Why, there he is. [*Mother Ingeborg looks toward the garden.*]

MOTHER INGEBORG: Has he been out already? Who is it with him?

ERLAND: The Constable. [*Enter Gudmund with the Constable.*]

CONSTABLE: Good morning, friends.

MOTHER INGEBORG: Good morning, Lars Jansson. Gudmund, where have you been? What has happened?

GUDMUND [*going over and kissing her*]: Don't be frightened, mother. I'm arrested, but—

MOTHER INGEBORG [*with a stifled shriek*]: Arrested?

GUDMUND [*putting his hand on her shoulder soothingly*]: Yes, but it's a mistake. Only on this particular morning, you see, it's awkward.

ERLAND [*stepping forward and facing Gudmund*]: Tell us, Gudmund, what have you done?

GUDMUND: You see, I don't know. That's the difficulty.

ERLAND: You don't know?

CONSTABLE: The young gentlemen were very drunk.

GUDMUND: We'd been drinking all the evening—Thorwald, Hugo and I— at the Blue Hen, you know. And a pedlar came in—one of those Swiss fellows—and maybe we got too rough with him, I don't know. Anyhow, he's dead, with the blade of somebody's pocket-knife in his skull. [*Erland utters a stifled exclamation. Mother Ingeborg looks at Gudmund with incredulous horror in her eyes.*]

MOTHER INGEBORG: Oh, Gudmund, but it was not you. It could not be. You never hurt a grasshopper in all your life!

CONSTABLE [*shaking his head sagely*]: Many a murder has been done without intention.

ERLAND: Is that all the comfort you have for us, Lars Jansson?

CONSTABLE: It is best to look first on the dark side of things, Erland Erlandsson. Because then, if all things turn out well, you have a pleasant surprise. If not—you are prepared for the worst. [*He wags his head knowingly and looks around the circle for admiration; but Gudmund is kneeling beside his mother with his arms around her body, which is shaking with silent sobs. Erland, gazing at them, hardly hears what the Constable is saying.*]

GUDMUND [*in a choking voice*]: Don't, Mother dear. We must think what can be done.

MOTHER INGEBORG: How can anyone think you did it?

GUDMUND: I wouldn't believe it *was* done at all, if I hadn't seen the knife in him. I *couldn't* have done it. Why, I wouldn't know how.

CONSTABLE: We must detain all the young gentlemen, until they can clear themselves. Very sorry. Especially today.

GUDMUND: It's all a delirium. How can we ever know?

ERLAND: You did not do it, my son. We may be sure of that. But to prove it— [*He breaks off with a despairing gesture.*]

CONSTABLE [*judicially*]: The knife blade is the only clue, so far.

ERLAND [*impatiently*]: Well?

GUDMUND: That doesn't seem to help much either. Hugo's knife has a broken blade, but it does not fit the one in the pedlar's skull. Thorwald's knife has no broken blade. And my knife—is missing. [*Erland groans involuntarily and drops his head.*]

CONSTABLE: Don't give up hope, Erland Erlandsson. I have seen men saved who were nearer the gallows than he. [*Gudmund winces at the word and Mother Ingeborg raises her bowed head proudly.*]

MOTHER INGEBORG: Do not say such things, Lars Jansson. Gudmund is innocent and no harm can come to him.

ERLAND: But what did you do with your knife? You always carry it.

GUDMUND: Yes, in this pocket. But it is not there.

ERLAND: Can't you remember what you did with it?

GUDMUND: No. Of course it looks as if I had got rid of it after sticking the Outlander. But I was too drunk to go out of the room, I'm sure.

CONSTABLE: It is nowhere on my premises,—I have made thorough search, since daylight.

MOTHER INGEBORG: But the wedding! Hildur! What shall we do about—

ERLAND: They may have started already. I'll go and meet them.

GUDMUND: Why should you do that? Do you want to stop the wedding?

ERLAND [*amazed*]: Why—can the wedding go on, now? [*Looks at Constable.*]

CONSTABLE: If you will sign this bond for your son, [*producing a legal document from his pocket*] he can remain at liberty till six o'clock this evening. He seems to think it important.

ERLAND: Would you marry Hildur before—

GUDMUND [*squaring his shoulders*]: I am innocent. Why should I not marry Hildur? When you have signed this bond, the Constable will leave me and come for me at Alväkra at six o'clock tonight. Hildur need not know till then.

MOTHER INGEBORG: You would not tell her till after the wedding?

GUDMUND: I would not. Why should I shame her before all the country-side? If I had killed the man, it would be different; but I am innocent and this will be proved.

ERLAND: Yes. You are innocent; but until you are proved so— However, you can decide this when I have signed the bond. Let me have it, if you please. [*Turns to the Constable and takes the bond from him.*]

CONSTABLE: Sign here, if you please, Erland Erlandsson.

ERLAND: Very well. [*Sits at the table and reads the bond.*]

CONSTABLE: We must have two witnesses—not members of the family. I will be one and one of the servants will do for the other.

GUDMUND: Here is Helga, I'd rather ask her. [*Helga is seen approaching through the garden. Gudmund opens the door to her.*] Good morning, Helga. What brings you here so early?

HELGA: Good morning, Gudmund. I have come to wish you happiness on your wedding day. Good morning, Mother Ingeborg and Father Erland.

MOTHER INGEBORG }
ERLAND   } : Good morning, Helga.

HELGA: I had to go to market with the peat, so I came to wish Gudmund happiness. [*She smiles frankly at him. Gudmund chokes and turns away.*]

MOTHER INGEBORG: Thank you, my child. He will need your good wishes today.

HELGA: Why, what is the matter? Is something wrong, Gudmund?

GUDMUND: It is better now, Helga, since you have come. Something hard in me broke when you wished me happiness— Why are you so kind? You ought rather to be angry with me for making it impossible that you should remain here.

HELGA: Why no, Gudmund. Surely you were not to blame. But tell me what has happened. Why are you not dressed?

GUDMUND: You shall hear, Helga. But first, will you be a witness to this bond that my father signs for me?

HELGA: Certainly I will.

CONSTABLE: As soon as Erland Erlandsson has signed, you must write your name. [*Erland signs and motions Helga to take his chair at the table. Helga sits. The Constable, points to a line on the paper*]: Here. [*Helga signs her name, the Constable signs his, puts the bond in his pocket and moves toward the door. Mother Ingeborg sits bowed in her chair, her face hidden in her hands,*] *weeping silently. Helga kneels before her chair and puts both arms around her.*] Good morning to you. At Alväkra at six tonight.

GUDMUND: I will be ready. Good morning. [*Exit Constable.*] Father, I have changed my mind. [*Mother Ingeborg and Helga look up. Helga rises and stands with clasped hands, looking steadily at Gudmund.*] I must tell Hildur, before the wedding. It would be unjust to drag her into my misfortune. I must have been mad to think of it.

ERLAND: Good. And I may as well tell you now, my son, that I should have told the Councilman, if you had not. The Alväkra folk are jealous of their honor, and I could not have stood silently by while Hildur married a man under accusation of murder.

HELGA [*clasping her hands together in dismay*]: Murder?

GUDMUND: I have not killed anyone, Helga.

MOTHER INGEBORG: That he has not.

GUDMUND: But—is it too late to see Hildur before she leaves Alväkra?

MOTHER INGEBORG: They must already have started.

ERLAND: It will soon be over, Gudmund. I believe that the Councilman will understand what it costs you to do the right thing and they will all be kind.

GUDMUND: It does not matter.

ERLAND: I have heard something of this sort before.

MOTHER INGEBORG: Not like this, surely.

ERLAND: Yes— There was a bridegroom once who happened to shoot a comrade to death during a hunt. It was not discovered that he was the one who had fired the fatal shot; but he went to the bride and said, "This marriage cannot take place. I do not wish to drag you into the misery that awaits me."

HELGA: This is what Gudmund will say.

ERLAND: And the bride took him by the hand and led him into the drawing room where all the guests were assembled for the ceremony. There she related in a clear voice what the bridegroom had just said to her. "I have told of this," she said, "that all may know you have practised no deceit upon me. Now I want to be married to you at once. You are what you are, even though you have met with misfortune; and whatever awaits you, I want to share it equally with you."

HELGA [*flashing at Gudmund a radiant smile of friendly confidence*]: That is just what Hildur will do!

GUDMUND [*shrugging his shoulders incredulously*]: It will not end so for us.

ERLAND: Who knows? [*The wedding party approaches, Hildur wearing*

her bridal gown, veil and crown; the Councilman, the Councilman's wife, and
Karin, in resplendent costumes, closely following. Gudmund opens the door for
them. Helga slips quietly over to the fireplace and stands there unobserved by the
newcomers.]

GUDMUND: Good morning, Hildur. I bid you welcome all.

HILDUR: Good morning, Gudmund. Why, you are not dressed!

ERLAND: Welcome, honored guests.

MOTHER INGEBORG: Good morning, my friends.

THE COUNCILMAN
THE COUNCILMAN'S WIFE } : Good morning, good morning all.

KARIN [*with a flourish*]: Way for the bride! She does me credit, doesn't
she? [*She looks around the circle for admiration.*]

THE COUNCILMAN'S WIFE: But how is this? Gudmund not dressed yet?

KARIN: Shame upon him! If I were you, Hildur, I'd take one of the others
in his place.

THE COUNCILMAN: Is anything wrong?

ERLAND: My son has something to tell you.

GUDMUND [*as though he were repeating a lesson*]: I was at the Blue Hen
last night, drinking out my last night as a bachelor with Thorwald Larsson
and Hugo Andersson. And a man was killed—

THE COUNCILMAN [*sharply*]: What? Who killed him?

GUDMUND: No one knows. We were all too drunk. But there is a broken
knife blade in his skull that will tell. And my knife is missing. [*Helga, who has
been listening attentively, starts and makes as if to rush toward the group, then
checks herself, clasps her hands together and looks with joyous expectancy toward Hildur.*]

KARIN: But, Gudmund! That's simply absurd!

[*The Councilman and his wife glare at Gudmund with furious anger. Gudmund looks steadily at Hildur, who stands motionless with her eyes on the
ground. As if unconsciously she pulls out one of the large pins which holds her
crown in place and lifts her hand as if to remove it.*]

GUDMUND: So I must go to prison, until the case is judged. [*Seeing
Hildur's action, he stops speaking; she looks up at him, and in confusion puts the
pin back in place.*]

THE COUNCILMAN'S WIFE: Upon my word! This is what comes of such a
connection!

THE COUNCILMAN: A wretched business, indeed. But it is well that we
have not been dragged into it.

KARIN [*almost sobbing*]: Don't let them talk so, Hildur.

HILDUR [*looking at her with cold steadiness*]: One can easily see that you are not concerned in this, Karin.

ERLAND: It is not proved that Gudmund was the slayer; but I can well understand that you would wish the wedding postponed, until he has been cleared of the charge.

THE COUNCILMAN: It is not worth while to talk of postponement. It is better to decide now that all is over between him and Hildur.

KARIN: No, Father!

THE COUNCILMAN'S WIFE: Certainly! That is the only thing to do now. But what a dreadful disgrace. Oh, my poor child! Come, let us go at once.

GUDMUND [*going over to Hildur and extending his hand*]: Won't you say farewell to me, Hildur?

HILDUR [*staring coldly at him*]: Was it with that hand you guided the knife?

GUDMUND [*turning to the Councilman*]: You are quite right. It is useless to talk of a wedding. [*To Erland.*] Now I will go back to the prison and give myself up. [*Puts on his hat and exit by the garden.*]

THE COUNCILMAN'S WIFE: Come, Hildur, let us go. Good morning, Anna Olafsdotter, and Erland Erlandsson. [*They all bow ceremoniously, the Councilman opens the garden door and they start to go out, when Helga moves impetuously toward Hildur.*]

HELGA [*breathlessly*]: May I speak with you, Hildur Ericsdotter? It is a matter of great importance.

THE COUNCILMAN'S WIFE: Do not keep us waiting, Hildur. This girl can have nothing to say to you.

HELGA [*clasping her hands in entreaty*]: Oh, do let me speak with you, alone, only for a moment. You will not be sorry.

HILDUR [*surveying her coldly*]: Very well. I will join you at the carriage, Mother. [*The Councilman and his wife go out slowly, pausing several times to look back and shake their heads together. Karin follows them with drooping aspect, as if ashamed.*]

MOTHER INGEBORG: Wheel me to my room, Erland. [*Exeunt, while Helga waits, looking anxiously at Hildur. Before the door is fully closed, she begins to speak, going close to Hildur and looking earnestly in her face.*]

HELGA: Before I speak, I must know one thing—do you love Gudmund?

HILDUR [*wincing slightly*]: Why else do you suppose I ever wished to marry him?

HELGA: I mean, do you still love him?

HILDUR [*slowly*]: I think, perhaps, I have never loved him so much as today.

HELGA [*clapping her hands in childish joy*]: Oh then, run quickly, dear Hildur. He cannot have gone far. If you call to him, he will stop.

HILDUR [*drawing back from her*]: Why should I do that?

HELGA [*drawing her impulsively toward the door*]: Don't wait,—not a moment,—or he will be out of call.

HILDUR [*resisting her*]: What do you mean?

HELGA [*eagerly*]: If you tell him, now, that you love him more than ever, and that you will wait for him while he is in prison,—

HILDUR: But that is impossible. I don't wish to marry someone who has been in prison.

HELGA [*staggering back, as if Hildur had struck her*]: But I don't understand. Surely if you love him—And besides, he is innocent.

HILDUR: Do you know this for certain, or is it only something that you believe to be true?

HELGA: I know it for certain. When he spoke about the knife, I could see at once—

HILDUR: The knife?

HELGA: It was not the blade of Gudmund's knife that killed the pedlar—

HILDUR: How do you know?

HELGA [*takes from her pocket Gudmund's knife which she shows to Hildur*]: This is Gudmund's knife.

HILDUR: Yes, I know it well.

HELGA: It has been in my pocket since yesterday morning. Gudmund lent it to me to cut the wild apple boughs which I strewed in the drive before you. And I left Närlunda without giving it back, so he did not have it in his pocket last night.

HILDUR: Then he is innocent, after all!

HELGA: Did you not know it, before this?

HILDUR: No, Helga, I was not sure.

HELGA [*proudly*]: Gudmund is no murderer.

HILDUR [*looking keenly at Helga*]: Have you told anyone of this?

HELGA: No. It is only now that I learned it. I shall go straight to the Judge and he will release Gudmund. But first you must speak with him,—oh do, dear Hildur! that all may be well between you two.

HILDUR: First? Before he knows that you can prove him innocent?

HELGA: Yes, indeed! You must never let him know I have spoken to you; else he cannot forgive you for what happened just now.

HILDUR: I was very angry with him, because he had brought me into disgrace. But no doubt I was too hasty.

HELGA: Then come, at once, Hildur. Your father's carriage will soon overtake him.

HILDUR: But there is much in all this that I do not understand. Do you know that it was I who wanted you to leave Närlunda?

HELGA [*simply*]: I knew, of course, that it was not the folk at Närlunda who wished me away.

HILDUR: I can't comprehend that you should come to me today with the desire to help me.

HELGA: Gudmund has been very kind to me. I want him to be happy.

HILDUR [*after a pause, looking keenly at Helga*]: Why did you keep Gudmund's knife?

HELGA [*confused*]: I—there was so little time before I left Närlunda and I was much distressed—

HILDUR [*with quiet persistence*]: Did you forget it?

HELGA: No, that was not the reason. I wanted to keep it just for a few hours. I had nothing else which belonged to him.

HILDUR: I see.

HELGA: Yes. You see, Hildur. And I am not ashamed that you should see. Nobody can help loving Gudmund. He is so generous and good.

HILDUR: But why, then, are you trying to make it up between us?

HELGA [*sharply*]: What could I be to him? You know very well, Hildur, that I am only a poor Croft girl, and that's not the worst about me. He's as far above me as Mount Otterhällen is above our marsh.

HILDUR: Well, I will go speak with Gudmund. But we shall not overtake him now.

HELGA: Will your parents let me ride to the town with them, Hildur?

HILDUR: I will tell my father to take you whenever you wish.

HELGA: I will go to the Courthouse, or to the Judge's house, if the Court is not sitting now. And he will let Gudmund go home at once. If you wait by the Crossroads, till he goes by, you can't miss him.

HILDUR: At the Crossroads? In my wedding clothes?

HELGA: Leave the crown and the veil here. Then they will be ready for the wedding when you return. Your mother has on a dark cloak, hasn't she?

HILDUR: Yes. [*She removes crown and veil and lays them on the table.*]

HELGA: Slip it over this dress and no one will notice. Oh, come, let us go at once, to set Gudmund free. [*She pulls Hildur toward the door.*]

CURTAIN

ACT III

Scene 1

The Courtroom, arranged as in the Prologue, but with no spectators present. Time, one-half hour later than the end of Act II. The Judge is discovered sitting at the table with papers spread before him. Helga stands in front of the table and the Constable at one side of it. Both men lean toward Helga in attitudes of absorbed attention.

JUDGE: This is very important, Helga. Will you swear in court to what you have just told me?

HELGA: Indeed I will.

JUDGE [*to Constable*]: Bring Gudmund Erlandsson here at once. [*Exit Constable.—To Helga.*] It is well that you are the one to tell me this. If it were some other person I should wish first to make sure that his knife is really Gudmund's and that it has been in your possession since yesterday morning; but I know that one may believe what you will say.

HELGA: You may believe this, your Honor.

JUDGE: Have you told anyone else about the knife?

HELGA: Only Hildur Ericsdotter, Gudmund's betrothed. She is waiting for him now at the Crossroads.

JUDGE: Then Gudmund does not know that his knife was in your possession last night?

HELGA: He must have forgotten, or he would have spoken of it. [*Door opens.*]

JUDGE: Well, we will see if he cannot remember.

[*Enter Gudmund with Constable. He looks as if he had made a toilet, but still wears his torn suit of clothes. He bows gravely to the Judge, and then with some surprise, to Helga.*] You have a friend here, you see. [*Door again opens and Erland enters. There is an elation in his face and bearing which he cannot conceal.*] And here is Erland Erlandsson. What can I do for you, my friend? [*Erland bows low to the Judge and glances at Gudmund and Helga.*]

ERLAND: I have a piece of evidence to lay before you in this case, your Honor.

JUDGE: I will hear it in a moment. But first let us finish the business in hand. [*To Constable*]: Take note of what is said. [*Constable bows—To Gudmund.*] Tell me, Gudmund, do you not know where your pocket knife is?

GUDMUND [*looks troubled and slightly shakes his head*]: When my head stops aching I can probably remember. But I thought it was in my pocket. I always carry it there.

JUDGE: Have you no better knife that you sometimes carry?

GUDMUND: No. Only this one. It was given to me by my father when I was twelve years old. I have always used it since.

JUDGE: Describe it to me.

GUDMUND: It has one large blade and one small one, and a horn handle with a silver plate on it.

JUDGE: Is the plate marked?

GUDMUND: Yes, by my initials, G. E.

JUDGE [*corroboratively*]: When did you use it last?

GUDMUND: Shaving kindlings, I think, yesterday morning—I can't remember having it since.

JUDGE: Did anyone else use it afterwards?

GUDMUND [*after a pause, starts and looks at Helga*]. Why yes, of course. Helga borrowed it of me to cut apple blossoms. How stupid of me to forget that! You remember, don't you, Helga? [*Helga nods smilingly at him.*]

JUDGE: Did she return it to you?

GUDMUND: You didn't, did you, Helga? [*Helga shakes her head.*] Our guests came very soon, and Helga went away that afternoon.

JUDGE: Is this the knife you lent her?

GUDMUND: It is. [*He takes it in his hand and opens the two blades.*] Neither blade broken—[*with a boyish chuckle that breaks into something like a sob*] I didn't stick the Outlander, did I?

HELGA: Of course you didn't. We all knew that.

JUDGE [*to Erland*]: Can you swear to it, as your son's knife? [*Shows it to Erland.*]

ERLAND: I can— O, your Honor— [*His voice breaks, he turns abruptly from the Judge, goes to Gudmund, puts both arms around him and conceals his face against Gudmund's arm.*]

GUDMUND [*patting Erland's shoulder*]: It's all right now, Father. I didn't kill him, so, of course—

ERLAND: No, thank God! You didn't kill him.

GUDMUND: But who did? Not Thorwald or Hugo, surely.

JUDGE [*who has been ostentatiously looking away from them, with a softened expression on his keen face*]: That we shall see. But this clears you, Gudmund. When you have signed this paper, binding you to appear as witness at the trial, you may go home. [*Helga clasps her hands in an ecstasy of happiness.*]

GUDMUND [*in a shaken voice*]: I thank your Honor.

JUDGE [*who has been scribbling on a blank form, pushes it toward Gudmund and puts a pen in his hand*]: It is Helga whom you must thank.

GUDMUND [*signing the paper and clasping Helga's hand*]: I do thank her from my heart.

[*Enter Martensson. Seeing Gudmund and Helga, he hesitates at the door.*]

JUDGE: Come in, Martensson. Can you wait a few moments? I will not keep you long, but some unexpected matters in connection with this case have delayed me.

MARTENSSON [*half sullenly*]: I would rather come back later.

ERLAND: I will wait, your Honor. Shall we go into the next room?

JUDGE: Thank you, Erland. But you need not withdraw. [*Erland, Gudmund and Helga seat themselves. Martensson approaches the table.*] Now, Martensson, all I want of you is to find out what took place between the pedlar and the three young gentlemen while you were with them. Try to remember exactly.

MARTENSSON [*after a pause, as if endeavoring to recollect*]: The young gentlemen insulted the pedlar several times—at least Gudmund Erlandsson did.

JUDGE: What did he say?

MARTENSSON: "Keep your distance, Isaac, I can smell you from here," was one thing.

JUDGE: What else?

MARTENSSON: "You may be honest, but you're not decent," I think, or something like that.

JUDGE: Did the pedlar reply to these insults?

MARTENSSON: I didn't notice that he did.

JUDGE: Did either of the others address the pedlar?

MARTENSSON: I think not.

JUDGE: Try to remember what else was said. Gudmund has been cleared of the deed, so we must find some other clue.

MARTENSSON [*startled*]: Cleared?

JUDGE [*darting a swift glance at him*]: Yes. Why not?

MARTENSSON [*sullenly*]: How has he been cleared?

ERLAND [*coming forward*]: Your Honor, may I give you my evidence now? I wish Martensson to hear it.

JUDGE: Sit down, Martensson. Say what you know, Erland.

ERLAND: Last night, from my window, I saw someone passing our house throw into the marsh opposite a small object. This was at one o'clock, for I heard the chimes as I was getting back into bed.

JUDGE: A small object? Perhaps a cigar stump.

ERLAND: It seemed heavier than that. I thought nothing of this circumstance until this morning when Gudmund told us about the knife. Then I went into the marsh, where I thought it might have fallen, and caught on a hummock, I found—this. [*He takes a knife from his pocket and lays it before the Judge. The Judge examines it in silence, while the Constable comes from the door and leans over the table to look, too. Martensson half starts from his seat, but sits back again with an obvious effort.*]

JUDGE: An M- on the handle—mmmm— Did you recognize the man who threw the knife?

ERLAND: Yes. [*Looking straight at Martensson.*] The moon was bright and I saw—Per Martensson.

MARTENSSON [*springing from his chair*]: It's a lie!

JUDGE [*sternly*]: Sit down, Martensson. You can defend yourself in due time. [*He makes a sign to the Constable, who goes over and stands near Martensson. Then he unlocks a drawer of the desk, takes from it a small object wrapped in paper, and fits it with the knife. With an expression of solemn exultation, he holds the knife and the blade together, raising them above the table, so that all present may see.*]

CONSTABLE [*in his excitement moving closer to see*]: By glory! [*Martensson makes a dash for the door.*]

JUDGE: Arrest him! [*Constable pursues Martensson through the door. Helga covers her face with her hands and turns away.*]

ERLAND [*involuntarily*]: Poor fellow!

GUDMUND [*perplexed*]: But I don't understand—

JUDGE: It will all be cleared up at the trial. [*He rises with papers in his hand and shakes hands with Helga.*] Good-bye, my child. Are you going back to Närlunda, now?

HELGA: No, your Honor.

GUDMUND [*authoritatively*]: Yes, Helga, you are coming home with me.

HELGA: No, Gudmund, I shall go to the Marsh Croft. [*To the Judge.*] Mother Ingeborg has given me weaving to do at my home.

JUDGE: That is good. Come to me, if you should need help at any time.

HELGA: I thank your Honor. [*Enter Constable, puffing and blowing.*]

CONSTABLE: I caught him, your Honor, just at the door of the jail. He's locked up tight enough now.

JUDGE: Thank you, Constable. Bring the girl Olga this afternoon at two— [*Exeunt together, the Judge still talking.*]

ERLAND [*shaking hands with Helga*]: Helga, my child, can you not overlook all that is past, and come home with us again?

HELGA: You have overlooked so much in me Erland Erlandsson, that surely I— But I cannot go back to Närlunda.

GUDMUND [*impetuously*]: You *must* go back, Helga—

HELGA: Oh, do not stay here talking, while Mother Ingeborg weeps at home. Go quickly and tell her that you are free.

ERLAND [*turning to the door*]: I will drive to the door and take you both with me. [*Exit.*]

GUDMUND [*turns to Helga, takes her hands in his and suddenly pulls her to him, clasping her in his arms and kissing her wildly. She pushes him away with a little cry of terror.*]

GUDMUND [*still holding her but ceasing to kiss her*]: Don't push me away, my Helga. It is you I love. Long ago I might have known this.

HELGA [*twisting out of his hold*]: No, no, Gudmund. Don't say so. It is Hildur— You must go to her.

GUDMUND: Hildur! I want nothing from her.

HELGA: Surely you do not mean that, Gudmund.

GUDMUND: Of what are you dreaming? Hildur is done with me. She told me so, herself.

HELGA: But she did not mean it, Gudmund. I am sure she did not mean it. She was so startled with your news that she did not know what she was saying. No doubt she regrets it bitterly at this very moment.

GUDMUND: Let her regret it as much as she likes for all of me! I know her now! She is the sort who thinks only of herself. I'm glad I'm rid of her.

HELGA [*putting out her hand to stop his words*]: Gudmund, you must not speak so of Hildur. Wait till you have seen her—then you will understand.

GUDMUND: I have no intention of seeing her. I want you for my wife. Will you marry me, Helga? [*He tries to take her in his arms again, but she slips out of them.*]

HELGA: No, no, Gudmund. You must not say such things to me. Please go. Your father must be at the door.

GUDMUND: Do you not love me, Helga?

HELGA [*hesitatingly*]: Do not ask me, Gudmund. I can't love anyone now.

GUDMUND [*slowly*]: Do you mean since—? Surely you don't care for him, still. [*Helga turns away in silence.*]

GUDMUND [*hoarsely*]: Tell me, Helga. Do you love that—Per Martensson?

HELGA [*with averted face*]: I can't bear to hurt you, Gudmund.

GUDMUND [*after a moment's silence*]: You cannot love a man like that, Helga. You are deceiving yourself.

HELGA [*simply*]: I am not clever enough for that, Gudmund.

GUDMUND [*in a hard voice*]: You love the man who has given you nothing and taken everything! And I—the damned scoundrel!

HELGA [*faintly*]: Why should we speak of him, Gudmund? Go quickly and tell your mother that you are free.

GUDMUND [*with a harsh laugh*]: Free! Yes, I am free. But you—

HELGA [*almost sobbing*]: I am not free and never shall be. Now go— Don't keep her waiting a moment more.

GUDMUND [*after gazing at her fixedly a moment, turns to the door, pausing after he opens it.*]: Good-bye then. We must go our separate ways, you and I.

HELGA: Good-bye, Gudmund. [*Exit Gudmund. Helga stands for an instant with hands clenched at her sides, making a desperate effort for self-control. Then she shakes herself together with a resolute gesture, begins, as at the end of the Prologue, to slip off shoes and stockings, and hangs shoes over her shoulder. While she does so, she forces herself to hum in a shaky voice the folksong she sang at the opening of Act I., breaking off several times and swallowing hard to regain her self-control. Finally, she sings more strongly, opens the door, looks out as before, and exit, with an air of more settled cheerfulness.*]

CURTAIN

ACT III

Scene 2

Half an hour later. The Crossroads. At right front two roads cross. A grassy knoll with a few gnarly trees on it rises gently from their intersection and occupies the greater part of the stage. Behind on the left, the knoll descends and reveals a fjord in the background.

Hildur is disclosed sitting on a low mound a little above the road. She wears her wedding dress, and a long dark cloak over it. She rises and peers anxiously down the road, but when she hears wheels and sees Erland and Gudmund approaching in the cart, she seats herself again on the mound and turns her face away. Gudmund sees her and stops involuntarily, then bows silently and starts the horse again. Erland bows gravely to her, but does not speak. Hildur rises and extends her hands to Gudmund, in an attitude of supplication.

HILDUR [*in a faint voice*]: Gudmund.

GUDMUND [*stopping the horse again*]: How do you come here, Hildur?

HILDUR: I would have a word with you.

GUDMUND [*indifferently, after a slight pause*]: Very well.

ERLAND: I will drive on and tell your mother.

[*Gudmund jumps out of the cart and walks toward Hildur, while Erland drives off the stage. Gudmund seats himself at a little distance from Hildur, who has sunk down upon the bank again. He remains silent, gazing off abstractedly down the road. Hildur looks at him and then away again.*]

GUDMUND: Well, Hildur.

HILDUR [*begins to speak after a pause and with a perceptible effort*]: I was—yes, it was much too hard—what I said to you this morning.

GUDMUND [*kindly*]: It came upon you so suddenly, Hildur.

HILDUR: I should have thought twice. We could—it would, of course—

GUDMUND: It was to be, Hildur. But you are kind to speak as you do.

HILDUR [*covers her face with her hands, then looks straight at Gudmund*]: No, I am not kind. I was—contemptible, this morning. You see I thought you might be guilty.

GUDMUND: That was natural, I suppose.

HILDUR: No one who loved you, believed it. And I would not believe it now.

GUDMUND [*warmly*]: Would you not, Hildur? I am glad of that. We have all changed much since this morning.

HILDUR: But I did not change of myself, Gudmund. I don't want you to think I am better than I am. Someone has told me that you are innocent.

GUDMUND: Why, how could anyone know? We have but just come from the Judge.

HILDUR [*in a low voice*]: Helga showed me your knife before she took it to town.

GUDMUND: It was Helga, then?

HILDUR: And she urged me to see you at once that I might make things right between us again. I wish I had thought of this before I knew about the knife—but I did not. But I have longed for you all day—and wished that things were with us as they were before this happened.

GUDMUND: Do not wish that, Hildur. It is probably best as it is.

HILDUR [*puts her hands to her face, draws a breath deep as a sigh, then raises her head again*]: I understand that you can never forget how I behaved to you this morning.

GUDMUND: I shall forget it sooner than you, Hildur. But you must not reproach yourself, for it was really a stroke of good fortune that all has been ended between us.

HILDUR: You think this, Gudmund?

GUDMUND: Yes, for today it has become clear to me that I love someone else; and it would have been a great misfortune to us both if this had come to light after our marriage.

HILDUR: Who is it, Gudmund?

GUDMUND: You would not understand. But I cannot marry her, so the name does not matter.

HILDUR: Why can you not marry her?

GUDMUND: She does not care for me— that is all . . But I shall never marry anyone else.

HILDUR [after a long pause, raising her head proudly]: I want you to tell me, Gudmund, if it is Helga whom you love.

GUDMUND: Why do you think so?

HILDUR: Because I do understand, better than you think. And if you are speaking of Helga, why do you suppose she came to me and taught me what I should do, that you and I might come together again? She knew you were innocent, but she did not say so to you or to anyone else. She let me know first.

GUDMUND [looking her steadily in the eyes]: Do you think this means that she—

HILDUR: You may be sure of it, Gudmund. No one in the world could love you more than she does.

GUDMUND [starting up and walking hurriedly back and forth along the bank]: And you—why do you tell me this?

HILDUR: Surely I do not want to stand beneath Helga in this too! [Enter Helga along the road, shoes about her neck. They do not see her and she attempts to hurry by during Gudmund's speech, but Hildur discovers her.]

GUDMUND [placing his hands on Hildur's shoulders and shaking her gently]: Oh, Hildur, you don't know how happy you have made me. You don't know how much I like you!

HILDUR: See, there she is, Gudmund.

GUDMUND [running to intercept her]: Helga, oh Helga!

HELGA [turning to smile at them both]: May I wish you happiness?

HILDUR [coming to her and taking her hand]: I wish you happiness, dear Helga, with all my heart—you and Gudmund.

GUDMUND [taking her other hand]: Yes, Helga, you can't escape from me any more.

HELGA [looks from one to the other, with a questioning gaze, then turns to Hildur]: But Hildur, why will you not marry Gudmund?

HILDUR [*smiling down at her*]: Because he does not want to marry me, Helga. You would not have him marry me against his will, would you?

HELGA [*looking at Gudmund in utter amazement*]: But surely you can forgive—

GUDMUND [*heartily*]: Indeed, I can!

HILDUR: He has forgiven me, Helga, I am sure. But he does not any longer love me. You can see how that might be.

HELGA [*anxiously searching the faces of both for confirmation of this statement and finally accepting it with drooping head*]: Oh, I am *so* sorry!

HILDUR [*impulsively putting her arms about Helga*]: What have you done to us, Helga?— I believe,—why, I believe I really *want* you to marry Gudmund!

GUDMUND: So do I, Helga.

HELGA [*radiant with joy*]: Is it for me, then?— Oh, are you *sure*? [*She looks from one to the other with childlike appeal.*]

GUDMUND [*tenderly*]: Why not, little one?

HELGA [*seizing upon Hildur in a kind of panic*]: But I'm not fit, Hildur. You *know* I'm not fit to be mistress of Närlunda.

HILDUR [*sincerely*]: You are fit to be Gudmund's wife and mistress of his house. [*Gudmund reverently kisses Helga's hand.*] Listen, Helga. My veil and crown are at Närlunda. You have given me much and I want you to wear them, at your wedding. Will you? [*Helga puts up her face and Hildur kisses her. The sound of violins, flutes, and other musical instruments is heard approaching. Hildur and Helga, startled, draw apart.*]

GUDMUND: It's the bride's escort. No one has told them.

HILDUR: I will tell them.

[*A number of young men on horseback enter, followed by a carriage containing several musicians with their instruments.* One of the riders leads a beautiful horse with a woman's saddle on it. Another horse with a man's saddle on it is led by another rider. The men are in Swedish costume, their hats decorated with ribbons of bright colors and with flowers. Some of them carry guns. The first riders stop as they see Hildur and signal to the musicians to cease.*]

1ST RIDER: Why, here is the bride. A joyous wedding to you, Hildur.

2ND RIDER: Have you come so early from Närlunda? We were to fetch you thence at twelve.

OTHER RIDERS: Good luck to Gudmund and Hildur! Good luck! Good luck!

*The escort and the musicians may be on foot, if necessary. If horses are dispensed with, the speeches referring to them must be altered.

HILDUR [*raising her hand as if to push away their words*]: Thank you, my friends. We have come from Närlunda, it is true. But I am not the bride today. Here she is. [*She takes Helga's hand and draws her forward. Helga clings close to her and looks down in confusion.*]

1ST RIDER: What?

2ND RIDER: Has Gudmund married Helga?

HILDUR: Not yet. But they go now to Närlunda for the wedding.

1ST RIDER: Are you playing pranks with us, you two?

2ND RIDER: Has there been no wedding at Närlunda?

1ST RIDER: What do you mean? [*They crowd close about Hildur and become very still. Gudmund steps forward. Thorwald enters, unobserved, and stands in view of the audience, listening.*]

GUDMUND: It means that there has been no wedding at Närlunda. Hildur has decided not to marry me, after all. [*Murmurs of incredulity and disapproval from the crowd. Thorwald steps forward and confronts Gudmund.*]

THORWALD [*hotly*]: Do you accuse Hildur of breaking faith with you?

HILDUR: Let me speak, Gudmund. I will tell them the truth. [*She raises her head proudly and looks straight at Thorwald as she speaks.*]

—Since last night Gudmund has stood in the shadow of disgrace and death.—And I would not stand there with him.—But Helga came and set him free. So they found that they loved one another and today they will be married. [*Turning to the escort.*] Give Helga a salute with your guns and then escort her to Närlunda. [*Thorwald stands gazing at Hildur as if in a dream. After an instant of amazement, the escort fires a salute. All the riders and musicians doff their hats to Hildur, and the rider who leads the unmounted horse, approaches Helga. Dismounting, he holds the two horses while Gudmund swings Helga into the saddle. Gudmund kisses Hildur's hand and mounts beside Helga. The horsemen surround Gudmund and Helga. Thorwald moves toward Hildur.*]

GUDMUND: But you, Hildur? You will come with us, will you not?

1ST RIDER [*dismounting*]: Will you not mount with me, gracious Hildur? My horse has often carried double.

THORWALD [*pushing impatiently forward*]: If only you would walk with me!

HILDUR [*smiling at him and giving him her hand, which he kisses, then turning to the First Rider*]: Thank you, my friend. But I think I would rather walk.

THORWALD [*exultantly, to the horsemen, still holding Hildur's hand*]: We will follow you to Närlunda.

[*At a signal from the 1st Rider the musicians strike up and exeunt before the riders, who fire another salute, and then sing:*

Safe shall we lead her,
The bride of thy choosing,
From all ill defend her,
To thy hands commit her,
O bridegroom triumphant.

[*While they sing the first two lines, Hildur and Thorwald exeunt in close converse in the wake of the musicians. At the end of the fourth line the riders gallop off the stage, still singing.*]

CURTAIN

17   The Funeral

from *Poems and Plays*,
edited by Laura Johnson Wylie (New York: Duffield, 1922), 167–184.

In these pages from The Funeral, *an unfinished novel, Buck sketches a community where politics and money influence education as much as truth and morality. The main character, Dr. Fowler, seems to represent Buck's ideal academic who lives out a sound philosophy of life. The eulogy at the funeral stuns the town, and one professor comments, "I suppose it does us good to hear harsh truth sometimes." Fowler's response seems to summarize Buck's teaching method and rhetorical theory. "Speaking the truth in love," mused Dr. Fowler. "I wonder if it really does good, spoken in any other spirit?"*

There was a great funeral in Forsythe that afternoon. The late Mr. Ira Cox had been wont to boast that his name spelled more dollars with fewer letters than that of any other man in town. He had been sole owner and manager of three of Forsythe's cardiac enterprises,—the *Morning Gazette*, the Cox Windmill Company and the Gilt-Edge Creamery.

Before the hour set for the funeral the employees of these three companies gathered outside their respective places of business and marched in a body to the church. Gurney, passing the three groups, one after another, noted their clumsy suits of borrowed black, their non-committal expressions of decorous self-importance, and wondered cynically how they really felt. Did they excuse to themselves now Ira Cox's hardness and his greed, perhaps even swelling a little over what a good business man he had been—at their expense? Or did they hate him dead as they had hated and feared him living?

Two of the oldest printers bore between them a creation of the florist's art representing in black and white immortelles the first page of the *Gazette* as it had appeared on the morning of Mr. Cox's death, with each of its columns heavily black leaded. Two of the veteran piece-men in the Windmill factory, whose wages, Gurney happened to know, had not in twenty-two years risen above ten dollars a week, carried an equally appropriate and even more imposing replica of a Cox windmill done in white carnations and candytuft,—"pump handle and all complete," as admiring spectators noted. These triumphs were inspected with pride by all the contributors thereto, but the employees of the Gilt-Edge Creamery felt that their committee had discharged its office in a poor and unimaginative spirit with the purchase of a plump pillow of white roses lettered I. C. in purple violets.

At the head of Main Street Professor Gurney overtook Dr. Fowler, and the two were soon joined by Professor Rawley, the Seminary gossip, who emerged from his doorway with news exuding from every pore. He was a bald, florid, bustling little man, impatient of ceremonies.

"Heard about the old rapscallion's will?" he demanded without salutation. The tips of his stiff mustache bristled with importance and indignation.

"No," answered Dr. Fowler tranquilly. "Has any one?"

"Ah, how d'ye do, Rawley," broke in Gurney maliciously. Rawley did not waste a look on him.

"Everybody knows. It was read this morning. He had it endorsed to be read on the morning of the funeral. Jim Leavens says he told him that his poor relations had no call to camp down in his house for the best part of a week waiting to hear the will,—the old skeezicks!"

"I take it he has cut the Seminary off with a shilling?"

"Yes. How did you know? I thought you hadn't heard."

"I hadn't, till you told me. —I mean," he hastened to add, seeing Rawley's blank expression and Gurney's twinkle of appreciation,— "I guessed it from what you said. Where does the money go?"

"To the widow—every nickel. Did you ever hear anything so outrageous— so unprincipled?"

"Well, I don't know. What do you say, Gurney?"

"It's like the old chap, isn't it? A good deal of a practical joker."

"If you call this a joke—", exploded Rawley.

"Well," conceded Dr. Fowler, placably, "no doubt he knew why he was made a trustee."

"Well, if he did, wouldn't a decent sense of honor lead him to satisfy the expectations he had raised, yes, repeatedly raised? You know as well as I do how many times he has refused to contribute a dollar to some crying need of ours and how invariably he has put us off with 'When I am gone, you'll see that I haven't forgotten the Seminary.' You've heard him, time and again. And now—it's false pretenses, or something worse. I hope the trustees will break the will."

"I don't just see on what grounds."

"Well, a lawyer could see. And I hope they'll consult one. Oh, there's Dempsey." And he shot off without a word of farewell as the lank, drooping figure of the professor of homiletics turned into the street just before them.

Rawley bobbed up and down beside him, "like corn on a hot shovel" as Gurney observed, occasionally seeming to pop with indignation.

"Too bad to stir Dempsey up just before preaching," he commented further.

"No doubt he's heard it before," Dr. Fowler assured him. "I imagine from the way he shakes his head, that Rawley is talking about contesting the will. I don't wonder he's so hot, poor chap. It's one under the belt for the Seminary."

"And how it does serve us good and right," observed Gurney.

"It does that. Providence really couldn't lose a chance like this for a moral lesson. Any self-respecting secular college would have hesitated to put him on its board of trustees; but a theological seminary has no sense of humor."

They had reached the church, which was fast filling with towns people, theological students and faculty. Dr. Fowler was seated next to President Hampson, who wore his customary expression of aristocratic boredom. Mrs. Hampson leaned forward and scintillated an individual greeting from her eyes to each of the two men. She made a point of marked cordiality to those who were in her husband's bad books. Was not this the whole duty of a president's wife,—to keep things socially pleasant, whatever the necessities of official discipline might be?

Across the aisle from them and a little in front of the mourner's pew was Mrs. Cox, quite alone except for an old woman servant. The poor relatives had unanimously left town, it would seem, after the reading of the will. The widow's rotund person gave no effect of being bowed by grief. Her brilliant cheeks glowed even through the dense crepe veil. Gurney, watching her from behind, was teased by the same question that the faces of the gathered employees had suggested. How did she really feel? But no satisfying answer was written in the trim crepe-bound lines of the erect figure, the slightly lifted head, the straight-forward gaze of the eyes toward the coffin and the pulpit above it.

The preliminaries of hymn-reading and prayer fell to the lot of the Reverend Dr. Henry Runciman, the pastor of the church. His large, thick-featured face, hung with flabby folds of sodden flesh, wore an expression of studied sweetness, as it would say, "Behold how a manly man bows his strength to become as a little child in the kingdom." He prayed that on this sad occasion our hearts might be opened to receive their lesson, namely that Death is no respecter of persons. Rich and poor, high and low, old and young, he spares none. Our time may be tomorrow—even tonight the Death Angel may knock at our door. Are we ready? Help us to answer, each for himself, this solemn question. Help us to be ready, to keep our light trimmed and burning. Help us to learn the lessons of the life that has passed from our midst, to note how often, as in the case of our brother, great, even surpassing, business ability is joined with the highest integrity of character, with unfailing respect for God's laws and institutions, with regular attendance upon the means of grace. Our departed brother was no less a business man for those admirable qualities,—nay rather a greater financial success and a nobler example to our youth. Success is gained not by transgressing but by obeying God's laws. May we all remember this and be better men and women for this lesson. Bless and comfort the heart of the sorrowing widow, that dear wife who made a happy home and place of refuge for our brother from the heat and burden of the business day. May she be enabled to look through her tears to a happy reunion in the land where there is no night and no parting forever.

And then he prayed it all over again in partly different words and sat down while the choir sang "Crossing the Bar," covering his large fat face with a large fat hand, the stumpy fingers radiating upward to the edges of his fluted hair.

Then Professor Dempsey uncoiled himself and stood behind the desk, silent for a long moment while he looked at the audience as if it were not there. His slender figure had the tenseness of a bent bow. His eyes were caverns of smouldering protest.

"We are gathered here," he began, in an intense, smothered voice, which grew clearer and higher as he went on, "to perform the last rites for one who has often been denominated the foremost citizen of Forsythe." In crisp, pictorial sentences, as unlike as possible to his usual flamboyant circumlocutions, he narrated the events of Ira Cox's early life; how he had at the age of ten run away from a stepmother who had systematically ill-treated him, and begun his business career on the streets of Forsythe by selling matches obtained on credit from a friendly elder boy; how he had risen from matches to newspapers, thence to the proprietorship of a news-stand, thence to reporting on the *Gazette* and finally to its management and ownership, with the control of the town's two most important industries. "At the time of his death,"—the words came more slowly now, as if dragging behind them some weighty meaning,—"he was paying to more than twelve hundred inhabitants of Forsythe, men, women and children, the wages which bought their daily bread. He was thus, in wealth and in the power which wealth brings, our foremost citizen."

The speaker paused, until every eye in the congregation fixed itself upon him. Then a swift challenge shot from his somber eyes to theirs.

"But in the house of God and in the presence of God, I ask you, what more than this can we say of Ira Cox, our foremost citizen? Was he foremost in all that makes a man truly useful in his life and truly lamented at his death? Who among you will answer yes?"

President Hampson glanced uneasily away from the speaker and then back to him again, gradually steeling his face into an expression of aloofness and irresponsibility, faintly tinged by surprise. Mrs. Cox had paled suddenly and her rotund figure had wavered a little, before it stiffened determinedly into the lines of her previous attitude. She had given a swift involuntary glance at the vestry door, as if meditating flight, but checking the impulse, had forced her eyes again to the speaker's face. Thus she sat, as one searing sentence followed another, her cheeks and lips bloodless in the intensity of her listening, rigidly upright under the lashings of Dempsey's words and the glances that leaped upon her from every quarter of the church.

"He had such power," the vibrant Celtic voice went on, "over the lives of other human beings as few men wield. Did he use it for their welfare and happiness, for the glory of a compassionate God? We pass over his business dealings, since this great game of business is supposed by those who play it successfully to have its own rules, apart from and inconsistent with the laws of human kindliness. Yet the game was here in Forsythe largely in the hands of Ira Cox, and its rules might have been so modified by him as to yield him profits only a little smaller and his employees a living wage. If he had sometimes, in his prosperity, remembered the little boy who sold matches and slept in the streets at night, who was never warm or well-fed until he had wrested these goods from the hands of a hostile world, would he not have been, perhaps, content with slower gains? If he had remembered what his young eyes saw of the life of the poor, would he not have endeavored, even at some small sacrifice of mere money, to put color into the faces of the women who worked for him, and to lift from men's shoulders the intolerable burden of daily anxiety lest the bare bread of poverty should fail? But none of these things were by-products of the business enterprises carried on by Ira Cox in this town. They made money, but they made no strong and self-respecting men, no intelligent and hopeful women, no happy children. Do we ask too much of business, do you say, in asking these fruits from it? In your hearts you know that this is not true. This is what business exists for, not to enrich one man while it impoverishes and enslaves the many. Business is, like all the rest of life, our Father's business.

"This truth, however, Ira Cox never, in his earthly life, came to know. Nor did he understand the true values of life outside of his business relations. I search my memory in vain, and I have in vain searched the memories of other men who knew him well, for one instance of public-spirited benevolence performed by him, for one offering made out of his abundance to relieve the necessities, or to lessen the hardship of any other human being. Can any one here recall such an instance? If so, in God's name let him speak. Is there in this congregation a young man who owes to Ira Cox his education or his start in a business career? Or one whom Ira Cox's kindly counsel saved at a moment of sore temptation and need? If there be any such in this audience, I conjure him to rise and let us know that this man's life was not lived in vain."

The speaker paused in a tingling silence and looked searchingly over the audience, from pew to pew, over the lower floor, then along the galleries. At length he dropped his eyes with a low sigh of relinquished expectation.

"Is there no one? Is there not, then, perhaps, a man to whom Ira Cox once lent a helping hand when ill health and discouragement were dragging him down to failure? Is there not some one who can say out of a full heart, 'The man who lies in yonder coffin gave me courage to go on in the darkest hour of my grief, by a warm clasp of the hand, a word of genuine sympathy?' "

Again the long pause, and the slow searching of the audience, the disappointed relinquishment of the quest.

"Cannot some widow here rise and tell us that in the anguish of her bereavement and her apprehension for the future, Ira Cox came to her, giving her time for the payment of her mortgage and offering her work or temporary aid to keep the family together? Will not even some child recall a punishment remitted or the tears of fright wiped away by this man who can never now lighten the grief of any? Surely no one here would hesitate to rise in his place in defense of one who is forever silent.— But no one speaks.— There is no one who can honestly say that this man, living all but the first ten of his seventy-two years in this community, has enriched it by one word or deed of loving-kindness. The wealthiest and the most powerful man in Forsythe, he has gone out from among us, leaving no monument but one of granite in yonder cemetery. Poorer than that of many a humble man or woman whose life 'smells sweet and blossoms in the dust,' his spirit has been summoned to the bar of eternal justice. May God have mercy upon it."

He stood for a moment with eyes that looked beyond the audience, and then dropped quietly into his seat. The Reverend Dr. Henry Runciman arose with a perturbed air, his child-like sweetness temporarily obscured, while in a voice which did not quite succeed in sounding as if nothing had happened, he read the closing hymn, "How Firm a Foundation." It rose feebly from the congregation at first, but soon swelled into tremendous volume, as if the familiar words and tune had put solid ground under foot once more in a world strangely shaken. Then the unprotesting body of Ira Cox was borne out, followed by those who were to attend it to the grave, and the audience melted away, moved by a common, unacknowledged impulse to tell the tale to those who were not present and to gain time for reflection before committing themselves to an opinion upon it.

Dr. Fowler made his way out of the church before the Hampsons could detain him. He knew the President's practice of saving his own mental energies by getting some radical's view of any current event and then setting his own opinion in the opposite direction. Linking his arm into Gurney's, he said no word until they stood at his own gate. Then,

"What do you make of it, Ned?" he asked abruptly.

"It was certainly a magnificent exhibition of courage," answered Gurney. "And every word he said was true. I suppose it does us good to hear harsh truth sometimes."

"Speaking the truth in love," mused Dr. Fowler. "I wonder if it really does good, spoken in any other spirit?"

Gurney made no answer.

"Would he have preached that sermon, do you think," pursued Dr. Fowler, "if Cox had left a hundred thousand to the Seminary?"

"No, I can't think he would have seen it all so clearly," admitted Gurney.

"And the suffering of that defenceless little widow, impaled on all those eyes,—" Dr. Fowler left his sentence unfinished as Ellen ran down the steps and approached them.

"How do you do, Professor Gurney?" she called. "Won't you come in and have dinner with us? We're going to have fried chicken."

The mask of the clown slipped down over Gurney's face. He smacked his lips appreciatively.

"I just wish I could, Ellen; but little Lovejoy is coming to supper with me—if he keeps his courage up till six o'clock—and it wouldn't do for me to turn up missing."

"O well, some other time," said Ellen easily.

"When you have fried chicken," agreed Gurney longingly. "Do you have it every day?"

Ellen laughed at him and turned toward the house with her father. At dinner he told her and Courtney the story of the funeral. Their comments and questions were in full tide when Mrs. Cox was announced, "to see Dr. Fowler on a matter of business."

She sat very upright in one of the padded library chairs, dressed as she had been in the afternoon. Her eyes, however, were swollen with weeping and her round cheeks were almost colorless.

"I s'pose you're surprised to see me, Dr. Fowler," she said, with an attempt at sprightliness.

"I am very glad to see you, Mrs. Cox," answered Dr. Fowler heartily. "I hope there is something I can do for you."

"Yes, there is." Mrs. Cox was visibly relieved at this opening. "You heard what that man said this afternoon."

Dr. Fowler nodded.

"Well, he had no right to say it." Color began to burn darkly in her firm cheeks. "It was true, of course. But there was more to it."

"I thought there must be more," said Dr. Fowler.

"There was," asserted Mrs. Cox fiercely. "And that pin-headed fellow had no call to say what he did aginst Iry. Iry didn't want to be like that. But he didn't know how to act different. He never let on to me, but I knew it. He wanted folks to look up to him and he was top of the heap, but they didn't. He knew they didn't. And now he's dead—" Her voice broke, but her eyes were quite dry.

"I'm sure what you say of him is true," Dr. Fowler said gently. "I wish we could have helped him more."

She searched his eyes dumbly, then nodded to herself as if satisfied.

"Most likely nobody could," she declared, hopelessly. "But I'm not goin' to have him spit on now by them that licked his hands when he had money to give." She was fierce again in her maternal attitude of defense. "I'm goin' to give all his money to the Seminary to be a memorial to him, and show up that pin-headed feller for a liar. But I ain't goin' to give them a penny of it without they kick him out and that stick o' wood of a president that backs him up."

Dr. Fowler sat dazed in a torrent of new ideas. Mrs. Cox watched him anxiously.

"I kin do it, kin't I?" she asked at length, since he did not speak.

"Yes," said Dr. Fowler, rousing himself, with a half-audible sigh. "You can do it, quite legally, no doubt. There is nothing to prevent your making any conditions you choose."

"Then I'm goin' to do it. There ain't no sense in my havin' such a pile of money myself. I couldn't spend it. I don't know how. I'm fifty years old now. When I was young I could of learned, and mebbe I would of liked it. But I've learned to live close now, and I couldn't live no other way. And there's some, old as I be, would marry me for the money."

"Not if you see the possibility so clearly, I imagine." Dr. Fowler's voice showed no glint of amusement.

"Well, I wouldn't resk it. I'm as like as any other woman to be made a fool of. I can have all I want on five hundred thousand, and the Seminary can have the million and odd, if they do what I say. Will you make out the papers, Dr. Fowler? I want it put straight to them. They must fire Dempsey and Hampson and I want they should make you president."

Dr. Fowler sat very still for a moment. Then he said slowly, "I thank you for thinking of that, Mrs. Cox. But the fact is, I don't want to be president. There's nothing in it but the name. And I don't care a fig for that."

"Oh," ejaculated Mrs. Cox, disappointedly.

"And besides," went on Dr. Fowler still gently, "I couldn't take it, you know, if it were bought for me. If the trustees and faculty and students all thought I was the best man, without being bribed to think so, I might take it, even though I'd rather teach. But that's not in the question."

Mrs. Cox brooded darkly. "Most people'd jump at it," she opined.

Dr. Fowler did not discuss the point.

"Do you mean you won't take it, even if I put it in the papers?" she persisted.

"I mean just that. But I'll write the letter to the trustees, if you like, which you can sign, stating the amount you wish to give and the terms of the gift. A lawyer will have to make the deed of gift, of course."

"Well," conceded Mrs. Cox. "But will you see that he says what I want him to?"

"I'll tell you if he hasn't said what you want, if you show the deed to me before signing it."

"Look here." Mrs. Cox emerged with a jerk from a darkened silence. "There's something you don't like about this, and I don't know what it is."

Dr. Fowler nodded acquiescence, but did not speak.

"Ain't it a good thing," she demanded, "to use Iry's money for a memorial to him and throw that feller's lies back in his teeth?"

"I think it's a fine thing, Mrs. Cox, to make us remember him by such a gift. And I agree with you that it's the sort of thing Mr. Cox would have liked to do, if he had known how. But why do you choose the Seminary rather than any other institution?"

"Why it's the only thing he was ever trustee of. Of course I could build a big hospital or something. But if I give it to the Seminary, I can make them fire Dempsey and Hampson."

"Yes." Dr. Fowler's voice was so low that she had to lean forward in her chair to catch his words. "But is that the kind of memorial you want to leave for Mr. Cox? He was not a mean man or a revengeful man."

"No, he wa'nt. But that skunk Dempsey—I'll get even with him, if I spend the last cent of Iry's money."

"Think it over, Mrs. Cox, will you? What if you should get 'way ahead of him, instead of merely even with him? And I can't think of anything better for that than to give this money to the Seminary without any conditions, unless, perhaps, you wanted to provide that the name be changed to the Cox Theological Seminary."

"Dr. Fowler, you're workin' me," accused Mrs. Cox. Dr. Fowler laughed,

"No, Mrs. Cox, I'm not, unless you choose to be worked. I'm only giving you the advice I'd like to have somebody give me in the same place. It's nothing to me, you know, one way or another. But I wish you'd think it over, to-night."

"Now, Dr. Fowler, you don't reely think I'm goin' to take that skunk's back-talk against Iry, and hand him out a boquet for it. That ain't common sense."

"It seems to me like uncommon sense, though. I believe it would set Mr. Cox's name higher in the community than any gift that had a touch of spite in it."

"Why they might even think he got the money for the Seminary by his low-down talk," expostulated Mrs. Cox.

"No, I hardly think so. You see it's not the usual way of meeting an unkindness. And Mr. Cox so often spoke of leaving the Seminary something in his will, that I should think you would be quite justified in saying that you give the money to carry out intentions which he had frequently expressed. I'll put that in the letter if you like."

Mrs. Cox gripped the arms of her chair. "Land sakes, Dr. Fowler, you certainly had ought to be president of something. I declare I have to take a holt of my chair to keep from saying aye, yes and no, just as you want me to. But I ain't goin' to give up seein' Dempsey squirm, no, I kin tell you."

"If I were Dempsey, I think I should squirm more if you gave the money over my head, so to speak," declared Dr. Fowler, with a chuckle. "Anyhow, it's a memorial to Mr. Cox, isn't it? and not to what Dempsey has said or hasn't said. But don't say aye, yes or no now. Think it over till morning and let me know."

"Well, I'll think it over," promised Mrs. Cox, rising from her chair. "But I don't guess I'll see it your way when I'm by myself."

"All right, Mrs. Cox," as they shook hands vigorously. "You must see it in your own way. But I know you'll see it straight."

Before breakfast the next morning, Mamie brought up to Dr. Fowler a note which she said Mrs. Cox had left at the door. It ran thus:

"Dr. Fowler. Dear Friend.

I expect your right. I don't want anybody to think Ira was mean. Maybe Dempsey will feel worst this way. You can say in the letter they can have it if they call it Cox Theological Seminary. Thanks very much.

Respectfully,
Mrs. Minnie J. Cox."

VI Working Documents

Buck's letter of 1919 to President MacCracken explicates her views on the priorities of education and contains a paragraph or two where she carefully advises the president how to act. Her request in 1920 for release from three hours of teaching per week must have been written while she was not in the best of health. The tone of MacCracken's refusal is official and it is hard to estimate the toll on her health the extra work took.

The department report of 1900 was handwritten by Buck to President Taylor because Laura Wylie, the chair, was not well enough to draft it herself. It outlines the courses Buck taught, summarizes the way her textbooks were used, and outlines the specific space and salary needs of the department. The 1915 report, written by Wylie, addresses MacCracken during his first year as president of Vassar College. She records the history of the department, before and during her leadership, describes the emphasis put on smaller class sizes, wider range of courses, and asks for more faculty and staff to continue to do fine work. Her 1921 report differs in tone considerably, for she holds nothing back in giving Mac-Cracken her opinion of the way finances have been handled by the college. This report is also notable for stating specifically that cooperation was the key to governance of the department. Wylie stepped down as department chair in 1922–23 and retired at the end of the 1923–24 school year.

These documents all exist in typescript. I have silently corrected obvious typographic errors; handwritten insertions appear, in angle brackets, at the place in the text indicated by the author.

CORRESPONDENCE

112 Market Street
Poughkeepsie, New York

January 6, 1919

My dear Dr. MacCracken,

I am hoping that you will finally decide not to present to the trustees the plan you outlined to me of equalizing and increasing the salaries by means of a reduction in the teaching staff. This plan is not, so far as I can see, based upon a sound, self-consistent educational policy. Half of it leans to the principle of education first, finance second, the other half to the contrary and wholly irreconcilable principle of finance first, education second.

Justice demands the equalization and the increase of salaries in each rank. This should be recognized by the trustees and made a preferred claim upon the Fiftieth Anniversary Fund. But this equalization and increase should not take place until it can be made without impairing the efficiency of the teaching now being done. You may say, as you did to me, that to reduce the number of teachers will not impair the efficiency of the educational work of the college; but no one on the faculty will believe you, if advanced courses are to be withdrawn or the numbers of students in a section increased.

To cut out advanced courses is to deal a blow at higher education. It nullifies the intention of our recently adopted legislation as to continuity in election, and makes it necessary for *all* students to do what so many of them unintelligently did under our old system, namely, elect nothing but relatively elementary courses in several subjects and never pass beyond the rudiments in any field.

The evils of phalanx-teaching are too well understood to need discussion. Any increase in the size of sections would certainly be opposed by every department that is trying really to teach its students, instead of merely going through the forms of instruction; and this opposition would be justified by every educational authority in the country.

When I spoke of the necessity for solidifying your support, I meant not trying to "please everybody",—which is a fatal mistake,—but seeing so clearly the educational issues involved in every question that you are not deflected by financial or tactical or any other minor considerations. This singleness of purpose is the only thing that gives confidence in a leader, because it is the only thing that deserves confidence. Your supporters all stand, not for you as an individual, but for you as representing better than any other party to the present struggle, a policy of real educational advance in the college; and if you seem to further such a policy in one breath, while "selling it out" in the next, those who whole-heartedly believe in it will see no reason for holding their place in the ranks.

Please accept my frank statement of opinion in the spirit of good will in which I make it, as an observer of this situation, who deeply desires your success—in the best, the only real sense, of the word. As a member of the faculty, I know I should not be induced, by a proposition for equalizing and increasing salaries, to acquiesce in the crippling of the academic work to which I am giving all I have. Nor do I believe that the business men on the board of trustees will be conciliated by the reduction-of-staff article in your measure. In fact, by trying to "please" everyone, I fear that you will fail to secure the confidence of either party.

Please understand, however, that I do not suggest your defining and holding to a just and progressive educational policy as a measure of expediency. I should hope that you would maintain such a policy as just and progressive, whether expedient or not. But I am trying to point out what seems to me the fortunate coincidence, in this case, of right with expediency.

May I wish you the best of all New Years?

Sincerely yours,

Gertrude Buck

Vassar College
Poughkeepsie, N.Y.
Department of English

June 3, 1920

Dear Dr. MacCracken:

May I supplement the memorandum of your talk < with Miss Wylie and me> on May 21st by the following:

1. The Community Theatre is recognized by dramatic experts such as Professor Baker, Stuart Walker and the New York Drama League, as an educational experience of notable significance to other communities and as an example of what all colleges should do for their communities. An endorsement of its general plan will appear in the July issue of the Theatre Arts Magazine, the official organ of the Drama League, and a fuller account of it in a succeeding number.

2. To insure the success of this experiment, I must devote a great deal of time at the beginning to making connections with the school system, Lincoln Center, and all other educational bodies in the town. No one but myself can do this work successfully. The director has virtually two people's work, in rehearsing for both the children's and the adult plays, and in supervising the work of the untrained committees on the two productions, using to best advantage the work of all members of the community who are interested and developing their latent powers. The task of acquainting various groups in the community of the opportunities opened to them in this enterprise, must fall to some one who knows both the organization proposed and the community. The careful adjustment of the plays produced to the taste and growing capac-

ities of the audiences, is the most important single piece of work to be done; and this requires a special knowledge of the dramatic field as well as of the particular social situation.

3. The opportunity to render such a service as this does not occur more than once in a life-time. I feel that I must render it, at whatever sacrifice to me, personally. But my energies are not limitless. And I shall be able to serve the college and the community longer if I may be allowed to apply three hours of college time to this work, instead of adding it to a full-time schedule plus at least one-third of a full-time schedule given to the Workshop productions that must be continued for the first semester. I have during the past four years been heavily overworked, but this was by my own choice and I do not grudge the strength and time given,—[although it has made any work of my own quite impossible]. It does not, however, seem quite right to continue indefinitely a program so over-weighted. In addition to a full schedule of classes, I have had the correlation and supervision of the work of the entire freshman course in English, and the establishment and direction of the Vassar Dramatic Workshop. The Workshop has abundantly justified itself by raising materially the standard of play-writing and play-production in the college, sending out Vassar plays to all parts of the country, and thereby increasing not only the prestige of the College but its usefulness. If the three hours of relief to my program can be given only for the first semester next year, I can continue my work for the freshman course and the workshop and add the effort necessary for successfully establishing the Community Theatre without endangering my capacity for future service, or seriously crippling the academic work of the department.

4. If such a privilege is granted me, it will not serve as a precedent for other requests from the faculty, if it is clearly understood that this special service to the community is directly in line with my particular department of teaching. General service to the community such as might be given by any other equally intelligent member of the faculty does not constitute a parallel case. I should not ask a time allowance for doing Americanization work or public health work, or anything out of my especial department. The fact that this community theatre work is a direct extension of my own especial line of teaching into the community, constitutes its claim.

Sincerely yours,
Gertrude Buck

GB/EJ

June 8, 1920

My dear Miss Buck:

The Committee on Faculty and Studies gave full consideration to your request for part time allowance for work in connection with the Community Theatre, but they did not feel that they could grant the request at this time.

After long personal thought on the matter I coincided with their judgment, chiefly because of the precedent which would be established. I read very carefully your remarks with respect to this point, but it is possible that should similar requests arise in other fields the administration of our budget might become extremely difficult.

You have, as you know, my own interest in your plans, although it must be unofficial.

With cordial regards and best wishes for the summer, I am,
Sincerely yours,
[no signature, although presumably H. N. MacCracken]

DEPARTMENT REPORTS

Vassar College
Poughkeepsie, NY
Department of English

May 17, 1900

To the Honorable Board of Trustees:

There are no fundamental changes of plan to be chronicled in the work of the English department during the past year. The advances made within the large outlines of policy and method already familiar to you should, however, be briefly noted.

The publication of two text-books written for use in the required courses by Miss Buck, with the assistance of Miss Woodridge, last year a member of the department, has been of service to us in several ways. It has made possible, with less directive effort than before, an approximate uniformity of program among the various teachers in the freshman and sophomore classes; it has enabled the new instructors to gain a more rapid and accurate familiarity with these courses as a whole; and it has placed in the hands of the students a body of illustrative literary material, the accumulation and printing of which on our own account was previously a considerable drain upon the time and energy of the department at the beginning of each year.

One gratifying result of the publication of these text-books has been that the department meetings which before had of necessity been given over almost entirely to planning and unifying the work of the required courses, could this year be devoted to the discussion both of the general principles and the specific problems of English teaching. I believe that the teaching throughout the English department stands with the very best in the college. Its informality and genuineness, its real sympathy with the students' point of view, its strenuous spirit and intellectual clarity are frequently remarked even by casual and wholly disinterested observers. But these qualities cannot be maintained and increased in our teaching without some direct and centralized effort to that end. Convinced of this fact, the department has carried on throughout the year a series of pedagogic conferences at which certain problems of English teaching were fully and carefully discussed on the basis of a report prepared beforehand by some one of the teachers. One enclosed program of these meetings will serve to indicate further, the range and character of the subjects discussed. In alternation with these conferences have also been held similar meetings at which the recent publications likely to be of service to us in the teaching of literature, rhetoric or linguistics have been briefly reviewed and their relations to our own work emphasized. While these meetings have involved on the part of the teachers a considerable expenditure of time and effort, they have proved themselves invaluable in quickening and broadening the teaching done by the department, in bringing the new instructors into immediate and vital relations with our plans and in helping to further that spirit of sympathetic cooperation without which the highest efficiency is impossible.

In pursuance of suggestions made in these department meetings the first step has been taken toward establishing close relations between the required courses in college and the preparatory work in English. Inquiries have been sent out to one hundred and twenty-seven schools which prepare students for Vassar College, asking information as to the extent and character of their work in English. A copy of the questions mailed to each of these schools is enclosed herewith. A large proportion of the schools thus interrogated have replied very fully and by careful examination and comparison of the answers received we hope to gain some information which shall prove useful not only to ourselves but to the preparatory teachers of English whose students enter Vassar. When these reports have been thoroughly sifted, we shall issue to the preparatory schools a bulletin of printed suggestions as to their English work which may serve at least to prevent some misdirected effort and to give us students with less to unlearn.

Let me say, in passing from the subject of our required work, that never before have so many evidences presented themselves of its essential sanity and fruitfulness. Not only the advanced students in writing but those in literature as well, in their keenly critical appreciation, their clear thinking, and vivid expression have borne witness to the excellent substructure of their training in English. The numerous inquiries concerning our required courses which have come to us during the year from both colleges and preparatory schools throughout the country are also gratifying as some indication that the lines of our work are not without suggestiveness to those who in other institutions are attempting to solve the problems of English teaching.

In accordance with the policy announced in my report of two years ago the energies of the department have up to this time been concentrated upon the required work. Until this had been thoroughly reconstructed and placed upon firm foundations of intelligent and thorough teaching the extension of the elective courses was necessarily postponed. The time has now come, however, when the further development of our advanced work can no longer be delayed if we are to hold our own with institutions of equal rank. In the number of elective courses in English announced by our catalogue we are conspicuously inferior, to such women's colleges as Bryn Mawr, Wellesley and Smith. But not even all the courses announced by us can be actually given until our teaching force has been increased. The courses in Chaucer, the development of the essay and the theory of the drama could not be offered for election last year in spite of numerous requests from strong students; the course in Middle English, though elected, had to be withdrawn because of the unusual size of the freshman class; and the course in nineteenth-century prose could be given only by such rearrangement of the required work as involved a change of sections and of teachers for many of the freshmen and seriously overburdened the instructors in the prescribed courses.

Such facts as these indicate very plainly the need of a considerable increase in the number of our teachers whose training has been adequate for the more highly specialized courses. I would therefore ask that such increase be made as rapidly as possible, and that ability to do advanced work when shown by instructors now in the department be recognized by promotion in rank or by very considerable additions to the salaries now paid them.

The specific recommendations I wish to make are four in number.

1. That an associate professor be appointed whose special field of investigation and teaching shall be that of rhetoric and composition. I recommend the appointment of an associate professor at this time because of the urgent need of the department for another executive officer. The size of the English

department and its complexity of structure, including as it does three subjects usually differentiated in colleges of Vassar's rank, make the organizing and administrative work of its head far heavier than can be accomplished by any one person. And I recommend that this associate be a specialist in rhetoric and composition since my own work is primarily in literature and the next professorship created in the department should represent the rhetorical side of English, which maintains in all our courses a relation with the literature at once coequal and complementary. It may be remarked in passing that the same intimate and mutually dependent relationship exists between these subjects and the linguistic branch of English, and our next forward movement must be to strengthen materially this side of the department by the appointment of an able associate professor in English philology.

2. That a secretary or assistant to the head of the department be made a regular appointment. The mere record-keeping and routine office business essential to the conduct of a department so large and involving so much prescribed work has this year occupied half the time of the graduate student who has served me as secretary. Without such assistance as has thus been rendered the management of the department by one person who also teaches several hours a week would be physically impossible. For next year and thereafter, however, it seems highly desirable that an assistant should be appointed who beside these secretarial functions shall be competent to do the additional critical work which from one cause or another arises every year incident either to large, freshman or sophomore classes or to larger electives or to such a complication of circumstances as might for instance allow Miss Buck to teach one freshman section whose writing she could not by her schedule of hours criticise. The great loss involved to the classes in case of a teacher's illness when all the members of the department are too heavily burdened by their own work to add hers to it might this year have been avoided had an assistant in training and personality capable of filling the breach for a few days or even weeks been a member of the department.

3. Our greatest material need is for a department room in Rockefeller, the Main Building, or even in Music hall, where the large pictures from the art portfolios and other similar apparatus used in the freshman work can be displayed and where essays may be filed. In the freshman and in one of the large elective courses in writing many reproductions of famous pictures, statues and buildings are used as a basis for the writing. These reproductions have been hitherto hung in two small one-windowed offices in Rockefeller Hall, each of which could comfortably and hygienically accommodate no more than four or five students at a time. They are, however, during several

weeks of the year packed almost every hour with twenty five to thirty girls—as many as can gain a bare standing place—who emerge from the foul air and the pushing crowd physically exhausted—and it need not be said incapable of any intelligent or vigorous writing. These conditions cannot, of course, continue. Furthermore I shall be obliged next year, since I am to live in Poughkeepsie, to reserve one of these offices for my own use; and the other is ours only by suffrance, likely to be at any moment withdrawn. A room somewhere upon the campus which is of respectable size, and fairly well-lighted, which can be open all day and during the evening seems an absolute necessity. Such a room might ultimately be given us in connection with the library, the books of rhetoric and linguistics finding shelf-space there. In any case, as soon as a room is assured to us we will gladly undertake the task of raising money from outside sources to equip it with dictionaries and other requisites for a laboratory of English.

4. This year we have devised a somewhat primitive filing apparatus by which all the written work of each student can be preserved throughout his required and elective courses. Such preservation, essential to an exact knowledge of the student's progress in every stage, has justified itself not only in our experience but in that of numerous colleges and preparatory schools in which the plan has for some years been followed. In addition to the department room for harboring these files we need a small appropriation of about one hundred dollars for wall cases in which they may be occupied away from all but the instructors in the department. Until we have such cases a proper security of the files is impossible.

The recommendations in regard to the present teaching force I will copy from the report sent to President Taylor in February.

"That Miss Buck be made associate professor of English (or rhetoric). This is to the credit of the college to have more than one officer of professorial rank in the department including literature, rhetoric and linguistics. The actual work of organization in so large a department is more than any one person can do and should be provided for by an appointment above the rank of instructor. Miss Buck has not only done a very large part of the shaping work of the last three years but has carried senior and graduate courses and represented the college ably by her writing. She has, moreover, by her devotion to the common good and her sympathy with the general policy of the department proved conclusively her ability to work successfully with me and at Vassar.

"Miss Bacorn has made steady progress as a teacher. An uncommon delicacy and acumen in her dealings with her students and her devotion to improving herself and her work have assured her position as a valuable and reliable member of the department. I therefore strongly recommend that her salary which was originally small be next year increased one hundred dollars.

"Of Miss Adams' work I can hardly speak too highly. She is proving herself an excellent teacher, at once originative and faithful and possesses much executive power which she uses at all times for the common good. I therefore recommend that her salary be raised not less than fifty dollars and should feel that double that amount was no more than a fair recognition of her value to the college.

"Miss Keys is a teacher, of real ability and ability of a rare quality. She will, I think, more than fulfill the promise of this year."

In concluding this report I must ask indulgence for the short comings on the ground of my recent illness from which I am not yet fully recovered. It has been written by Miss Buck, partly from my dictation, partly from mere suggestion, hence under serious difficulties of construction. The recommendations made I have very much at heart and I regret deeply the necessity for presenting them less adequately than might have been possible under more favorable conditions.

Very respectfully yours
Laura J. Wylie

My dear Dr Taylor: Miss Wylie has authorized me to sign this for her. She would have done so had I been able to copy the document before leaving her. The recommendation in regard to Miss Keys is blank in the rough draft of Miss Wylies' February report from which she asked me to copy. Can you supply the omission from your copy of that report?

Very truly yours,
Gertrude Buck

Report of the Department of English
January 30, 1915

President Henry Noble MacCracken,
Vassar College,
Poughkeepsie, N.Y.

My dear Mr. MacCracken:—

Before making my recommendations for next year I should like to state briefly what has been the policy of the department of English since I have had charge of it, and to indicate, as clearly as I can, the point we have now reached in our development.

The single principle, which, in my management of the department of English, I have tried to apply to all questions of practical organization has been the necessity of providing for every student the best individual training possible at the time. In the late nineties faith in mass-work in education was at its height and large classes and much cheap teaching were accepted as matters of course. From the fad of the day we were saved, leaving out of account any genuine teaching-ability, in part by my long connection as student and teacher, with Professor Backus, who was pedagogically modern in practice, though with a most non-modern scorn of theory; in part by the tradition of excellent individual teaching which he had established at Vassar and which remained a force in its intellectual life a dozen years after he had left the college; and in part by the fact that Professor Buck, who had studied under both Professor Dewey and Professor Scott, brought to Vassar not only a strong professional spirit but a wide acquaintance with the most progressive educational theory. Our feet were thus early set in the right path; but we were able to advance in it very slowly, since distrust of a new point of view, the expense involved in working out our ideas, and the difficulty of finding teachers who understood our aims were obstacles that could only be gradually over-come. The development of our ideas demanded constant and varied experiment, but followed, in the main, three lines; the formation of a body of teachers scholarly in ideal and skilled in developing the power of the students; the division of those students into classes or sections small enough to allow of truly individual teaching; and the getting of offices and such other material equipment as made the knowledge and skill of our instructors available to the uttermost.

Our first effort was to raise the scholarly and professional standing of the members of the department. At my coming to Vassar in the fall of 1895 the head of the department was the only member of it holding professorial rank, and of the six members of the existing force three were in reality assistants, who criticised papers and met no class whatsoever. The position of assistant has been entirely done away with since 1908, none but experienced teachers being since then in charge of any part of our work. We have now, in a department numbering fourteen, two professors of full rank, and one associate and two assistant professors. Eight of our number are doctors of philosophy; two others, Miss Barstow and Miss Lyons, are within a year of getting their doctorate; and every one of the English instructors has had at least one year of advanced study. The larger number of highly trained teachers we have in recent years been able to secure has enabled us to offer a number of new courses, and so in part to solve the difficulties of congested elections. Eager to carry on their work in special fields, they have frequently been willing to carry for several years a larger number of hours than was required of them and thus to introduce into the curriculum courses in which they were particularly interested. Associate Professor Fiske, Assistant Professor Wood and Assistant Professor Peebles have rendered especially valuable service in this way.

The division of classes into sections small enough to permit of real teaching has been a task of peculiar difficulty and perplexity. When I first came to the college the lecture-system was almost universally in force and large classes were taken as a matter of course. In my first year at Vassar I taught four sections of freshmen averaging forty-five students each, and two classes in argumentation, then required of sophomores, averaging sixty each; thus meeting in all more than three hundred students in class weekly, while the bulk of their written work was criticised by assistants. Under such conditions good teaching was so manifestly impossible that soon after taking charge of the department I was able to reduce the size of the freshman sections to a maximum of twenty-five and to make seventy-five the maximum number of students assigned to a teacher doing only freshman work. This system, which antedated the Princeton tutorial system by some years and was intended to bring about somewhat the same results, marked a real educational advance at the time it was put into operation. Educational opinion has, however, moved faster than Vassar. We still adhere to our old numbers. But President [M. Carey] Thomas about three years ago, solely in the interest of efficient teaching, lowered to forty the maximum number of students assigned to one instructor in freshman English; the English Conference of the Associations of Colleges and Preparatory Schools in the Middle States and Maryland, in November, 1913, "indicated fifteen in each section as the maximum number of college students for the attainment of the best results in composition teaching";[1] and the National Council of Teachers of English at its last meeting passed the resolution here quoted, which makes sixty the maximum number of students to be assigned to each teacher;

"It is the sense of the National Council of Teachers of English that in order to secure satisfactory results in college English it is essential that the maximum number of students in Freshman English Composition assigned to a single instructor should in no case exceed 60; and that when such an instruc-

1. Professor Buck's report for 1914, page 5, has a fuller discussion on this whole subject.

tor has classes in other subjects, a corresponding reduction should be made in the number of pupils assigned to him in English composition."

It has been so difficult to cut classes or sections to compassable size in elective work that we have here hardly passed beyond the stage of experiment. The problem has, of course, been simplified by changes in the general curriculum, such as the opening of courses in Economics and Biology to sophomores, the addition of Italian and Spanish to the languages offered by the college and the establishment of the department of Psychology and Political Science. But such changes as these, acting automatically and unintelligently, have rather tended to prevent the development of the various smaller classes in which the best teaching could be done than to reach the real difficulty. I made the first attempt to distribute the elective work more equally when in 1908 I exchanged the course in Nineteenth Century Poetry, then numbering over one hundred and fifty, for the course in Nineteenth Century Prose, which was less attractive in subject-matter and elected by about twenty students. Professor Buck two years ago put into operation a plan by which the size of her sections in writing courses were limited to twenty. She is thoroughly satisfied with the result of the experiment, and the students, who continually urge that they want small classes, acknowledge the benefit of the change. A slight expansion of our elective work may, we hope, render arbitrary limitation in any course practically necessary and at the same time allow for a normal growth in elections. The apparent exception in our general plan of working for small elections is my own course in Nineteenth Century Poetry. It would undoubtedly be for the good of the students to recite in small groups, but the subject is an important one, the interest in it fairly keen, and the unlikelihood that several teachers would approach it from a similar point of view is very great. I am hoping by group-work and conferences to overcome the worst evils incident to the large-class-assistant-system so long as it seems impossible to change the character of the course to advantage.[2]

The material equipment of the department is of course a much less important matter than its teaching-force or its educational philosophy. When I first took charge of it most of the recitation-rooms were still in the Main Building and professors and teachers used their own rooms for business purposes,—though many of us even then objected to the discomfort in which

2. It is perhaps worth while to note here that the work of the English teachers is wherever possible assigned with regard to the number of students taught rather than the hours spent in the class-room, and that classes less than six in number, defined by the trustees as "small" classes, have, with rarest exceptions, been carried as extra hours or combined with another small course.

we worked. With the opening of Rockefeller Hall, I got one small office; and later Professor Buck, by the courtesy of the German department, got a second one. As the teachers began to live "off campus", there arose an increasing need for offices, which has in part been met by giving teachers living out [of] the college conference-rooms—or a part of one—in the main building. There is, however, no question that the space assigned to all teachers of English is inadequate. A large part of their work consists of interviews and it is extremely inconvenient to have but a single room in which to sleep, study, and carry on one's business and one's social life. I shall not be satisfied until the trustees recognize the situation by providing either an office or two living-rooms for every instructor in English. There is, furthermore, serious need of a Department Office for filing, committee-meetings, and other business purposes. My office, though far too small, is now so used, with the result that I have to see students and teachers on private or semi-private matters in an empty recitation-room, or failing that, in the hall or on the stairs. It would, moreover, be of great advantage if some rooms of tolerable size could be available for use in the evenings for readings, group-conference, and other such meetings. I, myself, this year had to give up a plan for reading with some of my students because I could find no suitable and comfortable room for use in the evening; and I know that other members of the department have had a like experience. A few years ago we brought before the trustees our need of an English building, the plan for which was for a time favored by Dr. Taylor though later he objected to it on the ground of departmental favoritism and expense in running. Our chief desire in the matter was to provide offices and rooms in which we could work effectively, and I sincerely hope that when increased recitation-facilities are contemplated, the need of offices and suitable business-rooms for our department may be thoroughly investigated. I also wish that the trustees might immediately consider assigning two rooms, if possible adjacent to each other, to all English instructors.

The Alumnae Council has asked me to nominate from the department of English a teacher who can give one-third of her time to the Publicity Work of the college. There is no over-estimating the importance of this work and I should, even at great inconvenience, be glad to arrange for it. Fortunately there is no real difficulty in the way. Dr. Helen E. Sandison is willing to undertake it and seems in every way fitted to carry it on. I do not know whether her salary is to be entirely paid by the trustees or whether the alumnae are responsible for one-third of it.

The brief review of the past shows that while we have worked hard and accomplished much, there is much still to be done. The trustees have always, to the best of the financial ability of the college, supported our endeavors to give the students the best English training attainable; but our department has had its due share of the delay and limitation unavoidably due to the poverty of the college. I sincerely hope that the Fiftieth Anniversary may mark the beginning of an era, when, our physical wants being fairly well supplied, we may spend more freely on educational salaries and equipment. Money is, I know, but one of many difficulties in the way. Fine teachers, for instance, and especially fine teachers of writing, are as hard to find as is the money to pay their salaries. But if we are to move more rapidly toward our end than we have hitherto done, it must be by having the power to secure good teachers when we find them, and to recognize good work more promptly and liberally than we have hitherto been able to do.

In view of our present situation, I therefore recommend:

1. That sections of freshman English be reduced to a minimum of fifteen and maximum of twenty students each, or a total of forty-five to sixty students to a single teacher, even if such reductions require the services of an additional teacher or teachers.

2. That in order to meet the reasonable demands of the students and to allow for normal growth in elective courses, without over-crowding our classes, we look toward the appointment of such teachers as may enable us to offer a few additional and much needed courses, which, whether given by the present members of the department or by new-comers, would certainly involve the addition to the staff of highly trained and highly paid teachers. Courses for which the students have for several years been asking, and which it seems to us desirable to offer as soon as possible, are:

(a) A course in Bible as English literature.

(b) A course in the development of the novel.

(c) A course in newspaper writing, which would be in no sense a technical course, but would offer liberal training through study and practice in the best type of newspaper-writing.

(d) A course in the structure and technique of the drama, which might well supplement our courses in Shakespeare and the history of the drama.

(e) A course in the theory of argumentation, which would enable us to make our present course somewhat more elementary while offering advanced training to a few students.

3. That the need of our teachers for offices be considered and that a second room be assigned to each as soon as possible.

4. That Miss Sandison take charge of the Publicity Work of the college, giving one third of her time to that work, and two thirds as at present to the department of English.

Of the teachers of the department I shall not speak at length. You will meet and know them soon. I cannot, however, forbear saying that it would be hard to find a group of women marked in a higher degree by devotion to their work, scholarly enthusiasm, and loyalty to the college. In matters individually concerning them I recommend:

1. That Professor Buck's request for a year's leave of absence be granted on the terms for which she asked it. Professor Buck has been at the college since the autumn of 1897 with one half year of absence. We shall miss her beyond words; but there is no doubt that she has earned the year of freedom.

2. That Associate Professor Fiske be made professor. Dr. Fiske has now worked eleven years at Vassar, is a woman of maturity, scholarship, and rare intellectual initiative and force. This recognition of her service should, in my judgment, be delayed no longer. <not approve.>

3. That Assistant Professors Wood and Peebles be re-appointed with due increase of salary.

4. That Dr. Winifred Smith be appointed assistant professor. Dr. Smith's scholarship, intellectual initiative and power as a teacher would more than justify this appointment. <4 or 5 yrs.>

5. That Miss Ballard, Miss Tylor, Dr. Sandison, Miss Dodge and Dr. Thayer be re-appointed with due increase of salary.

6. That Miss Rourke's resignation be accepted. We look forward with hope to Miss Rourke's return when her period of writing and possible study is over. She is a strong moral and intellectual force among the students and is especially valuable to the department on account of her interest in writing and ability to teach it.

7. That the resignations of Miss Barstow and Miss Lyons be accepted. These ladies have been with us only one year and wish to continue their studies at Yale and Chicago.

8. That Miss Katharine Warren—who taught at Vassar from 1895 until 1901, and who substituted for us during the illness of Miss McCloud in 1906–7, and who took part of Professor Buck's work during her one absence,—be appointed instructor next year for two thirds of her time. We shall probably withdraw Professor Buck's course in Literary Criticism, and possibly that in Advanced Writing, and Miss Warren can thus take the part of Professor Buck's work that will be offered next year.

9. That Miss Mary Yost, who will in June have completed her work for the

doctor's degree at the University of Michigan, be appointed assistant professor; or, if this is impossible, that she be assured of promotion after another year. Miss Yost has taught at Vassar from 190_ until 1913, and has proved herself a valuable member of the department and an excellent teacher. She is in every way fitted for an assistant professorship.

10. That Miss Alice D. Snyder, who will before June have completed all, or most, of her work for the doctor's degree at the University of Michigan be appointed an instructor. Miss Snyder has done excellent work with us as an English teacher and showed marked power of development and much intellectual grasp. She will, I am sure, be a very strong member of the department.

11. That President MacCracken and the Head of the Department be empowered to fill the third vacancy and to provide for such changes or additions to the force of the department as they find necessary.

Respectfully submitted
Laura J. Wylie

May 2, 1921

REPORT OF THE DEPARTMENT OF ENGLISH

My dear President MacCracken:

In adjusting its work for next year to the limitations of a reduced budget, the Department of English has endeavored to maintain the integrity of its teaching standards, and to follow the general principles on which its work has hitherto been conducted. But the result of this attempt is profoundly discouraging, even though we believe that there is no intention of prolonging the present regime of drastic retrenchment many years. We are squarely confronted by the fact that not only is our situation at present less advantageous than it was a few years ago, but that the present budget-limitation is but the culmination of a series of administrative measures all tending in the same direction. The financial pressure has been increasing for the last five or six years, until we are to-day at a point where there must be not merely amelioration of a bad situation, but a radical change in administrative policy towards the department, involving a considerable enlargement of our resources, if the coherence of our department organization is to be preserved and the educational ideas on which it is based are to develop freely in response to the new demands of the college as a whole. It is, therefore, in no spirit of rebellion against an immediate and evident necessity that we lay our conclusions before the President and the Trustees' Committee on Faculty and Studies, but rather with the conviction that the body ultimately controlling the educational policy of the college should have a chance to know what seem to us the educational issues involved in present retrenchment.

The most evident results of the present limitation of the budget are: the failure of five members of our department to get the promotion, with corresponding increase in salary and intercollegiate dignity, to which long and recognized service should have entitled them; the transfer of the librarian, who ranked as a professor to an associate professorship in our department; and the fact that, since we are not permitted to replace Miss Hincks, we shall be no better off next year than this, when we have undertaken to carry additional work in order that Miss Smith might have a semester's leave of absence without asking the college to provide a full-time substitute. Our present proportion of teachers to students, moreover, falls below what it was in 1914–15 or 1915–16, and still further below what we have for years considered an adequate teaching force. This condition is the more difficult because for the last six or seven years, we, with other members of the faculty, have been giving liberally of our time and strength to help the college bear the financial burdens inevitable in time of war. Willing as we have been to tax ourselves to the utmost so long as the emergency was pressing, the time would seem to have now arrived when we might reasonably expect the restoration of normal conditions. Instead, however, the relief from strain to which we had long looked forward, we are met by the necessity of heavier work than at any time during the war. We are also keenly aware that the budget for labor and for material equipment has been exceeded again and again. In other words, the administration will face a deficit to meet material, but not spiritual or intellectual, necessities; and it would seem that a co-operative spirit on the part of teachers makes them inevitable victims of retrenchment when coal dealers or hand workers get their price.

In face of a situation educationally precarious we have felt it necessary to review, with especial reference to the budget, the principles on which, so far as money and personnel allow, we have as a department hitherto tried to work. These principles are so simple and familiar that nothing short of such a practical issue as the present one would justify us in dwelling long on them.

In the first place, we believe that English is primarily an art, and that, whether considered from the point of view of literature or of writing, it should be so studied and taught.

In accepting this principle, we recognize our kinship in nature and method with the departments of language, ancient and modern, in so far as they go beyond the elementary mastery of tools, and our relationship to music and painting, sculpture and architecture in so far as they are studied as arts of expression. Yet, although intimately related to these subjects, English has its peculiar place, because as their mother tongue, it is the art most necessary to the training of all our students, and offers them the single tradition through which they can enter into possession of their racial or national inheritance in the humanities.

The conception of English as an art involves important practical consequences. In the first place, if it is to meet the requirements of art-study, it must be taught as individually as possible and must concern itself with the imaginative and perceptive hardly less than with the intellectual training of the student. For these reasons we have made every effort to have small classes, and to allow opportunity for individual teaching. My early annual reports insisted year after year on the necessity of working with small groups. But inasmuch as comparison with studio work was then out of the question, I dwelt, in season and out, on the parallel between our work and that in the sciences offering laboratory training, urging that we be given an equally liberal allowance of teaching time per student, as well as such office and other equipment as was needed for carrying on effective conferences. Fortunately for us, the earlier organization of the department favored individual teaching, the "interview" having been established with a relatively large corps of teachers to carry on the work, as early as the coming of Professor Backus to Vassar in 1867. It was after repeated consideration of these facts that, not later than 1899, we established as a reasonable basis of class work for each instructor, nine hours weekly in the class room with six additional hours devoted to conferences; and set the number of students to be assigned to each teacher as sixty. We have, it is true, approached this norm only in 1914–15 and 1915–16, when our students averaged respectively 63.5 and 63.8 per teacher; but that our estimate was not too high for the time at which it was made, would seem to have been indicated by the *Report on the Cost and Labor of English Teaching* issued by the Committee of the Modern Language Association of America and the National Council of Teachers of English in 1913. According to this report "the individual statements of 397 high school teachers, averaged, make 81 pupils the upper limit of proper assignment to a single teacher; and similarly 265 college teachers average 61 as the corresponding limit for college freshmen."[3] This report thus not only recognizes in freshman teaching the number we had set as the college norm, but indicates the decreasing number of students that can be handled by a single teacher as their work becomes more advanced; for the obvious reason that the greater bulk of work done by

3. Report, p. 8.

more mature students takes not only more time for criticism, but demands a corresponding increase in study and responsibility. The report quoted makes the norm we had set for our work the maximum number that a freshman teacher could carry. Our estimate, based on a careful study of our own teaching, we knew to be the highest possible. How much we had conceded to the exigencies of the Vassar budget was made evident by the action of Bryn Mawr, which announced in 1913 that forty was the ideal number of freshman students per teacher, the teacher holding only four classes a week, and giving the rest of her time to interviews.

It is to be noted that both the Report and the Bryn Mawr decision have to do with the teaching of composition rather than of literature, while we, from the first, have applied the same norm to classes in literature as to those in writing. We have frequently, it is true, been compelled to carry from twenty-five to forty or more students per section in literature, but this we have always regretted, believing that the teaching of writing and of literature should be more closely connected than they usually are. In our literature classes, furthermore, we work consistently to develop in the students a sort of critical power, involving both research and reproduction of idea in literary form, attainable only by careful individual oversight. We were in the first fifteen years of this century working out a plan, developed from the system earlier established at Vassar, which aims essentially at the same ends as those sought by the preceptorial system established in Princeton in 1905, and the tutorial plan adopted at Harvard for the class of 1917 in the division of History, Government, Economics, and extended for the classes of 1922 and following to all subjects. The striking difference between our system and those two seems to be that with us the class-teaching and conference or tutorial work are in the hands of the same person,—a difference that is, in our opinion, wholly in our favor.

Our conviction that all our teaching must be done by the best people has important consequences. If we are to teach English successfully as an art we must not only increase our proportion of teachers to students, but the teachers we have must be experts in the fields of writing or research or both. In 1895, as in the earlier years of college history, all, or most, of the theme correction was done by "critics," whose position corresponded in rank, at least in the 90's, to that of assistants in departments of science. Since 1899 there have been no assistants in the department of English, and we have worked steadily, and in the face of very great obstacles, for a larger proportion of teachers of professorial rank on our staff. If the college is to send out the best type of graduate there can be no question that it must employ teachers gifted with scholarship, personal power, and range of culture.

The need of an experienced staff is the more important because the second article of our education creed is the co-operative or democratic organization of the department.

From 1896 at least, we have worked co-operatively whenever co-operation was possible. Matters affecting the interests of the whole group have in every case been made subjects for joint discussion, and whenever it was practicable have been jointly determined. Smaller units acting together in any capacity have invariably made the organization of their common task a definite part of their work. The sharing by all teachers in departmental activities has always been considered part of each teacher's work, for which provision was made and which she was bound to render as a part of her service to the college. Incoming teachers have invariably had their attention called to the fact that department and group meetings were as much required of them as their hours of teaching and conferences, and this, not from any mere sense of formal value, but because an understanding of our common ends seemed necessary to the best teaching. It is, we believe, only through this joint organization of their common work that the members of any department can act effectively toward the development of a coherent educational policy.

The demands of any democratically organized department on its members are so little understood that I may be pardoned for dwelling in detail on some of our departmental activities in order to illustrate my point. These activities vary from such seasonal occupations as the supervision of the Dana Prize or the classification of students who have studied literature in secondary schools, to permanent jobs, such as the adjustment of our work to entrance requirements and to conditions in elementary schools, or to the development of a whole line of outside activity like the Vassar Workshop. Such work is, in many colleges, conducted perfunctorily, or with a view to the interests of the individuals conducting it; it is the peculiar distinction of the English department at Vassar that its members work disinterestedly and intelligently for the common good, and through this intelligent co-operation make the ideas on which we act effective in the various spheres to which they are applied.

The results of long-continued co-operative work, evident in the conduct of courses taught by two or more teachers, is perhaps especially notable in the course of freshman English. Nine teachers, besides Miss MacColl who gives us invaluable help with the below-grade students, are this year teaching this course, and the two hours a fortnight usually spent in considering its problems are none too long for the task. About six years ago we began to assign the students to sections, as far as was practicable with existing schedule limitations, according to their capacity and type of mind, and since then have devoted much effort to adjusting the work of each type of section to its peculiar needs. The problems of the low-grade, excellent, and middle-class sections are almost equally difficult and important; and the choice of the one book or essay ordinarily read by all sections each semester and the setting of an examination paper stimulating to the able and yet compassable by the weak, compel such close consideration of the ends and methods in different classes that we seldom fail to come to some understanding both of common aims and of individual difficulties. The *Sampler*, established in 1917–18, was begun primarily as a means to bring the students and teachers of diverse sections into closer connection, but has proved so valuable in developing a sense of literary values and a respect for technique, that the time spent on it— one third of an instructor's teaching and conference hours—seems more than justified by the results. The *Sampler*, however, since a regular time-allowance is made for it, is perhaps the least taxing part of this common work. Miss Buck, as chairman of the freshman teachers and Miss Yost as vice-chairman, make the improvement of existing aims and methods subjects of careful and constant thought, and there is hardly a meeting when several members of the group do not report on some special subject.

This co-operative management of the department, though at first sight remote from questions of budget, is in fact intimately bound up with it. In the earlier years of my connection with Vassar the other members of the English staff co-operated rather in carrying out policies outlined by Professor Buck or me than in initiating activities or modifying those suggested; but for the last dozen years or more they have increasingly taken a vital share in the management of the department, with the natural result that, while I carry less personal responsibility than formerly, the other members carry considerably more. Such departmental organization as ours seems to me to be just now especially necessary if Vassar is to advance towards the democratic government rapidly developing in most of our colleges and universities. Democratic government—i.e. general departmental and faculty control of educational policies—is possible only when the members of the faculty share in ultimate educational responsibility. Such responsibility requires time and energy as well as interest; and if the college is to benefit by the best service of its faculty, the work involved in joint management of common business must be recognized as an integral part of the teacher's task. Such work can assuredly not be done by people exhausted by excessive demands whether of the classroom, of the additional conference-hours made necessary by sections that are too large, or of an over-burden of administrative detail. It is true, too, that these more general activities, essential as they are both to the well-being of the college and to the teacher's grasp of large educational policies, ordinarily meet with scanty recognition either administrative or scholarly.

The review of our present situation, briefly outlined above, seems to prove that we are at present suffering from a long-continued pressure of overwork, with little prospect of relief; that our work is, and has long been, conducted on principles that involved a tolerably high per capita cost per student; and that so far from seeing any way to lessen our present demands for money we believe that we must have a larger appropriation than at present if the quality of our work is not to be still further impaired. Up to this year we had considered only the educational demands of our work, leaving to the trustees the assignment of a sum as nearly as possible adequate to our needs. The statement made a few months ago that it would be necessary to reduce our expenses, and that it would be wise, if possible, to cut the number of our students accordingly, set us seriously to the work, first, of learning just what we cost Vassar relatively to other departments, and, second, of deciding how far methods of teaching and number of elective students should be determined by budget conditions. Fortunately, the material for a comparative study of departmental costs in recent years was available, since records of the number of students and teachers have long been kept in the office of the dean, and, from 1916 on, the teaching budget has been on file in the President's office, where it is accessible to all members of the faculty. Furthermore, Miss Flick not only made it as easy as possible for us to use this material, but generously undertook to help us in our tabulations, and, when necessary, to advise with Miss Newcomer, a trained statistician. The material to which we had access concerned the three items common to all departments: the faculty payroll, the personnel of the teaching force, and the number of students. It is, of course, true that our results must be, to a degree at least, inaccurate, inasmuch as peculiarities of department organization can not always be fully reported to the central office, or classified according to a common plan. But our conclusions are at least impartial, are based on material open to all interested members of the faculty, and concern the one item which is the same for all departments—the cost of teaching. Our own extra-teaching expense is probably below the average, as the salary of our secretary is included, in these calculations, in the teaching-budget, and our six offices and use of the library almost make up the sum total of our extra-teaching cost.

The results of our investigations prove the fallacy of the current impression that the Department of English is among the most expensive in the college. It undoubtedly has the greatest number of students, the greatest number of teachers, and the largest salary budget at Vassar, but an estimate based on the number of student-hours per teacher, which is now accepted as the only fair way of computing teacher-costs for colleges and universities, shows that in cost per student-hour we are the fourth from the cheapest of Vassar's twenty-four departments.[4] Below us in cost are Economics, French, and Political Science. Of these three departments, it is to be noted that French, the only language in this group, would rise in the scale were a considerable part of its teaching not done by exchange students, whose tuition is not reckoned in department charge, and that Economics and Political Science conduct their work on the lecture and quiz method, which is radically different from ours. Our own case, we submit, is parallel neither to that of departments using the lecture system nor to those dependent on student-assistants. Both of these methods have certain advantages, and, when they can be used with educational profit, serve the double purpose of lending variety to the curriculum and of making less demand on the college purse. In English, however, the general adoption of either method would be profoundly unsatisfactory, in view of the nature of our subject-matter, which demands expert training on individuals by a corp of trained and experienced teachers, and is allied with that of the practical arts. Here, however, we have no definite basis of comparison in the records accessible to us; and so we turn to the laboratory sciences with which, because of the individual training given, we may best measure our relative cost. Comparing ourselves with this group we find that we are below the cheapest. Even Psychology, which has a very small amount of laboratory work, costs $6.10 per student-hour as against our $5.44, while Physics, which costs $9.53, is a little over one and three-fourths times as expensive in its teaching budget as English.

As our teaching-cost depends directly on the number of students handled by each teacher, it may be worth noting that we not only rank fourth from the lowest in money spent, but that only five departments carry a larger number of students, or of student-hours, per teacher. In students per teacher, English

4. These statistics count English Speech as a separate department since its work is based on a different system of credit.

Speech is first, with a record of 115.1 per semester, followed by Political Science, 93.7, French, 92.5, Economics, 87.8, History, 74.4, as against our 74.3.[5] Here again the nature of the instruction given must be carefully analyzed before any conclusion can be drawn as to the relation between numbers and work. Physics, with which we above compared ourselves in price and method, has 27.2 students per teacher as against our 74.3 from which high water mark of the laboratory sciences, the number falls gradually to 17 in Astronomy and to 14.3 in Botany. We emphasize the high teaching cost of the sciences in comparison with the small number of students carried by each teacher only to point the fact that for twenty-five years we have been trying in vain to approximate to a standard of work as individual as theirs, while at the same time we have been forced to carry considerably more than twice as many students to each teacher as the highest student-averaging department among the purely laboratory sciences. The history of our attempt to reach this point is noteworthy. In 1898, the first year in which records are available, when we were beginning to define our student-teacher unit, we averaged 72.5 for each of our eight teachers.[6] In 1905–06 the number had risen to 85.4 for each of eleven teachers. From this time the number of students per teacher gradually decreased, owing chiefly to an increase in size of the teaching staff, till, in 1914–15, we fell to 63.5, and in 1915–16 to 63.7, for each of our fourteen teachers. We have since then somewhat increased our number of students and decreased our number of teachers till this year we have 75 each for twelve and five-sixths teachers,[7] or more than 18 per cent. above our closest approximation to standard reached in 1915–16. This lowest point, it will be remembered, was still more than three students per teacher, or five per cent. above the maximum fixed by us as a norm more than twenty years ago, when ideas as to the importance of individual teaching were much less developed than they are to-day.

The conclusion gained from this statistical study is irresistible; we are asked, on the basis of students taught,—without regard to such other demands as the need of advanced courses and fuller departmental co-operation—to work a fifth harder than we did six years ago, when we, for the first time in our history, even approached our early estimate as to numbers,—

5. If neither Mr. MacCracken and his twenty-five students, nor Miss MacColl and her twenty-four students, are counted, the students per teacher in English are 74.2.

6. In the following computations the records used are those kept by the department.

7. This counts neither Mr. MacCracken and his twenty-five students, nor Miss MacColl and her twenty-four students, since are not counted in the department budget. If they are counted we have 75.1 students for thirteen and one-sixth teachers.

English Department Statistics compiled by E. M. Jones, April, 1921.

Year	Professors	Prof. rank	Instructors	Total no. Teachers	Total no. Students	Students per Teacher	
						Year	Sem.
1898–9	1	1	7	8	1322	145.1	72.5
99–0	1	1	7	8	1214	151.7	75.8
1900–1	1	1	7	8	1434	179.2	89.6
01–2	1	2	7	9	1417	157.4	78.7
02–3	1	2	7	9	1559	173.2	86.6
03–4	1	2	7	9	1466	162.7	81.3
04–5	1	3	8	11	1704	154.9	77.4
05–6	1	3	8	11	1880	170.9	85.4
06–7	1	3	9	12	1735	144.6	72.3
07–8	2	3	9	12	1812	151	75.5
08–9	1 (GB)	2	10	12	1772	147.6	73.8
09–0	2	3	10	13	1841	142.8	71.4
1910–1	2	4	9	13	1857	142.8	71.4
11–2	2	3 (FK)	10	13	1757	135.1	67.5
12–3	2	4	9	13	1725	132.6	66.3
13–4	1 (LJW)	4	9	13	1797	138.2	69.1
14–5	2	5	9	14	1780	127.1	63.5
15–6	1 (GB)	5	10	14⅓ (BJ,KW ⅔)	1827	127.4	63.7
16–7	2	8	6	13⅓ (BJ,KW ⅔)	1744	130.8	65.4
17–8	2	8	7	14 (BJ,KW,ALR,⅔)	1872	133.7	66.8
18–9	2	8	7	14 (BJ,KW,ALR,⅔)	1849	134.9	67.4
19–0	2	8	6	13 (BJ,KW,ALR,⅔)	1782	137.0	68.5
1920–1	2	10	4	12⅚ (BJ,ALR,⅔,WS,½)	1928	150.1	75.0
1916–7	Plus Dr. MacCracken ⅓			13⅔	1821	133.3	66.6
17–8	Plus Dr. MacCracken ⅙			14⅙	1938	136.8	68.4
18–9	Dr. MacCracken not teach						
19–0	Plus Dr. MacCracken ⅓ and Miss MacColl ⅙			13½	1879	139.1	69.5
20–1	Plus Dr. MacCracken ⅙ and Miss MacColl ⅙			13⅙	1977	150.2	75.1

Note: Teachers whose names are in parentheses were absent on leave and have not been counted in these statistics.

Teachers on part time were counted as on full time for *Professorial rank column*, but in adding them to obtain the number of teachers *in toto* the part time was considered as noted in parentheses.

The figures of the *number of students column* were taken from the English Department records.

Figures are for the whole year except in the last column.

In the first set of figures Dr. MacCracken and Miss MacColl are not counted since they are not paid out of the department budget.

an estimate which, as we were even then convinced, was too high for truly efficient teaching.

The study of our economic history has impressed upon us the desirability of change in at least two methods of administration. From a study of comparative departmental costs, it is evident that each department is a separate unit with demands primarily growing out of the nature of its material or some temporary condition that makes its needs and expenses peculiar to itself. This is chiefly significant as making difficult anything like a departmental average in determining the budget. The sciences, with their high teaching-cost and demand for the upkeep of laboratories, are undoubtedly the most expensive of the departments; yet they vary from a minimum of $6.10 in Psychology, with little laboratory work, to $15.76 in Botany. The languages, again, show peculiar divergence in their teaching, varying from $4.23 in French, to $7.70 in Greek and to $19.34 in German. English, as we have before noted, is dearer only than French; and in the arts group it stands at the bottom as concerns expenses and at the top as concerns the average number of students.

These departmental differences, impossible to reduce to common terms, would seem to make it desirable that the various departments might have more control of the disposition of their own budgets. We have suffered not only from having too little money for the kind of work that we are doing, but also from having too little control over the money spent for, but not by or even with the advice of, the department. The case of Miss Kitchel is much to the point. Miss Kitchel left us a year ago after two years of an instructor's service, and is to return next year to an assistant professorship, which considering the fact that not a single promotion could be made within the department, is evidently a higher position than we should have offered her had she stayed with us. There is no question that we, one and all, want Miss Kitchel to return and that we rejoice in her promotion. But six people, all of whom have records of very much longer service than hers, are left next year without any recognition whatsoever; and, in view of this most discouraging fact, there is grave question whether the salary for an assistant professorship should not have been applied to insuring two promotions, together with the appointment of an instructor of less experience but of high capacity and promise. Even if in the end the action taken had been the same, the whole subject might well have been canvassed, and the grounds of the action defined, if the budget-system was to further any other end than that of a capricious or routine-bound economy. Certainly some means should be devised for the intelligent co-operation of each department, within certain well-defined limits, in determining the financial policy which is to affect its whole development, and should, therefore, have some relation to its peculiar needs.

After consideration of the budget we are convinced that it would be to the interests of both parties concerned to separate English Speech entirely from the English department proper. Our relations with what is now regarded as sub-department of English are most cordial, and we are hoping that as time goes on we may be able to co-operate with it more frequently and more effectively. But the friendliness of our relations and our departmental similarity in methods and ends do not seem to us a sufficient reason for including in a single unit two departments so loosely connected that they cannot function effectively as one. The administrative connection between the two is necessarily very slight, since neither one can take responsibility for defining the methods, outlining the work, or choosing the teachers of the other. Such joint knowledge and responsibility are necessary to real unity, and we are therefore convinced that entire separation, with the co-operation inevitable in fields so closely related, will work for the best interests of us both.

Our recent enforced study of our educational versus our economic situation has strengthened our conviction:

That in our effort to give our students thoroughly individual training, we have been, and still are, in the line of educational advance;

That we have never had proper equipment, either in numbers or in rank of staff, for the kind of work we have tried to do;

That our demonstrated cheapness has meant great hampering of our work and, in spite of our utmost effort, some loss in its quality;

That the best interests of our classrooms and the college alike demand that we be actively occupied in research or some form of creative writing. We have all of us been obliged to sacrifice our own research and writing in order to do the individual teaching we believe in, under conditions which make it all but impossible.

We are doing our best to meet the situation entailed next year by college poverty. We shall continue to teach somewhat too many freshmen; to have unmanageably large classes, especially in literature; to refuse, in so far as we must, the increase of advanced courses demanded by the students, and, where necessary, even to withdraw courses already established. We recognize that this action involves the further delay of most of our plans for writing and research, a delay that must ultimately react most unfavorably, after our long years of pressure, on the teaching, scholarship and reputation of the college as well as on the interest and ambition of most of us.

In accepting our burden for next year we would, however, respectfully call to your attention the fact that in only two of the last twenty-five years (1914–15 and 1915–16) have we approximated tolerable working conditions; that to live up to the standard, set about a quarter of a century ago, we should this year have sixteen teachers and six promotions, all belated; and that if this pressure continues much longer, our own scholarly capacity and hence our value to the college will be somewhat impaired. We are convinced that our condition must be radically changed in the near future by a considerable increase of our staff in numbers, and by a policy that will allow for the promotion of all those who have won distinction as teachers and scholars. In no other way can we be sure of having a scholarly and efficient English faculty. As a department we believe that we should be excellent teachers and productive scholars, and that we should have a firm grasp of the educational problems of the college and of the community. We very earnestly hope that provision can be made in the near future to enable us to work towards these ends more effectively than has in the past been possible.

This report has grown directly out of your request that the Department of English consider plans and methods in relation to the budget, with a special view to retrenchment wherever such retrenchment was possible. It is, therefore, the result of much discussion. Miss Snyder and Miss Reed have acted as a committee with me to consider the points to be taken up and the form in which they should be presented; and the report, when early finished, was read to the whole department, except the one member who was absent, and has had the benefit of much suggestion and criticism.

Respectfully submitted,
Laura J. Wylie

Works Cited

Allen, Virginia. "Gertrude Buck and the Emergence of Composition in the United States." *Educational Biography, Vitae Scholasticae* 5 (1986): 141–59.

Baker, George P. "Address." *Vassar Miscellany Monthly* 9 (1923): 10–15.

———. *The Principles of Argumentation*. Boston: Ginn, 1895.

Barbour, F. A. "The Psychology of the Diagram." *School Review* 5 (April 1897): 240–42.

Bennett, Helen. "Seven Colleges—Seven Types." *Women's Home Companion* 47 (November 1920): 13.

Berlin, James. *Writing Instruction in Nineteenth-Century American Colleges*. Carbondale: Southern Illinois University Press, 1984.

Bizzell, Patricia. "Opportunities for Feminist Research in the History of Rhetoric." *Rhetoric Review* 11 (1992): 50–58.

Brody, Miriam. *Manly Writing: Gender, Rhetoric, and the Rise of Composition*. Carbondale: Southern Illinois University Press, 1993.

Buck, Gertrude. "Another Phase of the New Education." *The Forum* 22 (1896): 376–84.

———. "Anti-Suffrage Sentiments." *The Masses*, June 1913, p. 9.

———. "Athletic Education for Women." *The Inlander* 6 (April 1896): 291–301.

———. *A Course in Argumentative Writing*. New York: Henry Holt, 1899.

———. Rev. of *The Elements of English Grammar*, by G. R. Carpenter. *Educational Review* 15 (1898): 404–06.

———. "The Ethical Significance of 'Coriolanus.'" *The Inlander* 6 (March 1896): 217–22.

———. "The Foundations of English Grammar Teaching." *Elementary School Teacher* 3 (1903): 480–87.

———. Letters to Fred Newton Scott. 23 April 1910; 24 January 1914. Fred Newton Scott Papers. Bentley Historical Library, University of Michigan, Ann Arbor.

———. Letters to Henry Noble MacCracken. 18 November 1918; 6 January 1919; 19

April 1920; 3 June 1920. Special Collections, Vassar College Library, Poughkeepsie, N.Y.

———. "Make-Believe Grammar." *School Review* 17 (January 1909): 21–33.

———. "Marks in Freshman English." *The Vassar Miscellany News* 21 February 1920.

———. *The Metaphor: A Study in the Psychology of Rhetoric.* Contributions to Rhetorical Theory 5. Ann Arbor, Mich.: Inland Press, 1899.

———. *Poems and Plays.* Ed. Laura Johnson Wylie. New York: Duffield, 1922.

———. "The Present Status of Rhetorical Theory." *Modern Language Notes* 15 (March 1900): 84–87.

———. "The Psychological Significance of the Parts of Speech." *Education* 18 (1898): 269–77.

———. "The Psychology of the Diagram." *School Review* 5 (April 1897): 470–72.

———. "Recent Tendencies in the Teaching of English Composition." *Educational Review* (November 1901): 371–82.

———. "The Religious Experience of a Skeptic." n.d. *The Vassar Miscellany Monthly* 9 (1923): 21–28.

———. "The Sentence-Diagram." *Educational Review* 13 (March 1897): 250–60.

———. *The Social Criticism of Literature.* New Haven, Conn.: Yale University Press, 1916.

———. "Some Preliminary Considerations in Planning the Review of Grammatical Terminology." *English Journal* 2 (1913): 11–17.

———. "What Does 'Rhetoric' Mean?" *Educational Review* 22 (September 11901): 197–200.

Buck, Gertrude, and Kristine Mann. *A Handbook for Argument and Oral Debate.* Orange, N.Y.: Orange Chronicle Co., 1906.

Buck, Gertrude, and Harriet Scott. *Organic Education.* Boston: Heath, 1899.

Buck, Gertrude, and Fred Newton Scott. *A Brief English Grammar.* Chicago: Scott Foresman, 1905.

Buck, Gertrude, and Elisabeth Woodbridge. *A Course in Expository Writing.* New York: Henry Holt, 1899.

Burke, Rebecca J. "Gertrude Buck's Rhetorical Theory." Occasional Papers in Composition History and Theory. Ed. Donald C. Stewart. Kansas State University, 1978. 1–26.

Carpenter, George Rice. *Elements of Rhetoric and English Composition.* New York: Macmillan, 1899.

CCCC Committee on Professional Standards for Quality Education. "CCCC Initiatives on the Wyoming Conference Resolution: A Draft Report." *College Composition and Communication* 40 (1989): 61–72.

Clifford, Geraldine Jonçich, ed. *Lone Voyagers: Academic Women in Coeducational Institutions, 1870–1937.* New York: Feminist Press, 1989.

Connors, Robert. "Mechanical Correctness as a Focus in Composition Instruction." *College Composition and Communication* 36 (1985): 61–72.

———. "Personal Writing Assignments." *College Composition and Communication* 38 (May 1987): 166–83.

———. "Rhetoric in the Modern University: The Creation of an Underclass." In *The Politics of Writing Instruction: Postsecondary.* Ed. Richard Bullock and John Trimbur. Portsmouth, N.H.: Boynton Cook, Heinemann, 1991. 55–84.

———. "The Rise and Fall of the Modes of Discourse." *College Composition and Communication* 32 (1981): 444–55.

Crowley, Sharon. *The Methodical Memory: Invention in Current-Traditional Rhetoric.* Carbondale: Southern Illinois University Press, 1990.

Damon, L. T. Letter to Gertrude Buck. 22 April 1905. Fred Newton Scott Papers. Bentley Historical Library, University of Michigan, Ann Arbor.

Ellis, Constance Dimock, ed. *The Magnificent Enterprise: A Chronicle of Vassar College.* Compiled by Dorothy A. Plum and George B. Dowell. Poughkeepsie, N.Y.: Vassar College, 1961.

Furness, Caroline. Letter to James Taylor. 9 March 1909. Special Collections, Vassar College Library, Poughkeepsie, N.Y.

Genung, John. *The Working Principles of Rhetoric.* Boston: Ginn, 1900.

Gerlach, Jeanne Marcum, and Virginia R. Monseau, eds. *Missing Chapters: Ten Pioneering Women in NCTE and English Education.* Urbana, Ill.: NCTE, 1991.

Glenn, Cheryl. "sex, lies, and manuscript: Refiguring Aspasia in the History of Rhetoric." *College Composition and Communication* 45 (1994): 180–99.

Gunner, Jeanne. "The Fate of the Wyoming Resolution: A History of Professional Seduction." In *Writing Ourselves into the Story.* Ed. Sheryl Fontaine and Susan Hunter. Carbondale: Southern Illinois University Press, 1993. 107–22.

Halloran, S. Michael. "Rhetoric in the American College Curriculum: The Decline of Public Discourse." *Pre/Text* 3 (1982): 245–69.

Harris, Barbara. *Beyond Her Sphere: Women and the Professions in American History.* Westport, Conn.: Greenwood Press, 1978.

Hill, A. S. *The Principles of Rhetoric.* New York: American Book Co., 1895.

Horowitz, Helen Lefkowitz. *Alma Mater: Design and Experience in the Women's Colleges from Their Nineteenth-Century Beginnings to the 1930s.* New York: Knopf, 1984.

Jarratt, Susan C. "Performing Feminisms, Histories, Rhetorics." *Rhetoric Society Quarterly* 22 (1992): 1–5.

Kitzhaber, Albert R. "Rhetoric in American Colleges, 1850–1900." Diss. Univ. of Washington, 1953.

Mulderig, Gerald. "Gertrude Buck's Rhetorical Theory and Modern Composition Teaching." *Rhetoric Society Quarterly* 14 (1984): 96–104.

Paton, Lucy A. "Gertrude Buck." N.d. Special Collections, Vassar College Library, Poughkeepsie, N.Y.

Raymond, John. "The Demand of the Age for a Liberal Education for Women and How It Should Be Met." In *The Liberal Education of Women*. Ed. James Orton. 1873. New York: Garland, 1986.

Reed, Amy L. "Opening Address." *Vassar Miscellany Monthly* 9 (1923): 1–2.

Ricks, Vickie (Weir). "Revisioning Traditions Through Rhetoric: Studies in Gertrude Buck's Social Theory of Discourse." Diss. Texas Christian University, 1989.

Rosenberg, Rosalind. *Beyond Separate Spheres: Intellectual Roots of Modern Feminism.* New Haven, Conn.: Yale University Press, 1982.

Scott, Fred Newton. "Address." *Vassar Miscellany Monthly* 9 (1923): 3–7.

——. "Two Ideals of Composition Teaching." In *The Standard of American Speech*. New York: Allyn and Bacon, 1926. 35–47.

——. "What the West Wants in Preparatory English." *School Review* 17 (1909): 10–20.

Shinn, Millicent Washburn. "The Marriage Rate of College Women." *The Century Magazine* 50 (1895): 946–48.

Smith-Rosenberg, Carroll. "The Female World of Love and Ritual: Relations Between Women in Nineteenth-Century America." *Signs* 1 (1975): 1–29.

Swain, George. Letter to James Taylor. 8 March 1913. Special Collections, Vassar College Library, Poughkeepsie, N.Y.

Taylor, James Monroe. "The 'Conservatism' of Vassar." N.p.: 1909.

——. Letter to M. Carey Thomas. 9 January 1908. Special Collections, Vassar College Library, Poughkeepsie, N.Y.

——. Letter to Faculty. 24 March 1909. Special Collections, Vassar College Library, Poughkeepsie, N.Y.

——. Letter to Parent. 4 June 1912. Special Collections, Vassar College Library, Poughkeepsie, N.Y.

——. Memorandum to Faculty. 19 March 1909. Special Collections, Vassar College Library, Poughkeepsie, N.Y.

Tyler, Moses Coit. "The Experience at the University of Michigan." *The Liberal Education of Women*. Ed. James Orton. 1873. New York: Garland, 1986.

Vicinus, Martha. " 'One Life to Stand Beside Me': Emotional Conflicts in First-Generation College Women in England." *Feminist Studies* 8 (1982): 603–28.

Warren, Katharine. "In Remembrance of Gertrude Buck." *Vassar Miscellany Monthly* 9 (1923): 17–20.

——. "The Retirement of Miss Wylie." *Vassar Quarterly* 10 (1924): 1–6.

Wellesley College President's Report, 1907–1908. Wellesley College Archives, Wellesley, Mass.

Wendell, Barrett. *English Composition*. New York: Charles Scribner's Sons, 1891.

Woodbridge (Morris), Elisabeth. "Address." *Vassar Miscellany Monthly* 10 (1923): 8–9.

Wozniak, John. *English Composition in Eastern Colleges, 1850–1940*. Washington, D.C.: University Press of America, 1978.

Wylie, Laura Johnson. Letters to Henry Noble MacCracken. 30 September 1916; 19 April 1920; 3 June 1920. Special Collections, Vassar College Library, Poughkeepsie, N.Y.

——. Letter to Fred Newton Scott. 23 November 1921. Bentley Historical Library, University of Michigan, Ann Arbor.

——. "Report of the Department of English." 1900–1921. Ts. Special Collections, Vassar College Library, Poughkeepsie, N.Y.

——. "Some Early Writings of Gertrude Buck." *Vassar Miscellany Monthly* 10 (1923): 21.